*Civil Wars in Africa:*
*Roots and Resolution*

A collection of case studies of African countries, *Civil Wars in Africa* provides a comparative perspective on the causes of civil strife and the processes by which internal conflict may be resolved or averted. The book analyses the situation in Ethiopia, Liberia, Mozambique, Rwanda, Somalia, Sudan, and Uganda as well as the experience of Tanzania and Zimbabwe, where civil war was averted, to determine conditions under which conflict can most successfully be managed.

Part I looks at civil wars in which force has been the major means of resolution (Uganda, Ethiopia and Eritrea, and Rwanda). In part II contributors examine civil conflicts decided principally by negotiation (Liberia and Mozambique). Part III analyses the protracted civil wars in Somalia and Sudan. In part IV, authors look at the way in which Zimbabwe and Tanzania have avoided armed internal conflict. Part V offers an overview of the resolution of conflict in post–Cold War Africa and a conclusion about the findings of this study.

TAISIER M. ALI, formerly professor of political economy at the University of Khartoum, is a visiting scholar in the Department of Political Science, University of Toronto, and a member of the executive and secretary-general of the Sudan Alliance Forces (SAF).

ROBERT O. MATTHEWS is professor of political science, University of Toronto.

# Civil Wars in Africa

*Roots and Resolution*

Edited by

TAISIER M. ALI AND
ROBERT O. MATTHEWS

McGill-Queen's University Press
Montreal & Kingston · London · Ithaca

© McGill-Queen's University Press 1999
ISBN 978-0-7735-1777-6 (cloth)
ISBN 978-0-7735-1883-4 (pbk)

Legal deposit first quarter 1999
Bibliothèque nationale du Québec

Printed in Canada on acid-free paper
Reprinted in paperback 2000, 2003, 2007

This book was first published with the help of a
grant from the Humanities and Social Sciences
Federation of Canada, using funds provided by the
Social Sciences and Humanities Research Council
of Canada. Funding was also provided by the
Cooperative Security Program of the Department
of Foreign Affairs.

McGill-Queen's University Press acknowledges the
financial support of the Government of Canada
through the Book Publishing Industry Development
Program (BDIDP) for its activities. It also acknowledges
the support of the Canada Council for the Arts for its
publishing program.

MAPS

Maps on pp. 52, 122, and 222 derived from Larry
Diamond, Juan J. Linz, and Seymour Martin Lipset,
eds., *Democracy in Developing Countries.*

Maps on pp. 2, 194, 122, 12, and 168 derived from
Raymond W. Copson, *Africa's Wars and Prospects for
Peace*, pp. 28, Map 1 – Africa's Wars since 1980; 32,
Map 2 – Sudan; 39, Map 4 – Mozambique; 49, Map 6 –
Uganda; 51, Map 7 – Somalia respectively.

All maps drawn by Audrey Mona Christman.

---

**Canadian Cataloguing in Publication Data**

Main entry under title:
Civil wars in Africa: roots and resolution
Includes bibliographical references and index.
ISBN 978-0-7735-1777-6 (cloth)
ISBN 978-0-7735-1883-4 (pbk)
1. Africa – History – 1960– . 2. Africa – Politics and
government – 1960– . 3. Civil war. I. Ali, Taisier
Mohamed Ahmed, 1946– . II. Matthews, Robert O.
DT21.5.C58 1999    960.3'2    C98-900898-3

*To the voiceless victims of civil wars*

# Contents

Maps   ix

Preface   xi

Introduction   3
TAISIER M. ALI AND ROBERT O. MATTHEWS

PART ONE: FORCE AS THE MAJOR INSTRUMENT
OF RESOLUTION

1   Managing Political Change: Uganda under Museveni   13
JOHN KIYAGA-NSUBUGA

2   Liberation Politics in Ethiopia and Eritrea   35
JOHN PRENDERGAST AND MARK DUFFIELD

3   Civil War, the Peace Process, and Genocide in Rwanda
53
BRUCE D. JONES

PART TWO: NEGOTIATION AS THE PRIMARY
INSTRUMENT OF RESOLUTION

4   The Civil War in Liberia   89
ELWOOD DUNN

5   Inside from the Outside? The Roots and Resolution of
    Mozambique's Un/Civil War  123
    JOHN S. SAUL

    PART THREE: PROTRACTED CIVIL WARS

6   Somali Civil Wars   169
    HUSSEIN M. ADAM

7   Civil War and Failed Peace Efforts in Sudan   193
    TAISIER M. ALI AND ROBERT O. MATTHEWS

    PART FOUR: CIVIL WARS FORESTALLED

8   Leadership, Participation, and Conflict Management:
    Zimbabwe and Tanzania   223
    HEVINA S. DASHWOOD AND CRANFORD PRATT

    PART FIVE: SECURITY, CONFLICT, AND PEACE

9   Redefining "Security" after the Cold War:
    The OAU, the UN, and Conflict Management in Africa
    257
    JAMES BUSUMTWI-SAM

10  Conclusion: Conflict, Resolution, and Building Peace
    288
    TAISIER M. ALI AND ROBERT O. MATTHEWS

    Contributors   313

    Index   317

# Maps

Africa 2

Uganda 12

Ethiopia and Eritrea 36

Rwanda 52

Liberia 88

Mozambique 122

Somalia 168

Sudan 194

Zimbabwe and Tanzania 222

# Preface

The idea of drawing together a collection of essays comparing civil wars in Africa grew out of our common interest in the long-standing conflict in Sudan. Having been deeply involved in the efforts undertaken by the trade unions and political parties to restore peace to that nation from 1985 to 1989, Taisier Ali was anxious to reflect on the causes of the civil war and the reasons why all attempts at finding a peaceful settlement had failed. Having written his doctoral dissertation on conflict in Africa, Robert Matthews welcomed the opportunity to join Ali in that enterprise, examining in particular the regional and global dimensions of the conflict.

Together we applied in 1993 for a Cooperative Security grant from Canada's Department of Foreign Affairs. We proposed two separate but related stages to our study: the first to focus on Sudan alone, the second to cast the net wider in a comparative study of a number of civil wars in Africa. We were convinced that each project would benefit from the insights gained from the other.

We were fortunate to obtain generous funding from the Department of Foreign Affairs to last us for two years, 1993–95. That support allowed us to carry out the needed research on Sudan's civil war and to plan and organize a conference. We are extremely grateful to the department and to the administrator of the Cooperative Security Programme, Roger Hill, for allowing this entire project to get off the ground.

Having chosen the people who would contribute papers to this conference and ultimately to this volume, we decided to develop a common framework for the case studies at a one-day workshop in November 1994, made possible by generous donations from the Anglican and United Churches of Canada, Project Ploughshares, and the Department of Political Science at the University of Toronto. Six months later, in May 1995, we convened a two-day conference on civil wars in Africa.

We are extremely grateful to a number of organizations without whose support it would have been impossible to hold that conference and to a large number of scholars and activists whose participation ensured that the outcome was a tremendous success. The organizations included the Canadian International Development Agency (CIDA), and within it especially Calvin Piggott; the International Development Research Centre (IDRC), and Necla Tschirgi; the Ford Foundation, and Humphrey Davis; the Steel Workers of America, and Gerry Barr; Oxfam Canada, and John Saxby; and, at the University of Toronto, the Department of Political Science, the Faculty of Arts and Science, and the African Studies Programme. The list of individuals contributing to the conference is too lengthy to include here, but we would like to thank here those who commented formally on the papers, as their comments helped the contributors prepare final drafts for this volume. The commentators included Douglas Anglin, Abdullahi An-Na'im, Lee Cassanelli, Francis Deng, Kassu Gebremerim, Rhoda Howard, Nelson Kasfir, Ann Mosely Lesch, Paul Martin, Ken Menkhaus, Nakanyiki Musisi, Marina Ottaway, Janice Stein, and William Zartman.

Following the conference we decided to include an additional case study in the volume, that of Mozambique. We were particularly fortunate to enlist the services of John Saul for that task. His words at the conference made it obvious to us that Mozambique's experience would be particularly useful as a reference point to many of the other studies. Sincere thanks are due also to our contributors for their patience and cooperation. We are grateful to Professor Cranford Pratt for his candid and stimulating comments on several parts of this manuscript. Particular thanks go to our two anonymous readers for McGill-Queen's University Press for their constructive reports.

Finally, we would like to thank Carolynn Branton, Hyla Levy, and Marian Reed, staff members at the University of Toronto's Department of Political Science, who helped make all the arrangements for the conference. Their support was invaluable.

Taisier M. Ali and Robert O. Matthews
Toronto
February 1998

*Civil Wars in Africa:*
*Roots and Resolution*

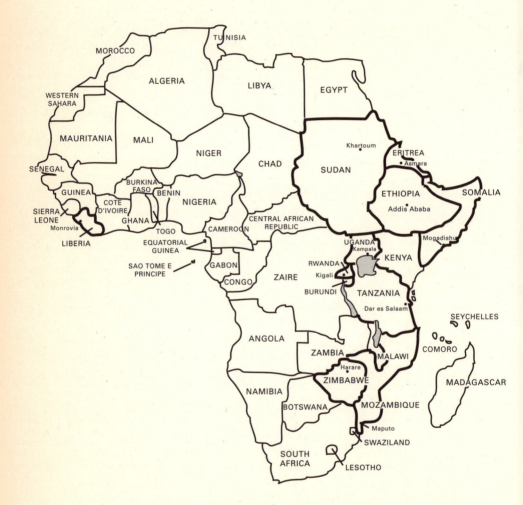

Africa

Political boundaries of countries under study are highlighted.

# Introduction

TAISIER M. ALI AND
ROBERT O. MATTHEWS

The editors of this volume have for some time now been engaged in
a study of the civil war that has plagued Sudan virtually since its
independence in 1956. In this study we explore the underlying and
proximate causes of that war and trace the numerous attempts made
to resolve it. Our particular interest lies in accounting for the repeated failure of both Sudanese and disinterested third parties to find a
peaceful solution.

While Sudan's civil war has the distinction of being Africa's longest
civil war, it clearly is not its only one. Since achieving independence,
African nations have had a long history of civil wars. Beginning with
Sudan in 1956, Congo – Leopoldville (later Zaire, now Congo) in
1960, and Nigeria in 1967, and ending with the most recent, though
probably not the last, in Rwanda and Sierra Leone, these wars have
wreaked untold havoc on the lives of Africans, destroying their
economies, dissolving their political institutions, and undermining
the fabric of their societies.

Our underlying purpose here is to examine a number of these civil
conflicts in a comparative context. Though not an exhaustive study of
Africa's civil wars, this volume, unlike most earlier books on the same
theme, does not limit itself to a single or several cases. Instead it
examines seven instances of civil war and two instances in which civil
war was averted. By comparing the root causes of these wars and the
processes by which some have been resolved, we hope to see whether
or not there are generalizations that we can make about the sources
of conflict and the methods of conflict resolution. By examining two

cases where the potential for large-scale civil strife existed but was avoided, we want to begin the task of identifying the policies most likely to prevent the outbreak of violent conflict and thus the conditions under which conflict can most successfully be managed.

Following a workshop during which we developed a common framework for this volume, the contributors were asked to address two general issues – the underlying causes of each civil war and attempts at resolution. First, while analysis of root causes necessarily involves a description of the historical background, going back to the colonial period, we encouraged the authors to concentrate on the post-independence years. The colonial legacy cannot be ignored, for colonial rule has helped to define and shape the societies from which have emerged civil wars, but it alone does not provide a sufficient explanation.

Beyond the impact of colonialism, to what extent are the wars rooted in the socioeconomic structures of post-colonial society – the result of such factors as ethnic/communal cleavages, ideological/political differences, disparities in economic wealth, intra-elite rivalries, general weakness in national societies, and environmental problems? Alternatively, the conflicts may be the consequence of the policies and practices of the ruling elite. According to this explanation, the conflicts emerge less from the long-term structural factors listed above than from the failure of governance, from government's mismanagement of ethnic divisions, racial discord, religious differences, and regional economic disparities. While the first explanation directs attention to the cleavages that divide societies, the second rests on governing elites, the policies they pursue, and their vision of the future.

Civil wars may result not only from the impact of domestic social forces and the failure of governance by local elite. They can also emerge from forces, events, and activities originating outside the country, from the surrounding region or the world at large. Certainly most governments faced with internal challenges to their authority have not hesitated to assign blame for the problems they confront to foreign intervention and intrigue. Our interest then lies in assessing the extent to which external forces and actors have served as convenient scapegoats, allowing a governing elite to divert attention from its own mismanagement, or have actually helped initiate civil conflict. Obviously the relative importance of regional and global actors will vary from case to case, though we contend that most civil wars in Africa are derived largely from internal sources.

Second, our ultimate interest lies in the resolution of these wars. In this context we examine the efforts made both by the parties themselves and by disinterested third parties to curb, dampen, and resolve them. Are most civil conflicts brought under control by the parties themselves, either through military victory or through negotiated settlement? What role, if any, do third parties play? On occasion, they act in such a manner as to prolong conflict, by identifying with and supporting one side or the other; at other times, they may intervene to promote a peaceful solution. When, how frequently, and under what conditions have third parties helped initiate reconciliation?

We want to determine whether the end of the Cold War has had a salutary or baleful influence on the management of conflicts in Africa. Do our cases confirm the view that the end of Soviet–American rivalry in Africa has created an environment more conducive to peaceful settlement than towards a military solution, or, alternatively, do they substantiate the contrary contention – that, with the decline of interest, by the two superpowers, internal conflicts that previously were contained are now likely to erupt?

Not only do we explore the kinds of actions taken by domestic leaders and third parties to end the fighting, but we examine how the bases of a permanent peace can be nurtured. It is generally acknowledged that peace is not just the absence of war. If the structures of peace are not well established and even strengthened, civil unrest is likely to smoulder and erupt into violence again. The collapse in 1983 of the Addis Ababa accord, which ended eleven years of relative non-violence in southern Sudan, shows that peace is easily reversible if the underlying causes of the conflict are not seriously addressed. Therefore, in those cases where the military struggle has largely wound down, as in Ethiopia, Mozambique, and Uganda, our focus is of necessity on the difficult stage of transition from war to enduring peace. There is clearly a close parallel between the peace-building initiatives undertaken by the governments of these three countries and the policies pursued by Tanzania and Zimbabwe since their independence to prevent civil war in the first place. As we see, peace-building and war prevention involve similar, if not identical activities.

Unfortunately, several wars have persisted over a considerable period; neither side is able to win militarily, and negotiations are all but ruled out. In some such instances, one or both parties may proclaim an interest in talking with the other party but make it quite clear, through their actions, that they have no intention to negotiate in good faith. In either case, the outcome is protracted conflict rather than conflict resolution. Our intention in such instances is to examine the impediments to peaceful or even forceful solutions. To what extent are these latter cases the result of forces beyond the control of competing leaders – an explanation suggested in the phrase "unripe for resolution" – or to the myopia and ideological rigidity of one or both sides in the conflict?

In deciding which case studies to include in this volume, we were influenced by several factors. First, we were anxious to examine conflicts in which the apparent roots vary and the processes by which they were resolved (if at all) differ. Second, we wanted to select cases in which third-party involvement ranged across the spectrum, from little or no participation to active engagement. Third, we chose countries that in all but one instance shared borders with at least one of the other countries under investigation here, thus drawing out the regional dimensions of internal conflict in Africa and showing how conflicts in adjacent countries actually feed on one another. Finally, we recognize that others have written about some of the cases we selected, but, as William Zartman points out, such studies "tend to be either historical or polemical."[1] We believe that our emphasis is neither purely historical nor polemical. In the end, we chose seven cases of civil war – Ethiopia, Liberia, Mozambique, Rwanda, Somalia, Sudan, and Uganda – and two instances involving potential rather than actual violent conflict – Tanzania and Zimbabwe.

In the first three chapters the civil wars examined are ones in which the main actors sought to achieve their ends chiefly by force. As John Kiyaga-Nsubuga demonstrates in chapter 1, Uganda's whole history since independence has been punctuated by civil war, until in 1986 the conflict was finally brought under control largely through military force, without any noticeable assistance from outside. Though Tanzania did intervene militarily in the late 1970s, the Ugandans themselves have had to settle their own differences. Since coming to power Yoweri Museveni and his National Resistance Movement regime have engaged in the difficult task of transforming Uganda from a condition of continuous political instability and widespread violence to one of relative peace. Indeed, Kiyaga-Nsubuga devotes much of his chapter to the analysis of this peace-building in a society that has suffered extensive dislocation and to the tension that arises from a government opening up the political process to include a broad range of participants while needing at the same time to exercise political control. In chapter 2, John Prendergast and Mark Duffield examine Ethiopia's experience with a long civil war. Launched by Eritrea in response to the central government's violation of an earlier commitment to regional autonomy, the war led to the final defeat of Mengistu and the Derg and to Eritrea's subsequent secession, crafted on the battlefield rather than at the negotiating table. As in Uganda, both Eritrea and the rest of Ethiopia now face the momentous task of establishing the conditions of an enduring peace. Prendergast and Duffield describe how that process of peace-building has been adversely affected by the liberation experience and the special role that non-governmental organizations (NGOs) and donor countries have in that process. In his study of Rwanda, in chapter 3, Bruce Jones offers another example of protracted conflict, ostensibly ethnic in nature. He outlines the various attempts at managing, if not resolving, the conflict – a process facilitated by a number of African and European states and capped by the Arusha Accords in the summer of 1993. As in Liberia, this case included external intervention, on this occasion through the deployment of a United Nations monitoring force, which was too small and lacked a proper mandate to prevent the collapse of the accords into a sustained period of genocide. The fighting was brought to a conclusion when the Rwandan Patriotic Front declared a military victory and a unilateral cease-fire.

The next two chapters focus on civil wars that have involved outside intervention to facilitate a negotiated end to bloody ethnic fighting, which threatened to spill over into neighbouring territories. Elwood Dunn's case study of Liberia, in chapter 4, provides an illustration of politically manipulated ethnic differences resulting in sustained civil war. The states of the Economic Community of West African States (ECOWAS) intervened with a regional peace-keeping force to reduce the level of violence and to fashion a settlement. Divided in its members' support of Liberian rival factions, the regional force delayed final resolution, which still remains to be fully implemented. Indeed, as the last year has demonstrated, the Liberian conflict is not likely to end. With a measure of good luck and sustained external support, it may be better managed. In chapter 5, John Saul reveals the peculiar mix of external and internal factors that explain the outbreak and continuation of the civil war in Mozambique. As in Liberia and Rwanda, external actors – especially a lay Roman Catholic church organization and the major Western donor countries – helped bring the parties together and reach a political settlement in 1992. As part of that agreement, a United Nations peace-keeping force was deployed to monitor the cease-fire, to provide humanitarian assistance, to oversee demobilization of RENAMO's military forces and their integration into a new national army, and to ensure that national elections were free and fair. Saul describes in detail the implementation of the peace accord and the role of Western powers in that process.

In the last two cases of civil strife, the wars have dragged on, with no apparent end in sight. In Somalia, as Hussein Adam vividly describes in chapter 7, the world witnessed the collapse of an authoritarian regime, which led to inter-clan and sub-clan rivalry on a national scale. The resulting civil war prompted international intervention to ensure provision of relief and to promote a negotiated settlement. The United Nations has now withdrawn, having brought relief to the Somalis, but the prospect of peace is as distant as ever. In chapter 7, in their study of Sudan, the two editors of this volume provide a case study of protracted conflict over forty years. Often portrayed as pitting an Arab, Islamic north against an African, Christian south, the reality is far more complex. Various attempts have been made to resolve this war, including intervention by individuals, other states, and regional organizations, and a settlement reached at Addis Ababa in 1972 lasted for eleven years, but none of those attempts has established an extended peace.

Our study of Tanzania and Zimbabwe, in chapter 8, involves two countries that largely avoided severe and sustained internal unrest without primary reliance on repression. In both countries, however, the potential for such a calamity existed and continues to do so. Hevina Dashwood focuses on the timely initiatives undertaken by the leaders of Zimbabwe to maintain stability and social peace and thus avert the tragedy that has befallen so many other African states. Cranford Pratt describes how Julius Nyerere developed policies and institutions that enabled Tanzania to chart a course over sixteen years that avoided the divisive force of ethnic, regional, and religious factionalism and intra-elite rivalries, as well as the corrosive effects of corruption.

It is often argued that contestation between the superpowers over spheres of influence has intensified nearly all inter- as well as intra-state conflicts in Africa. Yet the end of the Cold War and of superpower rivalry does not seem to have enhanced the capacity of African states to deal effectively with internal conflicts. Indeed, there is a danger that most ongoing civil wars will be allowed to drag on, as in Liberia, Rwanda, Somalia, and Sudan. This is an ominous reality, for not only are these countries deprived of the stability that is necessary for economic, social, and political development, but they also suffer from the rapid destruction of the institutions of civil society. The Cairo meeting of the heads of states of the Organization of African Unity (OAU) in 1993 created "a mechanism to prevent and resolve conflicts" as well as a fund for peace-keeping operations. In 1994, the thirtieth OAU summit meeting in Tunis issued "A Declaration on the Fundamental Principles of Relations between African States," which prohibited the arming, training, or financing of armed groups. It may seem premature to assess the effect of these developments within the

OAU and of similar ones in the UN system, but it is important to study the extent to which these measures can be effective in resolving conflicts and whether additional steps are needed. In chapter 9, James Busumtwi-Sam explores recent changes in the role of the OAU and the UN in resolving such wars and assesses the effectiveness of these new procedures.

In chapter 10 we attempt to draw out the similarities and differences among these various civil wars. On the surface, all the countries examined in this volume seem to have inherited deep ethnic cleavages that ruling elites have not hesitated to manipulate and exploit in order to strengthen their hold on power. To what extent are these civil wars grounded in what might be termed "instrumental ethnicity"? Once the civil conflicts have erupted, foreign interests are usually only too ready to intervene at their own initiative or to respond favourably to requests for support from one of the parties. Have outside forces in fact played a spoiling role, exacerbating strife and reducing the likelihood of peaceful resolution? Or have they instead offered their services as conciliators or mediators in the search for a negotiated settlement? In what instances and under what conditions does third-party intervention succeed? Finally, the signing of an agreement is not the beginning of peace, just a step in that direction. In those instances in which violent conflict has largely ended, what steps have newly formed governments taken to start the difficult transition from war to peace? Is there a difference in the set of problems that such new administrations face if they come to power through the barrel of a gun rather than via negotiated settlement? It is against the background of these questions that we draw out the conclusions to this volume.

NOTES

1. I. William Zartman, "Conflict Reduction, Prevention, Management, and Resolution," in Francis M. Deng and I. William Zartman, eds., *Conflict Resolution in Africa* (Washington, DC: Brookings Institution, 1991), 319. In addition to this volume, there are several other general studies of conflicts in Africa – for instance, Raymond Copson, *Africa's Wars and Prospects for Peace* (New York: M.E. Sharpe, 1994); David R. Smock, ed., *Making War and Waging Peace: Foreign Intervention in Africa* (Washington, DC: U.S. Institute of Peace 1993); and Peter Anyang' Nyongo, ed., *Arms and Daggers in the Heart of Africa* (Nairobi: African Academy of Sciences, 1993).

# PART ONE
## *Force as the Major Instrument of Resolution*

Uganda

# 1 Managing Political Change: Uganda under Museveni

JOHN KIYAGA-NSUBUGA

In assessing the reconstruction of societies that have suffered extensive dislocation, it is necessary to examine how reformist regimes try to liberalize the political process amid continuing instability. Since no two transitions[1] can unfold in the same way or lead to identical results – the character of each is determined by how the reformist regime got into power, the socioeconomic context within which it is operating, and the resistance that it has to overcome – analysis of reforms that are preceded and accompanied by high levels of political violence should pay attention to how reformist regimes try to engineer socioeconomic change without losing control of the process altogether. In doing so we might generate better understanding of the dynamics of political transitions in sub-Saharan Africa than analyses that examine political change in terms of some preconceived standard.

This chapter examines the struggle by Yoweri Museveni's National Resistance Movement (NRM) regime to reconstruct Uganda after seizing power in 1986, following a five-year guerrilla war against Milton Obote's second regime (1981–85) and that of his successor, General Tito Okello (1985). The account has two parts. The first provides an overview of the nature and effects of the intra-elite struggle that preceded the regime's seizure of power. The second discusses the regime's efforts to rebuild Uganda's economic and political institutions and processes against a background of severe elite discord. I argue that the regime's strategy for bringing relative stability to Uganda – which Gilbert Khadiagala describes as "a judicious mix of coercion and incorporation"[2] – is explicable in terms of elite[3] failure to agree on the rules of the game.

Uganda's experience suggests that the re-establishment of stability in a country that has suffered extensive, recurrent upheavals requires firm but nationally minded leadership, extensive broadening of the political process to include previously marginalized groups, intra-elite cohesion, and positive developments on the economic front. Only then can conditions be laid for addressing the structural imbalances that underlie social conflict. The dilemma during this latter phase, however, is that the need for political control is bound to clash with the logic of political liberalization.

Political conflicts in Africa are rooted in structural imbalances originating from the colonial practice of favouring development of some ethnic and religious groups or regions at the expense of others, and they are compounded by the failure of the post-colonial state to perform its expected developmental role. Keeping these conflicts within manageable bounds requires vast improvement in the developmental capacities of the state, as well as major changes in the distribution of political and economic power, both of which require broad agreement within the elite on the rules of political competition. If such consensus is lacking, the resultant zero-sum politics is likely to cause incalculable damage to socioeconomic institutions and processes. The problem of political change is then compounded: to address the underlying structural imbalances, the country must first be restored to normality, which cannot re-emerge in a context of zero-sum politics.

This dilemma is particularly acute in countries such as Uganda, which have suffered severe damage to their political and economic institutions and processes from prolonged intra-elite conflict. Even if the shattered infrastructure and state institutions can be rebuilt – which is no easy task – re-establishing political normality is often complicated by the ever-present "insecurity dilemma," as "individuals and groups acting against perceived threats to assure their own security or securities consequently create an environment of increased threat or reduced security for most, if not all, others within the borders of the state."[4] This situation greatly inhibits emergence of elite consensus over the parameters of political discourse. Moreover, since fall from power threatens political incumbents with loss of access to state patronage, as well as imprisonment, exile, or even death, they are hardly likely to put themselves at considerable risk when they embark on political liberalization. In the absence of elite agreement over the rules of the game, political liberalization is more likely to be "guided," as incumbents seek to rebuild the economy and establish new democratic institutions without losing control of the political process.

Ever since Dankwart Rustow highlighted the close relationship between elite consensus and the transition to democracy,[5] numerous studies have pointed to elite pact-making as crucial during the initial stages of the transition.[6] Most of these studies, however, treat incumbent's actions as the main – if not the only – impediment to liberalization. Yet they are just one dimension of the problem, equally significant is the behaviour of counter-elites and the dynamics set in motion by previous regimes.[7] Thus the analysis of socioeconomic reconstruction in highly destabilized countries must also focus on intra-elite behaviour, because of the elite's centrality to the political process – both as facilitators and as impediments to social change.[8] I discuss these issues in Uganda's context by reviewing the political dynamics that gave rise to the NRM regime and the political struggle that ensued after the regime came to power in 1986.

BACKGROUND

Prior to the NRM's seizure of power in 1986, Uganda had experienced a long history of political upheavals, with military coups in 1971, 1979, and 1985, war with neighbouring Tanzania in 1978–79, and civil war in 1981–85. The underlying causes of this turbulence were colonially derived regional, ethnic, and religious imbalances. Buganda had been the first region with missionary schools and commercial agriculture, which eventually enabled the Baganda to be dominant – among native Africans – in Uganda's civil service, agriculture, petty trade, the transport sector, and the professions. Buganda also received greater administrative autonomy than other regions in the 1900 and 1955 agreements with Britain,[9] which set it further apart in political terms. In contrast, the development of the northern region was largely neglected, forcing most of its workforce to migrate to the south, where relative affluence was all too evident. At the same time, recruitment into the military, police, and other security agencies was biased in favour of northerners, allegedly because they were "martial."[10] Meanwhile, the end of the religious wars in 1889 had given rise to Protestant hegemony at the expense of the Catholic plurality,[11] which led the Catholics eventually to form the Democratic party (DP) in 1956 in order to champion their grievances.

The key problems after independence, therefore, were how to relate Buganda to the rest of Uganda and how to redress regional imbalances and Catholic grievances. While Buganda's strong corporate identity and centrality to Uganda's socioeconomic life enabled it to acquire a privileged, semi-federal arrangement in the independence constitution of 1962, it also deepened anti-Buganda sentiments elsewhere, which had earlier led to formation of Milton Obote's Uganda People's Congress (UPC).[12] However, even though "[a]t independence (1962), Uganda had one of the most vigorous and promising economies in Sub-Saharan Africa (SSA),"[13] this situation could not hide the gross disparity between north and south. These various cleavages called for development aimed at rectifying the underlying structural imbalances, not solely at expanding the economy. Yet, apart from Obote's ineffectual "move to the left,"[14] and Amin's disastrous "economic war,"[15] no other major attempt was made to alter the economic relations inherited at independence.

These cleavages also called for a type of politics that emphasized negotiation, compromise, and inclusion, not one that aggravated existing anxieties or created new ones. However, not much effort was made to generate intra-elite cooperation that transcended ethnic, regional, and religious attachments. Instead, political control was sought either through tactical coalitions, such as UPC's ill-fated alliance with Buganda's Kabaka Yekka (KY) party in 1962–64, or through use of state coercive machinery to reduce political space for contending elites – which Nelson Kasfir refers to as "departicipation."[16] At times the latter included outright murder of political opponents, as during Idi Amin's regime, when tens of thousands of people were killed, including such notables as the vice-chancellor of Makerere University, the governor of the Bank of Uganda, the chief justice of Uganda, and the Anglican archbishop of Uganda.

Not until Amin's overthrow in early 1979, through the combined actions of Tanzanian troops and Ugandan exile groups, did the opportunity arise for restructuring politics anew. Yet, even after being coaxed by the Tanzanian government into forming the Uganda National Liberation Front (UNLF), the competing elite groups (more than twenty of them) still failed to overcome their petty factionalism to lay the foundation for a smooth transition to democratic politics. In their rush to gain control of the state machinery from Amin's crumbling regime, they failed to devise an effective formula for sharing power during the two-year transition to the scheduled elections, an initiative that would have addressed most of the deep-seated insecurities and prevented the immediate resumption of zero-sum politics. Consequently, the entire UNLF period (1979–80) saw heightened instability and violence – evidenced by the coups against Yusuf Lule and Godfrey Binaisa in 1979 and 1980, respectively – as each group tried to safeguard its interests by altering the political balance in its favour. Even though the UPC had the best organization nationally and virtually controlled the political process by mid-1980, its leaders still blatantly manipulated the elections to their advantage.[17] Thus, when the UPC returned to power in 1981 with Obote at the helm, all the ingredients for civil war were in place.

The political violence that brought down Obote's second regime followed from three interrelated factors. First, prospects for intra-elite cooperation were greatly eroded both by the sharp post-Amin struggle, in which key elite factions sought control of state patronage and coercive machinery, and by the bad taste left by the manner in which the UPC "won" the 1980 elections. Second, the country's total institutional and economic collapse made it extremely difficult for the regime to guarantee people's physical security and material well-being.[18] Third, in addition to confining state patronage and meaningful political participation to the UPC faithful – particularly Obote's kinsmen, the Langi – the regime rejected reconciliation with its opponents,[19] even though the key to stability lay in allaying the anxieties of opposition groups, whose access to the state had been cut off by the regime's ascendancy, and of the Baganda, whose centrality to the country's political economy and long-standing grudge against Obote made them formidable opponents. It was these factors, together with internal splits within the regime, that led to Obote's overthrow in July 1985 by the Acholi faction, led by the army commander, General Tito Okello.

Far from resolving the political crisis that had engulfed the country, Obote's overthrow generated greater instability, because it created a power vacuum, which the triumphant Acholi faction was too weak to fill by itself. Rather than bringing all the major players into the political mainstream, where they could collectively devise a new political direction for the country, the coup leaders simply tried to neutralize political parties and other armed groups[20] by incorporating them into a political structure that lacked shape or purpose. For instance, all armed groups retained their separate commands, and each was allocated control of a separate section of the capital. When this scheme failed, because the most powerful group – the NRA – refused to be a party to it, the regime then tried to negotiate a power-sharing formula with the NRM in a series of peace talks organized in Nairobi by the Kenyan president, Daniel arap Moi. The negotiations, which ran from 26 August 1985 to 17 December 1985, concentrated on distribution of positions on the new military council and the number of soldiers that each armed group would have in the new army.[21] In the end, General Okello's side accepted the NRM's demand for parity in the planned new military council, after the NRA had demonstrated its power by setting up a rival administration in the southern and western parts of the country.[22]

These talks constituted a significant advance for Uganda's political development. Even though they were rushed, providing little opportunity to erode the deep mistrust between the two polarized sides,[23] they introduced the crucial precedent of negotiated power-sharing as a method of conflict management. They did not lead to peace, because General Okello's regime miserably failed to improve civil–military relations, it lacked any sense of direction, and its Acholi leadership was deeply mistrusted by most of its coalition members and the NRM because of its past close association with Obote. By the time the agreement was signed, the balance of power had clearly shifted in the NRM's favour, enabling it to overthrow Okello's military council regime with relative ease.

### THE NRM IN POWER

When the NRM took power in January 1986, Uganda was in a political and economic crisis caused by the ravages and deep psychological wounds inflicted by the preceding civil war. The objectives that the regime set for itself – to restore law and order, to reverse economic ruin, to establish democratic rule, and to promulgate a widely acceptable constitution – and the manner in which it tried to attain them cannot be understood without reference to earlier failure by contending elite factions to agree on the fundamentals of political discourse.

Three factors shaped events: the relentless intra-elite struggle for control of state patronage after Amin's fall, the decisive power shift from "northern" to "southern" hands that the NRM's ascendancy engendered – for the first time the military and government were dominated by southerners – and the sheer economic dislocation suffered during the civil war. All three combined to compel the regime to adopt a strategy of compromise, negotiation, and political inclusion and constitutional consultation vis-à-vis competitors. This approach was not induced by what William Zartman calls a "hurting stalemate,"[24] since the NRM had achieved preponderance over other competing groups – at least in a military sense. Rather, as Mahmood Mamdani observes, the regime correctly recognized that its monopolization of political power would have led to disaster, given that political imbalances had long been part of the problem.[25]

Yet even as the regime liberalized the political process, it also restricted certain forms of political participation, particularly the resumption of overt party activities. The explanation for this contradiction lies in the uncertainties of the very transition that the regime had set in motion. The NRM was a hegemonic alliance between two ethnic groups – the Banyankore and the Baganda – whose armies, Museveni's People's Revolutionary Army (PRA) and Lule's Uganda Freedom Fighters (UFF), respectively, had merged in the bush in 1982 to form the NRA. Its leadership was an umbrella movement, within which different tendencies would participate in politics as the country reconstructed itself. To function smoothly, however, this arrangement required initial agreement between the major participants over the key elements of the transition, especially the formula for power-sharing, the nature of political competition during the interim period, and the long-term relationship between the NRM and political parties.

However, because the rapid collapse of the Okello regime enabled the NRM to capture power when competitors were relatively weak, the transition did not start with protracted negotiations over the essence of the democratization process. The NRM extracted only a "gentleman's agreement" from other forces to suspend political activities until the adoption of a new constitution. This lack of prior harmonization of expectations created uncertainties which influenced subsequent developments: while the NRM regime was unsure of any lessons that other groups might have learned about political competition which awarded all the spoils to a single winner, its competitors were equally suspicious of its intentions.

## THE POLITICS OF INCLUSION

While previous regimes had sought political control through departicipation, the NRM worked for inclusion, because its leaders recognized the impossibility of achieving economic reconstruction against a background of sharp adversarial politics.[26] This inclusion took several forms, of which four were most prominent – appointment to cabinet of representatives of different political tendencies, expansion of the NRA, promotion of grassroots discourse through people's Resistance Committees, and inducement of widespread participation in the drafting of a new constitution.

There were nine major players when the NRM took power. The four political parties were the Democratic party (DP), the Uganda People's Congress (UPC), the Uganda Patriotic Movement (UPM), and the Conservative party (CP). The five armed groups, excluding the NRA, were the Uganda Freedom Movement (UFM), the Federal Democratic Army of Uganda (FEDEMU), the Uganda National Rescue Front (UNRF), the Former Uganda National Army (FUNA), and the

Uganda National Liberation Army (UNLA). During the "Obote 2" regime only the UPC had been represented in cabinet because of the winner-take-all arrangement on which the 1980 elections had been organized.[27] In contrast, Museveni's cabinet was more representative of diverse political tendencies. Except for the UPC, whose leaders were still in disgrace, and FUNA, whose leaders the NRM refused to have anything to do with on account of their past association with Amin's regime – its head, Major-General Isaac Lumago, had been Amin's chief of staff – all political parties and major armed groups were represented.[28] The basic strategy was one of cooption: the regime invited into its fold all tendencies, regardless of their philosophies, the objective being to generate sufficient peace to permit reconstruction. As Museveni put it: "The groups which were threatening me would bring me a list of twenty bad people, and to preserve peace I would have to choose two or three of the least bad of them."[29]

This same rationale also operated in the expansion of the NRA. At the time the NRA captured Kampala its full strength stood at approximately 15,000 troops. By 1992, however, it had expanded to over 100,000, leading external donors to put pressure on the regime to reduce it to approximately 50,000.[30] This phenomenal increase was the result of the leadership's decision to stabilize the situation by incorporating into the NRA thousands of fighters from the other groups, including UNLA soldiers who had surrendered when the NRM seized power, and even from rebel groups formed to fight the NRM regime – such as the Uganda Peoples Democratic Army (UPDA) and the Uganda Peoples Army (UPA).[31] While drafting these groups into the NRA en masse was bound to create numerous disciplinary problems,[32] the alternative of thousands of armed men roaming the countryside was considered far worse.

A third method by which the NRM pursued political inclusion was through people's Resistance Committees (RCs). During the guerrilla war the NRM had introduced RCs where it operated, in order to undermine local administrative structures and to gain valuable intelligence. Later, it extended RCs all over the country to form the basic link between the regime and the populace and to provide people with an unprecedented say in local affairs. As in the old administrative system, the RC structure had five levels – village, muluka (parish), gombolola (sub-county), ssaza (county), and district. Whereas chiefs had previously been appointed from above and were therefore direct representatives of central authority, RC officials were elected from below.

All residents in a village who were eighteen years or older constituted an electoral college, which elected nine members, including at least one woman, who formed the village resistance council (RC1). The members of each RC1 executive committee in a parish formed an electoral college and from among themselves elected nine members – again, at least one a woman – who made up the parish's resistance council executive committee (RC2). This indirect election was repeated at sub-county (RC3), county (RC4), and district (RC5) levels. Atop this structure sat the National Resistance Council (NRC) – or parliament – which was at first elected indirectly from RC5 but was chosen in national elections in 1989. The primary purpose of RCs was to handle local disputes, oversee security (for instance, all visitors to the village, including soldiers on leave, had to report first to the secretary for defence), serve as watchdogs against corrupt chiefs and police, vet police and army recruits, and deal with local development.[33] In theory, RC officials could be voted out of office at any time, though this was more likely at the RC1 level, where elections were direct.

The regime's fourth inclusive measure involved unprecedented consultation in the drafting of a new constitution. Previous exercises had been confined to elite circles. The independence constitution of 1962 had been drafted at Lancaster House in London, England, by representatives of the colonial government, Uganda's major political parties, and the Buganda government. When Milton Obote abrogated that constitution in 1966, he replaced it with one that he had drafted with a few close associates, which was then rubber-stamped by an intimidated parliament.

In comparison, the NRM regime made a constitution in a markedly different way. From December 1988, when the NRC enacted the Uganda Constitution Commission Statute, to January 1993, when the Constitutional Commission submitted the draft document, individual and group submissions were received from all interest groups, even from Ugandan communities abroad. For the elections of 28 March 1994 for the constituent assembly, which was to discuss the draft constitution, there were no restrictions on who would run; candidates were required to stand as individuals, not as representatives of political parties or even the NRM itself. Stringent measures were also taken to prevent a repeat of the electoral malpractices that had marred the 1980 elections. Only one ballot box was used at each polling station (to prevent stuffing of party boxes with extra ballots), vote counting was done at the polling station on the same day, and gerrymandering was eliminated by using existing counties as electoral constituencies.[34] The outcome strongly favoured pro-NRM candidates, who swept Buganda, the west, and most of the east. Only in the UPC stronghold in the north and parts of the east was the NRM decisively rejected,[35] but not because of electoral malpractices, as in the past.

How should all these measures be interpreted? On the basis of his analysis of the NRC election of 1989, Nelson Kasfir argues that the regime's handling of the liberalization process cast serious doubts on its overall commitment to democratization, because it prevented political parties from campaigning and fielding candidates openly and did not put itself at genuine risk (68 of the 279 NRC members were appointed – thirty-eight "historical" members, twenty presidential appointees, and ten NRA representatives).[36] Similarly, Oloka-Onyango argues that the NRM's "grassroots" approach was stillborn because the regime flatly rejected party politics, designated the NRA as the ultimate guarantor of the political system, and placed RCs, which were meant to serve as watchdogs, under the overall supervision of district administrators, who were themselves political appointees.[37] To implement meaningful socio-political change, he contends, the regime should have removed "the strictures that prohibit the working class and the peasantry from functioning autonomously."[38] Thus he emphasizes control in assessing the nature of political change.

But there is another side to consider, too. Even as the regime firmly set the parameters within which the system had to evolve, it also incrementally liberalized the process. As indicated above, RCs were expanded throughout the country, bringing millions of people into active local politics for the first time. Also, NRC and CA elections increased participation beyond what party representation would have allowed.[39] The press was accorded unprecedented freedom,[40] and women's political mobilization was greatly increased, reversing earlier, exclusionary policies, which had denied them participation in national affairs. Earlier, Amin's decree setting up the National Council of Women in 1978 had also banned other women's organizations; as well, Obote's second regime had deliberately stunted the activities of women's organizations whose leaders were not allied to the UPC.[41] However, the NRM regime designated one place for a woman on each RC in the country, set up a ministry of women in development (and later merged it with that of culture and community development) and drew more women into the expanded NRC and the CA. Whereas there had been only one woman out of 152 members of parliament during Obote's second regime, the NRC had thirty-eight women out of 263 members.[42] For the CA, each district was allowed to nominate one woman representative, in addition to women who had won seats in their own right. Even though this affirmative action took place largely at the level of public politics, it provided women with a platform from which to struggle for further changes in order to reduce the extreme gender inequality in the country.[43]

Another of the regime's actions intended to increase political participation was its policy on exiles. Hitherto the tendency had been for exiles to stay abroad until the incumbent regime fell and then to induce a new set of exiles themselves after taking power. The NRM regime reversed this by enticing exiles back in order to reduce the cost of keeping them at bay and to enable them to contribute to the development effort. As a result, there was a steady return from exile of many of the government's high profile opponents.[44] The regime also showed an inclination towards negotiation, compromise, and respect for majority decision – as demonstrated by deliberations within the CA. One major bone of contention was whether Uganda should adopt a federal structure similar to that under the 1962 constitution, as most Baganda wished, or be governed by a unitary arrangement, as the rest of the country wanted.[45] Though itself opposed to federalism, preferring decentralization of powers to the districts under a unitary government, the NRM leadership negotiated a compromise solution with the Lukiiko (Buganda's parliament) in February 1995, under which, at the adoption of the constitution, Buganda's eight districts would be deemed to have formed a de facto federal state.[46] Another controversial issue was whether the country should continue under the NRM umbrella arrangement or return to a multi-party system with the new constitution. Though the NRM had long opposed parties, and even used its majority in the CA to suspend party activities for a further five years following inauguration of the constitution,[47] its leaders wanted the matter to be resolved by referendum at the end of that period.[48]

Also to consider in assessing the political changes are the actions of competing groups. First, the decisive shift in the control of state power from "northern" to "southern" hands, which the NRM ascendancy engendered, generated great bitterness among former beneficiaries of the "Obote 2" and Okello regimes, some of whom assumed a hostile and uncompromising attitude to the new changes. For example, the UPC refused to contribute any proposals during the drafting of the new constitution or to nominate its two representatives to the CA like other parties, even though this move would have improved its image, badly tarnished by its earlier constitutional miscues. Second, while the regime's inclusive politics attracted individuals and groups receptive to broad-based politics, it also created internal destabilization and intrigue.[49] Third, the incorporation into the NRA of large numbers of fighters from various armed groups weakened military discipline, with serious political consequences. For instance, the rise of the Uganda Peoples Democratic Army (UPDA) and Alice Lakwena's Holy Spirit Movement (HSM) in

1986–87 in Acholi resulted largely from local alienation caused by the lawlessness and revenge killings perpetrated by unruly elements of the expanded NRA.[50]

Finally, none of the regime's competitors presented a viable alternative to the NRM's broad-based structure other than calling for the immediate return to winner-take-all politics. Even when some of them formed the National Caucus for Democracy (NCD) to put pressure on the regime to allow resumption of multi-party politics,[51] they did not indicate how political control by a single party would prevent the country from relapsing into chaos. Part of the problem, I have argued, was that lack of negotiation over the terms of the transition at the beginning led to divergent expectations. The NRM leadership wanted to maintain a broad-based system until sufficient stability had returned to warrant a return to divisive, multi-party politics. The UPC and DP leaders, in contrast, wanted a rapid return to conventional partisan politics, because prolonged NRM hegemony undermined the long-term viability of their parties' political fortunes.

The failure to reconcile these divergent positions at the beginning made inevitable a rupture in the NRM's broad-based regime during the final phase of the constitution-drafting process, as eventually happened. In June 1995 Ssemogerere resigned as second deputy prime minister and minister of public service in order to run against Museveni in the forthcoming general elections. More important, the DP and the UPC entered into a tactical alliance by fielding Ssemogerere as their sole candidate against Museveni, in order to avoid splitting the opposition vote, as had happened in neighbouring Kenya the year before. The move badly backfired. Museveni successfully pinned Obote's ghost on the alliance and swept every region except Obote's stronghold in the north, where, ironically, Ssemogerere was fully embraced. The overall result was: Museveni 74.2 percent; Ssemogerere 23.1 percent, and little-known Muhammad Kibirige Mayanja 2.1 percent. The new cabinet did not contain any multi-party advocates, and once again politics became characterized by highly publicized intra-elite conflict – precisely what the NRM leadership had wanted to avoid.

If the regime was subjected to so much pressure from the main political parties and from an assortment of armed groups, why was it able to retain control of the political process and bring relative stability to the country? One major factor was that it enjoyed the full backing of the National Resistance Army, and its roots in the countryside were still quite deep. Of equal importance, as I indicate below, the regime managed to generate a sustained economic upswing.

## THE ECONOMIC DIMENSION

One of the most significant developments during the NRM's rule was the regime's relative success in turning around key sectors of the economy. By the first five-year mark, according to the World Bank, it had made "impressive progress in those aspects of its agenda that required immediate attention."[52]

This was in sharp contrast to the unsuccessful attempts by Obote's second government to halt the economy's backsliding and generate sustainable forward momentum. The severe drought in 1984 and the disruptions of the civil war, among other factors, had caused the GDP which had increased by 8.2 percent in 1983, to decline by a precipitous 7.7 percent in 1984, after which it rebounded by a modest 1.4 percent in 1985.[53] Reductions in coffee proceeds and the IMF's suspension of its support program in 1984 had also greatly reduced import capacity.[54] By the time the NRM seized power, the country's gross reserves stood at a mere U.S.$23 million,[55] while annual inflation exceeded 120 percent.[56] Infrastructure decay was also pronounced: roads were full of potholes, schools and hospitals were in an advanced state of disrepair, most industries were idle because of lack of inputs, government offices had been looted of materials and equipment, and vehicles for transporting produce were in critically short supply – most having been destroyed or looted by fleeing UNLA troops. These adverse developments were complemented by a welter of institutional weaknesses. For years government had been run by a demoralized civil service whose overall size and efficiency had not been fully investigated; revenue administration was woefully inadequate; there was little idea about the country's manpower needs; and the economy's overall performance could not be accurately assessed because of the earlier collapse of the statistics department in the Ministry of Planning and Economic Development.[57]

Though serious problems still remained by the end of 1994 – notably poor tax administration, budgetary fiscal and financial indiscipline, a demoralized civil service, continuous reliance on coffee for over 80 percent of export earnings, and low managerial capacity in the public sector – the economy had stopped its backward slide and had entered the reconstruction phase. Among other things, between 1987 and 1994 GDP expansion averaged 5 percent annually, with most of the recovery taking place in agriculture, mining and quarrying, manufacturing, electricity, construction, commerce, transport, and community services.[58] The reorganization of the public sector was also under way following a series of studies that determined the required reforms.[59] Inflation, which had reached a staggering 273 percent in 1988, had been reduced to single digits.[60] Moreover, while revenue collection in 1986/87 (excluding export taxes on coffee) was equivalent to 3.4 percent of GDP, in 1993/94 it had climbed to 8 percent of GDP.[61] This turn-around was possible because of the regime's strict application of the tough IMF/World Bank stabilization and structural adjustment program that it had been forced to adopt in late 1987.[62]

Thus, even though one cannot say that by 1996 the economy had fully recovered – rural poverty was still at staggering levels, and urban workers still found it difficult to live on their salaries and wages – sufficient momentum had been registered in key sectors to warrant optimism that the country was on the way to recovery, and even to dampen some sources of potential conflict. The rehabilitation of infrastructure, together with increases in agricultural production permitted more food crops to reach urban areas; increases in imports, along with expanded industrial output, made basic commodities such as sugar, salt, and soap more available; and the phenomenal growth of the housing sector in urban areas relieved some of the housing shortages. Together with the inability of the opposition to come up with credible alternatives, these factors earned the regime sufficient political capital with which to handle domestic and external pressure.

CONTINUING INSTABILITY

A constant during reconstruction was instability. The NRM's overwhelming political position following the 1996 elections induced further opposition from vanquished elites and energized former foes, indicating clearly that the culture of democratic choice that the regime was cultivating was still a long way from taking root. In addition to Joseph Kony's Lord's Resistance Army in the north and Lieutenant- Colonel Juma Oris's West Nile Front in the northwest, a new rebel group called the National Democratic Alliance opened another front against the army in the southwest, on the border with Zaire. At the time of writing these and a sprinkling of other armed groups were engaged in frequent combat. Thus the regime was not only under pressure to implement economic reform but also had to maintain a stable political environment within which the program could be implemented. While it had to handle challenges to its authority with firmness, it also had to minimize intra-elite conflict in order to reduce defence expenditure.[63] Stabilizing the country called for complementary political and economic policies rather than those that worked at cross-purposes.

CONCLUSION

Political developments in Uganda under the NRM regime reinforce the argument that the struggle for political power among contending elites has to be resolved if highly destabilized countries are to rebuild themselves. Of course, political conflict is always deeply rooted in structural imbalances, which have to be addressed. But this realignment is a long-term prospect. During the process of re-establishing normality a significant part of the challenge lies in facilitating intra-elite cooperation in order to create a predictable environment for positive economic reform. If different elite factions harbour deep-seated ill-will and mutual mistrust, the situation calls for inventive measures that allow all participants to participate, not arrangements that award all spoils to the victorious party. Firm, nationally minded leadership and inclusive policies are indispensable at this critical juncture.

NOTES

1 My concern here is with the transition from authoritarianism to democracy.
2 G.M. Khadiagala, "State Collapse and Reconstruction in Uganda," in I.W. Zartman, ed., *Collapsed States: The Disintegration and Restoration of Legitimate Authority* (Boulder, Col.: Lynne Rienner Publishers, 1995), 39.
3 By "elite" I mean "the principal decision makers in the largest or most resource-rich political, governmental, economic, military, professional, communications, and cultural organizations." John Higley and Richard Gunther, eds., *Elites and Democratic Consolidation in Latin America and Southern Europe* (Cambridge: Cambridge University Press, 1992), 8.
4 B.L. Job, "The Insecurity Dilemma: National, Regime, and State Securities in the Third World," in Brian L. Job, ed., *The Insecurity Dilemma: National Security of Third World States* (Boulder, Col.: Lynne Rienner Publishers, 1992), 18.
5 Dankwart A. Rustow, "Transitions to Democracy: Toward a Dynamic Model," *Comparative Politics*, 2 (April 1970), 337–63.
6 See G. O'Donnell, P. Schmitter, and Laurence Whitehead, eds., *Transitions from Authoritarian Rule*, 4 vols. (Baltimore: Johns Hopkins University Press, 1986); L. Diamond, J.J. Linz, and S.M. Lipset, eds., *Democracy in Developing Countries*, 4 vols. (Boulder, Col.: Lynne Rienner Publishers, 1989); and Higley and Gunther, *Elites and Democratic Consolidation*. South Africa provides a most recent example of "elite pacting" at the start of a political transition. See René Lemarchand, "Managing Transition –

Anarchies: Rwanda, Burundi, and South Africa in Comparative Perspective," *Journal of Modern African Studies*, 32 no. 4 (1994), 581–604.

7 As Bratton and De Walle observe, "the nature of the preexisting regime shapes the dynamics and outcomes of political transitions." See Michael Bratton and Nicolas Van De Walle, "Neopatrimonial Regimes and Political Transitions in Africa," *World Politics*, 46 (July 1994), 454.

8 For an elaboration of this dual role, see P.J. Schraeder, "Elites as Facilitators or Impediments to Political Development? Some Lessons from the 'Third Wave' of Democratization in Africa," *Journal of Developing Areas*, 29 no. 1 (Oct. 1994), 69–90.

9 See D.A. Low and R.C. Pratt, *Buganda and British Overrule 1900–1955* (Oxford: Oxford University Press, 1960).

10 Actually, the Acholi (who were preferred) were considered easy to control because they were segmentary and politically acephalus, while the Baganda and Banyoro from the central and southwestern regions were considered security risks because they had constituted powerful kingdoms in the past. See Amii Omara-Otunnu, *Politics and the Military in Uganda, 1890–1985* (London: Macmillan, 1987), 10; and A. Mazrui, "Ethnic Tensions and Political Stratification in Uganda," in B.M. du Toit, ed., *Ethnicity in Modern Africa* (Boulder, Col.: Westview Press, 1978), 50.

11 According to the 1959 census of the African population, 34.5 percent were Catholics, 28.2 percent Protestants, and 5.6 percent Moslems. See Kathleen G. Lockard, "Religion and Politics in Independent Uganda: Movement toward Secularization," in J.R. Scarrit, ed., *Analyzing Political Change in Africa: A New Multidimensional Approach* (Boulder, Col.: Westview Press, 1980), 24.

12 On the formation of UPC as an anti-Buganda party, see D.A. Low, *Political Parties in Uganda* (London: Athlone Press, 1962), 48; Dan Mudoola, "Political Transitions since Idi Amin: A Study in Political Pathology," in H.B. Hansen and M. Twaddle, eds., *Uganda Now: Between Decay and Development* (London: Heinemann, 1988), 284; D.A. Low, "The Dislocated Polity," in H.B. Hansen and M. Twaddle, *Uganda Now: Between Decay and Development* (London: Heinemann, 1988), 41; Senteza-Kajubi, "The Historical Background to the Uganda Crisis, 1966–86," in P. Wiebe and C.P. Dodge, eds., *Beyond Crisis: Development Issues in Uganda* (Kampala: Makerere Institute of Social Research and African Studies Association, 1987), 38; D. Mudoola, "Problems of Institution Building: The Uganda Case," in P. Wiebe and C.P. Dodge, eds., *Beyond Crisis: Development Issues in Uganda* (Kampala: Makerere Institute of Social Issues and African Studies Association, 1987), 63; T.V. Sathymurthy, "The Social Base of the Uganda Peoples' Party, 1958–70," *African Affairs,*

73 no. 297 (Oct. 1975), 442–60; and Francis A.W. Bwengye, *The Agony of Uganda* (London: Regency Press, 1985), 77–80.

13 World Bank, *Uganda: Growing Out of Poverty* (Washington, DC: World Bank, 1993), xi.

14 See S.D. Ryan, "Economic Nationalism and Socialism in Uganda," *Journal Commonwealth of Political Studies*, 11 no. 2 (July 1973), 140–58; I. Gershenberg, "Slouching towards Socialism: Obote's Uganda," *African Studies Review*, 15 no. 1 (1972), 79–95; and J.J. Jorgensen, "Structural Dependency and the Move to the Left: The Political Economy of the Obote Regime in Uganda," in T. Shaw and H. Kenneth, eds., *The Politics of Africa: Dependence and Development* (London: Longman, 1979), 43–72.

15 See Will Kaberuka, *The Political Economy of Uganda: A Case Study of Colonialism and Underdevelopment* (New York: Vantage Press, 1990), 249–82.

16 Nelson Kasfir, *The Shrinking Political Arena: Participation and Ethnicity in African Politics, with a Case Study of Uganda* (Berkeley: University of California Press, 1976). For instance, once the UPC was firmly entrenched in power it dissolved the alliance with KY, manipulated and eventually controlled the security agencies, enticed opposition parliamentary representatives to cross to its side, placed Buganda under a perpetual state of emergency, banned all other parties in 1969, and imprisoned the leaders of opposition groups.

17 DP candidates in West Nile, Lira, Kotido, and Kasese districts were prevented from registering in time, which enabled the UPC to claim to have won seventeen seats from these areas "unopposed." More blatantly, when it appeared that the DP was likely to win, Muwanga – the de facto head of state and Obote's front-man – prevented the electoral commission from announcing the results, saying that he would personally have to verify who had won. See Minority Rights Group, *Uganda: Report No. 66* (London, July 1989), 8 and 28.

18 Cherry Gertzel, The Politics of Uneven Development: The Case of Obote's Uganda, Discussion Paper No. 20 (Flinders University of South Australia, July 1988), 1–66.

19 Just two months before Obote's overthrow he refused to negotiate with the rebels who were closing in on the capital because he believed that doing so would be tantamount to appeasement. See Milton A. Obote, Communication from the Chair, *Mandate for Recovery and Development*, Delivered at of the Opening of the Fifth Session of Parliament, 23 April 1985 (Kampala: Government Printer, 23 April 1985), 8–9.

20 Five armed groups had formed to fight Obote's regime – Yoweri Museveni's National Resistance Army (NRM), which operated in the Luwero triangle in the central region; Dr David Lwanga's Federal Democratic Army of Uganda (FEDEMU) and Dr Andrew Lutakome Kayiira's Uganda

Freedom Movement (UFM), both of which operated in Mpigi District, also in the central region; and Brigadier Moses Ali's Uganda National Rescue Front (UNRF) and Major-General Isaac Lumago's Former Uganda National Army (FUNA), both of which operated in West Nile province. The political parties incorporated into the regime structure were the DP, the Conservative party (CP), and Museveni's Uganda Patriotic Movement (UPM), formed a few months prior to the 1980 general elections.

21 Omara-Otunnu, *Politics and the Military*, appendix 3.

22 See "Uganda: The Squeeze," *Africa Confidential*, 26 no. 24 (27 Nov. 1985), 1–3.

23 The talks were at times conceived as a medium through which to outwit the other side. See Y.K. Museveni, *The Path of Liberation* (Kampala: Government Printer, 1989), 3.

24 I. William Zartman, *Ripe for Resolution: Conflict and Intervention in Africa* (New York: Oxford University Press, 1985), especially chap. 1.

25 Mahmood Mamdani, "Uganda in Transition: Two Years of the NRA/NRM," *Third World Quarterly*, 10 no. 3 (July 1988), 1168.

26 This was similar to what happened in Zimbabwe, when Robert Mugabe's Zimbabwe African National Union (ZANU) offered cabinet portfolios to influential whites after winning the country's first general elections. See Victor De Waal, *The Politics of Reconciliation: Zimbabwe's First Decade* (London and Cape Town: Hurst & Company and David Philip, 1990), 44–7; and 133.

27 Obote's cabinet consisted of twenty-eight ministers (Obote was president and minister of finance and also of foreign affairs), eight ministers of state, and eleven deputy ministers of state – a combined total of forty-seven. Fourteen were from the eastern region, twelve from the west, fourteen from the north, and four from Buganda. All, however, belonged to the UPC. See Colin Legum, ed., *Africa Contemporary Record: Annual Survey and Documents 1981–82*, vol. 14 (London: African Publishing Company, 1981), 303–4; and Francis A.W. Bwengye, *The Agony of Uganda: From Idi Amin to Obote* (London: Regency Press Ltd., 1985), 250–8.

28 The DP leader, Dr Paul Ssemogerere, was first appointed minister of internal affairs before being promoted to second deputy prime minister and minister of foreign affairs; the leader of CP, Joshua Mayanja-Nkangi, was first appointed minister of education, was then switched to the Ministry of Planning and Economic Development, and later to the expanded Ministry of Finance and Economic Planning (several other senior officials in the DP were also given cabinet posts); Dr David Lwanga, the leader of FEDEMU, was appointed minister of environment; the two leaders of UFM – Balaki Kirya and Dr Andrew Lutakome Kayiira –

were appointed to the Ministries of State in the President's Office and Energy, respectively; and Brigadier Moses Ali, the leader of UNRF, was appointed minister of tourism and wildlife. Key leaders of UPM (for example, Bidandi-Ssali, Ruhakana Rugunda, Cripus Kiyonga, and Kirunda Kivejinja), were also part of the NRM hierarchy. For the evolution of Museveni's first cabinet, see James Tumusiime, ed., *Uganda 1986–1991: An Illustrated Review* (Kampala: Fountain Publishers, 1992), 10–11.

29 *Weekly Topic* (Kampala), 26 Oct. 1988: 1.

30 The demobilization involved the discharge of previously screened personnel, each of whom received U.S.$714 in cash and building and agricultural implements for resettlement to his home area. The funds were provided by several donors, including the World Bank. See "Demobilization Programme Explained," *New Vision* (Kampala), 20 Sept. 1993: 12–13; and Nat J. Colletta and Nicole Ball, "War and Peace Transition in Uganda," *Finance and Development*, 30 no. 2 (June 1993), 36–9.

31 See *Munno* (Kampala), 29 April 1988; and *Africa Research Bulletin*, 25 no. 5 (15 June 1988), 8892.

32 A most graphic example concerned UFM and FEDEMU troops in the 35th battalion, which was stationed in Kitgum district in Acholi in 1986. They resorted to lawlessness and revenge killings, which so alienated the local population that the situaton led to the formation of the UPDA. *Africa Confidential*, 27 no. 18 (3 Sept. 1988), 3.

33 These activities were backed by three statutes: The Resistance Committees (Judicial Powers) Statute of 1987; the Resistance Council (Judicial Powers) Statute, 1987, Second Schedule; and the Resistance Councils and Committees Amendments Statute, 1988, Section 2A. See Apolo R. Nsibambi, "Resistance Councils and Committees: A Case Study from Makerere," in H.B. Hansen and M. Twaddle, eds., *Changing Uganda: The Dilemmas of Structural Adjustment and Revolutionary Change* (London: James Currey Ltd., 1991), 288–9.

34 See *Monitor* (Kampala), 5–8 April 1994, 8–9.

35 Museveni's interpretation of this election result was that the NRM had used the Zulu "horn formation" to defeat its enemies (Zulu military strategy was based on a solid centre and two outflanking wings). See *Monitor* (Kampala), 5–8 April 1994, 1.

36 Nelson Kasfir, "The Ugandan Elections of 1989: Power, Populism and Democratization," in H.B. Hansen and M. Twaddle, eds., *Changing Uganda: The Dilemmas of Structural Adjustment and Revolutoinary Change* (London: James Currey Ltd., 1991), 261–2.

37 J. Oloka-Onyango, "The National Resistance Movement, 'Grassroots Democracy,' and Dictatorship in Uganda," in Robin Cohen and Harry Goulbourne, eds., *Democracy and Socialism in Africa* (Oxford: Westview Press, 1991), 126–35.

38 Ibid., 141.

39 In the CA elections some constituencies had as many as twelve candidates. See *New Vision* (Kampala), 14 June 1994: 13–17.

40 The best example is the bi-monthly *Uganda Confidential*, which describes itself as "The paper which splits the atom"; its sharp investigation of public figures had no precedent in Uganda's history.

41 Aili Mari Tripp, "Gender, Political Participation and the Transformation of Associational Life in Uganda and Tanzania," *Africa Studies Review*, 37 no. 1 (1994), 114–15.

42 Ibid., 116.

43 See R.E. Boyd, "Empowerment of Women in Contemporary Uganda: Real or Symbolic?" *Labour, Capital and Society*, 22 no. 1 (April 1989), 19–40; and Josephine Ahikire, "Women, Public Politics and Organization: Potentialities of Affirmative Action in Uganda," *Economic and Political Weekly*, 29 no. 44 (29 Oct. 1994), 77–83.

44 For instance, General Tito Okello returned to Uganda in March 1993, and Edward Rugumayo, Dan Wadada Nabudere and Omwony Ojok (three of the "gang of four") the same year. By early 1995 the following had also returned: General Mustapha Adrisi (Amin's vice-president); Peter Otai (minister of state for defence during Obote's second regime, and leader of the rebel Uganda People's Army – UPA); Masette Kuuya (minister of rehabilitation in Obote's second regime); Major-General Gowon (Amin's former chief of staff); and Colonel Wilson Toko (vice-chairman of the Military Council regime). Three other important exiles returned to Uganda in 1996: Joel Alrio Omara (minister of commerce during the second Obote regime); Tony Olanya Olenge (deputy minister of culture and community development in the same regime); and Dr Albert Picho Owiny (minister of state for foreign affairs in the same regime).

45 For these competing views see Republic of Uganda, *The Report of the Uganda Constitutional Commission: Analysis and Recommendations* (Kampala, May 1993), 244–5; Uganda, *The Report of the Uganda Constitutional Commission: Index of Sources and People's Views* (Kampala, Dec. 1992), 375; and Apolo Nsibambi, ed., *Managing the Transition to Democracy in Uganda under the National Resistance Movement. Report of the Uganda Democratization Study for the Global Coalition for Africa and the African Leadership Forum* (Kampala, Dec. 1939), 139.

46 See Agreed Positions Concerning the Creation of a Regional Tier (Memo to CA members, Feb. 1995).

47 See *Monitor* (Kampala, 30 June–3 July 1995), 1.

48 According to Museveni, if people voted to a return to a multi-party system, the NRM would transform itself into a party too to compete directly against the rest. *Monitor* (Kampala, 28–30 June 1995), 1.

49 For example, in October 1986 twenty six people were arrested and charged with conspiring with FEDEMU and UFM units within the NRA to try to overthrow the government. They included senior army officers, Dr David Lwanga (the minister of environment and leader of FEDEMU), Dr Andrew L. Kayiira (the minister of energy and co-leader of UFM), and Evaristo Nyanzi (minister of commerce, and DP treasurer). *Africa Research Bulletin*, 24 no. 3 (April 1987), 8446.

50 *Africa Confidential*, 27 no. 18 (Sept. 1988), 3; Heike Behrend, "Is Alice Lakwena a Witch? The Holy Spirit Movement and Its Fight against Evil in the North," and L. Pirouet, "Human Rights Issues in Museveni's Uganda," in H.B. Hansen and M. Twaddle, eds., *Uganda Now: Between Decay and Development* (London: Heinemann, 1988), 162–77 and 197–209, respectively.

51 The NCD was led by Professor Dani Wadada Nabudere, a key participant in Lule's overthrow in 1979, UPC's Cecilia Ogwal, and Sebaana Kizito, a leader of the DP.

52 World Bank, *Public Choices for Private Initiatives: Prioritizing Public Expenditures for Sustainable and Equitable Growth in Uganda*, vol. 1, (Washington, DC: World Bank, 12 Feb. 1991), 4.

53 Uganda, *Rehabilitation and Development Plan 1988/89 – 1991/92*, vol. 1, 2nd ed. (Kampala: Ministry of Planning and Economic Development, Dec. 1989), 15.

54 The value of imports was U.S.$428 million in 1983, but the corresponding figure for 1985 was only U.S.$264 million. P.S. Mulema, Minister of Finance, *Budget Speech* (Kampala: Ministry of Finance, 1986), 1 and 5.

55 World Bank, *Uganda: Towards Stabilization and Economic Recovery*, Report No. 7439-UG (Washington, DC: World Bank, 26 Sept. 1988), 12.

56 Uganda Economic Study Team, *Economic Adjustment and Long-Term Development in Uganda* (Ottawa: International Development Research Centre, 1986), 36.

57 According to Mulema, the NRM's first minister of finance, the first budget, which he presented in August 1986, was compiled from "rough estimates based on few statistics and lots of assumptions." Mulema, *Budget Speech* (1986), 1.

58 Dr Kiyonga, Minister of Finance, *Budget Speech* (Kampala: Ministry of Finance, 2 July 1991), 1; Uganda, *Rehabilitation and Development Plan 1988/89–1991/92*, 15; Uganda, *Background to the Budget 1990–1991* (Kampala: Ministry of Planning and Economic Development, July 1990), 12; Uganda, *Background to the Budget 1994–1995* (Kampala: Ministry of Finance and Economic Planning), 3–18.

59 See Uganda, *Report of the Public Service Review and Re-organization Commission 1989–1990* (Kampala: Ministry of Public Service and Cabinet

Affairs); and Uganda, *Rehabilitation and Development Plan 1988/89–1991/92.*

60 J. Mayanja-Nkangi, Minister of Finance and Economic Planning, *Budget Speech* (Kampala, June 1993), 2.

61 Ibid., 25.

62 Initially, the regime was very much opposed to SAP, which had been introduced earlier in 1981 by Obote's second regime. However, after failing to restart the economy by itself, and following considerable pressure from the World Bank and from representatives of some key Western governments, the NRM reversed itself and adopted SAP with surprising gusto. See John Kiyaga-Nsubuga, "Political Instability and the Struggle for Control in Uganda," PhD thesis, University of Toronto, 1995), 254–61.

63 During the financial years 1988/89 and 1989/90 Uganda spent 30.2 percent of its budget on defence, while expenditures on social services (education, health, and so on) and economic services (infrastructure, agriculture, and so on) were 23.1 percent and 29 percent respectively. In comparison, during the same period, Kenya, Ghana, and Malawi allotted, on average, 7 percent of their budgets to defence, 33 percent to social services, and 40 percent to economic services. While the three countries" defence expenditures averaged 1.5 percent of GDP, Uganda's was twice as much, at 3 percent. World Bank, *Public Choices for Private Initiatives*, vol. 1, 30–5.

## 2 Liberation Politics in Ethiopia and Eritrea

JOHN PRENDERGAST* AND
MARK DUFFIELD

Conventional diplomatic efforts have had much less influence on the course of conflict in Eritrea and Ethiopia than have external assistance and its integration into the political programs and military strategies of the ruling Eritrean People's Liberation Front (EPLF) and the ruling Tigrayan People's Liberation Front (TPLF), which dominate the two countries. Analysing conventional diplomatic channels probably reveals much less than does an examination of aid patterns and how they have helped underwrite the political philosophies of the major factions. These philosophies put minimal stock in negotiation and compromise with opposition interest groups, including political parties.

This chapter traces the historical evolution of the political programs of the currently dominant parties in Ethiopia and Eritrea. It argues that these programs, solidified by years of material support from Western donors to the factions during their years as liberation movements, explain their present lukewarm attitudes towards independent political and civic organizations. Their principled, messianic leadership has its origins in decades of cell-by-cell political organizing in the face of genocidal counter-insurgency campaigns by Mengistu's regime. We focus on Ethiopia as a case study. We demonstrate how liberation strategies have translated into governance, and we describe

---

\* This chapter was written before John Prendergast joined the National Security Council in Washington, DC.

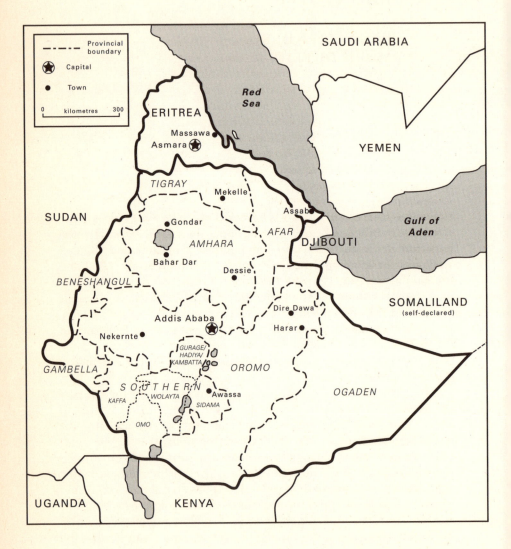

Ethiopia and Eritrea

the current state of the political process. In conclusion, we point out the potential for conflict as well as for its resolution.

Ethiopia is still one of the largest countries in Africa, roughly the size of France and Spain combined, and the second most populous, with more than fifty million people. Ethiopia's modern history was dominated by Emperor Haile Selassie, who ruled from the mid-1920s until the mid-1970s, when he was overthrown by the military council of Mengistu Haile Mariam, known as the Derg, which ruled until 1991.

It was during the Derg's rule that the TPLF was born (1975) and one of the most deadly famines in the country's history occurred (1984–85). The EPLF, officially formed in 1973, had been fighting for independence since the early 1960s. The EPLF and TPLF were primarily responsible for defeating the Derg.

### PUBLIC WELFARE AS A POLITICAL IMPERATIVE[1]

The manner in which the EPLF and the TPLF fought the long-standing armed struggle calls into question the conventional wisdom on the consequences of war and famine – that war is the antithesis of development. Though the contribution of counter-insurgency activities to famine is increasingly acknowledged, in the Horn of Africa the EPLF and TPLF turned social dislocation and privation into a means of mass mobilization and political consolidation. In other words, the war, while visiting untold suffering, also provided the basis for internal development and social change with few parallels in contemporary Africa.

It is clear that the cross-border operation from Sudan into Ethiopia and Eritrea would not have taken place, or would have followed a much more limited trajectory, without the active cooperation and support of the EPLF and TPLF and the relief organizations they established (the Eritrean Relief Association, or ERA, and the Relief Society of Tigray, or REST) and a background of long-standing regional animosity, which effectively sanctioned the violation of Ethiopian sovereignty from Sudanese territory.

Sudanese cooperation in providing a conduit for supplies to areas held by the EPLF and the TPLF proved a lifeline for those movements to the outside world. In Khartoum, for over two decades, three military regimes and one elected government maintained an open-border policy, with only a few short-term interruptions. Besides facilitating the flow of humanitarian supplies, Sudanese support was also part of the larger Cold War drama, which involved large transfers of military aid to the regimes in Addis Ababa and Khartoum, as well as being caught up in regional confrontation, which included Ethiopian support for the rebel Sudan People's Liberation Army.

The cooperation of the Fronts was crucial and signifies the emergence, during the 1970s, of strong, indigenous systems of disaster management in Eritrea and Tigray. These systems, with their emphasis on participation, planning, and social and economic analysis, were in advance of the main approaches among international relief agencies. As well, the political imperatives of the Fronts, in which public welfare was central, stood in strong contrast to the predatory relationship between combatant and non-combatant populations characteristic of successive Ethiopian regimes and, more widely, to the logic of internal war that is all too prevalent in Africa today.

A full appreciation of indigenous political responses in Ethiopia to public welfare and internal war has yet to be written. So far, much of the literature has concentrated on the role of the international community. However, analysis of internal politics is vital, given its importance to the success or failure of relief operations. In the solidarity literature that has grown up around the Fronts there is a good deal of material demonstrating their effectiveness and organizational skills. Less often encountered are references to how the Fronts were able to sustain themselves economically and at the same time pursue political mobilization. The available evidence suggests that the Fronts, using similar strategies but with different aims, established a political economy of liberation capable of simultaneously providing effective famine relief, engendering political support, and pressing the war.

The strength of the resulting economies lay in their essential duality, in which political support and public welfare were organically linked, often through the same organizations, in a mutually reinforcing structure. Public assistance cemented political support, and growing political success facilitated increased humanitarian aid. When pitched against the divisive politics of the contemporary opposition, this "virtuous circle" has had proven effect. Therein, however, lie the seeds of present concerns about the ability of such a directed structure to manage a transition to peace and reconstruction. In such a transition, "transparency," competing visions, and diversity are much more difficult to control.

### SELF-RELIANCE AND RECIPROCITY

Self-reliance is more than a slogan. Since it implies popular participation in problem-solving, it is primarily a matter of organization. In the case of the EPLF and TPLF, this involved establishing a system of civilian administration which could serve as both a means of organization and a channel for voluntary material and political support. The economy of internal war is dependent on the productive capacity of the civilian population. For this reason, civilians are the main target of counter-insurgency campaigns. When, as under semi-subsistence conditions, productive assets are thinly spread, such campaigns can assume genocidal proportions. Since political evolution within the EPLF and TPLF had propelled them to harness civilian productive capacity through voluntary means rather than exaction, the process underscored the need for organization, education, and civilian assistance.

In the mid-1970s, zonal geographical structures were created in Eritrea and Tigray that linked elective village committees to area organizations. Large towns, where they were controlled, had a similar elected administration. Both Fronts developed civilian departments, interconnected with these vertical structures, responsible for the main aspects of public policy: health, education, transport, economy, social welfare, and so forth. Finally, the EPLF and TPLF established horizontal mass political organizations based on the main socio-economic groups: women, peasants, workers, and professionals, for example. Not only did the mass organizations link administrative and public structures, they were the means through which more ambitious social programs, such as land reform and women's equality, were advanced.

In Eritrea, contributions destined for civilian relief were handled by the village committees. Contributions to the military struggle, because of their more political nature, went through the mass associations. Assistance that had not passed through such popular channels would not be accepted.[2] Without this voluntarism, the virtuous circle collapses. Literacy programs and political education meant that civilians could understand the nature of their situation.

Voluntarism, however, demanded reciprocity between movements and people under their control on the part of the EPLF and TPLF. In addition to necessitating political and economic reform favourable to the main agricultural and commercial classes, which was vulnerable to the vicissitudes of the war, reciprocity required urgent attention to public welfare. Early developments in health, for example, meant that by the late 1970s, despite the conflict, both Eritrea and Tigray had achieved historically unprecedented levels of health coverage.[3] In 1975, the EPLF was spending 20 per cent of its total budget on medicine, four-fifths of which was being dispensed to the civilians within its jurisdiction.

Reciprocity also involved food aid and other relief assistance. In the early 1970s, the EPLF established the principle of fighters' sharing their rations with destitute war victims. As social dislocation grew, this direct assistance became more systematic, with the Fronts devoting whatever transport and other resources could be spared to relief purposes.[4] Up to the mid-1980s, the Fronts and the civilian population were probably supplying the bulk of the limited amounts of food relief available in Eritrea and Tigray. In Tigray, for example, in 1983, as famine began to peak but before international assistance became significant, the TPLF, with civilian help, managed to supply 55 per cent of the 11,200 metric tons of food aid distributed.[5] By this stage, however, this was only a fraction of the assistance that was necessary.

## THE ECONOMY OF LIBERATION

While they were ultimately dependent on the civilian population, the Fronts' principles of self-reliance and reciprocity demanded that they establish an economy that provided a strategic resource base independent of an already hard-pressed civilian population. Though the Middle East's support for the Eritrean Liberation Front (ELF) can be readily discerned, both the EPLF and TPLF avoided direct dependence on foreign political backers. For both the EPLF and TPLF, the extensive Ethiopian losses on the battlefield were a major source of military hardware. Information on the nature and extent of the Front economies, however, is sketchy and impressionistic. Even though a number of sources of income can be identified, material has yet to be released that would permit a confident quantitative appraisal. Despite various forms of income, in the last analysis the Fronts were dependent on contributions in kind from the civilian populations of Eritrea and Tigray. To a large extent, reciprocity involved the reallocation and moulding of this assistance into programs of public provision.

Reflecting different conditions in Eritrea and in Tigray, ERA and REST related in different operational ways to their respective Fronts. The EPLF would consolidate a liberated area, including towns, which then was defended and expanded by means of conventional battles. Though both the EPLF and TPLF developed extensive logistical operations and food-targeting systems based on village committees and the use of socio-economic information to distinguish those families in most need, from 1975 the EPLF established internal, self-managing camps for the displaced. The TPLF, in contrast, controlled a larger, changing sphere of influence, surrounding government-held towns, and engaged in mobile guerrilla warfare rather than conventional battles. From the early 1980s, TPLF relief policy involved the management of large-scale migration and repatriation and the internal purchase and allocation of surplus sorghum.

## THE POLITICAL USE OF FOOD AID

For international agencies a key issue in consigning relief supplies to ERA and REST was concern over possible diversion of that aid to military use. Donor governments frequently imposed accounting criteria on the cross-border operation in excess of that required in a conventional emergency. The result was that throughout the 1980s ERA, REST, and their non-governmental organization (NGO) partners (especially the Emergency Relief Desk consortium) directed a good deal of their activity to furnishing monitoring reports and accounts to indicate how the aid was used. While onerous and one-sided, this pressure to prove accountability continually was practically useful in establishing the international credibility of ERA and REST. From an analytical point of view, however, the above analysis would suggest that concern was somewhat misplaced.

Political support for the Fronts sprang largely from their ability to defend civilian populations and meet their economic and welfare needs. From the mid-1970s, the possibility of receiving foreign relief assistance was seen as an important adjunct to this relation of reciprocity. Hence the conscious decision by the Fronts to establish relief associations. Because of the international isolation of Eritrea and Tigray, foreign relief became an important psychological boost for the stressed civilian population.[6] It indicated at least that some outsiders knew of their plight. ERA, for example, had the freedom to advertise the foreign origin of its relief supplies, which was discussed with beneficiaries and on radio broadcasts. It can be argued that any substantial diversion of relief to other ends would not only have contradicted the political logic of the Fronts but would also have undermined their political base and hence their ability to press their aims. The historic and political significance of the Front's welfare policies has yet to be fully appreciated. It is clear that in choosing to assist civilians with various public welfare programs, they effectively reversed the Asian model of guerrilla warfare, in which the rural producers were the source of material support for the political and military movement.[7] To the degree that this shift is representative of the second wave of liberation in the world, it would suggest that this approach is of central importance in charting a future, indigenous solution to the wider African crisis.

Though the direct appropriation and control of food aid by the military establishment were not a feature of the Fronts' political dynamic, international relief perhaps allowed them to stabilize populations and expand their resource base. What about fungibility, or the ability to redeploy resources freed in one area to another? In so far as the cross-border operation reduced the Fronts' burden of supplying public assistance, their military capability probably was significantly enhanced.

Fungibility, however, together with voluntary civilian donations, should not be confused with direct military appropriation or diversion of relief assistance, which was a significant practice of the Ethiopian government. In contrast with the extensive cooperation that the relief associations and Fronts showed towards the international community, direct military appropriation would have weakened the participatory relief-management structures that had been established. Civilian productive capacity would have declined even further, and the levels of suffering been worse. Given the kinship ties between fighters and the peasantry, direct appropriation would therefore have undermined the Fronts' political base and hence their aspirations as well as their performance.

### THE FAILURE OF NEGOTIATIONS DURING THE MENGISTU ERA

Numerous cease-fires were pursued during the last few years of the rule of Mengistu Haile Mariam. African Rights, a London-based human-rights organization, argues that it was fortunate that they did not succeed: "Had there been a cease-fire in 1990 or early 1991, Mengistu would have been able to pursue a new war strategy ... This comprised mass mobilization on the basis of an appeal to ethnic chauvinism. ... Mengistu would thereby have succeeded in turning a war between a military dictatorship and an array of liberation movements into a largely ethnic conflict, and the bloodshed would have been far greater still. The best possible solution for Ethiopia was the rapid and decisive military defeat of Mengistu, and this was duly achieved."[8] Had the war continued for another year, the former scenario might well have unfolded. Because of the tinderbox that ethnicity represents when manipulated by the likes of Mengistu, it is fortunate that the war ended when it did, even if it did lead to the uncontested assumption of power by the TPLF and EPLF.

The only successful mediation effort during Mengistu's rule came in the area of humanitarian diplomacy. In 1990, the government and the liberation movements agreed to corridors of tranquillity for the delivery of relief assistance. This "Joint Relief Partnership" survived the end of the regime and continued into the transitional period.

One other noteworthy sequence of diplomatic events under Mengistu came a few months before his overthrow. A group of fourteen

Ethiopians who became known as the Ad Hoc Committee for Peace and Development approached most of the significant armed and unarmed parties and secured agreement to hold a reconciliation meeting in Switzerland. Days before the conference was to be held, U.S. Assistant Secretary of State Herman Cohen asked the committee to postpone its meeting because of U.S. efforts to secure a peaceful transition of power. As well, at the time of the transition the dominant opposition throughout Ethiopia was made up of resistance movements organized along ethnic lines, and this elite ethnic polarization – realized through the alienation and de-participation of the leadership of ethnic opposition groups – has only increased since the fall of Mengistu.

Negotiation efforts since then, involving the (U.S.) Carter Center, the U.S. Congress, various ambassadors in Addis Ababa, and numerous bilateral initiatives, have failed to entice most opposition parties back into the electoral process.

### COMPETITION FOR POLITICAL AND ECONOMIC POWER

After the fall of Mengistu and the capture of Addis Ababa and Asmara, the Ethiopian People's Revolutionary Democratic Front (EPRDF) and EPLF charted very different political courses of action. The EPRDF chose to make an immediate foray into multi-party politics but placed obstacles in the way of opposition parties. The EPLF was less sanguine about Eritrean society's ability to withstand the inevitable religious and ethnic fragmentation that accompanies multi-partyism and kept a tight leash on the political process from the beginning. Still, the diversity of Eritrea – which contains an even split between Muslims and Christians, as well as nine major ethnic groups – pales in comparison to the ethnic and religious smorgasbord in Ethiopia.

The remainder of this paper focuses on the situation in Ethiopia. (All the remaining quotations come from interviews carried out during field trips to Ethiopia in February, July, and October 1995.) The above analysis of the development of the TPLF's political philosophy is critical in understanding its current course of action. From its inception, the TPLF undertook mass mobilization based on its singular political vision, forged in the context of constant siege and consistent internal and external competition. In this atmosphere – which lasted no less than fifteen years – there was little room for compromise. In the context of massive civil conflict and the genocidal policies of the Mengistu regime against Tigrayan peasant communities, victory went to the strongest, the best organized.

The purse strings of a poor nation reside primarily in the hands of those who control the state. This makes political power more desirable than ever, especially when drought and famine create scarcity that intensifies competition and can be manipulated by politicians to mobilize support.[9] State power is a major cause of conflicts in the Horn, and identities, religions, and nationalism are all used to support this cause.

In the Horn, development has contributed to conflict primarily in response to state decisions about investment in export sectors, especially agriculture and livestock. The state has steered investments towards areas controlled by the ruling elites. Resulting investment patterns have led to extraordinary regional disparities in economic opportunity. These disparities have been intensified as the state provided social services primarily to the same areas. This post-colonial continuation of a colonial trend intensified inequalities among social groups and regions; and resulting tensions fed larger civil conflicts. The most conflict-prone areas in the Greater Horn are nearly all areas that have been excluded from the fruits of state investment.

Ethiopia in 1991 witnessed massive change in the control of state power. Shoan Amhara domination ended, and a clear era of Tigrayan rule and Eritrean independence commenced. To gain and maintain political power, the Tigrayan People's Liberation Front (TPLF, the main organization comprising the ruling EPRDF) has for over a decade supported the creation of associated parties in different regions to act as partners in a larger coalition. These regional parties produce the administrators and cadres for the regional governments. The abuses by some of these local operatives against older regional parties – combined with the strength of the EPRDF – pushed most of the major opposition parties out of the electoral process after 1991. By the 1992 local and regional elections, most opposition groups began a boycott of the process. This continues until the present.

The Oromo Liberation Front (OLF) left the political process for a complex set of reasons, including harassment and intimidation throughout Region Four, favouritism shown to the Oromo People's Democratic Organization (OPDO) by the EPRDF, a long history of disagreement and rivalry with the TPLF, a perception by the OLF that the odds were not in its favour in the electoral process, and the OLF's belated fear that agreements that it had negotiated in 1991 with the EPRDF had nevertheless given the latter the upper hand politically; the Southern Coalition (a grouping of small parties based in the southern parts of Ethiopia) was removed from the government after it signed a resolution calling for the formation of a new government.

The All Amhara People's Organization (AAPO) is the youngest of these major groups, and its leader, Professor Asrat Woldeyes, has been in prison since July 1994 because of his inflammatory writings and speeches, which the government felt incited ethnic hatred and which represent a brand of "hate politics" that has an explosive history in the Horn.

These and other organizations have not gone beyond their unified anti-EPRDF platform into developing alternatives or coordination mechanisms among themselves. This vacuum has left Ethiopia largely without a significant "loyal opposition." With the political elite sidelined, civil society's leaders were left to lead any political opposition. Meanwhile, the EPRDF has accelerated its internal revolution by winning overwhelming electoral victories from the national level (1995) down to the zonal level (1996). A perverse reality results: non-EPRDF dissent is not voiced within the system, but it is tolerated to an extent outside the system in the Addis Ababa-based press. But in the latter, there is no accountability to the public, and little constituency-building. Nevertheless, there exists extensive room for debate and public participation within the EPRDF structure itself, in which many different points of view are accommodated. This is the hallmark of "movement-based democracy," epitomized by Eritrea, Ethiopia, and Uganda.

One structural problem for the future of the political process in Ethiopia is the boycott of elections by the major opposition parties and their perception that they have no legal means by which they can participate freely and gain power. They are hitching their fortunes to an all-or-nothing strategy: either the whole game begins over, or they don't play at all. Another structural problem is the division and fragmentation of the opposition itself, making it more unlikely that huge blocs of political opponents will re-enter the legal process. This situation is in contrast to the strength of the EPRDF across the country.

The post-transition potential for conflict in Ethiopia is difficult to gauge. There is little credible analysis of what level of armed resistance these and other organizations might offer. The Ethiopian National Patriotic Front, for example, may try to tap extremist sentiment in some form of a terrorist campaign. Al-Itihad and OLF units have used violence against the state. Given the current strength of the government's army, fairly widespread support among the peasantry in many locations, and the solid support of donors, major armed conflict is unlikely in the near future at the national level in Ethiopia. Political motives are often ascribed to banditry, but it may be impossible to decipher the actual level of politically inspired violence.

Another issue that will certainly be contentious is the gradual restructuring of the government army in an attempt to widen its representation to a more national base. In recent years many EPRDF officers have been pensioned off, while members of minority ethnic groups were encouraged to join the forces. The strong, centrally controlled army remains an anchor of power for the EPRDF.

The economic dimension of state control is less clear. The opposition continues to allege that disproportionate resources flow to Tigray. This is countered by the fact that the EPRDF leadership frowns on personal enrichment through government service. The economic arena is subject to contestation for control in much more subtle ways. Two issues stand out: post-conflict development and privatization. Regarding the former, EPRDF-affiliated parties have formed and supported associated development organizations designed to assist the process in their regions. The Tigray Development Association, the Amhara Development Association, and the Oromo Development Association are the most prominent. Some international NGOs perceive an increasingly less hospitable environment in which to operate in some regions, perhaps signaling the government of Ethiopia's (GOE's) desire to channel more development assistance directly to these indigenous development organizations associated with the ruling party.

The process of privatization presents a much less clear portrait of consolidation of assets and economic power by the ruling EPRDF. The sacking of Deputy Prime Minister Tamrat Layne on charges of corruption was an abnormal case of personal enrichment and profligate influence-peddling. The real story of economic concentration or diffusion is much more difficult to discern. The economic context of the last five years has included a commitment to a market economy by the GOE and a brisk pace of privatization. Parallel to this process of economic liberalization has been the rapid creation of non-government-owned enterprises controlled through majority shareholding by members of the TPLF and to a lesser extent by other EPRDF-affiliated parties, particularly the OPDO and the the Amhara National Democratic Movement (ANDM). The largest of these TPLF-controlled enterprises is the Endowment Fund for the Rehabilitation of Tigray (EFFORT), a charity run by Siye Abraha, a member of the TPLF's central committee. EFFORT obtained large blocks of shares in numerous key companies formed by leading TPLF members. Profits end up under the control of the EPRDF members. These companies represent what is likely the largest concentration of capital and assets within Ethiopia.

Questions are being asked about the extent to which other elements of the private sector can compete with this ruling-party-affiliated conglomerate, which is quickly infiltrating the most profitable sectors of the economy – namely, production, services, trade, and transport. Credit, import and export licences, government contracts, and access to international sources of capital are all areas where advantages might be realized. For example, the Tigrayan trading company GUNA has cornered the market on the distribution and sale of fertilizers and other inputs in Tigray through the Global 2000 program.

The counter-argument finds that market-oriented management of these companies has produced efficient, profitable operations. The EPRDF's objectives are served more efficaciously through directed development than by an unfettered, often parasitic private sector unleashed after years of socialist rule. The TPLF's development vision engages the private sector, and public- and private-sector goals are harmonized, minimizing competition and disarticulation of the development process. Profits from these enterprises are ploughed back into the country's development rather than being subject to large-scale capital flight at the first sign of economic stagnation. Most important, though shareholders are largely EPRDF members, access to capital is spread much more widely throughout society. This is a fundamental element of the EPRDF's economic program, aimed at democratizing capital formation. A more public debate about the aims and composition of these companies would serve to reduce misperceptions and misinformation and more fully explicate the EPRDF's comprehensive vision of directed development and economic democracy.

## FEDERALISM

Throughout Africa attempts to liberalize political processes – specifically when introducing multi-party elections – have been incomplete and fraught with difficulty. Liberalization is risky. Change of any sort can cause conflict, at least in the short term. Understandably, then, certain approaches to political liberalization in formerly authoritarian states can increase instability.

In analysing the effects of introducing electoral processes, numerous issues must be differentiated, including electoral laws, state institutions, and types of electoral systems. But election laws are only part of the democratization equation. Basic fundamental laws related to freedom of expression and association are critical as well, as are procedures for redress. The depth of the liberalization process is also key in averting violence. When non-executive components of government – parliaments, local governments, and so on – are perceived to be relatively powerless, there are less opportunities for the formal democratic institutions to channel broad societal demands and to bring extremists into compromise positions. It may not be necessary for one ethnically based party to win the presidency, but as long as that party's members feel they can have some degree of local autonomy and control over their own lives through empowered local government structures or participation in parliament, then they may not resort to violence. The strength of democratic institutions such as political parties and civil society organizations is also key.

This is where the debate regarding Ethiopia intensifies. One line of analysis criticizes the EPRDF for not allowing electoral democracy a full chance, maintaining that there is a single-party state where the imbalances of power at the national and regional level make it difficult or impossible for other major parties to re-enter the democratic process.

A competing framework of analysis notes the participatory local structures that the EPRDF is developing, as well as the process of devolving administrative power away from the centre (the arena in which USAID and other donors may have the greatest impact). It also acknowledges a different vision of participation shared by governments such as those in Ethiopia, Uganda, and Eritrea, as opposed to multi-party models.

After the fall of the Derg in 1991, the EPRDF quickly acceded to donor's demands for a classic multi-party transition. Nevertheless, the election process has been subordinate to the EPRDF's implementation of its own internal version of democratization. The national level machinations related to the electoral process have been in many ways a distraction from the real processes of decentralization and ethnic federalism aimed at restructuring the Ethiopian state and discrediting the old elites.

The Ethiopian state had been over-centralized for decades. The EPRDF believed that, in order to move forward with any political liberalization, it had to dismantle that centralized empire-state. Its leadership felt that if it let go of the reins in certain regions, the country would have splintered, especially in regions 4 and 5. The EPRDF needed to rely on allied parties to maintain control over the process of decentralization.

Now that the transition is over, with the EPRDF entrenched in the centre and its associated parties paramount in key regions, it is possible that the system will further liberalize. The end of the transition process found the TPLF leadership's primary goal accomplished: the consolidation of its power in the system it envisioned creating nearly two decades ago.

Ethiopia is experimenting with a unique democratization process, which creates an "ethnic federalism." There is mixed reaction to this policy, which is devolving administrative responsibilities to nine regions based on nationalities. Supporters are encouraged by the recognition of local languages and cultures, welcome the breathing room from a history of central government and Shoan Amhara domination, and believe over-centralization impractical in such a huge, populous country. The EPRDF views "ethnic federalism" as a means, not an end – its attempt to prevent a single economic class from dominating the poor majority and to avert domination by a single ethnic group. The hope is that if the economy is decentralized, the political arena will change to reflect that new reality, and that local development and local enterprise will be supported.

Detractors say this brand of ethnic politics threatens peace, fails to protect minority rights in the regions, and has led to increased divisions among different groups living in the same region. Some charge that ethnicity that used to be culturally expressed – religion, rituals, festivals, language, and so on – has now become politicized to the extent that it has become an ideology of opposition and exclusion. The OLF and ONLF certainly exploit the divisive elements of this ideology.

Because of regionalization, human rights problems may emerge in some of those regions where judicial and police structures are exceptionally weak. Checks and balances are ill-formed: insecure areas create the need for more central control and more military presence. A particular flashpoint for violence in some places will be taxation policy, especially where roadblocks are established to collect duties. Resource constraints are enormous. Future problems will probably centre around land disputes, regions' versus the central government's taxing power, and transfer of funds from the centre to the regions.

Part of the brilliance of the regionalization policy has been that it regionalized conflict that might have been expressed at the national level. During the more violent early years of transition, 1991–93, limited ethnic cleansing was carried out at the local level in a few regions, and power struggles were played out locally. In Region 4, OLF, the Islamic Front for the Liberation of Oromia (IFLO) and OPDO have battled each other at times, with the EPRDF forces involved in low-intensity counter-insurgency operations against OLF positions. In Region 5, the Ethiopian Somali Democratic League (ESDL) and ONLF battle politically, while military confrontation between the EPRDF and ONLF also occurs sporadically, as well as between the EPRDF and al-Itihad.

There have been major fallouts in trying to redraw boundaries according to ethnicity. People have been forced from lands their families have tilled for generations. Ethnic claims over minerals, lands, and water will continue to be explosive. In some cases, ethnic segregation imposed from the top is difficult for peoples of different ethnicities who have coexisted peacefully for many generations. In other cases, long-standing ethnic tensions have simply been exacerbated. In yet other areas, tensions have been reduced because of increased commerce and access to decision-making structures. Minorities in particular regions have at times claimed to be completely marginalized. In other places, zonal administrations allow minorities to exercise control over language, education, culture, and village councils. Predictably, Ethiopia's diversity produces diverse results.

CONCLUSION

There are certainly difficult contradictions. Decision-making processes are being decentralized and broadened at the base, while national policy-making remains largely under a single party. There has been empowerment of ethnic groups at the regional level but opting out of the main ethnic opposition at the national level. Peasant farmers have gained greater freedom to produce and market their surpluses, but at the cost of repression and control of the former political elite. EPRDF member-controlled companies are increasing its control of the development process but also widening access to capital formation to economic classes that up to now have been largely excluded from such opportunities. Depending on the perspective one chooses, these juxtapositions are either revolutionary or a recipe for disaster. But contradictory perspectives have to be factored in, because all these processes are ongoing simultaneously. The result of the political transition in Ethiopia is a political structure marked by counter-balanced regions which are empowered to varying degrees, though none is strong enough to dominate the centre. This situation clearly is in flux, and many changes lie ahead.

The position of the current Ethiopian and Eritrean governments owes no small debt to the substantial humanitarian assistance clandestinely provided by NGOs for a decade preceding their ascendancy. Because this support involved very little engagement or conditionality, the EPLF and TPLF moved forward with their mobilizing programs with little external manipulation, direction, or interference. This makes current efforts by external groups to affect the process of economic and political liberalization fraught with difficulty. Ethiopian visions of democratization, participation, and economic liberalization differ from conventional models. Rhetorical gamesmanship often results, confusing to those not familiar with the well-developed political philosophies of the movements.

Approaches to aid conditionality that press Western-style democracy combined with official efforts to bring major opposition parties back into the election process will probably yield few results in the current Ethiopian context. Combining support to the decentralization process and long-term civic education and institution building are more appropriate for social reconciliation.

More important, rather than adapting the political process in Ethiopia to fit Western models of democracy, there should be more dialogue among donor governments, international NGOs, UN agencies, Ethiopian civil society organizations, and the Ethiopian government with those steering the process in Addis Ababa over their long-term objectives and vision regarding the political process. Diplomatic efforts should then be expended in widening the participation of social groups in that process, recognizing the uniquely Ethiopian character of that process. Similar dialogue should take place with and about post-revolutionary leaders in Eritrea, Rwanda, and Uganda, all of whom – like Ethiopia's – have very specific ideas about widening participation that do not necessarily include multi-party electoral systems.

Finding the right external mix of supportive and challenging diplomatic and developmental inputs could prove the antidote to new rounds of destructive warfare in a country whose citizens have known little else.

NOTES

1 This and the following three sections come primarily from Mark Duffield and John Prendergast, *Without Troops and Tanks: Humanitarian Intervention in Ethiopia and Eritrea* (Trenton, NJ: Red Sea Press, 1994).

2 Fritz Eisenloeffel, "The Eritrean Durrah Odyssey 1983," *Dutch Interchurch Aid* (July–Aug. 1983).

3 K. Wright, "Relief for Tigray: Report on a Visit, February–March 1979," May 1979.

4 M. Dines, "Eritrea: The Current Situation," *EuroAction Accord*, London (June 1979).

5 REST, "Emergency Relief Desk Evaluation," Khartoum, 1 Feb. 1984.

6 Interview by the authors with Dr Nerayo Teklemichael, ERA director, Asmara, 3 Feb. 1993.

7 Trish Silken and Sarah Hughes, *Food Security and Food Aid: A Study from the Horn of Africa* (London: CAFOD/Christian Aid, Sept. 1992).

8 "Humanitarianism Unbound?" *Africa Rights* (Nov. 1994), 12.

9 The work of John Markakis provides an excellent conceptual framework for deeper analysis.

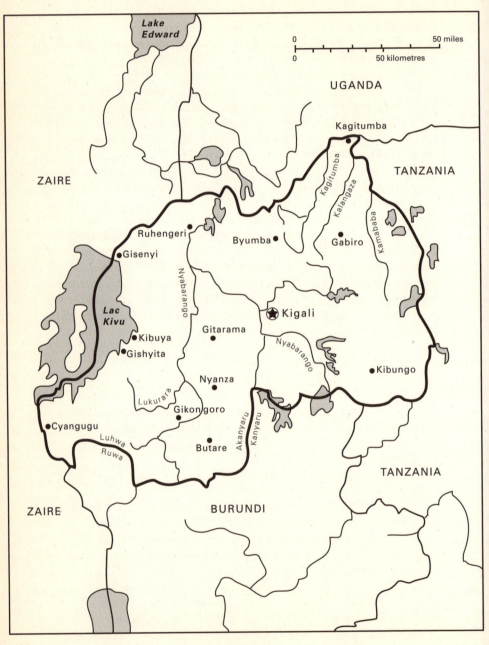

Rwanda

# 3 Civil War, the Peace Process, and Genocide in Rwanda

BRUCE D. JONES

In November 1993, an article about the civil war in Rwanda accurately referred to it as a "Forgotten War."[1] Five months later, the world's media flooded to that nation to cover the savage killings of 1994, in which up to one million Rwandans were butchered in three months. As a result of this uneven coverage, perception of "conflict" in Rwanda is dominated by images of genocide. The civil war that preceded it, dating from October 1990, remains little known and less explored.

This disjuncture in our knowledge of these events has a serious consequence: Rwanda has come to be seen as paradigmatic of the problems of international order in the post-Cold War era. Along with Somalia and Yugoslavia, it is part of the perceived one-two-three failure of the UN.[2] Events in Rwanda are taken to reflect the inappropriateness of existing tools for humanitarian action and the retraction of Western support in the face of unmanageable conflicts in situations of state collapse. They are seen particularly to reveal the international community's inability to anticipate and prevent emergent conflicts – to engage in early warning and preventive intervention.

Taking "conflict" in Rwanda to include the earlier civil war makes the implications of the events of 1994 quite different. For the civil war – a low intensity affair by regional standards, which ran from 1990 to 1994 – in fact provoked a series of third-party interventions designed to mitigate and transform the conflict. These attempts ran the gamut from informal mediation, through a formal peace process, to a series of neutral international monitoring and peacekeeping forces. The centre-piece was an international peace initiative known as the Arusha process, which brought together regional powers and members of the international community in a joint effort to stop the fighting and resolve the conflict. Our question should be not why there was no effort to manage the conflict, but why these attempts went so disastrously wrong.

The purpose of this chapter is to reconstruct elements of the third-party process, so as to place the Rwandan genocide in the context of the regional and international efforts to halt the civil war.[3] First, I expose the background to and root causes of both the civil war and the genocide. Second, I discuss the nature of the peace process to show how the conflict was transformed through negotiation. Third, building on an understanding of the roots of the conflict and of this transformation, I draw some initial conclusions about the central question – was there a causal relationship between the efforts to contain the civil war and the savage events that unfolded in their wake?

The main conclusion of this essay is that the third-party processes actually helped to spawn their own destruction and hence the butchery of 1994. By failing to resolve adequately a fundamental aspect of the conflict – the role of hard-line forces in Kigali – the Arusha Accords missed a critical opportunity to contain their violent opposition to Rwanda's peaceful transition. Despite warnings from various third parties, the accords deviated from the theoretical and historical argument that the groups which form the problem must either be made part of the solution or be decisively contained. They did not make hard-line forces in Rwanda part of the solution, and the peacekeeping phase that followed failed to contain them. This double flaw left peace in Rwanda open to the violent repudiation that followed in 1994.

Between the roots of the conflict and the possibility of its resolution lay political elites willing to destroy a society rather than concede their own power. Rwanda is a drastic example of a perennial problem faced in conflict resolution – hard-line opposition to peaceful transition. This case confirms the argument that solutions to this problem must be incorporated directly into settlements, which otherwise run the risk of being overturned. This thorny issue has frustrated peacemaking efforts for as long as they have been undertaken; if future tragedies are to be averted, efforts at conflict resolution in Africa and elsewhere should take seriously the lessons of this tragic case.

ROOTS AND CAUSES OF CONFLICT

The civil war in Rwanda began on 1 October 1990, when an armed band of Rwandan exiles launched an attack from southern Uganda.

Fifteen hundred to two thousand members of the Rwandese Patriotic Front (RPF), or Inkotanyi ("the fighters"), quickly fought half-way to Kigali, taking the major northern city of Gabiro. Rwandese President Júvenal Habyarimana, who at the moment of the invasion was addressing the United Nations in New York, flew directly to Europe to request military support. Reinforced in Kigali by three hundred French, six hundred Belgian, and over one thousand Zairian troops, the Forces armées rwandaise (FAR)[4] engaged the RPF in the north and by 1 November had pushed it back into Uganda. Radio Rwanda announced that the "October War" was over and victory achieved. However, the next three years would see continued, sporadic fighting between the two armies, interrupted by a series of partially observed cease-fires. In April 1994, the launching of genocide by Rwandan extremists collapsed a long-running cease-fire and brought the two sides back to war. Three months of fighting saw the RPF achieve a rout of the former Rwandan army, but not before almost a million Rwandans perished.

To explain the outbreak of the civil war, we must examine both the underlying causes – the historical roots – of social tensions in Rwanda and in neighbouring states, and the proximate, or immediate causes of conflict – those factors that translated underlying tensions into violent conflict in 1990. To do so in this case is to look at the troubled evolution of the Rwandan state, in the context of external forces that conditioned, constrained, or exacerbated the workings of domestic forces. The internal pressures at the heart of the conflict intersected with forces from a series of concentric circles, encompassing international, continental, and sub-regional actors.[5] The interactions between external and domestic forces at various points produced underlying tensions in Rwanda and helped lead to civil war. The war, once under way, occasioned massive transformations in Rwandan society, which again were amplified through international and regional pressures. These changes in turn contributed to the genocide in 1994.

CONCENTRIC PRESSURES

In Rwanda's relationship with the international community before 1990, its almost total economic dependence contrasted with its minimal relevance in strategic and political terms. Rwanda's economic dependence had two aspects: a high level of foreign aid throughout the 1980s, which underwrote what little economic activity the country generated, and the fact that a single export commodity – coffee – provided almost 80 per cent of export revenues and was a major component of the overall economy. In 1989 a steep decline in world prices for coffee precipitated a collapse of the Rwandan economy. This left the country unable to meet its balance-of-payment requirements, forcing it into a structural adjustment program – something it had managed to avoid throughout the 1980s.[6] As we see below, this economic decline exacerbated the impact of the civil war on Rwandan society.

On strategic and political fronts, Rwanda was very much on the margins of international politics. The effect of a lack of high-level interest in Rwanda can be seen via a comparison with other African conflicts – in Ethiopia and Mozambique, for example – where great power interventions transformed the nature and course of fighting and the prospects for resolution. The course of the peace process in Rwanda and the world's response to the genocide would reveal contradictory implications of Rwanda's marginal international position.

At the continental level, the context for the civil war was provided by the change in the political realities of Africa in the post-Cold War era, marked by a decline in Western intervention and super power competition.[7] Among the results was growing emphasis on finding "African solutions to African problems."[8] The Organization for African Unity (OAU) began to show willingness to transcend the previously sacrosanct prohibition on involvement in the internal affairs of member states and to develop mechanisms for conflict resolution to facilitate that involvement. Events in Rwanda were bound up in these developments, as we see below when we turn from the causes of the conflict to efforts to solve it.

At the sub-regional level, we must place the civil war and genocide in Rwanda in the light of the long-term balance of power of a regional "insecurity" system. Rwanda, along with Burundi, whose fate is intimately tied to that of Rwanda, forms a buffer between Zaire, Uganda, Kenya, and Tanzania. This insecurity creates a continuing struggle for pre-eminence among these four large states and intense personal antagonisms among their leaders. Highly porous borders between these states intersect ethnic groupings and have been penetrated by numerous refugee flows. Historically, conflict in one state has generated interference from others, with the most notable example being Tanzania's invasion of Uganda in 1979 – an episode directly relevant to the Rwandan civil war. The Tanzanian invasion, which returned Milton Obote to power, was in turn a spark that renewed Ugandan civil war between Obote's forces and those of Yoweri Museveni. Museveni's eventual victory over Obote was greatly aided by Rwandan refugees in Uganda, who later became key members of the RPF.

## HISTORICAL ROOTS OF CONFLICT: REFUGEE MOVEMENTS

The role played by Rwandans in Museveni's struggle illustrates an important currency in this sub-regional balance of power game – refugee movements, caused by what has been described as the "ethnic revolution and counterrevolution" in Rwanda and Burundi since before independence.[9] Political violence in each country has reverberated through the political life of the other and has produced large Hutu and Tutsi refugee populations in Zaire, Tanzania, and Uganda and in Burundi and Rwanda themselves. These refugees have carried with them the complex ethnic and social politics of their homelands and have been welcomed or rejected in large part in terms of their potential role in the dominant ethnic politics in the receiving states.

This pattern lies at the heart of both the civil war and the genocide in Rwanda. It reveals a longer, darker history of international involvement during the period of European colonization. Of particular importance was the transformation of Hutu–Tutsi relations resulting both from Belgian rule and from political competition by Rwandan political elites during efforts to end that rule.[10] In the pre-colonial period, the categories "Tutsi" and "Hutu" were complex, containing elements of ethnicity, lineage, clan, and social status, which were related in differing ways in various parts of the territory of the Rwandan kingships.[11] For reasons that combined deep prejudice with a desire for administrative simplicity, the Belgians in the 1920s introduced rigidities into these relations, essentially by equating Tutsi identity with ruling status, giving Tutsis privileged access to the state and economic opportunities, and introducing the now-notorious identity cards, through which Rwandans first came to be identified primarily through ethnicity.[12] These changes created a period of ethnic domination, the memory of which would survive systemic changes and still reverberates.

The high point of ethnic tension before independence came in the late 1950s, when emergent Hutu elites, given increased access to the state and economy in the wake of post-1945 decolonization movements, began to use Tutsi dominance as a focal point for generating political support. The crucible of political competition forged a new, combative set of relations between Tutsi and Hutu elites that ultimately became violent. Between 1959 and 1962, in what is known alternatively as "les évènements" or the "Rwandan Revolution," political violence left thousands of Tutsis dead and drove tens of thousands more into exile. The Hutu political elites succeeded in positioning themselves to take over from the Belgians when decolonization occurred in 1961–62. Following independence, residual tensions led to the killings of thousands more Tutsis and saw hundreds of thousands of them flee to neighbouring Burundi, Tanzania, and Uganda.

It is in this mass exodus of Tutsis, particularly to Uganda, that we find the long-term roots of the civil war. The Rwandans who formed the RPF, most of them Tutsi, were the descendants of the first wave of refugees – the "59ers." Having been born or raised in exile, this group developed a clear identity as Rwandans and as Tutsis, who were denied access to their homeland and spent much of their time in exile attempting to win the right of return. Over time, this group came to conform to the characteristics of what have been termed "refugee warrior communities" – exiled communities which, having fled violence at home, resort to violence to force their right of return.[13] In 1979, some senior members of the Rwandan refugee group in Uganda formed the Rwandan Alliance for National Unity, which was rechristened the Rwandese Patriotic Front (RPF) in 1987.[14] It was this group that attacked Rwanda from southern Uganda on 1 October 1990.

### PROXIMATE CAUSES OF WAR: SOCIAL CLEAVAGES AND ELITE POLITICS

Finding the immediate catalysts of the invasion entails determining what sparked the RPF invasion in 1990 and what accounts for its timing. We can posit a combination of two reasons, the evidence for each of which is partial but which, taken together, add up to a reasonable explanation. Major-General Paul Kagame, who for most of the civil war was the military leader of the RPF, has stated that the motivation behind the attack was sheer frustration with the failure of diplomatic efforts and the lack of international attention to the plight of the Rwandan refugees.[15] A more substantial explanation has to do with the fortunes of the Rwandan refugees in Uganda.[16] These had reached a low ebb in the early 1980s under President Obote, who at various times ordered attacks on the Rwandan population in Uganda. In response to these attacks, a number of Rwandans joined with Yoweri Museveni's National Revolutionary Army (NRA) and fought with Museveni until he overthrew Obote in 1985. (Indeed, two of the RPF's most senior military commanders, Fred Rwegyima and Paul Kagame, would rise in the NRA to the ranks of deputy chief of staff and deputy chief of military intelligence, respectively).[17] Having sided with the victor, the Rwandans saw their fortunes in Uganda rise after 1985.

However, while relations between Museveni and the Tutsi leader-ship remained strong, by the end of the decade many of the old antagonisms between the Rwandans in Uganda and their neighbour-ing populations had reappeared. Evidence for this tension is found in, among other things, the fact that the topic of the Rwandan refugees was discussed as a problem in Uganda's National Ruling Council in August 1990.[18] The council, which is not fully controlled by Museveni, decided to remove remaining Rwandan nationals from the NRA and to bar Rwandans in Uganda from owning land. More-over, Presidents Museveni, Mobutu of Zaire, and Habyarimana of Rwanda met in Kampala two weeks before the RPF invasion to discuss the issue and find a regional solution, which eluded them.[19] A letter from the Ugandan government to the Human Rights Watch Arms Project suggests, in a remarkable euphemism, that the Rwandan refugees in Uganda had become convinced "that they did not have a bright future in Uganda."[20] Though there is no concrete evidence of Museveni's support for the RPF invasion, it is widely believed that he did provide assistance. It would seem that he facilitated what amounted to an armed repatriation of the Rwandan refugees, both to repay the support of the RPF leadership and to solve an internal Ugandan problem.

The timing of the invasion also coincided with an increase in social and political tension in Rwanda in 1989 and 1990, precipitated by severe economic decline and exacerbated by intersecting interna-tional pressures. When the RPF invaded in 1990, the country was socially strained, economically and environmentally destitute, and politically fractured. The years since independence had seen a large growth in population and the consequent deterioration of an already difficult situation regarding population density and the availability of arable land.[21] Rwanda in the 1980s was one of the poorest countries in the world, had the highest population density in the continent, and had witnessed a decade of declining land productivity. Not surprisingly, it also experienced all the social ills associated with such circumstances, including high levels of corruption and high unem-ployment, especially among youths, resulting by the early 1990s in student protests and other forms of political unrest. A short rainy season in 1989 also led to widespread food shortages, and in some regions famine, in 1990. The situation was worsened by diminishing coffee yields and the dramatic fall in world coffee prices in July 1989. The beginning of negotiations over a structural adjustment program caused, in November 1990, a 40 per cent devaluation of the Rwandan currency. Rwanda's dependence on international financial organiza-tions, and its lack of international political clout, constrained its ability to limit the impact of these economic shocks. Thus, the RPF attack was timed (whether deliberately or not is not known) to exacerbate a rapid, massive economic decline, which would sap the state of its already limited strength.

Amplifying the social strains caused by a deteriorating economy was the intensification of regional and clan cleavages in Rwanda resulting from Habyarimana's politics. Rwandan society under him became fractured principally along north-south lines, though ethnic divisions continued. He had taken power in 1973 in a palace coup backed by northern Hutus, and in particular by members of his Bushiru clan from Ruhengiri province, in northern Rwanda. Over the next seventeen years, this small group consolidated its access to power to the detriment not only of Tutsis but equally of southern Hutus and Hutus from competing clans. Indeed, by 1980, 80 per cent of senior posts in the army were held by Bushiru Hutus from Ruhengiri province.[22] This group also dominated the political process through the Mouvement révolutionnaire national pour le Développement (MRND), which became the only legal party in Rwanda under the 1978 constitution.[23]

It was extremist members of this akazu (Little House), as it became known, who planned and controlled the genocide of 1994, targeting not only Tutsis, who were the principal victims, but also moderate Hutus, human rights workers, opposition politicians, moderate members of their own party, and competing militia groups, who became the first victims.

In their planning of the genocide we see a second reverberation of the memory of earlier ethnic domination. Like Hutu elites in 1959, the akazu used the fear of Tutsi domination as a tool to legitimate violence against Tutsis in Rwanda and the Tutsi-dominated RPF. Once again, the manipulation of social cleavages by elites in political competition would lead Rwanda to massive violence. But to understand precisely why the akazu used genocide to protect its own power in 1994, we need to understand the political transformations of the 1990s, caused both by civil war with the RPF and, more precisely, regional and international efforts to resolve or contain the fighting.

Attempts to limit the Rwandan civil war had two interlocking themes – democratization and negotiations towards peace. Together, these resulted in a massive shift in power from the old guard in Rwanda to a variety of new guards. Democratization came about partially as a result of international pressure in the late 1980s and early 1990, in the form of Structural Adjustment Program conditionalities, as well as agitation by Western governments over human rights problems. These twin pressures led Habyarimana to announce democratic reforms in early 1990, though these were quickly shelved at the onset of the RPF invasion. However, Rwanda's dependence on foreign aid (especially after November 1990) and its resultant vulnerability to Western pressure brought democratization back onto the agenda in 1991–92, when analysis by Western diplomats suggested that democratization must run parallel to peace negotiations if a viable peace were to be found.[24]

By 1991, several new political parties had registered in Rwanda. Under pressure, Habyarimana formed a nominally coalition government, which in fact had only one member from outside the ruling MRND. That government made only modest concessions to democratic principles. However, Western diplomats kept up the pressure, and in 1992 Habyarimana was compelled to bring the Parti libéral (PL), the Parti socialiste démocratique (PSD), the Mouvement démocratique rwandaise (MDR), and others into a real coalition government. The first act of the new government, in June 1992, was to agree formally to political negotiations with the RPF, thus launching the second theme of transformation, to which we now turn.

### PEACE-MAKING I: SUB-REGIONAL AND CONTINENTAL PRE-NEGOTIATION

A formal agreement in June 1992 to negotiate peace followed months of quiet negotiations, secret talks, and regional diplomacy. Indeed, efforts at resolving the conflict in Rwanda began within days of the RPF's invasion in October 1990. On 14 October, the Belgian prime minister, foreign minister, and defence minister traveled to Kigali on a peace mission and met with Habyarimana, Museveni, Mobutu, and Mwinyi of Tanzania.[25] The mission reflected Belgium's continued involvement in Rwanda as a former colonial power, albeit limited to diplomatic engagement. Brussels in fact attempted to send troops to Rwanda to respond to the October invasion, but parliament opposed the effort and limited the troops' role to protecting and evacuating nationals. The peace mission was a compromise, wherein the government sought to exercise its influence through diplomatic, rather than military means.[26]

The momentum generated by the mission was quickly taken up by sub-regional diplomatic mechanisms. The first locus of regional diplomacy was the executive assembly of the Economic Community of the Countries of the Great Lakes (or Communité économique de pays des Grands Lacs – CEPGL), which hosted a series of ad hoc regional summits. The neighbouring states all had interests in the conflict. Zaire had been a long-time supporter of the Habyarimana regime, and, as the senior statesman in the CEPGL, Zaire's Mobutu was asked to take on a role as mediator. Uganda's interests lay in competition with those of Zaire – Uganda supported the RPF's goals, hoping to see large numbers of Rwandan refugees return home. Burundi, whose population had the same ethnic mix as Rwanda, had concerns of possible reverberations from the conflict, which was taking on an explicitly ethnic dimension. Tanzania, long a power in the central and southern African security systems, was deeply concerned by instability on its borders, the resulting power struggles between Zaire and Uganda, and the prospects for refugee flows into Tanzanian territory. The combination of these fears and interests propelled the four states to engage in summitry, dialogue, and mediation to find ways of managing the Rwandan civil war.

Also quick to get involved in the peace process was the OAU. The activism of this continental organization was in some measures surprising, as it had in previous years often been reluctant to intervene in the "internal" affairs of member states. However, two factors made a difference in 1990. The chair was held by Uganda's Museveni, and the recently appointed secretary general, Salim A. Salim, was a Tanzanian, who had close contracts with the Ministry of Foreign Affairs in Dar-es-Salaam. Salim was trying to increase the OAU's capacity to find "African solutions to African problems," notably through revitalizing the OAU's Conflict Resolution Mechanism. This effort reflected heightened concern about the real and perceived withdrawal of international involvement with and concern for the continent following the end of superpower competition.[27]

After a series of gatherings of CEPGL members in 1990, the subregional and the continental processes came together early the next year. On 19 February 1991, at a meeting among Museveni, Mwinyi, and Habyarimana, the Rwandan agreed to the Dar-es-Salaam Declaration, accepting in principle the need for a cease-fire and negotiations. Critically, this declaration also outlined a solution to the refugee problem that underlay the invasion, which would be adopted in the eventual peace agreement itself. This declaration was witnessed by a representative of Mobutu, by Salim for the OAU, and by a representative of the United Nations High Commissioner for Refugees (UNHCR).

Habyarimana's willingness to agree to a cease-fire having been declared, the search for an agreement quickly got under way through the efforts of both the OAU and the CEPGL. An initial cease-fire agreement was reached on 29 March 1991, in N'Sele, Zaire.[28] Along with a cessation of hostilities, the N'Sele agreement called for the deployment of a monitoring force – the Neutral Military Observer Group (NMOG) – under the authority of the OAU and the leadership of Zaire.

NMOG was not deployed at this stage, however, as the N'Sele cease-fire itself lasted only for a matter of days, with violations on both sides leading to renewed fighting in April.

Fighting continued for some months, during which the FAR took heavy losses but blocked the RPF from advancing further into Rwanda. Renewed talks brought the two sides together in Gbadolite, Zaire, on 16 September, when the N'Sele cease-fire was amended and reissued as the Gbadolite cease-fire. The elements of the new agreement were not dramatically different than those of N'Sele but did restructure the NMOG, calling for a Nigerian chief officer with a Zairian deputy. At this stage, some eighty troops were deployed in northern Rwanda under NMOG. The switch from a Zairian chief officer to a Nigerian reflected a lack of trust, certainly among the RPF, in the neutrality of Zairian troops, who fought alongside the FAR in Kigali in October 1990.

This lack of trust was propelled by equal doubts about Mobutu's neutrality and effectiveness.[29] Indeed, the Gbadolite meeting saw the effective end of his role as mediator and a shift towards Tanzania's Mwinyi, who would later become "facilitator" to the talks. Mobutu retained the formal title of "mediator" but from this point on had little to do with the peace process. A full shift to Tanzanian facilitation would take several months, however, and in the interim the warring parties observed the Gbadolite cease-fire largely in the breach, and the prospects for sub-regional and continental diplomacy seemed limited.

### TOWARDS ARUSHA: LOW-LEVEL INTERNATIONAL DIPLOMACY

The relative failure of the regional peace process, despite early, high-level, sustained attention, suggests a general lesson. Much recent discussion of African conflict resolution has pointed to the need for greater levels of regional involvement in peace processes. As stake-holders, the argument goes, regional states have the interest and the awareness of the situation to ensure that solutions are found and adhered to. The experience of the regional and continental processes in Rwanda, however, highlights the problem posed by these actors' lack of neutrality. While there is never such thing as a truly neutral third party, concentrating peace processes at a regional level may amplify the problem of partiality.

In the case of Rwanda, it took a move out of continental and sub-regional processes, and into the international realm, to push the peace process forward, in the form of parallel talks at the U.S. State

Department and the French Ministry of Foreign Affairs.[30] Thus the results of continental and sub-regional diplomacy – the Dar-es-Salaam Declaration, the N'Sele cease-fire, and Gbadolite cease-fire – would in retrospect form pre-negotiation texts for the more substantial, and international, Arusha process.

That France and the United States became active at this stage requires some explanation. U.S. involvement in any form is perhaps surprising, given that it had neither strategic nor economic interests in Rwanda. With reference to the Rwandan civil war, as one American diplomat said: "We didn't have a dog in that fight." Thus U.S. engagement came not as a result of political interest but rather from a series of initiatives taken at the working level in the State Department and eventually reaching (but never transcending) Assistant Secretary of State for African Affairs Herman Cohen.

Having been approached by members of the RPF in Washington, the State Department was persuaded to use its influence in the region and its experience in African conflict management to revitalize the peace process for Rwanda. Its role is best characterized by the concept of technical support, which is what Cohen offered to both the RPF and the government of Rwanda to aid negotiations. Lack of American interests precluded deeper involvement, but even this low-level, bureaucratic participation did have an impact on negotiations. Being from neither a former colonial power nor a regional power, the American delegation was evidently trusted by both the RPF and the government's delegations and was thus able to make possible what regional diplomacy had failed to achieve – namely, an agreement to engage in full-fledged political negotiations, or the Arusha process.[31]

Rwanda's strategic marginality, in international terms, permitted low-level diplomatic efforts, free from political interference. As Chester Crocker, Herman Cohen's predecessor, has argued, the end of the Cold War has diminished political interest in Africa, creating a dilemma. On the one hand, the lack of strategic interest gives scope to bureaucrats and diplomats to forge peaceful solutions to conflict. Thus it may be easier to resolve conflicts in Africa now than during the Cold War. On the other hand, today there is little political will to back up peaceful solutions with the sort of engagement often required to ensure implementation. U.S. participation in 1992, determined by working-level contacts, lacking political involvement, and motivated almost exclusively by a desire to contain the conflict and produce a peaceful solution, illustrates the beneficial half of this dilemma. The American role in peacekeeping and implementation illustrates the negative.

Agreement on the Arusha process was not reached through U.S. intervention alone, however. France also took up the flagging momentum of regional and continental diplomacy. France, of course, had a substantial relationship with the Habyarimana regime and thus a direct interest in the outcome of the civil war. However, this friend of the regime helped broker peace talks with the RPF.

France's role was in fact considerable. Much has been written about its dark role in supporting the regime and thus in fostering genocide, and possibly training those who executed it.[32] However, French policy towards Africa is traditionally schizophrenic, and in Rwanda no less so than usual. While Rwanda was perhaps not a major player in French-African policy, it had at least made it into the inner circle of French foreign relations, becoming a "pays du champs," which gave it access to special loan provisions and meant that its relations with France were managed principally by the Ministry of Cooperation and the Africa Unit at the Elysée Palace, rather than by the Ministry of Foreign Affairs. The story of France's involvement in Rwanda seems to have been one of contradictory signals sent from the various French ministries.

While it is clear from subsequent analysis that the ministries of Cooperation and of Defence, with the backing of President Mitterrand, were actively supporting the regime, it appears that at the same time the Ministry of Foreign Affairs (MFA) was following a different path. According to MFA officials, they based their analysis of the civil war on an assessment that the RPF was capable of defeating the Rwandan government's forces in outright warfare. The Arusha process, which represented a sharing of power between the pro-French regime and the perceived anti-French RPF, seemed to them the cheapest and most effective way to maintain French access in Rwanda, given the alternative options of either outright RPF victory or large-scale military support to the government. The MFA thus actively supported the peace process, not because of humanitarian concerns or pro-RPF sympathies, but because peace was the best solution in terms of French interests.[33]

This being said, it is quite clear that the MFA perceived its role as one of lending support to the government of Rwanda and ensuring that negotiations did not jeopardize the regime's interests too much. Accounts of the Arusha process, to which we now turn, are replete with stories of the French delegation supporting the government when others were pushing for concessions, though participants also talk of France having persuaded its delegation to accept reasonable positions when it was otherwise unlikely to do so. This can easily appear another example of French support for a nasty regime, and, in a sense, it was precisely this. But it was also an effort to stop the political negotiations from going further than was acceptable to the core group around Habyarimana. In retrospect, there are reasons to wish that the French had been more successful in supporting the government delegation; the reasons for their failure become apparent below.

In any case, American and French interventions in the winter months of 1991–92, and the spring of 1992, eventually brought the RPF and the government of Rwanda together for a series of meetings, culminating in a Paris session in June 1992, at which the two sides agreed to political negotiations under the auspices of the OAU. The talks were to be facilitated by Tanzania and represented the effective coming together of international, continental, and sub-regional mediation processes.[34]

### PEACE-MAKING II: THE ARUSHA PROCESS

The story of the Arusha process is an extraordinary one of a sophisticated process of conflict resolution gone drastically wrong, because of a classic dilemma of conflict management and political transition – whether to integrate or marginalize hard-liners opposed to the resolution process. This section offers an account of the Arusha process, prefaced by a discussion of the Rwandan delegations and the Tanzanian facilitator, illustrating the manifestation of this dilemma in the Rwandan case. An analysis of the accords completes the section. The central conclusion is that the Arusha Accords themselves, having failed to resolve adequately the role of the hardliners, actually became one of the proximate causes of the genocide.

Among the issues that Arusha got right was the point that every party that should have been involved was. This included Belgium and Germany, with their historical interests (and important aid presence), the United States and France, the relevant regional actors (Zaire, Uganda, and Burundi), as well as the appropriate regional and international organizations (the OAU, the UN, and the UNHCR). As well, Senegal, Nigeria, and Zimbabwe at times played roles through their positions in the OAU.

Tanzania facilitated the process and coaxed from the third parties support for what seemed a comprehensive peace treaty. Three things need to be said about Tanzania's role in Arusha. First, the Tanzanian government devoted high-level attention and dedicated some of its best diplomats to the talks and in so doing succeeded in facilitating an effective peace process, in which it was judged for the most part to have played an honest-broker role. Second, its motivation for involving itself in a long and costly facilitation process combined a mix of self-interest, regional concerns, and humanitarian impulses. The self-interest had largely to do with its knowledge that conflict in either Rwanda or Burundi would result – as it had previously – in large refugee flows into Tanzania, with which it was ill-equipped to deal. The state's regional concern has been historically to have stable governments in neighbouring countries, and so it sought a tenable solution to the political crisis in Rwanda, which was compatible with its humanitarian concerns, for peace in Rwanda. Third, Tanzania was the only neighbouring country generally perceived to be neutral in the civil war. Its neutrality in the specifics of the struggle enabled it to use its regional status to broker a solution out of the internecine politics of the region.

Most important of all, of course, were the Rwandan delegations themselves – the RPF and the government of Rwanda (GoR). The nature of these delegations helps explain the course and outcome of the negotiations. First, as noted above, the decision to launch the Arusha process was taken by a coalition government, which had brought several major opposition parties into power-sharing arrangements in Kigali. These parties were represented in Arusha on the GoR delegation. Separate chains of command were thus in play – opposition moderates took their orders from the prime minister (a member of the MDR party), others were more clearly Habyarimana's men, and still others represented Hutu extremists in Kigali, communicating the progress of the talks back to those groups. The most notorious of the last-named was Colonel Theogene Bagasora, a government official who was known by some participants to be a senior member of the extremist Coalition for the Defence of the Republic (CDR).[35] These separate chains of command made for a fractured GoR team, which weakened its negotiating strength in Arusha.

The government's divided negotiating team stood in contrast to what many participants have described as a cohesive, professional, committed RPF line-up. The reasons behind the RPF's competence are not hard to find and lie with the enormous stakes that the RPF had in the negotiations. First, the lines of command from the Arusha team to the RPF leadership appear to have been clear and unitary, and the delegation was noted for its discipline and discretion, which gave it a negotiating advantage over the other side. Second, the RPF gained leverage from the fact that while it was serious about negotiations, it was also prepared to return to the field if talks failed. This position was in stark contrast to the government's – three years of war had savaged what was already an economy in deep retraction; domestic pressures for change were mounting; international pressure for change, from Western donors and from the international financial institutions, was equally intense; and the government was on its last legs and could ill-afford either a long, drawn-out peace process or a return to fighting. Thus not only did the composition and capacity of the two teams reflect a weakness–strength distinction, but the GoR was under substantially greater time pressures. The course of negotiations would prove this to be a critical variable.

## PROCESS AND CONTENT: TRANSITION BARGAINS AND VICTOR'S DEALS

The Arusha negotiations lasted thirteen months, from July 1992 to August 1994, and in that period stalled and recommenced several times, as the two sides reached agreement and then deadlock and then agreement again on a series of items. On 4 August 1993, the two sides signed the "Peace Agreement between the Government of the Republic of Rwanda and the Rwandese Patriotic Front," commonly referred to as the Arusha Accords. It incorporated the N'Sele, Gbadolite, and Arusha cease-fire agreements and included five protocols – on the "Rule of Law" (signed 18 August 1992); on "Power-Sharing within the Framework of a Broad-Based Transitional Government" (in two parts, agreed on 30 October 1992 and 9 January 1993); on the "Repatriation of Rwandan Refugees and the Resettlement of Displaced Persons" (9 June 1993); on "Integration of Armed Forces of the Two Parties" (3 August 1993); and "Miscellaneous Issues and Final Provisions" (3 August 1993).[36]

In the body of these protocols lie two contradictory agreements – a transition bargain between the regime and the opposition and a victor's deal for the RPF. The transition bargain, contained in the first three protocols, covered the political elements of the agreement. The first two set up the basis of a new political order, parliamentary rather than presidential; transitional institutions, notably a Broad Based Transitional Government (BBTG), and a new National Assembly; and the disbursement of seats in these institutions between the ruling MRND, the RPF, and the major opposition parties. Critically, the transitional institutions excluded the extremist Committee for the Defence of the Republic (CDR). This last point was the most contentious, and disagreement in Kigali stalled the signing of this accord from October 1992 until January 1993.

To say that these protocols represented a transition bargain is not to underplay their scope or significance, for together they would have realigned the political system and structure in Kigali. Indeed, Filip Reyntjens has argued that they constituted a "revolution" in the

Rwandan political system.[37] However, while they reduced the power of Habyarimana's regime and excluded extremist elements, they still kept the old guard in the government, if not precisely in power, and kept Habyarimana on as president, albeit with fewer powers.

Agreement on the third protocol, on refugee issues, came quickly and with relative ease, substantive agreement on the core issues having been reached in the pre-negotiation phase. The Dar-es-Salaam Declaration, which had been issued from the refugee conference in February 1991, formed the basis for most of its provisions.

In contrast, the fourth protocol clearly represented a decisive negotiating victory for the RPF, though one that would prove to be a costly tactical error. Negotiations on this issue started with the GoR delegation suggesting a 15 per cent share of the armed forces for the RPF, and the RPF, a 50–50 split. The RPF stuck to its position and won, eventually gaining the GoR delegation's agreement to a 60–40 split of the armed forces to the government's favour and a 50–50 split of the senior command posts. The two armies were to be integrated into a 20,000-strong national force, including a restructured gendarmerie.

This putative agreement was taken back to Kigali on 24 June by the government's negotiating team, where it was rejected by Habyarimana. An American participant observed at the time that the recommended division of the army would never be accepted by hard-line factions in the army, and threatened to collapse the talks. However, when the issue returned to Arusha, the RPF not only stood its ground but upped the stakes, calling for a 60–40 split in its favour. Eventually, on 26 June 1993, after considerable intercession by the Tanzanians, the two sides returned to the original 60–40 forces split and a 50–50 command split, but extended down to field commanders.[38] This extraordinary concession by the government would prove disastrous: this element in particular was impossible to implement in Kigali.[39]

### Analysis of Arusha

What accounts for this shift between the first set of agreements, which effectively forged a transition bargain, and the fourth protocol, which was quite justly perceived as a victor's deal for the RPF? How is it that the Arusha Accords went too far on this final issue, opening up the opportunity for the violent opposition that was to follow? The critical variable that explains this lop-sided result has already been alluded to – the superior position of the RPF.

The first reason for this situation had to do with the nature of the transition process. Because the RPF was struggling to gain powers in the possession of the government, it had the easier task of demanding concessions while the GoR delegation had the more painful task of making them. Second, as argued above, the RPF was both more disciplined and more motivated than the fractious GoR team. Third, the Rwandan state was under mounting time pressure, placed on it by the continued economic decline in the country, whereas the RPF, having spent thirty years in refuge, could afford to wait for a beneficial outcome.

The most important element, however, was the RPF's superior field position. This was illustrated by the tremendous success of a February 1993 RPF offensive. On 8 February, already frustrated with government intransigence at the Arusha talks, the RPF launched a major offensive against FAR positions, officially in response to the massacre of three hundred Tutsis in northern Rwanda. Over the course of two weeks of fighting, the RPF won victory after victory, doubled the territory under its control, and eventually moved to within twenty-three kilometres of Kigali.[40] Frantic requests by Habyarimana to the French brought some relief for the FAR in the form of four hundred paratrooper reinforcements, deployed in two phases. On the day after the second contingent of reinforcements arrived, the RPF declared a cease-fire. Tanzanian mediation resulted in the Kinihara cease-fire agreement, which saw the RPF return to its earlier position. Both sides agreed to return to Arusha, which they did on 16 March.

The two delegations returned, however, even more disparate in strength and position. The RPF had demonstrated overwhelming field superiority and in doing so had displaced over a million Rwandans from Ruhengiri and Byumba provinces, Rwanda's breadbasket areas, thus hugely increasing the pressure on the regime. The RPF delegation that went back to Arusha was thus in a position to sit and wait for capitulation; the GoR group was in no position to withstand the pressure and capitulated on the remaining critical issues. By July, the RPF had "won" on both counts: the CDR would be excluded from power, and the RPF would gain a disproportionate share of control over the armed forces.

RPF insistence on excluding the CDR from power and on the disproportionate split of the army was challenged by all the major third parties involved in the Arusha process. In particular, the Americans and the Tanzanians attempted to convince the RPF that it was in danger of winning phyrric victories at the negotiating table. Both the Tanzanians and Americans had encountered the problems posed by hard-liners in negotiations in Zimbabwe, South Africa, Namibia, and elsewhere on the continent. Both shared a metaphor: that if the hard-liners were not brought into the tent (the transition bargain), they would burn the tent down.[41] For Rwanda, the American negotiating team had come early to the realization that the Kigali hard-liners would pose a problem and should be dealt with by being given some stake in the transition bargain, since the option of removing or constraining them was perceived to be unfeasible. The Tanzanians agreed and on at least two occasions moved out of their neutral, facilitative stance to attempt to convince the RPF to relent on these questions.[42] Remarkably, even the Ugandans, who had backed the RPF, joined forces with the Americans and Tanzanians to support CDR inclusion and to moderate the proposed RPF share of control over the army.[43]

That even Ugandan pressure was unable to sway the RPF reveals the increasing strength of its position. Militarily, having advanced deep into Rwanda in the February offensive, the RPF was now not nearly so dependent on Ugandan support as when its principal base was inside Ugandan territory. Secure in its field strength, and strong in its negotiating position, the RPF rejected the advice and warnings of both neutral and allied third parties and refused to compromise. As a result, these elements of the Arusha agreements formed a victor's deal for the RPF, which would ultimately undermine the transition bargain forged in early protocols.[44]

The dynamics of the final stages of the Arusha process illustrate a major feature of conflict resolution – parties to a conflict bear the central responsibility for producing a settlement or resolution, as it is principally they who are capable of doing so. Outside pressure may push parties in a given direction, and when the parties are in fact merely fronts for powerful behind-the-scenes actors this responsibility shifts elsewhere. But when the parties are independent actors, they must resolve the conflict. Thus the parties to the Rwandan civil war, and in particular the RPF, much more than the international actors who supported their negotiations, bear responsibility for what would prove to be the stillbirth of the Arusha peace.

In August 1993, the RPF was winning the war and "won" the peace talks. Its strength on the battlefield and around the negotiating table outweighed the very careful and sophisticated negotiating process run by the Tanzanians. Because of RPF intransigence on the question of the CDR and on the army split, a well-conceived, neutral, and well-managed peace process produced an unsustainable result. The Arusha process, which in its first stages transformed a civil war into a political negotiation and succeeded in forging a transition bargain, in its final stages produced a victor's deal. The next sequence of events would see reaction to the deal thoroughly undermine attempts to implement the transition bargain.

## PEACE-"KEEPING": THE UN AND THE FAILURE OF IMPLEMENTATION

As international actors and moderates in Rwanda attempted to implement the the Arusha Accords, hard-liners in Kigali stepped up their reaction to the victor's deal.[45] For nine months, elements of the Rwandan political system, the UN, and some of the participants in the Arusha process struggled to implement its provisions. During the same period, Hutu extremist groups, led by members of the akazu, worked to undermine the peace and to solidify their plans for a violent repudiation of power-sharing.

### Implementing the Transition Bargain

The Arusha Peace Agreement called for the establishment of the Broad Based Transitional Government (BBTG) within thirty-seven days of the signing of the accord, as a first step towards integrating the RPF, the regime, and the opposition parties into one national government. Efforts to establish the BBTG began with the appointment of the MDR's Faustin Twagiramungu as prime minister, as agreed in the final days of Arusha. However, almost as soon as the process began, it began to derail. Critically, the opposition parties in Kigali began to splinter. As only a few members of each party would receive seats in the BBTG, factions within the parties struggled to place themselves in the lead to receive seats and power. Parties began to factionalize along regional and ideological lines. Attempts to convene the BBTG failed on 8 January 1994, because of deadlock within the opposition MDR and PL parties. By 10 February the deadlock within the PL was so intense that the other opposition parties, and the MRND, agreed to go ahead and establish the BBTG without the PL's participation. Before this could occur, Felicien Gatabazi, the leader of the PSD, was assassinated in Kigali, an event that led the following day to a revenge killing of Martin Bucyana of the CDR. Kigali was slowly but inexorably descending into chaos.

It was the UN's task to secure the transitional government and prevent its collapse. Though it had been a marginal actor in the pre-negotiation phase and early in the Arusha process, the UN had taken a more active role after the RPF offensive of February 1993. During the offensive, Uganda's President Museveni had written to the UN and invited it to deploy observers along the Uganda-Rwanda border to confirm that Uganda was not aiding the offensive. Its doing so had two results: the deployment of the UN Observer Mission for Uganda-Rwanda (UNOMUR) and a shift in the lead in conflict management away from the continental and sub-regional actors towards New York. Discussions during the Arusha process about a peacekeeping force during implementation considered proposals from both the OAU and the UN. An OAU bid was marred by lack of support from the UN and general loss of credibility in Rwanda occasioned by the poor perform-ance of the Neutral Military Observer Group. In the end, the UN was asked to compose a "neutral international force" to be deployed in Rwanda thirty-seven days after the signing of the accords.

The "neutral international force" was not even approved by New York within the original, unrealistic timetable. The target deploy-ment date of September was met with a reconnaissance mission, led by the head of UNOMUR, Brigadier-General Roméo Dallaire.[46] The mission's original assessment of the number of troops required for the mission was 4,500; the Security Council, whose members' limited interests in Rwanda restricted their financial commitment, approved 2,548. Dallaire was asked to lead the UN Assistance Mission in Rwanda (UNAMIR), which subsumed the smaller UNOMUR force. A lead party of UNAMIR troops headed by Dallaire eventually arrived in Kigali on 21 October 1993 – the same day that the Tutsi-dominated army of Burundi assassinated Burundi's newly elected president, Melchior Ndadaye, a Hutu, and commenced the killing of between fifty thou-sand and a hundred thousand Burundi Hutus. The contrast between the violence in Burundi and the late, partial arrival of the "neutral international" force could not have been more stark. Several close observers have since argued that the Rwandan peace never recovered.

The violence in Burundi had two deleterious effects on the security situation in Rwanda. First, the partially deployed UNAMIR force had immediately to send some of its personnel to the Rwanda-Burundi border, to ensure that refugees from the killings in Burundi did not, as had often happened in the past, destabilize Rwanda. Thus a force that for financial and political reasons was staffed well below its optimal level was diminished still further. Its resources stretched, UNAMIR was never able firmly to ensure security in the capital, let alone in the rest of the country. When the efforts to establish the BBTG were threatened by assassinations, the peacekeepers were able to restore only a superficial level of security, and not before a sense of chaos and impending catastrophe had pervaded the Rwandan politi-cal system.

Second, the assassination and killings in Burundi were rich material for the hard-liners in Rwanda, who used the events to lend credence to their claims that the Tutsis of the RPF were returning to Rwanda to re-establish their historic dominance over the Hutus. The degree to which Hutus should fear the once and future overlords, they argued (in the press, in demonstrations, in leaflets, and most effectively on the radio) could clearly be seen in the slaughter of Hutu brethren by Burundi Tutsis. Once again, the traditional Rwanda-Burundi cycle was in motion: political violence in one country was used to justify still more in the other.

### Reacting to the Victor's Deal

The Arusha Accords were never accepted by the hard-line forces in Kigali – the military elements of the one-party state who would have no authority, no place even, in a democratic regime. Specifically, senior military figures in the army and the Presidential Guard, members of the CDR, and extremist elements of the MRND, the senior ranks of which were all populated by members of the akazu, perceived the accords as a victor's deal for the RPF.

In particular, they reacted against the exclusion of the CDR from power and the military "agreements" of the armed forces protocol. As characterized by one Western participant, these two aspects of the deal imparted a profound sense of insecurity to hard-line forces. The military arrangements, and in particular the extension of the 50–50 command split down to field commanders, denied the hard-line military faction any control over the Rwandan security forces. What it had lost at the military level, it had failed to make up at the political level – exclusion of the CDR from institutions dominated by the new opposition parties would leave the security forces controlled by political groups that were far from being allies to the hard-liners. This double-edged loss gave urgency to hard-liners' efforts to undermine the peace process before other forces could establish the institutions that would deprive them of their power.

It was this group of political forces inside Kigali that was responsible for the assassinations and intimidations that were blocking the creation of the BBTG. This was part of a wider plan that had been in development roughly since the shape of the Arusha Accords had become known. The scheme had several elements, including the financing and coordinating of the training of extremist militia groups – the interahamwe and the impuzamugambi. Hard-liners also directed the dissemination of propaganda based on ethnic fear, transmitted through many media but notoriously the Radio Télévision libre des milles collines, or RTLM. Subsequent stages involved disrupting the establishment of the BBTG, compiling lists of Tutsis in Kigali for the purpose of their extermination, undermining UNAMIR by attacking Belgian peacekeepers, forcing withdrawal of the Belgian contingent, and overthrowing the government. This plan, parts of which were revealed to UNAMIR in January 1993, would eventually be executed faithfully, in every measure.[47] Its purpose, as conceived by the genocide's ideologues, was to destroy the RPF by wiping out its power base in Rwanda – the Tutsi population.

Focused on building the institutions of peaceful transition, the UN and the moderate forces in Rwanda underestimated the potency and deadly seriousness of both the propaganda and the planning. By February 1994, and particularly with the assassination of PSD leader Félicien Gatabazi on the 22nd, the hard-line forces had thoroughly undermined efforts to implement the transition bargain. Michel Moussali, a UNHCR special envoy, argued on 23 February that Rwanda would experience "a bloodbath of unparalleled proportions" if efforts were not made to salvage the peace process. But urgent communications from UNAMIR to this effect fell on ears in New York that, if not precisely deaf, were full of the sounds of other, ongoing crises in Somalia and Bosnia. The signals from Kigali could not compete with unfolding crises being managed by an overworked, understaffed Department of Peacekeeping Operations (DPKO) at the UN Secretariat. As a result, a critical opportunity to contain the forces of reaction was lost.

Even after the assassination of Gatabazi, last-ditch efforts were undertaken to salvage the Arusha deal. A special representative of the UN secretary general met with the RPF on 1 March to try to find ways to put the peace process back on track. Tanzania, the Arusha facilitator, also kept up efforts to persuade the two sides to implement the agreement. The Tanzanian facilitation team, which understood both the history of the Rwandan conflict and the depth of the tensions in that society, had all along been aware of the seriousness of delays. The Tanzanians attempted to communicate that urgency to the UN when that organization took the lead in the peace-making process. The OAU's secretary general, Salim, was also appraised of the depth of the threat to peace in Rwanda, and he tried to focus international attention on the brewing crisis. The sense of urgency that pervaded the sub-regional and continental levels was lost at the international level, where Rwanda was of marginal importance. Neither Tanzania nor the OAU had the clout where it mattered – the UN Security Council – to forestall the collapse of a once-celebrated peace deal.

Ultimately, Tanzania persuaded Habyarimana to attend a summit in Dar-es-Salaam on the crisis in Burundi, intending to press him to reaffirm his commitment to the BBTG. Habyarimana attended the meeting and did issue a statement reaffirming the Arusha agreement, but when he was flying back from this conference, on 6 April 1994, the plane carrying both him and President Ntariyamana of Burundi was shot down, probably by the Rwandan Presidential Guard, killing both men. The hardliners' violent repudiation of the victor's deal was thus launched into its final, brutal phase.

### Genocide and the Return to Civil War

The assassination of Habyarimana was not the spark to the genocide, but its first act. Before news of his killing had been transmitted, members of the Presidential Guard and extremist militias were setting up roadblocks around Kigali and commencing the program of assassinations that would wipe out the moderate and democratic political community. On 7 April, Agathe Uwilingiyama, who had been appointed prime minister in the absence of the BBTG, was assassinated in her home. Militia forces captured and then murdered thirteen Belgian peacekeepers, precisely according to plan, and achieved the desired result: Belgium announced the imminent withdrawal of its UNAMIR contingent. The RPF leadership, unconvinced that the UN could do anything to contain the killings, took its men out of their barracks and moved north into RPF-held territory. Rwanda was back at war.

For three traumatic months after 6 April, the RPF carefully fought its way across northern Rwanda, securing regions as it took them. Having secured its northern flank, and its supply routes into Uganda, the RPF fought down into Kigali, which fell entirely into RPF hands on 4 July. Moving south and west into the strongholds of the former government, RPF soldiers captured Butare on 5 July, Ruhengiri on the 14th, and Gisenyi on the 17th. On 18 July, two years almost to the day after the signing of the cease-fire that launched the Arusha process, the RPF declared victory and a unilateral cease-fire. In the final analysis, the civil war ended not through conflict resolution but in that age-old fashion, victory by one of the combatants.

As the RPF fought its way through Rwanda, the akazu and their militias executed their plan for a "final solution." Mobile gangs of militia youths, under the direction of Colonel Bagasora and other leaders of the CDR, swept through Kigali and then the countryside, rounding up suspected Tutsis and eliminating them en masse. Hutus were incited to identify their Tutsi neighbours and family members and were brutally killed if they failed to comply. Identity cards, which Habyarimana had promised but failed to eliminate, were used to determine victims' ethnicity. Fleeing to presumed sanctuary in churches, Tutsis were killed there in their thousands; the bodies of tens of thousands of victims were consigned to the Kagera River and would flow into Lake Victoria, bloated and naked; children and women and men alike were tortured and hacked to death. The final death toll from the genocide would be measured at almost one million.

In the process, the killers drove nearly half of the pre-war population into camps for refugees and internally displaced persons both in Rwanda and in neighbouring Tanzania and Zaire, the largest, fastest movement of refugees in modern history. Perhaps even more destructive, the perpetrators turned latent and historical ethnic emnities into a living, nightmarish reality of Rwandan society that is unlikely to dissipate, certainly not in the lifetime of the generation that watched the decimation of its society in the name of ethnic hatred.

### The International Non-Response

International response to the genocide was virtually non-existent. In the first days after the assassination of Habyarimana, the return to civil war and the apparent coup obscured the nature of the politicide in Kigali that preceded the wider genocide. General Dallaire's first efforts were aimed at preventing a return to civil war. He frantically attempted to contain the situation by convincing Kagame to keep his troops inside their own zone and struggled to bring the two sides together to forge a new cease-fire. As the dual nature of the violence became clear, his energy shifted to trying to cope with the deteriorating security situation with what resources he had and attempting in vain to convince New York to give him more resources – either troop reinforcements or at least proper equipment to make the best use of the troops he had.

The UN system failed to respond. A combination of preoccupation with other conflicts, a lack of strategic interests in Rwanda on the part of Security Council members, poor communication among DPKO, the secretary general, and the council, and the absence of contingency planning meant that the option of reinforcing UNAMIR never received serious consideration in New York. Instead, following the withdrawal of the Belgian contingent on 13 April, the Security Council voted on 20 April to pull all but 272 of UNAMIR's troops out of Kigali. In this decision, the United States in particular was guilty of reacting to events in Rwanda through the veil of its interpretation of the recent "peacekeeping" debacle in Somalia. The Americans were unwilling to engage in what appeared to be yet another bloody, internecine tribal war, and without American backing other members of the Security Council were reluctant to act.

In the end, some 470 UNAMIR troops remained in Kigali, and these vulnerable forces in fact managed to protect thousands of civilian

Rwandans. By May, the reports of genocide in Rwanda, and images particularly of bloated victims floating downriver into Lake Victoria, had generated such a public outcry worldwide that the UN was forced to reconsider its decision and vote to reinforce UNAMIR. Even then, however, the unwillingness of the Security Council's "Permanent Five" to contribute troops, or even to equip other nations' troops, meant that UNAMIR II, as it became known, was not fully deployed until mid-August, long after the civil war had ended and the genocide had claimed its victims.

In this sequence of events we see played out the fundamental irony of post-Cold War African politics. Chester Crocker has framed the situation as one in which the end of superpower competition on the continent has simultaneously increased the possibility of solving problems and reducing conflicts and at the same time diminished the political will to expend capital in so doing. In Rwanda, various Western states had been involved in conflict resolution through the Arusha process. That involvement was neither political nor high-level, however, and as a result it was largely free of the interest-based competition typical of much conflict resolution during the Cold War. However, when it came to a point in Rwanda when international political will was required to expend resources to secure the results of conflict resolution efforts – for example, by reinforcing UNAMIR – that will was absent among Western states with the needed capacity. Rwanda was caught between (mostly) African states with a motivation to respond but no capacity to do so and Western states with capacity but insufficient motivation. The black hole into which it was allowed to fall has frightening implications for the future of conflict resolution and peacekeeping on the African continent.

### CONCLUDING COMMENTS: ROOTS, RESOLUTION, AND REACTION

Between the roots of the civil war in Rwanda and its (temporary) resolution through victory, almost one million bodies lie testament to the failure of attempts to contain or mitigate the violence. Multiple efforts to those ends ultimately failed to protect those who died at the hands of genocide. The victims owe their deaths to those members of the akazu who chose to massacre them rather than relinquish their grip on power. In planning, organizing, leading, and executing genocide, the perpetrators committed an international crime against humanity for which they must be held accountable.

An account of the process of the negotiation and attempted implementation of the Arusha Accords provides some explanation for the failure of overall peace process – for why the accords collapsed in such a brutal fashion. Critically, the process failed to tackle the capacity of hard-liners – whose opposition to the Arusha Accords was widely known and publicly expressed – to challenge the construction of peace through violent resistance. Conflict resolution theory would suggest two options in dealing with such opposition – give those who lose in political transformation a stake in the new arrangements in order to minimize their destructiveness (for example, keeping minority whites in the political system in South Africa), or keep them out of new arrangements but find ways to ensure that they are unable to undermine the transition bargain (for example, pushing and pulling the military junta out of power in Haiti). The theory suggests that if hard-liners are not brought into the solution or pushed out of the picture, the "solution" is not whole and cannot be sustained.

Seen as a totality, the international peace efforts for Rwanda took neither the "Haitian" nor the "South African" option. Had the Arusha process given the Rwandan extremists a stake in power, perhaps the neutral peacekeeping mandate of UNAMIR would have secured the transition. As it was, Arusha resulted in a decidedly non-neutral transition bargain, with clear winners and losers. But having effectively removed the losers – the akazu – from power on paper, the international peacemakers should have conceived of means of pushing them out of power in fact – by disarming them or removing them from Kigali, under the supervision of a peace-enforcement force. Alternatively, if that option was unrealistic in terms of international willingness to supply a robust peace-enforcement presence, then alternative transitional arrangements could have given them some stake in power and thus an interest in maintaining the peace. By excluding them from transitional institutions but failing to tackle their power, the peace process forced hard-liners into a corner and then turned an unprotected back to them.

When genocide commenced, the UN withdrew its peacekeeping force, abandoning the peace and civilians to their fate. The reasons for the withdrawal had largely to do with the lack of great power interests in Rwanda and the resultant unwillingness of capable powers to risk troops in protecting the peace. It was also a conceptual and planning failure. Had the UN more fully understood the social roots of the conflict, the need for contingency planning vis-à-vis a forceful opposition would have been apparent. The broader failure, however, was a moral one on the part of UN members to respond to genocide, given the international legal right, clear moral responsibility, and ample military capacity to do so.[48]

What broader lessons does the experience offer? If the pattern is a valid indicator, future civil conflicts in Africa and elsewhere will generate well-intentioned interventions by a host of third parties seeking, through a variety of means, to move parties towards peaceful, negotiated solutions.[49] The paradox of a sophisticated peace process and a calamitous result in Rwanda does indeed suggest some wider lessons for these third parties, stemming as it does from a historical dilemma whose features are not specific to the Rwandan context and are bound to recur.

The experience of Rwanda suggests a general, a specific, and a conceptual lesson. The general lesson links the roots of conflict directly to resolution. Both threads of conflict in Rwanda – the civil war and the genocide – can be traced directly to the impact of manipulation of social cleavages, in this case ethnicity, by political elites in competition over power. Political manipulation of ethnic identities created the violence in Rwandan society in 1959 that drove the parents of the RPF's soldiers into exile. Manipulation of both ethnic and regional identities brought Habyarimana and his akazu to power after 1973. Ugandan and RPF leaders resorted to invasion to address social tensions between their populations, when other means were available. And the stirring up of ethnic fears and memories of old hatreds (themselves created by politics) allowed the akazu to perpetrate its genocidal plan in the summer of 1994. Peacemakers in Africa should recall the central role played by elites in transforming social tensions into violent conflict.

The specific lesson relates to the perennial dilemma of implementing peace in the face of hard-line resistance. If future collapses of negotiated peace settlements are to be avoided, third-party intervention must be grounded on an analysis of the historical roots and social causes of the conflicts they address. That analysis should pay particular attention to the role of elites in manipulating social tensions and fears to produce violent conflict in defence of their own, narrow political gain. It should focus on the issue of those who stand to lose out in transitional bargains and identify means of either coopting or neutralizing those forces. The composite elements of an overall peace process – negotiation, peace enforcement, implementation, peacekeeping, and reconciliation – should be coordinated by responsible actors to ensure that peacemakers do not adopt contradictory responses to the potential threat posed by hard-liners. Peacekeeping forces in particular should be prepared – both conceptually and materially – for the contingency of violent opposition by hard-line forces.

The absence of these elements in Rwanda resulted in the opening up of a space in which the akazu could plan its bloody opposition. In

Rwanda, opposition took the form of genocide; in other conflicts, it may be a return to civil war, a coup d'état against those who win power through negotiation, or terrorism. In any case, such opposition must be avoided or contained if peaceful solutions are to be sustained.

Finally, what becomes clear from Rwanda at a conceptual level is that conflict resolution is not a neutral exercise but forms part of a process of political transformation involving elites. While the original parties to conflict and transformation must retain the ultimate rights and responsibilities in that process, international peacemakers should be aware that they are engaging in an exercise that at least potentially creates losers. While the world has seen examples of transitions where a bargain is reached that protects the basic interests of the old guard while opening power to the new, such results cannot always occur. Efforts at conflict resolution should aim for such solutions – for the experience of South Africa, for instance – but be prepared to act to remove the old guard from a position in which it can threaten the new – to repeat the actions of Haiti, for example. Having failed to do the former in Arusha, peacemakers should have done the latter through UNAMIR. Doing neither, efforts in Rwanda left too great a scope to the enemies of the process and created an opportunity for the extremists to take the course they did. One million Rwandans paid the price. To avoid a recurrence, resolution of civil conflict in Africa must tackle directly the causes of violence and minimize the capacity of political elites to turn social cleavage into violent conflict.

NOTES

I would like to acknowledge financial assistance provided for parts of this research by a Social Sciences and Humanities Research Council Doctoral Fellowship and to thank Howard Adelman, Abdullahi An-Na'im, Emery Brusset, Rhoda Howard, Désirée McGraw, Bice Maiguascha, Beverly Neufeld, and Astri Suhrke for helping me produce this chapter, by allowing me access to their research or commenting on drafts.

1  Robin Lubbock, "Recalling Rwanda's Forgotten War," *Christian Science Monitor* (Feb. 1993).

2  Thomas G. Weiss, "Overcoming the Somalia Syndrome – 'Operation Restore Hope,'" *Global Governance*, 1 no. 2 (1995), 171–88.

3  The data on conflict resolution in Rwanda will never be complete; many key participants were killed during the genocide and civil war. This account relies on research that I conducted in Tanzania in December 1993 and January 1994 that generated documentary and primary evidence of the Arusha process as it was perceived at that stage; subsequent

interviews with Western and regional diplomats and UN officials involved in the peace process; and accounts of the process given by members of the RPF. I am particularly grateful to American, French, and Tanzanian officials who provided me with extensive interviews and access to documents, under conditions of confidentiality. I was part of a team of researchers investigating conflict resolution and early warning issues in Rwanda for a Multi-Donor Evaluation of Emergency Assistance of Rwanda. Much of the material gathered during the course of that research was confidential, and in this chapter I cite none of the interviews conducted or documents gathered during that process. However, the knowledge gained clearly forms part of the background to the analysis and conclusions of this paper.

4 The French name and acronym are used here in preference to the English – the Rwandese Government Forces (RGF) – because the latter is too easily confused with "RPF."

5 The term "continental" here refers to African states and institutions, including the Organization of African Unity, other than those that belong to the "sub-regional" category – Burundi, Kenya, Rwanda, Tanzania, Uganda, and Zaire.

6 Catherine Newbury, "Rwanda: Recent Debates over Governance and Rural Development," in Goran Hyden and Michael Bratton, eds., *Governance and Politics in Africa* (Boulder, Col.: Lynne Reinner 1992), 193–213.

7 On African international relations in the post-Cold War era, see Chester A. Crocker, "Afterword: Strengthening African Peacemaking and Peacekeeping," in David A. Smock, ed., *Making War and Waging Peace: Foreign Intervention and Conflict Resolution in Africa* (Washington, DC: U.S. Institute for Peace 1993), 263–70.

8 See Adotey Bing, "Salim A. Salim on the OAU and the African Agenda," *Review of African Political Economy*, 50, (1991); also confidential interviews in Dar-es-Salaam, Dec. 1993.

9 Aristide R. Zolberg, Astri Suhrke, and Sergio Aguayo, *Escape from Violence: Conflict and the Refugee Crisis in the Developing World* (New York: Oxford University Press, 1989), 45–9. This book contains an excellent discussion of the dynamics of refugee conflict, in particular the formation of "refugee warrior communities."

10 Rwanda was part of a German protectorate from 1899 to 1916. From 1916 until 1962, it was under Belgian administration, first as a League of Nations Mandate territory and after 1945 as a United Nations Trust Territory.

11 On the complexity of "ethnic" relations in Rwanda, see especially Catherine Newbury, *The Cohesion of Oppression: Clientship and Ethnicity in Rwanda, 1860–1960* (New York: Columbia University Press, 1988), chaps. 1–3. As Newbury makes clear, these relations varied not only by

region but also through time. Newbury is in agreement with other major scholars of the region, notably René Lemarchand, in finding strong support in Rwanda for instrumentalist accounts of ethnicity over primordial accounts. See René Lemarchand, "Burundi in Comparative Perspective: Dimensions of Ethnic Strife," in Brendan O'Leary and John McGarry, eds., *The Politics of Ethnic Conflict Regulation* (London: Routledge 1994), 151–71. On instrumentalist accounts of ethnicity, see Leroy Vail, ed., *The Creation of Tribalism in Southern Africa* (Berkeley: University of California Press, 1989).

12 How the Belgians decided who should be accorded Tutsi and Hutu status, given that these issues were not clear in Rwandan society, is an unresolved issue in the literature. I am grateful to Danielle de Lame, of the Musée royal de l'Afrique centrale, Belgium, for sharing her encyclopaedic knowledge of the literature on Rwanda with me.

13 Zolberg, Suhrke, and Aguayo, *Escape from Violence*, chap. 1.

14 Major-General Paul Kagame, Lecture to the Royal Institute of International Affairs, Chatham House, London, 7 Dec. 1994, printed in *Africa Research Bulletin* (Oct. 1990), 9874. Since achieving victory in the civil war, the Rwandese Patriotic Front has become careful to distinguish the Front from the Rwandese Patriotic Army (RPA). During the civil war period, however, there were virtually no references to the RPA, and where it was mentioned the two terms were used interchangeably, as they are in this paper.

15 Ibid. As Kagame rather devastatingly argued, there was more international attention paid to the plight of the gorillas in northern Rwanda than to the plight of Rwandan refugees in southern Uganda.

16 For the history of the RPF, see Catherine Watson, *Exile from Rwanda: Background to an Invasion* (Washington, DC: U.S. Committee for Refugees, 1991), and Rwandese Patriotic Front, "The Genisis of the Rwandese Patriotic Front" (Ruhengiri: RPF Department of Information, 8 May 1991).

17 Major-General Fred Rwegyima, who had also been a deputy defence minister in Museveni's cabinet, was the first military commander of the RPF and led the invasion of 1 October 1990. During that invasion he was killed by his second in command, Peter Bayingana, who was subsequently killed by Rwegyima loyalists. Kagame was recalled from the United States, where he was on a U.S. Department of Defense course at Fort Levenworth, to take command of the RPF. See *Africa Research Bulletin* (Oct. 1990), 9874.

18 Ibid., 9874.

19 Ibid., 9876.

20 Letter from the Ugandan Ambassador in Washington to Stephen Goose of the Arms Project, dated 26 August 1993, and reproduced in Human

Rights Watch Arms Project, *Arming Rwanda: The Arms Trade and Human Rights Abuses in the Rwandan War*, 6 no. 1 (Jan. 1994).

21 For this section, I have drawn extensively on Newbury, "Rwanda: Recent Debates," 193–213.

22 See *Africa Research Bulletin* (March 1992), 10512.

23 As Newbury makes clear, the quota system was publicly represented as a means of ensuring ethnic equality, but was in fact used to quite different effect. Newbury, "Rwanda: Recent Debates," 193–213.

24 This analysis originated with a French military attaché in Kigali, Lieutenant Colonel Galinie, but was quickly picked up by other Western donors. Confidential interviews, June 1995.

25 United Nations Economic and Social Council, Commission on Human Rights, Fiftieth Session, Item 12, E/CN.4/1994/7/Add.1, 11 August 1993, "Report by Mr. B.W. Ndiaye, Special Rapporteur, on his mission to Rwanda from 8 to 17 April 1993," 4. I am grateful to Dr Liesbet Hooghe, University of Toronto, for bringing the Belgian efforts to my attention.

26 The other former colonial power, Germany, played almost no role in this early stage. Germany's brief "occupation" of Rwanda had had far less impact than that of Belgium. Germany would end up as an observer to the Arusha peace process but even there played a minimal role.

27 Crocker, "Afterword," 263–70.

28 The timeline contained herein was developed, except where otherwise noted, through reference to confidential documents obtained on a visit to Dar-es-Salaam in December 1993 and January 1994; to discussions with American, Canadian, French, and Tanzanian officials; to *Africa Research Bulletin*; and to texts of the accords themselves, which are unpublished but not restricted.

29 Interviews with Rwandan, American, and French participants in the Gbadolite talks confirmed a general sense that Mobutu was ineffective and that his continued role was blocking further progress.

30 Interview with Carol Fuller, former desk officer for Rwanda, U.S. Department of State, and Herman Cohen, former under-secretary of state for Africa, U.S. Department of State, both in Washington, DC, in June 1995. Also, confidential documents from the French Ministry of Foreign Affairs.

31 Of course, the United States also had a certain power in the region that could be brought to bear, and was, particularly against Uganda, in an effort to press Uganda into ensuring RPF participation in the Arusha process. Interview with Herman Cohen.

32 See, for example, Human Rights Watch Arms Project, *Rwanda/Zaire: Rearming with Impunity*, 7 no. 4 (May 1995).

33 This argument is buttressed by several Western diplomats, including State Department officials, who speak of the cooperative and constructive role of the French diplomats in Arusha. Among other sources, a confidential interview with Carol Fuller, Washington, DC, Dec. 1994.

34 For more details on the pre-negotiation phase, particularly on the roles of France and the United States, see Bruce D. Jones, "The Arusha Process in Rwanda," Background Paper, Study II, Joint Evaluation of Emergency Assistance to Rwanda (Copenhagen: DANIDA, April 1996).

35 While some Western diplomats disclaimed any knowledge of Bagasora's connection to the CDR, the RPF, and the Tanzanians were aware of it (and knew him as "the Colonel of Death" for his involvement in appalling human rights abuses). It would be surprising if neither party had brought this information to the attention of other participants. One Western official described Bagasora as a "cold-hearted son-of-a-bitch"; a diplomat present in Arusha referred to him as a "loyal thug." The former epithet was more accurate; Bagasora appears to have been the principal architect of the assasination of Habyarimana. Confidential interviews, Dar-es-Salaam, Bergen, New York, and Washington, DC.

36 Peace Agreement between the Government of the Republic of Rwanda and the Rwandese Patriotic Front, 4 Aug. 1993, Arusha, Tanzania. The five protocols form appendices to the agreement, though each was released separately as it was signed.

37 Filip Reyntjens, *L'Afrique des grands lacs en crise: Rwanda, Burundi, 1988–94* (Paris: Khartala, 1994), 248–56.

38 Interview with Lieutenant Colonel Marley, Political-Military Advisor to Africa Bureau, U.S. Department of State, Dec. 1994.

39 The protocol on Miscellaneous Issues and Final Provisions was also signed during this final session; its contents are largely technical and did not contribute substantively to the agreement.

40 *Africa Research Bulletin* (Feb. 1993), 10902.

41 Interview with Tanzanian Foreign Ministry and U.S. State Department officials. A more colourful version of the metaphor suggested that it was "better to have the hard-liners inside the tent, pissing out, than outside of the tent, pissing in."

42 The French were taking the same position as these other third parties. While it is possible to interpret French support for inclusion of the CDR as support for the hard-liners, a nuanced account would note the correspondence of their position with that of the more clearly neutral American and Tanzanian delegations.

43 Confidential interviews, Dar-es-Salaam, Bergen, and Washington, DC.

44 It has been argued, especially by René Lemarchand, that the accords were negotiated by moderates, and only under intense international

pressure. It should be clear from this discussion, however, that Habyarimana's men and hard-liners were solidly represented on the GoR delegation to Arusha and that the accord was negotiated with their full knowledge, and that the ultimate positions in Arusha were taken precisely in opposition to the most direct international pressure. For a discussion of the role of hard-liners and moderates, see René Lemarchand, "Managing Transition Anarchies: Rwanda, Burundi, and South Africa in Comparative Perspective," *Journal of Modern African Studies*, 32 no. 4 (Dec. 1994), 581–601.

45 This section relies heavily on research conducted during the Multi-Donor Evaluation of Emergency Assistance to Rwanda and owes much to conversations with Howard Adelman and Astri Suhrke during the course of that research. For a more detailed account, see Jones, "The Arusha Process in Rwanda."

46 The Security Council voted unanimously on 5 October 1993 to pass Resolution 872, establishing the United Nations Assistance Mission in Rwanda. S/RES/872/5 Oct 93.

47 This plan was revealed to UNAMIR by an informant whose credibility was questionable but who turned out to be correct in every measure. UNAMIR's requests to New York for approval to follow up on the information were declined. Confidential interviews.

48 The UN Convention for the Prevention and Punishment of the Crime of Genocide (1948) gives member states the legal authority to use whatever means as necessary to prevent the conduct of genocide by other member states. It does not, however, create a specific legal obligation that they do so. See Multilateral Treaties Deposited with the Secretary General (New York: United Nations, 1989).

49 Indeed, such efforts are under way in Burundi, Sierra Leone, and elsewhere on the continent. Diplomats, UN officials, members of the development community, human rights organizations, conflict resolution NGOs, local community networks, diaspora groups, and church groups are some of the third parties seeking peaceful solutions in these situations of social conflict.

# PART TWO

## Negotiation as the Primary Instrument of Resolution

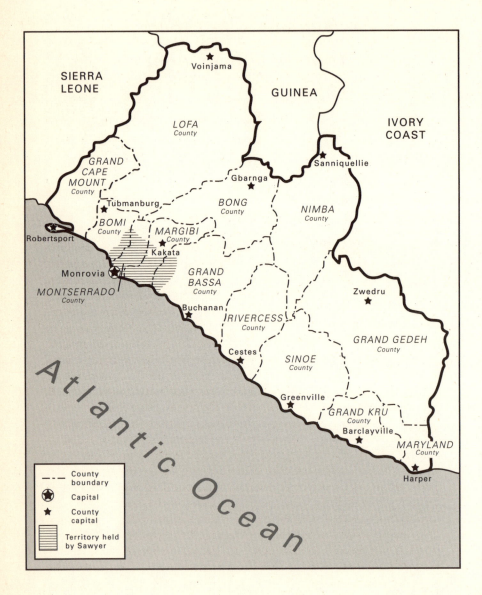

Liberia (1992)

# 4   The Civil War in Liberia

D. ELWOOD DUNN

In a perceptive 1978 study, Christopher Clapham proposed that "the most salient features of the post-World War II Liberian experience were political stability and economic growth." He concluded by suggesting that "whereas 'failure and promise' was the title of the volume, 'success and danger' might be a more appropriate verdict on the recent Liberian experience." Events transpired in rapid succession to bear out Clapham's warning of danger amid success. The "rice riots" of 1979 were followed by a military coup in 1980 and an attempted coup in 1985, with a bloody aftermath. Civil war erupted on Christmas eve 1989. The Abuja peace agreement (Abuja I) of 19 April 1995, which had to be revised in August 1996 (Abuja II) stands as the current, if problematic framework for containing the conflict.[1]

Is Liberia a special case, or does it share essential features with civil wars in Africa and elsewhere? We begin with the assumption that the conflict arose from "the tugs and pulls of different identities, the differential distribution of resources and access to power, and competing definitions of what is right, fair and just." The contenders in the political contest of "who gets what, when and how?" of the things of value in society, by resorting to violence to solve complex political problems, sought to ensure their security and survival (physical and political) and a prominent place in any settlement. If such conflicts are to be resolved, issues of social justice have to be addressed, along with the fears of the participants – the fear of settlement itself.[2]

This chapter explores the civil war in Liberia in terms of both its root causes and its settlement prospects. The examination of underlying cause must take place within the context of Liberia's distinctive origins and of changes in the nature and intensity of the conflict. Against this background, what prospects are there for conflict management or resolution? What has been the experience to date? Why have internal and external efforts not achieved the desired results?

In searching for causes and prospects for settlement, it is tempting to revert to the analytical focus of comparative foreign policy on the nation-state, especially if one sees in the Liberian war a single, "tribal" determinant. But a single-factor explanation is not enough: other analytical levels must be explored. Accordingly, I have employed a level-of-analysis framework and added to the national level those of the region (the sub-region and the continent) and the system (international).

In their study of international relations, Kegley and Witkoff stress the need "to trace changes in world politics to different groups of actors, their attributes, and their activities and interactions. Levels are commonly determined by the relative size and scope of their composition."[3] The three traditionally identifiable levels are the individual, the nation-state, and the system – or, in Kenneth Waltz's phrase, "Man, the State, and War." My modified categories – national, regional, and international – subsume the idiosyncratic or individual under the national, which encompasses not merely the national state and its foreign policy but the nation-state and the broader issue of governance.

The system level in Kegley's schema addresses "the conditions that result from the interactions of nations and nonstate actors with one another around the globe."[4] I have divided this third level into separate regional and international components because of the peculiar circumstances of this case study. The end of the Cold War permitted regional assertion in west Africa, which has become a salient element in the Liberian war. Here we start with the national roots of the problem and then move into the subregional, outer limits to grasp the interaction of forces and ultimately into the wider community of nations, where we encounter a sort of permissiveness or tolerance of civil war. Because the system's principal actors perceive no "strategic" interest at stake in Liberia, not only are their interests markedly limited (arms supply excepted), but they send signals to the protagonists that they may fight to the finish or "work out their own salvation" as best they can.

If we can establish that the Liberian conflict has its roots in the make-up of Liberia, reinforced from the region (and the continent, by extension) and from the changing international system, we will have a foundation for a realistic evaluation of what gave rise to the civil war and how it might be resolved or at least managed.

TOWARDS UNDERSTANDING CONFLICT

*National Level*

When the forces of the National Patriotic Front of Liberia (NPFL), led by warlord Charles Taylor, launched an attack against the forces of the government of President Samuel Doe on Christmas eve in 1989, it was only the latest in a series of triggers of violent conflict in Liberia – the "rice riots" of 1979, the military coup in 1980, and the foiled invasion by exiled Liberians under the leadership of Doe's erstwhile military comrade Thomas Quiwonkpa in November 1985. In fact, 24 December 1989 is seen by some as a vindication of Quiwonkpa's incursion, even if the prolongation of the conflict has altered the character of the political contest.

But we must go beyond triggers to root causes if we are to understand why Liberians continue to employ arms against each other. Two considerations must serve as guides: the historical context of the political conflict and changes in the nature and intensity of the conflict. First, I examine the peculiar origins of Liberia in the African context and trace the evolution of power relationships involving settler, indigenous, and hybrid Liberians and the resulting pattern of conflict. Second, I analyse the social cleavages of ethnicity, class, religion, region, and so on that have both altered and intensified conflict.

Politics in modern Liberia has seldom been played out in isolation from external circumstances. Nineteenth-century "philanthropy" and U.S. government interests were involved from the inception, as were the interests of European slavers, legitimate entrepreneurs, and colonialists. More recently, Liberian politics has been influenced by changes in the regional and international environments, especially during the Cold War. Thus I have used the level-of-analysis framework for this study because the nature and intensity of conflict in Liberia are functions of complex interactions between the domestic and the external environments.

Two ideas are omnipresent in modern Liberia. The first is that Liberia is an outpost of the Western world in Africa, devoted to a civilizing and Christianizing mission. The second is that of an African nationality modified by Western and other influences. The pioneering-settler Liberian leadership opted "to preserve the ideal of western democracy ... and to ... extend it to broader sections of the population," rather than merging "at the outset the comparatively small advanced elements of the population into the mass of those who were at a more *primitive stage of development*."[5]

Yet modern Liberia is the product of a complex African past, little of which could be considered "primitive." That past witnessed a long relationship among three indigenous, language-based groups: Mel-speakers (Gola and Kisi); Kwa-speakers (Bassa, Belle, Dei, Grebo, Krahn, and Kru); and Mende-speakers (Bandi, Dahn, Kpelle, Loma, Mandingo, Mano, and Mende Vai). It was on this complex African past that a contrived structure was initially imposed. But the new state that emerged in west Africa in the early nineteenth century involved much more than the meeting of two cultures. Other factors were superimposed on the broad cultural dissimilarities: the ideological disposition of the nineteenth-century world; the chieftancy and acephalous indigenous political structures and their implications for both authoritarian and democratic politics; state imposition of the chieftancy structure and therefore of authoritarian politics on all indigenous peoples, especially those of an acephalous tradition; and the effects on indigenous peoples of centuries of contact with European traders prior to the arrival in the 1820s of repatriated New World Blacks.

Once established, the modern state faced a dilemma: "[T]o maintain its autonomy, it had to meet the requirements of the prevailing international system by demonstrating evidence of state control." In the process of forging a state, it had imposed two aspects of a new political order: the ideal republican government brought by New World Blacks and the chieftancy system among acephalous peoples. The first involved establishment of a system within a system – that is, settler representative government within a wider polity offering few rights to the indigenous majority. The second adapted native modes of governance (chieftancy and acephalous systems) to the politics of patronage. The net effect was the gradual "emergence of autocracy" in the early twentieth century. In the world of a decolonized Africa and the Cold War, autocratic governance seemed secure despite challenges to it in Liberia and elsewhere in Africa, especially during periods of economic hardship.[6]

One such period of economic difficulty occurred in the 1970s, a decade that witnessed the initiation of a national discussion about social justice and equity and the imperatives of democracy. The traditional historical setting in which such issues were raised – namely the settler-indigene divide – figured prominently. Opposition groups emerged to engage the government of President William Tolbert (1971–80), which oscillated between a disposition to change and maintenance of the status quo. A dangerous political vacuum was created, which was soon filled when non-commissioned officers of the Armed Forces of Liberia (AFL) staged a coup d'état on 12 April 1980. Given the unprecedented nature of the coup and its excesses of violence, many observers concluded that the act was revolutionary and that it would set in train a profound social transformation. For others, it was decolonization from "Black colonialism"; the way was now clear for the replacement of settler minority rule with indigenous majority rule or, better yet, majority rule, pure and simple. Liberia for many was poised for a new, hopeful beginning.

But Liberia was too heavy with history to conform to simplistic assumptions about its politics and society. Following a period of uncertainty under an inexperienced and unfocused military government and its civilian enablers – the Movement for Justice in Africa (MOJA) and the Progressive Alliance of Liberia (PAL), briefly transformed into the People's Progressive Party (PPP) – the process of sorting out the imperatives of a return to civilian rule was soon under way. Largely in response to pressures from the U.S. government, which was bankrolling the military regime in keeping with its Cold War requirements, a new constitution was drafted and approved by referendum. Elections were held on 15 October 1985. There is ample documentation that the elections were rigged and that the incumbent military leader, Samuel Doe, stole the election.[7]

Amid protests, which included Quiwonkpa's attempted coup in November, Doe's inauguration as first president of the Second Republic took place on 6 January 1986. Though some saw this as a new start for Liberia, many more were less sanguine. In fact, a small but determined number in various organizations at home and in political exile would soon begin sketching an agenda for political opposition.

Two trends became discernible. The first was the military's quest to re-establish the single-party dominance reminiscent of at least the last years of the First Republic (1847–1980), especially the "refinement" of autocratic governance under William Tubman (president 1944–71). The second was the effort by a disparate opposition to resist Doe and his National Democratic Party of Liberia (NDPL).

Doe's return to single-party domination began with the political elimination of his erstwhile civilian collaborators, notably those of MOJA and PAL. On the eve of the 1985 election, his opponents were on the periphery, and he and his "political fixers" held the initiative. Of the six parties that were initially selected out of the large number of political formations that declared their intentions to form parties when the ban on politics was lifted by the military in August 1983, only four – the NDPL, the Liberia Action Party (LAP), the Unity Party (UP), and the Liberia Unification Party (LUP) – were finally cleared to contest the elections. Two important parties, the Liberian People's Party (LPP) and the United People's Party (UPP), were banned by the electoral commission because they "espoused ideology foreign to Liberia."[8]

Doe launched the NDPL in August 1983. Its constituents consisted of those citizens of Grand Gedeh County who had benefited from Doe's incumbency, some former True Whig Party (TWP) faithful, and a presumed Bandi constituency, because Harry F. Moniba, a Bandi-Liberian diplomat, was Doe's vice-president. The party guaranteed in a general sense the well-being of the military, which was still in power.

LAP owes its creation in 1984 to a number of indigenous, settler, and hybrid Liberian liberals of the TWP and independent indigenous and settler individuals. It claimed to be a responsible party of professionals and ordinary people, experienced, competent, and ready to govern. Judging from reports of the 1985 election, LAP may have won the presidency though it was not allowed to come to power. This fact was not insignificant in sparking Quiwonkpa's attempted coup.

LUP, also set up in 1984, was led by William Gabriel Kpolleh, a Kpelle schoolteacher (the Kpelle are the largest single ethnic group in Liberia) with no known political background. The party's general goals included bringing together rich and poor, indigenous and settlers. Doe is reported to have paid the required registration fees for LUP in an effort to create a "loyal opposition." But following the election, Kpolleh joined with LAP and UP in a grand coalition against Doe's NDPL government.

UP was identified with Edward Beyan Kesselly, a perennial minister in Tolbert's government. With familial ties to the Loma and Mandingo peoples and some affiliation with the military because his father was a retired general, Kesselly was thought able to tap into these ties to build a political constituency. His vice-presidential running mate in 1985 was S. Jabaru Carlon, a Vai-Liberian who, it was presumed, would attract the Vai votes. For whatever reason, UP attracted a very small following.

Though the LPP was officially launched in August 1984, it was banned in July 1985 because the military government was unwilling to accept a party whose origins suggested sympathy for Marxist socialism. LPP's roots are in MOJA, a political movement initiated in 1973 at the University of Liberia and committed to transforming state and society. It developed into a significant force for radical change in the 1970s and projected an image as a champion of the rural poor and urban masses. The LPP soon disposed of the ideological baggage of MOJA and advocated a free-market economy that encouraged private initiative and individual creativity. After it was banned, some of its members sided with the LAP in the 1985 election.

UPP's origins and ideological roots lie in PAL (a political organization of Liberians in the United States, established in 1975 and transferred to Monrovia in 1978) and the People's Progressive Party, established in January 1980 as the first opposition political party in Liberia in twenty-five years. PPP was banned shortly before the coup of April 1980. Led by Gabriel Baccus Matthews of settler-Liberian provenance, PAL advocated a "revolutionary but not Marxist" socialism. Its message was a blend of a return to traditional values of cooperation with insistence on greater distributive justice in the cash economy. It was this message, directed in confrontational fashion at the Tolbert regime in the late 1970s, that stole the show from the supposedly more experienced and professional MOJA and led to the collapse of the government in the 1980 coup. When PAL was reborn as UPP, the message shifted from African socialism (cooperation over competition) to consensus-building among former PPP and MOJA adherents, liberals of the TWP, and people with no political affiliation. As with the LPP, the military government was not convinced that a real shift had occurred.

None the less the election went forward. When the results were revealed, deep disappointment quickly set in. Quiwonkpa's attempted coup cost him his life. Brutal and massive repression ensued. Because of Quiwonkpa's county of origin, Liberians of Nimba descent bore the brunt of Doe's brutality, though there was a general crackdown on all opposition. The attempted coup provided a ready excuse for reining in the opposition. But Doe could not silence or intimidate those in exile. However, he thought that he was strong enough to deter any opposition from those outside the country. Nor did he anticipate an insurgency. And so he continued to weaken (though not eliminate) political parties and other internal opponents, while guarding against external political attack.

A disparate opposition developed. Its elements included five political parties (LAP, LPP, LUP, UP, and UPP) and exile groups, including the Association for Constitutional Democracy in Liberia (ACDL) and the Union of Liberian Associations in the Americas (ULAA). While the activities of home-based groups can easily be documented, it is more difficult to trace the underground movements of those in exile. The culmination of all the efforts by these disparate groups was the politics of insurgency, which the NPFL came to embody after 24 December 1989.[9]

By the late 1980s the tragedy of Doe was becoming the tragedy of Liberia. The likelihood of a "national political catastrophe," given the overt tribalization of politics and the militarization of society, was predicted in 1988.[10] With poorly managed public institutions and a militarized, autocratic government, Liberia had no mechanism for resolving conflict peacefully. Morale in civil society, as in the military, was at an all-time low. The economy was in shambles as the U.S. administration, in response to pressure from Congress, began gradually to withdraw support from Doe's government because of its inefficiency and flagrant violations of human rights. The national debt grew, and international financial institutions suspended business with Liberia when it failed to meet its obligations. The society was on the verge of collapse when the insurgency gave it a final shove.

Moreover, the opposition groups mirrored the anarchic condition of the government, thereby ensuring that the immediate post-Doe era would be chaotic. The four official opposition parties – LAP, LUP, UP, and UPP – suffered from varying degrees of weakness and were unable to function in the highly repressive and physically dangerous domestic environment. Personality differences among members of these parties in exile, particularly those of LAP, led to internal wrangling. The reviving LPP did not fare any better, as an internal struggle for leadership between MOJA stalwarts Boima Fahnbulleh and Togba-Nah Tipoteh came into the open. Amos Sawyer, who was also a founding member of MOJA and would later head an interim government, had made known his reservations about Tipoteh's inordinate ambitions. The TWP continued to blame the "progressives" for the 1980 coup and seemed to welcome a politically conservative insurgency. It was therefore not surprising that when Doe was seized and tortured to death by Prince Yormie Johnson's Independent National Patriotic Front of Liberia, which broke away from Taylor's NPFL in September 1990, the country was plunged into deeper political problems.[11]

The *triggers* of the conflict can be found in Liberia's recent political history – the evident political void reached by 1979, which led to the 1980 coup, and Doe's actions, which transformed a traditional settler hegemony into dominance by a single ethnic group. And superimposed on these developments was the unremitting militarization of society during a period of economic depression.

Against this brief historical background, we can now explore *root causes*, or "deep politics" – "political response, protest, and conflict" consequent on "high politics," or the "procedures and practices of government."[12] In other words, what is beneath all this political conflict that normal politics could not resolve?

Cleavages and Related Causes

Both the scholarly literature and the popular press seem to be in accord in ascribing most, if not all, of the civil wars in Africa either to "tribalism," with its pejorative connotation of "primitiveness," or to the inability of "tribal Africa" to govern itself in the modern world. The reality is far more complex. In fact, few of the major rebel movements in current wars are known publicly to have justified their political action in terms of "tribal ambition." They all claim to be waging struggles for "broader human rights and political change in society as a whole," and they use the presence of adherents from outside the core ethnic group to justify their claims.[13]

Yet there is an ethnic component to these wars. That is to say, there are "primordial" or "prebendal" (a pre-modern state) ties that can be mobilized in situations of inadequately managed social cleavages. In many African states, as the gap between state and civil society widened primordial allegiances deepened. Hence "primordial ethnic or regional loyalty [has] represented a social identity that people [have] turned to as they defined themselves in the struggle" for social justice.[14]

Some sense of what social cleavages are, and seeking to relate them to the Liberian experience, will broaden our insight into the nature and intensity of the conflict. We can look beneath the political veneer to discover the "deep politics" of Liberia – political response, protest, and conflict culminating in civil war, which in turn took on a logic of its own and rendered conflict total.

Conventional wisdom about the social dynamics in Liberia has often been one-dimensional. To cite just one source: "Until the 1970s, Liberian history was the history of the American-Liberians, their settlement, establishment of the republic, how they incorporated the other Liberians mainly through conquest, and how they held on exclusively to power at the expense of the indigenous Liberians. From the day the first group of settlers set foot on Liberian soil, it has been a long history of American-Liberian conquest and domination and indigenous Liberian resistance and opposition."[15] If there is any truth in this statement, then the 1980 coup, which was to end "Americo-Liberian" minority rule and usher in indigenous Liberian majority rule, was a turning point. But the events of the 1980s and the 1990s have further lessons to reveal. For several decades, a complex social transformation has been undermining not just settler hegemony (of which some indigenes were a part and some settlers were not), but more significant all hegemony. That was the political agenda that gathered momentum in the 1970s. Once the coup occurred, the venting of social and political anger was such that euphoria quickly replaced a reasoned assessment of what had transpired socially and politically, especially in the 1970s.

But we must see the mistakes of the immediate post-coup period in conjunction with other factors. In Liberia, as elsewhere in Africa, civil war was a result of autocratic rule, of rulers' manipulative skills aided by an infusion of foreign aid driven by the imperatives of the Cold War, "errors of policy and conduct," ethnic and regional factors, "political belief and ideology," and such contributing factors as poverty and limited opportunities.[16]

## Tubman and the Cleavages

Clapham has used core–periphery imagery to characterize the pre-coup paramountcy of settler Liberians in terms of control of state power. How did the core (some 2 per cent of the population) control the periphery during the Tubman administration? Clearly there were limits to the use of force because the resources were simply not available. At that time the regular members of the armed forces were largely from the periphery, while most officers hailed from the core. And indigenous groups were relatively small and scattered. They were not monolithic, except later as a politically conscious group. But even in Tubman's time there was a cleavage between coastal indigenes (who had longer contact with the West in pre-Liberia and with settler-Liberians after creation of the state in 1822) and hinterland indigenes (who had less experience of contact with the West).[17]

So how was hegemony sustained? According to Clapham, effective control was possible because of "the existence of a political formula which treats all Liberians as formally equal, and which allows the development of political mechanisms which help to integrate the periphery into the state structure and reduce the need for any overt use of force to very small proportions."[18] These "mechanisms," or "assimilationist development strategies," some of them not of Tubman's making, have included at least four elements. *The apprenticeship system* was a method of socializing recaptives (intercepted Africans en route to slavery) and indigenes into settler culture by putting them under the guardianship of settler families. *Education through the civilizing-Christianizing ethos* produced a corps of indigenous intelligentsia, a small number of whom were critical of the experience. *Settlement policy* involved creation of settler communities within "native jurisdiction" as a "civilizing" influence. One consequence of this policy was that settlers came to admire the Mende hierarchical forms of organization, which they would later employ in their attempts to administer the hinterland. And *interior administration and "indirect rule"* imposed a hierarchical, institutional form on all indigenes in the hinterland, whether or not such forms were compatible with their traditional institutional structures. Mende forms were forced on Mel and Kwa societies.

To the foregoing we must add Tubman's defining policies – the Unification Policy and the Open Door Policy. In his first inaugural address, Tubman stressed the need for the "assimilation and unification of our various populations." The major features of his Unification Policy included reforms of hinterland administration, including the transformation of hinterland provinces in 1964 into counties, on an administrative par with the coastal counties; extending infrastructure such as roads, schools, and hospitals to the hinterland; constitutional amendment to extend the franchise to hinterlanders; and increased indigenous participation in government service. The Open Door Policy was a modern and more comprehensive version of the traditional economic policy of inviting foreign investment to exploit the country's natural resources. Its key features were that foreign investors could bring in capital and remit profits, dividends, and other earnings "without interference or impediments."

There were shortcomings in both policies. Some saw unification as a strategy designed primarily to keep Tubman in office. Others have suggested that because of his non-Monrovia origins Tubman resorted to hinterland and other indigenous support to strengthen his political power outside the traditional settler base, where he felt both questioned and threatened by his sponsor, former president Edwin Barclay, who attempted unsuccessfully to unseat Tubman in 1955. Then there was the economic rationale for unification, as it was an essential base for the Open Door Policy. Not only was social peace required for development, but most exploitable natural resources were in the hinterland.

While the results of the Open Door Policy were statistically impressive,[19] the boom was short-lived. It relied too heavily on a favourable world market for iron ore and rubber, the country's principal resources. When the market for those products all but disappeared in the 1970s, so too did the positive impact of the policy. The global oil crisis did the rest.

Overall, the integration efforts and assimilationist strategies resulted in time in a "revolutionary consciousness" not only among indigenous Liberians but among young settler Liberians and Liberians of mixed parentage who had reason to feel alienated and repressed.

### Tolbert and the Cleavages

Tolbert, Tubman's vice-president for almost twenty years, inherited a Liberia in which a minority core (admittedly expanding) still largely controlled the majority. A passive vice-president, Tolbert surprised many after Tubman's death in July 1971 thrust him into the presidency. It became clear rather quickly that Tolbert wanted to distance himself from Tubman's personality and style of government. He soon took steps to reform the pattern of patronage government he had inherited. Major proposed changes included civil service reform based on a merit system; policies and programs based on impersonal "social" criteria such as qualification and need; constitutional and political changes, including the removal of elements of nineteenth-century provincialism from the constitution and other state papers; and an economic policy focused on "rural development and urban reconstruction." Though this was a powerful declaration of intent, especially to those alienated by the politics of patronage and other authoritarian features of the Tubman era, Tolbert's attempts to implement reforms would in time encounter resistance. His inability to lead in the midst of the resistance resulted in his overthrow.

Perhaps Tolbert's major problem was the danger that an elitist governing system faces when it decides to embrace large measures of democracy. Tolbert had clearly signalled an opening to the traditional political periphery – indigenes (coastal and hinterlander), inquiring and radical intellectuals and students, even radical movements such as MOJA and PAL. And as these groups pressed for more political liberalization, Tubman loyalists began quietly to complain not that things were changing to their disadvantage but that this "tampering" with the system could lead only to misfortune for all.

A significant crack had occurred in the old establishment, and the forces unleashed were determined to press for thorough change. There was no umpire in this contest, which raged into the later 1970s and contributed to the decay of the state. The impact of the global oil crisis on Liberia, and an economic policy that did not fully reflect the political rhetoric of societal change, also contributed to the decline. Tolbert's misfortune, which became Liberia's as well, was that he embodied both the old and the new. And he was unable either to part company with the old or to institute new policies with which all might identify. There was no leadership from any side to step in and fill the void, to manage a transition from hegemonic rule to power-sharing.

## Doe and the Cleavages

Perhaps the course of Liberian history would have been different if those who seized power in 1980 had evaluated the politics at least of the 1970s and drawn appropriate conclusions. They might not have re-installed hegemonic rule; they might have seriously addressed the changing society; and they might have reasoned that ethnicity, class, regionalism, and religion had to be dealt with and, perhaps above all, that the traditional political culture of authoritarianism would have to be exorcised. But they didn't, and over time the settler core was replaced with Doe's Krahn associates, and by 1985 Krahn hegemony had become an issue. Eghosa Osaghae writes: "Two things are interesting about the post-1980 ruling class. First, it inherited and imitated the tendencies of the class it overthrew. Second, the new class had neither the organizational skills nor the unity of the American-Liberians to perpetuate itself. There were now more instances of intra-class struggle along ethnic lines. These intra- and inter-class struggles culminated in the civil war of 1989–90 which however had the character of a straightforward inter-ethnic struggle."[20]

Resources at the disposal of the elite in Tubman's and Tolbert's Liberia went beyond ethnicity to include such other social institutions as the family (leading ones), the Christian church, benevolent societies (Free Masons/Eastern Star, United Brothers of Friendship/ Sisters of the Mysterious Ten, Odd Fellows/Household of Ruth), and the True Whig Party. The new Krahn ruling class seems to have had few resources besides ethnicity on which to base its power. Exiled Liberians with access to Western parliamentary committees were also beyond Doe's grasp. The Doe administration thus galvanized into action both latent and incipient ethnic conflicts, and the masses of indigenes responded by "becoming ethnic champions and relating with each other on this basis."[21]

In his search for allies, Doe had made overtures to some Mandingo-Liberian leaders, many of whom are Muslim. There are creditable reports that he planned to dispose politically of his Bandi-Liberian vice-president, Harry Moniba, and replace him with the head of national radio and TV, Alhaji Kromah (who later would lead the warring faction ULIMO-Mandingo). The salience of religion in Liberia perhaps dates from this period. When the civil war started, Krahn/Mandingo were seen as arrayed against Dahn/Mano. And as the war developed and settlement efforts got under way, a religious factor was introduced that continues to play an important role.

*Regional Level*

Regional neutrality might have rendered civil war in Liberia impossible. The attitude of Liberia's immediate neighbours was crucial, because each seems to have had a stake in Liberian politics, especially since the 1980 coup. In Sierra Leone there was a well-founded fear that here too a sergeant could topple the regime – of Siaka Stevens. Besides, in 1985 Stevens had "made available military facilities at Camp Samu and Jui to Thomas Quiwonkpa's Patriotic Front." Because he was grateful for the support of the United Liberation Movement for Democracy in Liberia (ULIMO) against the NPFL and Sierra Leonean rebels, Steven's successor, General Joseph Momoh, allowed ULIMO to operate out of Freetown.[22]

Likewise, the Ivory Coast had demonstrated its sympathies for those who fled Doe's repression in 1985, and Houphouet-Boigny's regime seemed keen on aiding attempts to depose Doe and possibly install an NPFL government. The Ivorian leader and other senior officials enjoyed personal and cordial ties with the Tolberts in Liberia. Tolbert's eldest son was Houphouet-Boigny's foster son-in-law, and the Ivorians never quite forgave Doe for his unceremonious removal of this Liberian from the French embassy in Monrovia in the immediate aftermath of the 1980 coup. There were ethnic considerations as well. The Dahn, Mano, and other ethnic groups are divided at the Ivorian–Liberian border; those on the Liberian side were threatened by genocide. Ivorian motives also extended to the politics of the subregion and involved Ivorian–French interests in containing Nigeria's hegemonic tendencies, which had earlier inspired Ivorian and French recognition of Biafra during the Nigerian civil war. Now support of the NPFL was "subterranean, cleverly packaged as uncontrollable private business deals." It included provision of sanctuary to the NPFL and diplomatic support to its "government."

To the Ivorian effort must be joined that of Burkino-Faso, where Burkinabe President Blaise Campaore's ties with the Ivory Coast and its leader may account in large part for its support of the NPFL. There is ample documentation of Burkinabe regulars (the number has ranged from 400 to 1,000) fighting alongside Charles Taylor's forces, of Taylor's use of Burkinabe aircraft to shuttle to and fro in the subregion, and that Taylor's bulletproof state car is provided by the Burkinabe government. Taken together Ivory Coast and Burkina Faso's support for the NPFL is substantial indeed.[23]

Guinea has harboured ethnic and religious sympathies for Mandingo-Liberians, who were targeted by Dahn and Mano-Liberians in the NPFL because they were allied with Doe. But members of the Kissi, Kpelle, and Loma ethnic groups live on both sides of the Guinean-Liberian border. With the formation of the ULIMO faction, at one point led exclusively by Kromah, a Mandingo-Liberian whose grandfather is a Guinean, that support solidified. Though disclaiming support for any one faction, Guinea did not hide its sympathy for Kromah. According to the minister of the interior, René Alsoni Gomez: "Like many Liberians he [Kromah] originates from Guinea. His grandparents are in Guinea so we cannot prevent him from coming 'home' like many other Liberians."[24]

It is difficult to imagine how the Liberian insurgency could have gone forward in the absence of help from neighbouring states, which fuelled the internal conflict. However, the most significant external involvement was the intervention of the Economic Community of West African States (ECOWAS), which may have inadvertently inflamed rather than dampened the conflict. The resulting problems, essentially political in nature, stem from that body's inadequate appreciation of the internal political stakes that fuel the conflict and from serious political differences within its own ranks. If the parties to the conflict perceive ECOWAS as biased and can call on backers in the subregion, is it any wonder that conflict persists?

Shortly after the first talks officially convened by an ECOWAS Mediation Committee in Freetown, Sierra Leone, in mid-July 1990, an impasse resulted: there would be no further talks unless the warring factions agreed to a peacekeeping force. The NPFL made it clear that not only would it resist such a proposal, it would not permit an ECOWAS-sponsored interim government and it would not lay down its weapons until Doe resigned. The ECOWAS summit that followed on 5–7 August 1990 mirrored the divisions within the subregion and the determination of a few member-states, led by Nigeria, to proceed with what was to become known as the ECOWAS Peace Plan for Liberia, a recasting of the peace formula of the Inter-Faith Mediation Committee (IFMC), an initiative of Liberian Christian and Muslim leaders.[25]

ECOWAS's involvement is both political and military. Political peacemaking includes a series of diplomatic initiatives (with inadequate internal Liberian consultation) and installation and protection of a series of interim governments, while ECOWAS presses warring factions to create a political settlement. Though the results to date include significant power-sharing – after the thirteenth such agreement, which had to be revisited in August 1996 – the challenge of faithful implementation remains. For military peacekeeping and peace enforcement ECOWAS formed a Military Observer Group (ECOMOG). Since its forces landed in Liberia on 24 August 1990, "the military trajectory has shifted unsteadily between a defensive and an offensive strategy in an effort to implement the political objective" of the ECOWAS Peace Plan.[26] Perhaps it is a matter here of implementing peace agreements known as Abuja I and Abuja II of 19 August 1995 and 18 August 1996, respectively, though adjustments in the original peace plan must be acknowledged.

Had ECOWAS scrupulously adhered to its legal instruments and normal institutional and political processes, it would have remained as inactive as did the Organization of African Unity (OAU). But because ECOWAS, or part of it, decided to depart from convention and act, it engendered suspicion. Of its sixteen member-states, only seven attended the summit of August 1990: the heads of state of Gambia, Ghana, Guinea, Nigeria, and Sierra Leone and the foreign ministers of Mali and Togo. Ivory Coast and Burkina Faso did not participate and declared that creation of ECOMOG was contrary to ECOWAS's rules.

None the less, part of ECOWAS decided to proceed, and that decision made ECOMOG possible. The leading players in the process had links to the domestic Liberian situation, which surfaced once ECOMOG was in Liberia and became complicating factors. Nigeria had been a staunch supporter of Doe, though it would soon switch its support to Amos Sawyer and the Interim Government of National Unity, when IGNU was established in 1990. Ghana had a relationship of some duration with MOJA elements of IGNU. Guinea despised Taylor, in part because of NPFL attacks on Mandingo-Liberians, who were widely perceived to be of the Islamic faith. Sierra Leone and Gambia wanted Taylor's insurgency quickly contained because of the presence of dissidents from their countries within the ranks of the NPFL and their implied threat to national security in both countries. In Sierra Leone the danger became a reality with the beginning of an NPFL-linked insurgency in 1991 and the subsequent coup, which overthrew the Momoh government in 1992. Similarly, Gambian troops returning from peacekeeping in Liberia overthrew the long-standing regime of President Jawara in 1994. ECOWAS's decision to intervene therefore meant that certain Liberian groups were politically disadvantaged, and its action in the absence of community consensus was bound to engender suspicion. While mediator/facilitators were clearly needed, given the inability of the Interfaith Mediation Committee (IFMC) to fulfill that role, a perception of impartiality was essential if it was to have any credibility in the eyes of all parties to the conflict. It was a classic "Catch 22" situation: without ECOMOG Liberia risked descending, in the short run, into greater chaos; with it came intensified internal political rivalry, which stalled the resolution of the civil war. ECOWAS's intervention was flawed in at least six ways.

*Inadequate mediation and preventive diplomacy.* There should have been greater coordination of efforts between the IFMC and ECOWAS, with IFMC providing the domestic Liberian ingredients (appreciation of the nuances of Liberian politics) and ECOWAS consulting in the subregion with a view to developing some consensus. Beyond this, Ivory Coast and Nigeria should have been actively consulting at the highest levels rather than avoiding each other. Understanding between these two member-states, putative leaders of the linguistic blocs in the subregion, could have helped immeasurably to bridge the gulf between the Doe and the Taylor camps.

*Questionable legal basis.* In a letter of 14 July 1990 to the chairman and members of the Ministerial Meeting of the ECOWAS Standing Mediation Committee, Doe formally invited ECOMOG to Liberia.[27] But because his government had virtually collapsed by then, and Taylor exercised de facto control over most of the national territory, intense diplomatic efforts should have been undertaken to secure Taylor's consent for ECOMOG.

*Failure to mould a coalition of key member states.* Even if the full support of the membership of ECOWAS was not forthcoming, involving such key states as Ivory Coast and Burkina Faso, known supporters of Taylor, and balancing the ECOMOG force with units from those countries, might have materially enhanced the mission.

*Manner in which IGNU was established.* ECOMOG began landing in Monrovia on 24 August 1990, and the ECOWAS Mediation Committee sponsored an All-Liberia Conference in Banjul, Gambia, from 27 August to 1 September 1990. Among the problems was the timing of the meeting. ECOWAS would have been wise to delay the conference until it had secured a cease-fire, thereby allowing more opportunity for Charles Taylor and the NPFL to participate in the selection of an interim government. "By putting the cart before the horse, ECOWAS may have actually created unnecessary political tension between the Interim Government of National Unity and Taylor."[28] In fact, political tension already existed between Taylor and his political allies, on the one hand, and Amos Sawyer and his allies, on the other. The timing of the Banjul meeting and the choice of Sawyer to head IGNU, rather than someone perceived to be closer to the centre of the Liberian political spectrum, only exacerbated political tensions.

*Lack of close cooperation between ECOWAS and the UN Security Council.* If the provisions of chapter VIII of the UN Charter (regional arrangements) had been implemented and if the UN had declared that the ECOMOG intervention fell within the "Purposes and Principles of the United Nations," the legitimacy and impartiality of the action would have been enhanced, reducing the occasion for suspicion on the part of the contenders for power in Liberia.

*Failure of ECOMOG to control fighting between additional parties.* As for post-intervention action, it is an open secret that ECOMOG either looked the other way or facilitated the war-making efforts of ULIMO, the remnants of the Armed Forces of Liberia (AFL), and the Liberia Peace Council (LPC), parties not explicitly covered by the ECOWAS-sponsored cease-fire of 28 November 1990.

*Systemic Level*

Imagine the response during the Cold War if Libya had trained and armed insurgents to destabilize the Liberian government. Libya's involvement in the Liberian crisis is rooted in disaffection between Doe and Quaddafi in the aftermath of the Liberian coup of 1980. Libya was the first country to recognize the new military government, putting its faith in the revolutionary rhetoric of MOJA and PAL. This situation did not last, as Doe soon sent all socialist-inclined forces, both external and internal, packing. Before the NPFL launched the fateful assault on government forces in Nimba County, the Libyan leader had already switched his support to Taylor as the new incarnation of revolutionary fervour in Liberia. Libya thus came to serve as a training facility and source of arms for core NPFL forces.[29]

But the Libyan factor was a source of complacency for some Liberians, who held to the traditional reasoning that the United States would quickly contain the conflict. And true to form, U.S. military advisers were seen in the Nimba area, doing what they were in Liberia to do – provide security advice and undertake covert action in the interest of the stability of the regime. But human rights groups were quick to spot them, and the resulting publicity forced their premature removal and a denial by the U.S. government of any involvement.

U.S. ambivalence may have reflected post-Cold War circumstances. Doe's political excesses and his terrorism had not been firmly restrained, and once fighting started the United States took the lead in adopting a "hands-off" policy. This was a far cry from an earlier era in which the United States extended to Liberia its Cold War policy of containment. After the Cold War ended, U.S. policy became one of permissiveness – marginal involvement through making sizeable contributions to humanitarian assistance, but otherwise leaving the initiative for action to others.

Unlike the United States, France opted to get involved, albeit indirectly. Though French interest in Liberia has a long history, the current civil war provides it with a new opportunity. In any linguistic rivalry (francophone Africans versus anglophone Africans), France is understandably keen to ensure the edge for the francophones. This translates into French support for the NPFL and its francophone supporters (Burkina Faso and Ivory Coast). As Nigeria continued to lead the ECOMOG intervention in Liberia and its officials insisted on the subregion as primary to Nigerian interests, the rivalry with France and francophone Africa continued to fuel the conflict in Liberia.[30]

The role of the OAU in the Liberian crisis has not been large. Perhaps the non-interference clause of the organization's charter spurred use of ECOWAS's defence and security protocols. Or it may have been lack of resources and any successful experience with conflict resolution. In any case, the OAU contented itself with a "diplomatic presence" as others took the initiative.

In June 1990 an OAU delegation visited Doe in Monrovia to express concern about the developing crisis. By July 1990, the OAU's chair, Museveni of Uganda, expressed the OAU's readiness "to take an active part in efforts to bring an end to the tragic hostilities in Liberia." The OAU further expressed support for "the laudable efforts deployed by ECOWAS" and its "total" solidarity.[31]

Nothing concrete transpired before the Geneva/Cotonou Accords of 1993, which provided for an expansion of ECOMOG to include forces from outside west Africa. The OAU and the UN agreed to limited supporting roles, with the former appointing an "eminent person" to liaise with the ECOWAS Secretariat, while Tanzania, Uganda, and Zimbabwe agreed to supply troops. This last action, from which Zimbabwe quickly withdrew, was designed to address the perception of partiality in ECOMOG's relations with the Liberian parties to the conflict. By mid-July 1995 both Tanzania and Uganda had withdrawn their forces from Liberia, but Charles Taylor's visit to Nigeria in June engendered some hope about movement in the peace process. Subsequent developments soon bore out this guarded optimism.

The final element in international influence on the war in Liberia is the involvement of foreign business. At the height of the war, when Taylor's NPFL controlled the bulk of the national territory, there was a thriving export trade in diamonds, timber, gold, and agricultural products, made possible through a network of foreign firms, which were used to exploit and market these resources and to finance Taylor's politico-military enterprise.[32] Among the companies involved were the Agricultural Development Corporation (United States); Firestone Tire and Rubber (United States), whose parent corporation is Bridgestone of Japan; the Nimba Mining Company (NIMCO), a consortium consisting of Bureau des recherches géologiques et minières (France), Cyprus Minerals (United States), Liberian Iron Ore (Canada), Liberian Swedish Minerals Company (United States and Sweden), Sumimoto (Japan), and West African Mining Company of Liberia (Britain); and Sollac (France) a state-owned iron-ore supplier to state-owned Usinor steel mills.

## TOWARDS RESOLUTION OF THE CONFLICT

Several processes have been at work to resolve the civil war in Liberia, some running concurrently and interdependently, including the All-

Liberia conference series; the ECOWAS peace plan, involving intervention and negotiation; the Liberian Interfaith Mediation Committee;
and the UN. To these must be added the efforts of a host of governments, NGOs, and individuals, all with the common objective of
ending the war. A brief examination of the efforts/processes at all
three levels – national (the All-Liberia conference series and IFMC),
regional (ECOWAS), and systemic (UN) – is in order.

### National Level

The first attempt at mediating the Liberian conflict came from within
Liberia. The Interfaith Mediation Committee (IFMC) was a fusion of
the Liberia Council of Churches (LCC) and the Liberian Muslim
Council. The effort began some five months into the civil war, in May
1990, when it seemed clear that the Doe regime could not win the
war. Included on the IFMC were Rev. J.K. Levee Moulton (Baptist),
Archbishop Michael Kpakla Francis (Roman Catholic), Sheikh
Kafumba F. Konneh (Muslim), Bishop W. Nah Dixon (Pentecostal
Church), Bishop Ronald Diggs (Lutheran), and Rev. Canon Burgess
Carr (Episcopalian). The LCC component of IFMC had begun attempting political negotiations between Doe and his civilian opponents in the tense aftermath of the 1985 election. Several appeals for
dialogue came from LCC and later IFMC to the government.

Following mediation feelers to Taylor and Doe contingent on an
immediate cease-fire, the convening of a peace conference, and
assurances of security for the mediators by both sides, the first IFMC-
sponsored conference convened at the U.S. embassy in Freetown,
Sierra Leone, on 12 June 1990. Senior representatives of both Doe
and Taylor showed up. A statement issued on the fifth day
announced adjournment "to allow consultations between the delegations and their respective principals." While both parties committed
themselves to return to the talks later in the month, the second
round never materialized.

Perhaps the gulf that divided Taylor and Doe was already un-
bridgeable. Taylor's forces were by this time only 30 km outside
Monrovia and in virtual control of the rest of the country. Taylor
wanted nothing short of surrender. Doe recognized that he was in a
"no-win" situation, given the fate that awaited members of his Krahn
ethnic group, if he resigned or was defeated, but he apparently still
thought that he could defeat Taylor militarily in Monrovia, as he had
Quiwonkpa in 1985. The IFMC's efforts came to grief because the
parties were unwilling to negotiate in good faith and because the
Liberian nationality of the mediators "put them in the dubious

position of proposing solutions that could be viewed by Doe and Taylor as contrary to their interests, or worse, indicative of betrayal or treason. Ultimately, as Liberians, their personal security and the safety of their families could be affected by the actions they took as mediators."[33]

Meanwhile, Taylor announced the first "All-Liberia conference" to be held in Buchanan, Grand Bassa County, in June 1990, to bring as many leaders and opinion moulders as possible under one roof to deliberate on the nation's future. But because Buchanan was deep within the war zone, the conference was a non-starter, though Taylor would form what he had perhaps earlier envisaged – his National Patriotic Reconstruction Assembly Government (NPRAG), which became the political arm of the NPFL.

The second All-Liberia Conference (Banjul, August 1990), at which the Interim Government of National Unity (IGNU) was chosen, was convened under the auspices of ECOWAS as part of its Peace Plan for Liberia, though ECOWAS made it clear from the outset that the effort was a Liberian one. None the less, while ECOWAS officials did not participate in the deliberations following the formal opening ceremony, NPFL and other non-participants insisted that the effort was not national but regional, and narrowly so. The pertinent statement of the ECOWAS Mediation Committee reads: "That a broad-based interim government shall be set up in the Republic of Liberia to administer that country or organize free and fair elections, leading to a democratically elected government. The composition of the interim government *shall be determined by all parties and other interest groups.*"[34]

The circumstances of the establishment of the interim government are important because they provide the context for subsequent Liberian efforts at resolving the conflict and forecast a political shadow for post-Doe Liberia. As the civil war intensified in mid-1990, so too did the power struggle at home and abroad. The core group that eventually set up the interim government consisted of six political parties, one warring faction (INPFL), and representatives from at least eight interest groups, most hurriedly constituted for the meeting.[35] Taylor and his NPFL refused to participate.

Before the ECOWAS Mediation Committee issued a public invitation to Liberian politicians to gather in the Gambian capital to form an interim government, significant differences were already surfacing within such major political parties as LAP and MOJA/LPP, and political realignments were in the making. In mid-July 1990 a group of "Displaced Concerned Liberians in Sierra Leone" sought to establish contact with Liberian politicians in the United States to elaborate a common position on an all-party conference (in Buchanan or Tappita) "with a view to establish an interim government of Liberia." This group, largely politicians, endorsed "the NPFL to head an interim government to succeed President Doe," which had to be broad-based. As efforts began to convene a meeting of concerned Liberians in the United States, a response came from the LPP's Amos Sawyer and the UP's Edward Kesselly. This response illustrates the close collaboration between the UP and that wing of the LPP of which Sawyer was a part, but it also clearly articulates the views of "members of the Unity Party and LPP presently in the U.S., Europe and some parts of Africa."

After commending the NPFL for its efforts to remove the Doe regime, the statement from Sawyer and Kesselly continued: "Clearly, the efforts of the Front have built upon the protracted struggles of all democratic and human rights forces which have confronted the Doe regime, exposed its excesses, and delivered numerous 'body punches' which have left that regime weak, vulnerable, and totally discredited locally and internationally." This coalition supported an NPFL-led interim administration, provided that on its being constituted it would immediately commit itself publicly to a free and fair election under international supervision within a specified time. It would then call a conference "of all political parties including those from whom an illegal ban was recently lifted [LPP]." Leaders of the interim government would be ineligible to contest the election, and an international peace force would aid the NPFL in maintaining public order "until elections are completed and constitutional government installed."[36]

"A group of Liberian political leaders," again including Sawyer and Kesselly, reacted broadly to the ECOWAS Peace Plan and anticipated the Banjul meeting of August 1990 that would create IGNU. Against the backdrop of the problems encountered by ECOWAS, the presence of ECOMOG on Liberian soil, and the opposition of the NPFL to the intervention which kept it from attending, IGNU was constituted. It was mandated to "assume full powers for the governance of the State as provided for in the Constitution of Liberia. In addition, the National Conference mandated the performance of such primary functions as may be required to return the country to normalcy."[37]

The architects of IGNU were LAP, LPP, LUP, NDPL, UP, UPP and eight interest groups – the Association for Constitutional Democracy in Liberia, the Business Association, Concern Citizens, Higher Education, the Popular Front for Democracy (a MOJA breakaway led by Boima Fahnbulleh, who did not attend), the Press Union of Liberia, the Union of Liberian Artists, and the United Nimba Citizens Council. But because IGNU was not acceptable to all factions, it was born with a handicap. Taylor remained bitterly opposed to the entire arrangement.

IGNU took power over the opposition of the NPFL. The NPFL continued militarily to resist ECOMOG and confined it to Monrovia. Ivory Coast and Burkina Faso continued to support the NPFL. An ECOWAS-sponsored conference in Bamako, Mali, negotiated a cease-fire on the understanding that the leadership would be decided through an all-Liberia conference to be held inside Liberia. The cease-fire lasted for two years, but progress on the political front stalled. Meanwhile the all-Liberia conference took place in Monrovia between 15 March and 18 April 1991. But it did not achieve the desired results, as sharp differences emerged over the terms of reference. While the NPFL argued that the conference was intended to elect a new interim administration acceptable to all factions, IGNU (and its many supporters in Monrovia) maintained that it was only an opportunity to broaden the existing interim government.

After failing to obtain representation at the conference for the political subdivisions (then twelve of Liberia's thirteen counties) under its control, NPFL delegates walked out, leaving the conferees to endorse almost the entire IGNU. Only the vice-president (an Independent National Patriotic Front designee) was changed, and he resigned a few months later, charging that IGNU had not accepted him in the government. The seeds of continuing conflict were being planted.[38]

The fourth and (as of 1996) last All-Liberia conference held its first round in Monrovia from 23 August to 1 October 1994. The Liberian National Conference (LNC) was perhaps more broad-based and realistic, given the large Monrovia population of one million and the fact that IGNU had been politically diluted when it was replaced in 1993 (consistent with the Cotonou Accords) by the Liberian National Transitional Government (LNTG), which had representation from all major warring factions.

Though the conflict remains unresolved, it seems that this fourth effort could aid its resolution. The conferees claimed to be "those who bear no arms" and were unwilling to pass the destiny of the Liberian people "solely into the hands of the leaders of the armed factions and their agents." The fact that the LNC has been recognized as a party may bode well for the peace process.[39] Its elected representative is one of the three "civilians" on the Council of State of the LNTG.

Finally, the regionally negotiated Abuja peace agreement was announced on 19 August 1995. In keeping with its terms, a power-sharing interim government led by a Council of State and involving all the major warring factions and other parties to the conflict began exercising power in Monrovia on 1 September 1995. Its principal terms of reference were to create the climate for an early free and fair election to usher in a legitimate government. But the peace process stalled as violence erupted in Monrovia in April 1996. Abuja I (1995) was replaced by Abuja II (1996), which corrected some of the problems of the 1995 agreement. The objective of an elected government continues to be the goal of the peace effort, though the means to that end still seem ambiguous.

### Regional Level

Because the OAU, the UN, and the United States were, for a variety of reasons, unwilling or unable to deal with the Liberian conflict, it was left to ECOWAS to act. But what motivated ECOWAS? Reduced to their essentials, the motivations were ethnic (neighbours concerned about fellow ethnic groups in Liberia); personal (Doe's friendship with President Ibrahim Babangida of Nigeria, as demonstrated by Nigeria's donation of a million dollars for the establishment at the University of Liberia of a Babangida Institute of International Affairs; Momoh's anti-Doe sentiment taken to logical conclusion); national interest (Nigeria as regional hegemon, which affected the role of Ivory Coast and Burkina Faso); and institutional (Executive Secretary Abbas Bundu's desire to give a "political thrust" to ECOWAS as he embarked on a "high-risk political detour" to convince member-states that the community must be engaged politically if its stated economic goals were to be achieved). And there was the humanitarian motive, though other factors explain its political saliency.

So, how successful has ECOWAS been? Thirteen peace accords and more than thirty documents have been signed by parties to the conflict, now eight in number – AFL, LDF, LNTG, LPC, NPFL, NPFL-dissidents, ULIMO-K, and ULIMO-M. The key accords in this long process include the Bamako Ceasefire Agreement of 1990, the Yamoussoukro series of 1991, the Geneva/Cotonou Accords of 1993, the Akosombo series of 1994–95, the Abuja agreement of 19 August 1995, and the latter's revision in August 1996.[40]

Yamoussoukro called for continued observance of the cease-fire of November 1990; encampment and disarmament of troops and depositing of arms and ammunition in armories, all under ECOMOG's supervision; a five-member Elections Commission; a four-nation ECOWAS committee to enlist the cooperation of Sierra Leone and Guinea in restoring normality along their borders with Liberia; and a timetable for implementation.

The Geneva/Cotonou Accords envisaged the same essential features – cease-fire, an interim administration representative of the parties, and disarmament, followed by an election. They also provided for the addition of forces to ECOMOG from Tanzania, Uganda, and Zimbabwe, under the umbrella of the OAU. And while responsibility for ensuring implementation remained with ECOWAS/ECOMOG, there was to be a UN presence "to monitor the various implementation procedures in order to verify their impartial application."

As for the Akosombo series of 1994–95, its initial thrust was to marginalize the political factions and give primary responsibility for a settlement to the warring factions, using various formulae. When the political factions objected strenuously, charging regional and other facilitators with attempting to impose a military junta, a stalemate ensued. Under the auspices of the Ghanaian head of state, who became chair of ECOWAS, talks to hammer out a compromise ensued.

The pace of negotiations accelerated in 1995, culminating in the Abuja agreement. A military stalemate and war-weariness speeded the process, a regional initiative orchestrated by President Jerry Rawlings of Ghana helped reconcile Charles Taylor and the Nigerian military government, and the United States supported Rawlings' efforts because of its own bilateral difficulties with the Nigerian regime. Consistent with Abuja, a power-sharing Council of State was installed in Monrovia on 1 September 1995, representing all parties and charged with creating an atmosphere conducive to an early election.

To implement the Abuja agreement, ECOMOG was to be strengthened and expanded, and substantial material and diplomatic support was expected from the international community. But factional warfare in Monrovia beginning in April 1996 exposed the absence of good faith on the part of the warring factions, a weak LNTG, and inadequate support from the international community. The revised Abuja agreement addressed these shortcomings and carried forward the peace process.

One cannot emphasize enough the essential requirements for effective mediation in situations such as the Liberian conflict.[41] First, the third-party intervenor should be substantially more powerful than the protagonists, have a strong interest in reaching an accord, and be willing to commit substantial resources to implementing its provisions. This effort must be backed by major powers. Second, conflict resolution can be useful but should be viewed as complementary to the role of a politically powerful, highly committed third party. Third, all key actors with potential veto power over implementation of an accord should be integral to its negotiation.

Under Ghana's leadership and with considerable u.s. encouragement, ECOWAS appeared to be playing well the intervenor's role. All
major Liberian actors were aboard. But at least two complicating
factors threatened the peace process: the deteriorating domestic
situation in Nigeria, its effects on that nation's external relations, and
the effect this might have on its crucial role in ECOMOG; and, not
unrelated, the level of support expected from the rest of the world,
notably the European Union, the United States, and the UN. The
domestic players sensed the absence of leadership and international
resolve. In the absence of effective monitoring of the peace process,
spoilers need not fear any punishment. When one or more factions
sought undue advantage, reactions ineluctably led to hostilities. In
the end, if the regionally negotiated Abuja agreements are to bring
peace, only substantial and committed support from the systemic
level will provide the necessary incentive to the national and regional
protagonists to live up to their end of the bargain.

### Systemic Level

Stedman has suggested that "changes at the international level influence conflict and its resolution at the national and regional levels
by affecting actors' resources, opportunities for development, and
perception of identity and legitimacy."[42] How relevant to the Liberian
situation! The sea change in international relations was the termination of the Cold War. Doe lost resources and, more crucially, legitimacy. His loss was initially Taylor's gain, but soon other factors
intervened to alter the very texture of the conflict.

Regional involvement was possible because the United States was
preoccupied with the Gulf War and no longer concerned about
Soviet involvement in western Africa. At one time it had seemed
inconceivable that the Americans would tolerate efforts to destabilize
a Liberian regime, especially by Libya. Now Liberia was left to the
conflicting politics of the leaders of its subregion, which created
opportunities for the NPFL, as well as general political fragmentation.

Many international actors have been involved in varying degrees in
either expanding or containing the conflict. They include France, the
UN, the United States, NGOs, and foreign business interests. Yet all
those who want to contain or resolve the conflict have accepted the
regional peace plan and appear prepared to work within its framework. If the United States has been unwilling to take the leading role
that historical ties suggest and the world expects, and has instead
chosen to see Liberia as a "regional conflict" best dealt with by a
regional body, so too has the UN, which did not address the conflict
in political terms until November 1992, almost three years after its

eruption. It emphasied that the United Nations Observer Mission in Liberia (UNOMIL) would only monitor implementation procedures of the Cotonou accord "in order to verify their impartial application." Primary responsibility for keeping the peace is ECOMOG's.

Given such circumstances, what prospects are there for international involvement aimed at a resolution of the conflict? Perhaps not much, if the assumption is sustained that Liberia (and by extension west Africa and the rest of sub-Saharan Africa) are of little national interest to the United States and might best be treated (along with Somalia, Rwanda, and others) as an object purely of humanitarian concern. However, let us not forget what Bill Clinton said about the politics of humanitarianism. "Unless human tragedy is caused by natural disaster, there is no such thing as a purely humanitarian enterprise."[43]

There is, however, a view that makes the case for committed international involvement, not specifically in Liberia, but in similar conflicts. Chester A. Crocker, a former U.S. assistant secretary of state for African affairs, called attention to a "Global Law and Order Deficit," or "a shortfall of agreed principles, laws, institutions, mechanisms, and capabilities for building a more secure and less violent world." He asserted that changes in the international system have led to a growth in the deficit and that international mechanisms should be available to address political repression as well as liberalization, both of which can be destabilizing and possibly degenerate into violent conflict. Among the possible means requiring international attention Crocker listed:[44] creative programs of military demobilization, retraining, and weapons collection and destruction; an international inter-agency task force of ten to fifteen experts available to third-party mediators for prolonged service if necessary; training and internship in peace-making and peacekeeping; and a "margin of leverage" – "that subtle mixture of credibility, leverage, legitimacy, and outright political will that is so often necessary to break the back of a conflict. *It is not only the special skills, insights, and information of a dedicated mediatory task force that are required: it is often essential to back these up with real clout, influence, and symbolic authority so that warring parties take the peacemaker seriously, knowing that there may be benefits for cooperation as well as penalties for obstruction.*"

These are cogent suggestions that are in harmony with ideas from another source, the International Negotiations Network of the Carter Center of Emory University, which has addressed the "mediation gap" – the inadequate attention paid by the world community, especially to intra-state conflicts. Yet the "margin of leverage" required "to break the back" of the Liberian conflict seems to remain elusive despite the two Abuja agreements.

CONCLUSION

We began with the assumption that the civil war in Liberia was a consequence of a crisis of governance, of inadequate regional cooperation, and of post-Cold War vicissitudes. Employing the levels-of-analysis mode of examination, we drew out the conclusion that the conflict has its roots in Liberia (national level) and was exacerbated by forces in west Africa (regional level) and in the changing international system (systemic level). If such an assessment is correct, then resolution must turn on these same factors. We can hardly expect a conclusion to physical hostilities while political hostility remains at the three levels, for the civil war is in fact political conflict carried on by other means.

As one considers resolution, one must address the interrelationship among the national, regional, and systemic levels of a conflict. Does regional (read, "external") resolution of conflict presuppose its resolution at the national level? Conflict resolution must be pursued simultaneously across all levels. If peace is to persist in Liberia, domestic political differences must be resolved, and the intricate mix of personalities and ethnicity and the gross inequities in the distribution of resources sorted out. Further political fragmentation must be arrested, and an acceptable ruling coalition envisaged. And does this process address the "fear of settlement" on the part of at least some of the warring factions? At the regional level, Liberia's neighbours must be willing to place the interests of Liberia's peoples ahead of their own. Finally, the international community must put substance behind its verbal commitments.

Perhaps the outstanding problem is inadequate appreciation of the interrelationship among the levels of conflict, and therefore the unevenness with which the levels have been treated. Most seem so enamoured of ECOMOG as a prospective model for regional peacekeeping that they pay inordinate attention to conflict resolution at this level and display far too little appreciation of the need for national and international action. The desperation for ECOWAS/ECOMOG to succeed tends to mask its shortcomings. The international community (specifically the UN and the United States) appears anxious to pass the buck to ECOWAS in order to get on with what it considers more pressing matters. A significant segment of Liberian opinion led by IGNU and its successors, LNTG and the Council of State (COS), has pinned its hopes on ECOWAS.

The Abuja arrangements contain elements that go beyond the original ECOWAS peace plan. As unpalatable as it may appear, they acknowledge all major Liberian players and envisage their sharing in interim power. They make significant strides in addressing cleavages within ECOWAS. As a basis for a politically more realistic peace agreement, they assure a clearer, supportive role for the world community. Faithful implementation remained the challenge.

The pace soon quickened, with widespread reports suggesting that implementation was in fact under way. In late 1996 and early 1997 there were glowing, almost euphoric, commentaries about the speed with which the factions were disarming, with more than 80 per cent of all arms being handed over by late March 1997. Ambitious warlords resigned from the interim government and declared their candidacies for the elections scheduled for early June, though held only in July.

But unanswered questions remained. How were the original 60,000 armed Liberians to be reduced by half? What about the frequent reports of uncovered arms caches? What about the arrest on arms charges and then subsequent release of warlord Alhaji Kromah? Many questions remained as well about the details of disarmament, demobilization, and the climate for holding elections.

For some, such questions have become less important after the elections themselves which were held on 19 July 1997 and were won overwhelmingly by former warlord Charles Taylor and his National Patriotic Party. Yet countries devastated by civil wars are seldom transformed overnight from war to peace. The cases of Angola, Cambodia, Mozambique, and Rwanda speak for themselves.

In actuality, Liberia seems to be experiencing a tension between two imperatives of peace in our time[45] – conflict resolution, and democracy and human rights. Where "conflict managers" pressed for and eventually obtained a lopsided negotiated outcome, "democratizers" – who went along with the process – seem troubled by the failure of power-sharing safeguards built into the electoral process and the consequent weak foundation of a future democracy. Under the circumstances, the challenge for all parties (at all levels) to the conflict is to make peace sustainable by making it just.

NOTES

1 C. Clapham, "Liberia," in John Dunn, ed., *West African States: Failure and Promise: A Study in Comparative Politics* (Cambridge: Cambridge University Press 1978), 117–31. Abuja I was almost completely destroyed when factional fighting erupted in Monrovia in April 1996, claiming the lives of hundreds of civilians and causing considerable property destruction. In its aftermath, ECOWAS facilitated a revision of the 1995 accord. Abuja II includes a new civilian chair of the power-sharing Council of State, an

abbreviated and monitored timetable for disarmament and an election, and penalties against faction leaders who obstruct the process. Though the conflict was somewhat altered as we went to press, with the election of a National Patriotic Party government in July 1997, it is our view that that event only opens a new phase in the ongoing quest to address the issues that gave rise to the civil war. Consequently, we have not deemed it necessary at this time to alter our analysis to take account of the election and installation of a new government in 1997.

2 S.J. Stedman, "Conflict and Conflict Resolutions in Africa: A Conceptual Framework," in F.M. Deng and I.W. Zartman, eds., *Conflict Resolutions in Africa* (Washington, DC: Brookings Institution 1991), 398.

3 C.W. Kegley, Jr, and E.R. Wittkopf, *World Politics: Trend and Transformation*, 5th ed. (New York: St Martin's Press 1995), 39; K. Waltz, *Man, the State, and War* (New York: Columbia University Press 1954); and K.J. Holsti, *International Politics: A Framework for Analysis*, 7th ed. ( Englewood Cliffs, NJ: Prentice-Hall 1995), 16–18.

4 Kegley and Wittkopf, *World Politics*, 40.

5 C.L. Simpson, *The Memoirs of C.L. Simpson: The Symbol of Liberia* (London: Diplomatic Press and Publishing Company 1961), 240, emphasis added.

6 A. Sawyer, *The Emergence of Autocracy in Liberia: Tragedy and Challenge* (San Francisco: ICS Press 1992), 302.

7 See D.E. Dunn and S.B. Tarr, *Liberia: A National Polity in Transition* (Metuchen, NJ: Scarecrow Press 1988); Lawyers Committee for Human Rights, *Liberia: A Promise Betrayed: A Report on Human Rights* (New York: Lawyers Committee 1986).

8 J.G. Liebenow, "Liberian Political Opposition in the Post-Election Period," *Liberian Studies Journal* 13 no. 2 (1988), 245.

9 "Charles Taylor: The True Story," *New African* (July 1991), 22–3.

10 Dunn and Tarr, *Liberia*, 194–201.

11 Unpublished communications of August 1987 from Sawyer through Tipoteh to MOJA Consultative Session in Liberia, 10. Fahnbulleh, a young university professor, was a prominent member of MOJA in the 1970s and served as a minister in the military government but resigned while on a mission abroad. In addition to being a prominent member of MOJA as well, Sawyer chaired the National Commission that produced the original draft of the 1984 constitution. He subsequently clashed with Doe, was imprisoned, eventually released, and went into voluntary exile. Prince Johnson was a leader of the breakaway Independent National Patriotic Front of Liberia (INPEL). It was he who captured Doe and tortured him to death in 1990. He was subsequently outmanoeuvred by his political and military enemies and forced to deliver himself to ECOMOG, which then took him to Nigeria, where he remains in exile.

12 For a discussion of these issues, see Naomi Chazam et al., *Politics and Society in Contemporary Africa* (Boulder, Col.: Lynne Rienner Publishers 1988), part II, chaps. 6 and 7.

13 Raymond G. Copson, *Africa's Wars and Prospects for Peace* (New York: M.E. Sharpe 1994), 79.

14 Ibid., 80.

15 Eghosa Osaghae, Ethnicity, Class and the Struggle for State Power in Liberia, unpublished manuscript, CODESPIIA, Dakar, Senegal, 38–9.

16 Copson, *Africa's Wars*, 75–88.

17 On this coastal – hinterland indigene cleavage, see Osaghae, *Ethnicity, Class*, chap. 4.

18 Clapham, "Liberia," 122.

19 Robert Clower, George Dalton, M. Harwitz, and A.A. Walters, *Growth without Development: An Economic Survey of Liberia* (Evanston, Ill.: Northwestern University Press 1966).

20 Osaghae, *Ethnicity, Class*, 22.

21 Ibid.

22 S. Byron Tarr, "The ECOMOG Initiative in Liberia: A Liberian Perspective," *Issue*, 21 (1993), 79–80.

23 Tarr, *West Africa*, 4–10 May 1992, 756. Amos Sawyer put the number at 700, and Boima Fahnbulleh, at 1,000.

24 Tarr, *The News*, 5 no. 108 (Aug. 1994), 1 and 6; "Plot to Destabilize Guinea Uncovered: Sekou Toure's Son, Charles Taylor Linked," *New Democrat*, no. 91, 10–14 March 1995, 1 and 10.

25 Most Rev. Michael Kpakala Francis, "Liberia: Towards Peace and Reconciliation," Catholic Church of Liberia, Monrovia, Liberia (Oct. 1994), 13–14; for more on IFMC, see 149–50.

26 Clement E. Adibe, "Institutionalist Theory and the ECOWAS Intervention in Liberia," paper presented at the Annual Meeting of the African Studies Association, Toronto, Ontario, 4–7 Nov. 1994, 14–15.

27 A. Weller, ed., *Regional Peacemaking and International Enforcement: The Liberian Crisis* (New York: Cambridge University Press 1994), 60.

28 K.O. George, The Civil War in Liberia: A Study of the Legal and Policy Aspects of Humanitarian Intervention, unpublished manuscript, Washington, DC, 1993, 89–95.

29 Tarr, "The ECOMOG Initiative," *Issue*, 21 (1993), 80. For Libya's expansionist policy in west Africa, see Jeff Haynes, "Libya Involvement in West Africa: Quadhaffi's 'Revolutionary Foreign Policy,'" *Paradigms*, 4 no. 1 (summer 1990), 58–73.

30 For contemporary insight into this French policy of indirection, see Howard D. French, "Poor Land Is Exerting Big Weight in Africa," *New York Times*, 16 March 1995, A5.

31 Weller, *Regional Peacemaking*, 140.

32 William Reno, "Foreign Firms and the Financing of Charles Taylor's NPFL," *LSJ*, 18 no. 2 (1993), 175–87.

33 George, *The Civil War in Liberia*, 68–9.

34 See ECOWAS, First Session of the Community Standing Mediation Committee, Banjul, 6–7 Aug. 1990, Final Communiqué, emphasis added.

35 This writer was an observer at the Baujul conference in August 1990.

36 A. Sawyer and E.B. Kesselly, "The Displaced Concerned Liberians in Sierra Leone," Washington DC, July 1990, unpublished statement in author's possession.

37 Final Communiqué, National Conference of All Liberian Political Parties, Patriotic Fronts, Interest Groups and Concerned Citizens, Banjul, Gambia, 27–31 Aug. 1990, 10.

38 "Liberia's Elusive Peace," *New Vision*, 1 no. 2 (Aug.–Sept. 1992), 7–8.

39 "Conclusions and Decisions of the Liberia National Conference on Disarmament and Demobilization, the Governance of Liberia, the Electoral Process for Post-War Liberia and the Akosombo Meeting," *Inquirer*, 4 Oct. 1994, 3–7.

40 Ulimo-M and Ulimo-K are the Mandingo and Krahn ethnic subfactions, respectively, into which Ulimo was broken in 1994. NPFL-dissidents are certain senior former NPFL officials who denounced Taylor and have formed a new group. LPC is the Liberia Peace Council, a Krahn-based faction that appeared in late 1993. AFL is made up of the remnants of the Armed Forces of Liberia. And LNTG is the current (early 1995) government in Monrovia, made up of the defunct IGNU, NPFL, and Ulimo.

41 J.M. Richardson, Jr, and J. Wang, "Peace Accords: Seeking Conflict Resolutions in Deeply Divided Societies," in K.M. Silva and S.W.R. de A. Samarasighe, eds., *Peace Accords and Ethnic Conflicts* (New York: Pinter Publishers 1993), 190–1.

42 Stedman, "Conflict Resolutions: A Conceptual Framework," in F.M. Deng and I.W. Zartman, eds., *Conflict Resolutions in Africa* (Washington, DC: Brookings Institution 1991), 382.

43 A TV remark, June 1994, by President Clinton. See also Rakiya Omaar and Alex de Waal, "The Lessons of Humanitarian Imperialism in Somalia," *War Report*, London, no. 23 (Feb.–March 1993).

44 See C.A. Crocker, "Global Law and Order Deficit," *Washington Post*, Dec. 1992, C-1. C.A. Crocker, "Strengthening African Peace and Peace-keeping " in David R. Smock, ed., *Making War and Waging Peace: Foreign Intervention in Africa* (Washington, DC: U.S. Institute of Peace Press 1993), 263–9, emphasis added. See also David A. Smock and Chester A. Crocker, eds., *African Conflict Resolution: The U.S. Role in Peacemaking* (Washington, DC: U.S. Institute of Peace Press 1995). The ideas referred to come from a man who, as an agent of the U.S. government, helped

fuel the Liberian crisis by a policy of "constructive engagement" with the Doe regime. This was a policy that provided Doe the funds and the arms to militarize Liberian society, unleash terror, and render violent change inevitable.

45 See Pauline Baker, "Conflict Resolution versus Democratic Governance: Divergent Paths to Peace?" in Chester Crocker, Fen Hampson, and Pamela Aall, eds., *Managing Global Chaos: Sources of and Responses to International Conflict* (Washington, DC: U.S. Institute for Peace, 1996).

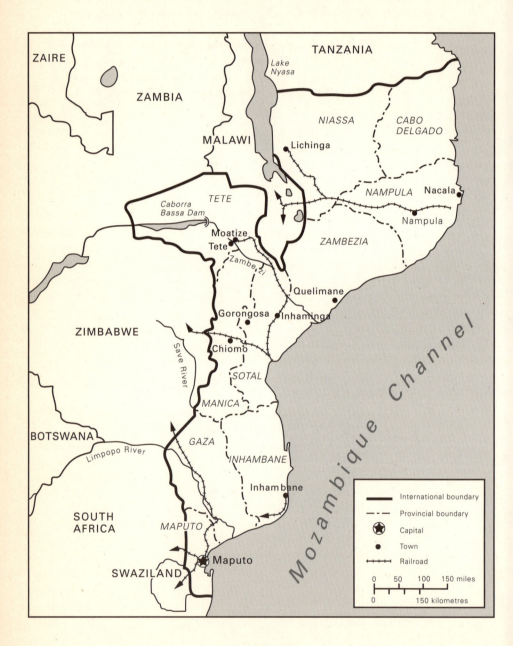

Mozambique

## 5 Inside from the Outside? The Roots and Resolution of Mozambique's Un/Civil War

JOHN S. SAUL

Recently students of "internal wars" in Africa have reacted against an earlier tendency, both on the left and the right, to explain domestic conflicts there in terms of external determinations – notably the machinations of the various global protagonists of the Cold War or, sometimes, those of a neighbouring "rogue state" on the continent itself that is understood to be meddling aggressively in the troubled nation's affairs. Any such analytical tendency was badly oversimplified, it is argued, even in the hey-day of the Cold War and has become all the more so in today's "unipolar" world. Moreover, as part of a general trend within African studies to give greater pride of place in our analyses to a sensitive understanding of the concrete circumstances and lived experiences of the African peoples themselves, this turning of the glass of understanding inward may seem to represent a valuable refocusing of emphasis for this reason alone. Small wonder that the editors of the present volume have encouraged just such an emphasis.

As we will see, the Mozambican case – important in its own right – can serve as a useful point of reference in this kind of analytical discussion. Certainly an earlier orthodoxy saw Mozambique's "internal war" as having been imposed largely from outside, by (albeit in some complex manner) "Western imperialism" and by (more straightforwardly) apartheid South Africa's regional strategy of "destabilization." More recently, in a brisk debate that has occurred both within Mozambique and without regarding this kind of interpretation, a number of observers have argued for a "new paradigm" that would place central responsibility for Mozambique's disastrous tumble into "civil war" on internal factors and internal actors. This chapter seeks first to illuminate the roots of the Mozambican conflict by alluding to this scholarly division over the relative importance of internal and external factors to that conflict's emergence.

Parallel concerns can also ground our analysis of the recent resolution of armed conflict in Mozambique. Thus the latter sections of this chapter trace the negotiations that, at their most formalized, saw Frelimo, the party in power, and Renamo, its counterrevolutionary antagonist, meeting in Rome between 1990 and 1992 to hammer out a peace accord. It will also examine the on-the-ground transition between 1992 to 1994 that saw the implementation of this accord, the winding down of the war and nation-wide, "democratic," multi-party elections. And, once again, we will see that in each stage of this "peace process," both internal and external actors played prominent roles.

## POLITICAL SCIENCE/POLITICAL ECONOMY

Inside? Outside? This analysis would be difficult enough to make if there were not a further complication that tends to be overlooked in much of the recent literature on both peace-making and the transition of democracy. This is the distinction between what I have designated elsewhere as the "political science" of such processes and their "political economy."[1] Certainly, one can comprehend both the emergence and the resolution of conflict in Mozambique in ways that privilege, almost exclusively, political explanations. This happens in part because such explanations do have some value. Mozambique's liberation struggle was indeed politically defined, representing a contestation between the Portuguese colonial authority and the country's key liberation movement, Frelimo (originally FRELIMO – the Frente da Libertação de Moçambique), for state power. Nor did the crystallization of Frelimo's anti-colonial project occur in isolation from broader political realities. It formed one front in what was, in effect, a region-wide struggle across southern Africa against the anachronistic structures of white minority rule.[2] Frelimo chose to play an active role in that broader struggle both before and after achieving independence in its own country, notably vis-à-vis Rhodesia – by operationalizing international sanctions, and by lending crucial logistical support to ZANU – and also (albeit in a far more modest way) vis-à-vis South Africa. And it was to pay a very high price for adopting, so high-mindedly, this set of regional policies.

Inevitably, too, Frelimo's struggle was framed by larger global geo-political realities – notably those defined by the Cold War. The Soviet

Union and its allies had been a major source of material support to Frelimo in the war against the Portuguese and continued to be a key actor in Mozambique in the post-liberation phase. This in itself would have been enough to place Mozambique on the enemy list of the Western powers, especially the United States. But the fact remains that Mozambique was on that list for another, though related, reason: because its own domestic project was some sort of socialist one, mounted in self-conscious defiance of the unquestioned hegemony of international capitalism. Indeed, Frelimo's "progressive" commitment across a broad front was actually a key reason for its associating itself, beyond its own frontiers, with the ongoing war for southern Africa in the first place (compare Mozambique's record in this regard to a Malawi or a Botswana, for example) and it was this commitment that also led it to look upon the Eastern bloc as its "natural allies."

It was also this commitment that helped increase the already high stakes in Mozambique for various external actors. Specifically, with the coming to power of Ronald Reagan, Mozambique found itself more clearly than ever in the line of fire for "roll-back," not merely as a "Soviet puppet" but, even more important, as a regime with (in the phrase of U.S. Assistant Secretary of State for African Affairs Chester Crocker) "Afro-Marxist fantasies" about domestic economic and political priorities.[3] It was no accident that South Africa moved to escalate its "destabilization" of Mozambique – a development so crucial to the fate of Frelimo's initial post-liberation project – within hours of Reagan's taking up occupancy of the White House. And it is also no accident that as Frelimo sought, under enormous military pressure, to sue for peace, it chose to run its attempts to do so in no small part through Washington – and to make that peace, to a significant degree, directly with international capitalism.

We will see that so interpreting Frelimo's original project – as at least in part defined, in its strengths and its vulnerabilities, by its socialist character – remains controversial. Nonetheless, it is the final point of the above paragraph that is the even more difficult one to make these days. For my argument will be, in essence, that the politics of peace-making in Mozambique have been framed by socio-economic processes, comprehensible only in terms of a "political economy" approach, that add up to a "recolonization" of the country. Of course, as regards the task of "peace-making," privileging political explanations that are at least in part independent of that recolonization process also makes some sense. By the late 1980s and early 1990s the country was in tatters,[4] and what had begun as a war largely imposed from outside had taken on many of the attributes of a "civil war." Therefore the political processes that brought Frelimo and Renamo together to negotiate and implement a peaceful resolution to their differences have been of great importance in their own right: not least because they have provided the vast mass of the population with, at minimum, some of the basic rudiments of personal security that full-scale war had denied them. But the fact remains that these processes were, in the end, greatly facilitated by Frelimo's abandoning virtually all vestiges of its progressive ideology, both domestically and internationally.

Why is it so easy to lose sight of this fact as being crucial to our understanding of "peace-making" in Mozambique? In part it is because Mozambique's original socialist project was plagued with so many problems and contradictions that the project itself may have come to seem merely improbable – and therefore more or less of an irrelevance to the "real" history of the country. More important, however, is the fact that it is now virtually impossible, more generally, to imagine an alternative to the conformity to a globalizing neo-liberalism that Mozambique's most recent socio-economic policies have come to exemplify. Indeed, most of the scholarly literature takes this latter as so commonsensical a premise about Africa (and beyond) that it scarcely bears commenting upon. As Colin Leys has recently argued, new and effective ideas about how to deal with Africa's problems could "seem rational only in a world that was in the process of rejecting the currently predominant ideology of the market ... [something] which is not yet in sight."[5] And in the meantime, in the climate that does prevail, the actual socio-economic content of such "peace" as is achieved in Mozambique – and such "democratic structures" as are established – tends to fall between the cracks of both observation and explanation. In a uni-polar world the one-eyed man is king. In this essay, in contrast, the processes of both "peace-making" and "recolonization" will be considered as having occurred, in Mozambique, very much in tandem.

### THE ROOTS OF WAR AND PEACE IN MOZAMBIQUE (1962–84)

To make the case we have evoked above implies a certain reading of Mozambique's recent history, and this is too complex an exercise to be easily summarized here. One thing is clear, however: as noted, the internal war that has plagued Mozambique had its roots in the original liberation struggle carried out by Frelimo cadres against Portugal's long and brutal colonial presence in their country. Founded in 1962, Frelimo launched its armed struggle in 1964 and, by the time of the Portuguese coup (1974) that paved the way to Mozambique's independence (1975), had established significant liberated areas in the northern provinces and a strong legitimacy in most other parts of the country. And, as also noted, the movement had committed itself to playing a continuing role in the further struggle to liberate the sub-continent. There is little argument that the other chief protagonist to internal war in Mozambique – the armed movement that was to become Renamo (Resistencia Naçional Moçambicana) – was, in the first instance, the creature of outsiders, comprised of a mix of Mozambican mercenaries and forced recruits mobilized and orchestrated by Rhodesia's security forces, and, with the fall of the Smith regime, by the South African military. Nor can there be any doubt as to the ruthlessness of the militaristic agenda set by such sponsors of Renamo: destruction of the infrastructure of economy and state and the heightened insecurity of the mass of the population.[6]

Much of Frelimo's initial legitimacy within Mozambique was cast in terms of a fairly conventional anti-colonial nationalism. But the leadership of Frelimo had become more radicalized than that during the armed struggle, setting an increasingly left wing agenda for itself. Something like a socialist project emerged which involved a growing defiance of imperial political and economic dictate and, at least in principle, the empowerment of the mass of peasants and workers in the society. As Jorge Rebelo, one of the early Frelimo leaders, phrased the point in a recent interview on the occasion of Mozambique's twentieth anniversary of independence: "We all agreed that we were going to gain independence, but this was not the ultimate object; that was in fact the creation of a progressive society which would bring an end to misery in our country. This was not merely a slogan. It was inside of us. ... But we can't help but be shocked by the distance between that which was our objective and what is the reality today."[7] Rebelo also recalled leaving a meeting at the Ponta Vermelha Palace just after independence and having President Machel say: "Now we have the power and we can finish with misery in Mozambique in two years." Someone said, "No, two years is too short a time." And Machel replied, "Okay, three years then." "We have to say now," Rebelo continued, "that this was a bit of voluntarism (voluntarismo) on our part. We were imagining things that in reality were not possible. But that's what we wanted to do."

Of course, Rebelo is signalling both the leadership's sincerity of intention *and* the fact that profound errors of judgment and mistakes in policy were made – springing, not least, from this kind of "voluntarism" and leading Frelimo to try to do too much, too fast. The early years did witness heroic efforts to transform Mozambican society: programs in the spheres of health and education are the most widely cited in this regard. But there can be little doubt that, in seeking to "mobilize" Mozambique's "workers and peasants" for "progressive" purposes, the Frelimo leadership also proved itself far too insensitive to the cultural complexities of the situation in which they found themselves. The party tended to ride roughshod over the various regional, ethnic, racial, and quasi-traditional faultlines that cut across Mozambican society, rather than finding more deft methods of political work to advance their project. In fact, Frelimo's arrogance of purpose, meshing with a firmly vanguardist bent (inherited, perhaps, from the movement's military past but also, once in power, all too easy to rationalize in classical "Marxist-Leninist" terms), drew the leadership towards markedly authoritarian practices. as well as a vision of socialism too exclusively cast in an eastern European mould.

Could Frelimo have righted itself and, left to its own devices, have discovered a socialist practice at once more realistic, more democratic, and more successful? This is too large and speculative a topic to be properly broached here.[8] Suffice to note, for present purposes, that it has now become quite fashionable to seek the principal roots of Mozambique's war in the weaknesses, even malignancy, of Frelimo's own project.[9] And there can be little doubt that the weaknesses in Frelimo's practice noted above did render it vulnerable to destabilization by Renamo and its sponsors as they moved to prey upon regional sensibilities and "traditional" loyalties in grounding their activities a little more firmly within Mozambique. In the end, however, Minter's finely balanced weighing of the evidence seems closest to the mark on this issue:

If one considers Angola and Mozambique at the time of the Portuguese coup in 1974 – imagining away both the regional southern African and the Cold War conflicts – what kind of wars, if any, might have resulted from internal factors alone, with the external environment similar to those of other African states. The most likely answer is: no war in Mozambique. ... In Mozambique it is simply not plausible that a coherent military organization such as Renamo could have emerged without external initiative. ... [T]he war came from outside. Once it started a variety of internal factors fed into the conflict, but they did not become responsible for continuing the war. Ethnic and regional tensions, while they existed, did not divide Mozambicans so deeply as to have sustained a war on these grounds. Nor were the policies towards peasants, economic ideology or the one-party state what the war was about. These were real issues, of course, but it is a bizarre misreading to see Renamo as fighting for a better deal for peasants or as speaking for the emergent civil society.[10]

Renamo had very little positive ideology, certainly, except a vaguely pro-Western predisposition. True, the relatively closed nature of the political structures sponsored by Frelimo lent credibility to the democratic claims Renamo came increasingly to employ to legitimate its war. But in view of its own brutal practices in the zones it controlled such claims, as made by Renamo itself, can only be seen as opportunistic. Nor (as we will emphasize below) were its "free market" proclivities long to differentiate its position from those of Frelimo as the latter came increasingly to share a neo-liberal agenda with its adversaries.

Indeed, what we find in Mozambique is a subtle slide from a war brought primarily from outside to a war much more internally sited – and also from a war cast in meaningful ideological terms (Frelimo's liberationist-cum-socialist project versus its array of enemies) to a struggle between two domestic protagonists for the spoils of office. Ironically this outcome was much less the result of any success Renamo may have had in rooting itself within the fabric of Mozambican society than it was a result of the slow but sure collapse of Frelimo's own project. Eventually the chief thing that would remain of Frelimo was its authoritarian propensities, these now drained to a very considerable degree of the "good intentions" and higher purposes in whose name such propensities have sometimes been explained and excused. As the war wore on and the socio-political situation in the country deteriorated, Frelimo's tattered armed forces, reduced themselves to living off the land, could seem to some parts of the population as almost as great a menace to their security as was Renamo. So, too, many Frelimo politicians and officials now seemed more preoccupied with looking to their own personal interests than ever they had in the past. If there was now increasingly less to distinguish Frelimo from Renamo in ideological terms there was also much less to distinguish the two protagonists in terms of their domestic political practices. Instead, what was now most visible on both sides was a naked desire to hold or gain power at almost any cost. Hence, in Minter's trenchant summary, "the popular perception in Mozambique – the more widespread the longer the war continued – of a war between two armies, with neither of them representing the people despite the overwhelmingly more abusive behaviour of one side [Renamo]."[11]

Here, in short, was a war that cried out, in the name of simple humanity, to be ended. Moreover, Mozambicans had become war-weary to a very considerable degree. Yet humanitarianism and war-weariness are not always sufficient reasons for conflict to cease. Nor was it sufficient that the main protagonists to the war would increasingly feel themselves to be stalemated – and therefore increasingly willing to think in terms of seeking to realize their interests by other means than continuing military confrontation. In the Mozambican case, other powerful actors had to shift their ground for a process of peace-making to take hold. By the end of the 1980s, as the peace-making process accelerated in Mozambique, the South Africa government – whose aggressive regional strategy of defence of apartheid had done so much to sew the seeds of war in Mozambique – was itself (with the passing of P.W. Botha from the scene and then with the release of Nelson Mandela) retiring to the sidelines of the regional war. And the same was true, for other but equally obvious reasons, of the Soviet Union and its Eastern bloc allies. Even more important, however, was the long-term shift in Western, principally American, evaluation of the nature of the Frelimo regime itself, a crucial point to which we will return

The key to this shift was, however, the "recolonization" of Mozambique referred to above. Whatever balance-sheet one strikes on this history of Frelimo's retreat and of Renamo's advance (an advance eventually to be signalled by that movement's relative success in the 1994 multi-party election in Mozambique), the fact remains that the process has left a Mozambique dependent in its poverty and its vulnerability on the behest of the World Bank, the IMF, and the external aid community. And it leaves a leadership which has certainly lost touch with the aspirations of ordinary people. As Graça Machel, the widow of Samora Machel and an important political actor in Mozambique in her own right as a minister in the first Frelimo government and now active in the NGO sector, put it forcefully to me during my recent stay there: "Workers and peasants don't count for anything in this country any more." True, in the 1980s, the Mozambican leadership did try to find ways of dealing with the external financial institutions which would protect achievements in social spheres like education and health while also keeping some kind of state involvement in the direction of the economy. Thus the country's first economic recovery program sought to finesse the World Bank and others into allowing space within which to give a more humane face to the compulsory restructuring that was going on. But this didn't last long, and soon privatization had become the alpha and omega of policy.

Much recent writing on Mozambique – as, for example, Joseph Hanlon's eloquent *Who Calls the Shots?*[12] or that by David Plank – focuses on the extent to which policy is, in these and other ways, being dictated from outside. Indeed, it is Plank who introduces the concept of "recolonization" most self-consciously into the discussion as something more than a mere metaphor, demonstrating, in his important article (cited above) and on the basis of his findings in

Mozambique, that "the most likely successor to post-colonial sovereignty will be neo-colonial vassalage, in which Western powers assume direct and open-ended control over the administration, security and economic policies of 'deteriorated' states under the banner of the UN and various donors."[13]

What this process of recolonization had begun to look like from the American angle can best be grasped, perhaps, from a reading of Chester Crocker's own smug account of the taming of the Mozambican revolution. By 1982, writes Crocker, "the Mozambicans sought U.S. understanding and diplomatic support in checking tough South African military and economic pressures" as well as "official encouragement of private investment ... [and] humanitarian and development aid from the Americans." As he continues, "Our priorities in these early encounters were to shift Mozambique away from its self-destructive confrontation with Pretoria, to foster rethinking about its ruinous domestic policies, and to explore its readiness to abandon its close Soviet and Cuban alignment."

By early 1983, this dialogue was paying off. In the months to come, U.S. food aid began to flow, and talks were held on an aid program to support the private sector and agricultural policy liberalization. ... Mozambique decided to freeze or curtail security ties to Communist states, to seek "associate" status with the European Community under the formula in place for other African states, and to apply to join the World Bank and International Monetary Fund. As a signal to the Western private sector, an oil exploration contract was signed with Exxon, and Lehman Brothers was signed on to provide advisory services on debt restructuring.

As for the regional front, "it was no longer difficult to persuade Machel, Chissano, Honwana and their colleagues that the primary victim of the Front Line State strategy of confrontation with South Africa would be the Front Line States themselves, and especially Mozambique." Indeed, writes Crocker, "we came to view the Mozambicans as partners."[14]

What did this partnership look like on the receiving end? Compare Crocker's account with the forlorn flavour of a remark made by President Chissano in a 1990 Maputo speech about the very first months of embarking on the formal negotiations process with Renamo: "The U.S. said, 'Open yourself to ... the World Bank, and IMF.' What happened? ... We are told now: 'Marxism! You are devils. Change this policy.' OK. Marxism is gone. Open market economy. OK, Frelimo is trying to create capitalism. We have the task of building socialism and capitalism here. We went to Reagan and I said, 'I want money for the private sector to boost people who want to develop a bourgeoisie.' Answer: $10 million, then $15 million more, then another $15 million. You tell me to do away with Marxism, the Soviet Union and the GDR and give me [only] $40 million. OK, we have changed. Now they say, 'If you don't go to a multi-party system, don't expect help from us.' "[15]

What could more starkly reveal just how supine Mozambique had been forced to become vis-à-vis Western dictate! Crocker also cites Chissano as visiting Washington, as early as October 1987, to assure Reagan of "his readiness to work with us and other countries to find a 'political solution.'" Ironically, Crocker and his presidential patron soon found themselves defending the Mozambican government against other right-wingers, in Congress and beyond, who chose to back Frelimo's antagonist, Renamo, unilaterally and uncritically. "In Washington," writes Crocker, "partisan strife over Mozambique became one of our biggest headaches during most of the second Reagan term. ... Amazing as it may seem the challenge we faced from within and beyond the administration was the demand that we abandon and cut off aid to the struggling Maputo regime and help Renamo as 'freedom fighters' under the Reagan Doctrine."[16] In response, Crocker and his officials sponsored and widely distributed a well-researched report by Robert Gersony documenting Renamo's brutal politics in order to disarm their critics and otherwise sought to press forward with their Mozambican agenda.[17]

Simply put, with the recolonization of Mozambique locked ever more firmly into place, the United States now emerged as a central protagonist of the unfolding peace process in that country – with internal war increasingly interpreted as undermining the stability of a new "partner" in the global enterprise of peace, capitalism and democracy. Indeed by the dawn of the 1990s the way was clear for various Western actors (further specified below) to follow the United States into the vacuum left by the withdrawal of both South Africa and the Soviet Union from the fray and by the taming of Frelimo's radicalism. In such a context, bringing together the two sides in Mozambique's "internal war," two sides increasingly indistinguishable in ideological terms, could now become the order of the day – with the "internationalizing" of the resolution of the Mozambican conflict which now occurred also to be valued as one further step towards ensnaring both of the country's chief partisan protagonists, Frelimo and Renamo, within "safe" and relatively predictable domestic structures, economic and political.

## RESOLUTION: THE NEGOTIATIONS PROCESS (1984–92)

### Pre-negotiations (1984–88)

In effect, then, the negotiations to end Mozambique's internal war had already begun in the early 1980s, and they occurred, as anticipated above, at two different levels simultaneously – levels that demand an understanding cast in terms of both political science and political economy. Politically speaking, Vines cites some preliminary outreach, from 1981 and 1982, by local Frelimo officials to Renamo forces, and to the people in Renamo-held areas. Nonetheless, the movement was still mainly perceived (and presented) in government circles as comprised of armed bandits. With some good reason the government chose to interpret Renamo's presence as being primarily that of a set of puppets. Consequently, its main strategy in the early 1980s was to seek to negotiate with the puppet-masters. This was, in fact, the essential back-drop to the 1984 Nkomati Accord, an agreement struck in the first instance with South Africa but framed by the first steps towards the substantial modification in broader socioeconomic strategy referred to by Crocker above. In signing this accord Frelimo agreed to step away from support of the African National Congress on the condition that South Africa would cease to support Renamo, the government's thinking probably being that it could then quite easily deal with the unsupported "bandits" who remained.

In the event the Nkomati strategy was only partially successful, even when evaluated in terms of the limited objective of lifting the state of siege that the country was enduring. It is true that it set the Frelimo government on the road towards its rehabilitation in Western eyes that Crocker writes of, and which would become so important to the politics of peace-keeping much later in the game. But, at the time, it failed to still the destabilization efforts of South Africa's military establishment, at best merely encouraging Pretoria (as was revealed in documents captured with the fall of Renamo's Casa Banana base in 1985) to seek to cover its tracks in Mozambique's war a little more effectively. Moreover, as Frelimo's own grip on things faltered, this continuing pressure would slowly but surely help Renamo to worm its way ever deeper into the decaying social fabric of the country. And, in the short run, it would also embolden South Africa later in 1984 to seek to force a political marriage between Frelimo and Renamo – one that Pretoria clearly hoped would compromise the Mozambican government even more fully than the Nkomati Accord had already succeeded in doing. Hence, the momentary surfacing of the so-called "Pretoria Declaration" (October 1984), apparently jointly sanctioned by delegations from both the Mozambican government and Renamo who also now appeared together in public for the first (and, for some years, last) time. It was soon apparent, however, that both Mozambican parties to this rather vague "agreement" interpreted it in diametrically opposed fashion (in each case as the virtual surrender of the other party). In the event the war was destined to grind on, at incalculable human cost, for many more years.

And yet, in the years of war that continued after this all too jerry-built "peace" initiative, the situation was also to alter in ways that would eventually bring the two sides back into political, as distinct from military, contact. Perhaps the context for this will by now have been made clear. Certainly, on the ground, both sides (Frelimo and Renamo) were eventually to lose erstwhile backers (the Eastern bloc fast fading from the scene and South Africa becoming ever more actively a force for settlement, for example). Both would begin to see some wisdom in seeking to resolve a situation of undeniable stalemate (albeit as much on their own terms as possible). And both would have increasingly pressing economic reasons for doing so: for Frelimo peace would soon become a necessary quid pro quo for its acceptance as a Western economic partner while, for Renamo, the ongoing drought would have, by the beginning of the 1990s, a particularly devastating effect on its ability to sustain itself in the rural areas.[18]

Equally interesting for present purposes, however, is the identity and role of other actors who now stepped forward to ease peace negotiations into existence. Most visible, perhaps, were the Mozambican churches, both Protestant and Catholic, Alex Vines, in particular, emphasizing the importance of the intermediary role these would now come to play.[19] Thus, "by 1984 the Mozambican Christian Council (CCM), the umbrella body uniting seventeen of the country's Protestant churches, became actively involved in the peace process, setting up a 'Peace and Reconciliation Commission' which reflected their view that 'dialogue is the way forward in any dispute.'" As Vines also notes, certain parallel initiatives by the Catholic church in Mozambique began about the same time.[20] Yet the CCM failed, in 1985, to get a "go-ahead" from then Mozambican President Samora Machel for "a low-key and confidential dialogue" with Renamo. It was only in late 1987 that Machel's successor, President Chissano, felt moved to give a green light to any such undertaking, and then only under quite restrictive conditions. Still, as Protestant and Catholic churches now (1988) joined together in peace-making efforts, a series of meetings with Renamo were planned and, even though a number of such planned meetings were aborted by Renamo,[21] enough contact was sustained – in Washington, in Kenya, in Gorongosa (in Renamo-controlled territory inside Mozambique) – to move the situation further along the road towards face-to-face talks (and a possible cease-fire) between Renamo and the Frelimo government itself.

## NEGOTIATIONS ABOUT NEGOTIATIONS 1989–90

Equally critical to the process, therefore, was the role played at this time by a pair of African heads of state, Daniel arap Moi of Kenya, whose government was quite sympathetic towards Renamo, and Robert Mugabe of Zimbabwe, whose troops were active inside Mozambique on behalf of Frelimo. There was even some sense, Vines suggests, that this might eventually lead to the more sustained mediating role of a larger group of African heads of state. Although this did not happen, and consolidation of the external loop of the peace-making process was to be taken increasingly out of African hands, Moi and Mugabe proved crucial players at this point, working together to facilitate the holding of preliminary talks in Nairobi and, through their joint "mediation," to set the stage for the more substantial negotiations to follow in Rome between 1990 and 1992. Indeed, the issuing of a joint communiqué in Nairobi (7 August 1989) by the two presidents – after some shuttling back and forth between Harare, Nairobi, Maputo and Addis Ababa and several talks between them – to the effect that they were "greatly encouraged by the spirit and willingness of the two sides of the conflict to undertake serious discussion to find a peaceful solution"[22] signalled the transition to a more formal, and quite promising, structuring of the peace process.

Interestingly, Frelimo and Renamo delegations were never to meet face to face in Nairobi. What was facilitated was important, however: a more substantive and sustained discussion between the churches' Peace and Reconciliation Commission and Renamo. The churches were now in possession of a document, the "12 Principles for Dialogue," setting out the Mozambican government's bargaining position, and soon, in their first round of talks (8–14 August) with Renamo within the now more formalized Nairobi setting, in receipt of an answering document, Renamo's "16 Point Declaration." The distance between the two sides was still substantial, however. Frelimo was agreeable to the eventual participation of Renamo members (in the context of amnesty and/or a peace agreement) as individuals in the political process but unwilling to accept Renamo's legitimacy as a political party; Renamo itself resisted this premise but also balked as the discussion proceeded, even recognizing the "legitimacy" of the existing Mozambique government.

Other outside actors began to weigh in throughout the year (1989) to break the resultant deadlock, the South African government putting pressure on Renamo, for example, and the ubiquitous Tiny Rowland of the British-based multinational Lonrho also popping up as a player of consequence in attempting to facilitate dialogue. Rowland had had economic dealings with Renamo from as far back as the early 1980s and was also pursuing a range of economic deals with the Mozambican government. For him political, and hence economic, stability was the order of the day and he judged the time to be ripe to consolidate this possibility, seeking aggressively to promote direct government–Renamo talks and canvassing a range of possible venues for such meetings. Even more important, however, was the role of the United States and u.s. Assistant Secretary of State for African Affairs Herman Cohen, who (according to Vines) "welcomed Rowland's peace initiatives" but was also prepared to take some initiatives of his own. Thus, on 7 December the United States presented Renamo President Afonso Dhlakama with a seven-point peace plan, copied to Moi and Mugabe. And on 8 December, Mugabe flew to Nairobi where, echoing the u.s. plan, he and Moi proposed direct Mozambique government–Renamo talks.

Clearly, the talks between Frelimo and Renamo were now to be ever more firmly internationalized – or, more accurately put perhaps, "Westernized." Thus it was during visits to Washington, London, and Lisbon in March and April 1990 that Chissano would make clear his willingness to meet directly with Renamo and to hint at a further opening up of the Mozambican political system. And, in Vines's formulation, it was "following strong u.s. and South African pressure on Renamo to be flexible over recognition of the Mozambique government [that] the final hurdle in the way of direct talks between the Mozambican government and Renamo was surmounted"![23] There was some skirmishing between the two sides over the locale of such talks, with Nairobi, Blantyre, Lisbon, and Munich being rejected in turn. Finally, for reasons to which we must now turn our attention, Rome was settled upon as the appropriate venue.

### NEGOTIATIONS (ROME, 1990–92)

*Protagonists.* Thus in July 1990, the two Mozambican protagonists came together in Rome for the first of a series of meetings that would culminate in the signing of a "General Peace Agreement" (4 October 1992). It was clear that, even as the site of formal negotiations now shifted from Africa to Europe, so too the African heads of state who had been playing an important role in the recent past – principally Mugabe on the Frelimo side, and Moi on the Renamo side – were to be displaced from centrality in the process. In the early rounds of negotiations Renamo did push for a key and continuing role for Kenya, but this was scarcely acceptable to Frelimo (who argued at first for direct talks, without any mediating presence whatsoever), and in any case the logic of a further internationalization of the peace process by now had a powerful pull of its own.

In the first instance the most visible external actors were once again representatives from the church, although this church involvement, too, was now rather more externally defined than previously. Central here was the role played by the Community of Sant'Egidio, a lay Catholic organization which was founded in the 1960s with a social activist agenda and which also had some history (since the mid-1970s) of links with Mozambique. Maintaining contact with both the Vatican and the Italian government (the latter would come to pay many of the expenses incurred during the ongoing negotiations), Sant'Egidio now offered its buildings as the site for talks. Moreover, in the process of facilitating such talks, two representatives from Sant'Egidio, Andrea Riccardi and Don Matteo Zuppi, took centre stage as "observers" at the negotiations – alongside the Mozambican bishop of Beira, Don Jaime Gonçalves, and Mario Raffaeli, a Socialist member of the Italian parliament named to this new role by Prime Minister Giulio Andreotti. An important further step was then taken when both Mozambican parties agreed, in the course of the first round of talks, to accept these four observers in the more formal role of official "mediators," even if, as Hume notes, it was not quite clear at first just "how much authority to organize the peace process the parties were actually willing to delegate to [such] mediators."[24]

It would be a mistake to downplay the extent to which the humanitarian concerns of the churches played a continuing role in pulling them into the fray in this way, of course. Indeed, any account of the peace process must emphasize the extent to which a broad range of external actors were moved to action by the self-evident horrors of the war and also, in the context of drought, massive starvation, and the continuing displacement of peoples, of the extent to which the very fact of the war itself – including, not least, the self-regarding calculations of military and political advantage on the part of the domestic protagonists (Renamo, in particular) – made relief efforts difficult. At the same time, it would be equally misleading to ignore a point raised earlier: the extent to which the larger context of Frelimo's rehabilitation as ward of the West helped frame such a development. For the humanitarian concerns now operative were far more easily cast in terms of bringing peace to a very troubled country than in any questioning of the ethics or long-term developmental efficacy of the march towards neo-liberalism that Mozambique was simultaneously undertaking. As we have suggested, this latter was the "common-sense" of the moment that, for better or worse, now bound virtually all actors in the negotiations drama together.

In addition, we must also be careful to qualify our preliminary characterization of the Catholic church as an external actor: things were rather more complicated than that. Certainly, the church had a stake of its own inside Mozambique itself and Mozambicans linked to the church had domestic political agendas to pursue. Vines suggests this to be true, in particular, of the one Mozambican member of the mediating quartet identified above, the bishop (later Archbishop) of Beira, Don Jaime Goncalves. As Vines phrases his point: "Long standing personal friendships and ethnicity significantly contributed to Sant'Egidio's ability to host the talks. Goncalves' close relationship with Sant'Egidio was crucial in bringing Renamo to Rome. Goncalves is not only from the same ethnic sub-group (the Ndau) as many of Renamo's senior leadership but is also from Renamo leader Dhlakama's home town, Chibabava (Sofala). Goncalves has also developed a reputation for Ndau chauvinism (which is a defining feature of Renamo's military leadership). ... Goncalves was also trusted by Renamo because of the government's dislike of him."[25] Nor was this the only domestic complexity of relevance to assessing the role of the churches: Renamo was itself suspicious of the role played, in the earlier rounds of pre-negotiations, by the Catholic archbishop of Maputo, Alexander dos Santos, for example.

As noted above, there was also considerable interplay between these church initiatives and the part taken by the Italian government – a link epitomized in the aforementioned presence of Mario Raffaelli as one of the four mediators. But the Italian role was, in any case, merely the tip of the iceberg of the growing involvement of Western countries in the ongoing peace process. Thus Cameron Hume's account makes graphic the extent of the American government's active engagement in cajoling (some might say bullying) both sides into compromise at various key points in the negotiations. Senior American officials such as u.s. Assistant Secretary of State Herman Cohen and Cohen's principal deputy, Jeffrey Davidow, are shown to be hovering in the wings throughout, and then there is Hume himself, author but also actor, and in constant attendance, it would seem, as U.S. "representative"-cum-"observer" to the talks. Moreover, as we will see, the evolution of the negotiations was eventually to bring not only the United States but a growing group of Western nations (eventually designated the "Contact Group") in from the margins and much closer to the centre of the entire peace process.

The most important of Mozambican actors, Frelimo and Renamo, both approached the negotiations process gingerly. Frelimo, the holder of state power, showed little real taste for multi-party democracy, for example, although it would soon move, however reluctantly, in that direction. Its chief interest was in ensuring the kind of cease-fire that would spike the guns of Renamo, whose historical role as spoiler Frelimo still deeply resented, once and for all. Frelimo was also reluctant, both for nationalist reasons and for reasons of more narrowly defined tactical advantage (qua party-in-power), to yield any more of its sovereignty-cum-legitimacy than was absolutely necessary, either to Renamo or to the "international community."

As for Renamo, as noted above, it never did have any very powerful independent ideological charge behind its activities, something that became all the more true as Frelimo began itself to mirror Renamo's own ostensible policy predilections. And even though Renamo drew much of its strength, at least at the leadership level, from regional and ethnic groupings rooted in the centre of the country (Manica and Sofala, in particular), this was a rather more amorphous and negotiable aspect of its political project than was true of the sub-national claims of some challengers to established political authority elsewhere in Africa. Certainly the movement did want to consolidate political space for itself: in consequence and in contrast to Frelimo's central preoccupation, consolidating the terms of a political settlement was a much more important priority on its negotiations' agenda than was the realizing of a cease-fire. But the leadership was also available, many suspected, to make deals of a rather more opportunist nature from quite early on.

In this respect, Vines argues, the Renamo leadership was to prove true throughout the negotiations period (and beyond) to its external origins and to its mercenary calling. Noting the considerable largesse extended by the Italian government to the Renamo delegation at the Rome talks, Vines suggests that this represented "an astute reading of probably the single greatest interest Renamo had, namely to extract maximum material, rather than political, benefits from the peace process." Moreover, "as the peace process progressed, so did Renamo's financial demands"![26] Hume deals with this aspect of things rather more circumspectly, but his formulations are nonetheless quite revealing. Thus he phrases a related point regarding one particular moment in the negotiations process as follows: "Dhlakama was worried about securing the wherewithal to change Renamo from a rural insurgency into a political party. In mid-March [1992] he went to Raffaelli, as representative of the Italian government and lead mediator, to say that Renamo needed a concrete guarantee of outside financial support. Italy was giving millions of dollars to Frelimo, so why could it not give 10 or 12 million to Renamo? However inelegant Dhlakama's solicitation, the need he expressed was genuine. For peace to take hold, Renamo would need help for its transformation into a civilian political party."[27] Yet note too his formulation elsewhere in his book: "In a meeting with the mediators Dhlakama raised the issue of guarantees for himself and Renamo. In this context 'guarantees' at times meant assurances of physical security once Renamo had laid down its arms, but it always meant the availability of resources *to pay for the entry of Renamo's cadres into the money economy.* Without such compensation, Dhlakama explained, he would seem to be getting nothing for his supporters while offering Frelimo the benefits of peace" (emphasis added).[28]

What was being established here, in short, was a pattern that would also continue into the implementation phase of the peace process in Mozambique, a pattern that has encouraged many observers to view Renamo as often merely holding the negotiations process to ransom for quite narrow purposes. The rationale for financial concessions to Renamo presented in the official circles frequented by Western governments and United Nations personnel was indeed (as Hume suggests) most often phrased in terms of giving Renamo the resources to become a "civilian political party." But this rationale tended to be offered up with a nudge and a wink, suggesting that private use was often being made of much of the money so granted.

*Process.* As for the talks themselves, the first phase – three rounds between July and December 1990[29] – saw negotiators from both Frelimo (led by Armando Guebuza) and Renamo (led by Raul Domingos) feeling each other out, confirming venue, and, as noted, sanctioning the installation of the four observers as formal "mediators" for the duration of the talks. Nonetheless, by the end of the third meeting (21 December) neither of the key issues that these talks would have to face if they were to be successful – agreement on the nature of any projected political transition (and of the political structures that would have to frame such a transition) on the one hand, the setting of the terms of a cease-fire (obviously central to any settlement) on the other – had been placed on the table. True, there was some meeting of minds on the need to delimit the continuing

Zimbabwean military role to a mere safe-guarding of the transport corridors to Zimbabwe and to Malawi through the centre of the country and to the establishment of a Joint Verification Commission (JVC) to monitor such an agreement.[30] In retrospect this can perhaps be seen as having been some kind of first step towards a more general cease-fire. Politically, however, the only significant development was made outside the frame of the negotiations, as the Mozambican government announced it was proceeding with the mounting of its new constitution. Even though this move confirmed the abolition of the one-party state, it is not surprising, perhaps, that Renamo leaders saw it as all too unilateral an initiative, and hence suspect.[31]

Thus, as a second phase of talks opened up in January 1991 (through to the signing of Protocol I in October), the difference of opinion, mentioned earlier, as to which should be prioritized, political settlement (as advocated by Renamo) or cease-fire (as advocated by Frelimo), hung in the air. Eventually, the mediators managed (assisted by Herman Cohen's interventions) to break the deadlock, obtaining agreement on an agenda that prioritized political issues – albeit in the "neutral," open-ended language favoured by the government. But such neutral language merely masked an even more fundamental disagreement that almost immediately threatened to deadlock the talks once more: this touched on the issue of the very legitimacy of the Mozambican government itself, in particular the nature of its continuing role (even existence!) during any transition that was to come. In consequence, the mediators soon found themselves conducting "bilateral discussions with both teams to find a way to bridge the gap between the government's insistence that arrangements for implementation not denigrate its legitimacy in any way and Renamo's refusal to acknowledge the government's legitimacy." Here, too, American intervention – the prominence of an October meeting between Davidow and Dhlakama is emphasized by Hume – was important. The result: agreement to Protocol I which affirmed (although the issue would pop up again from time to time) "that each side would retain its legitimacy: the government as government and Renamo as negotiating partner and opposition party."[32]

During the next phase of talks – a phase that would produce, between October 1991 and March 1992, both a "Protocol II" on "the formation and recognition of political parties" and a "Protocol III" on the election law – Davidow continued to play an important role in "helping the negotiations along" (in Hume's delicate phrase), most often by jogging by turns the arms of Frelimo, of Renamo, and of President Mugabe. From an early date the United States had been pressing for an even more prominent role for itself and other West-

ern states than the one they had come to assume,[33] Davidow having
floated with the mediators (at the time of his October 1991 meeting
with Dhlakama, mentioned above) the possibility of forming a
"contact group" of "interested governments" to oversee the peace
process as it advanced. And Davidow would again place the further
internationalization of the process on the agenda in early 1992, even
as the four existing mediators, still at the centre of the process,
worked overtime to bring about agreement on the electoral protocol.
He argued that such expanded internationalization would become
particularly appropriate as complex military and administrative
questions began to surface in subsequent rounds – and as the issue of
who would pay for the expenses to be incurred during the transition
process came to be addressed.

In the meantime, various draft proposals regarding possible
electoral systems were traded between the parties, State Department
experts were consulted, and a range of other "consultations" flour-
ished. And, as a sober undercurrent, the violence also continued.
Thus the military capacity of the government actually seemed to
deteriorate during much of this period, while for its part Renamo
appeared to be "in no hurry to end the war." Indeed, even as "the
talks proceeded at a pace virtually dictated by the rebels [in 1992],
their leadership continued to flirt with a return to the military option
in the belief that it could extract substantial concessions from the
government, and simultaneously further undermine popular support
for Frelimo by contributing to the deteriorating socio-economic
situation."[34]

The fact remains, however, that many other factors were also at
work in focusing the minds of the domestic political protagonists on
the peace process and that a certain logic of "peace-making" had
begun to take hold. Indeed, with the most "explicitly political items
on the agenda" dealt with, at least to some extent, in the first three
protocols, the stage was set for the next important phase of the negotiations. This round would see, among other things, an increasing
formalization (in June 1992) of the role of certain "observer governments" – France, Portugal, the United Kingdom, and the United
States – and also of observers from the United Nations, all of whom
now joined the talks. In Hume's view this reflected the fact that "the
Mozambican parties and the mediators had assumed that the international community would have many tasks to perform in implementing the peace agreement: monitoring a cease-fire, helping to form a
new national army, repatriating refugees, resettling displaced persons, providing relief supplies and development aid, and monitoring
elections. ... If representatives of several governments and United

Nations [now] participated in the negotiations, the international community would be in a better position to provide the resources needed for implementation."[35]

As noted above, a key task during this period (between March and August 1992) – a task which confronted mediators and observers alike – was to evoke from the Mozambican participants a greater sense of urgency as to the pace at which peace was being negotiated. And yet progress continued to be made on both the military and humanitarian assistance fronts. Thus the UN agreed (in line with a declaration of 16 July on "Guiding Principles of Humanitarian Assistance") to chair a committee that would coordinate and supervise the aid effort. Meanwhile, "the military experts of the Italian government and the observers ... had produced the basic draft of a protocol on military questions," including the model of a new, integrated army and proposals for reform of the police and security forces. However much remained to be done on these fronts, at least enough was achieved during this period to lay the groundwork for an "African Summit" meeting (4–7 August 1992) between Mozambique's President Joaquim Chissano, Renamo leader Afonso Dhlakama, and President Mugabe of Zimbabwe, a meeting which ratified, after lengthy debate amongst these participants and others, the progress made to date, and also set 1 October as the target for finalizing a Mozambican peace accord once and for all.

In the wake of this crucial meeting, two further processes were set in motion, one being the preparing of the UN for a key role in the transition that an accord would soon bring. Thus, "On August 7, just hours after the summit had concluded in Rome, UN Secretary-General Boutros-Ghali informed Security Council members that President Chissano had told him both parties now agreed on a UN role and wanted UN assistance for the peace process. The secretary-general explained that the UN role would include monitoring a cease-fire and demobilization and verifying an election, along the lines of the UN operation in Angola."[36] And UN teams were almost at once in Mozambique, investigating the organization's prospective role in implementing the peace agreement and soon dividing their efforts between concentrating on "the arrangements for elections" on the one hand and "the requirements for peace-keeping" on the other.

Meanwhile, in Rome, the work of dotting the "i"s and crossing the "t"s of the prospective accord also continued apace, especially as regards the structure of civil administration and military questions (including police and security matters and the terms of the cease-fire). This was not easy work, Renamo even being inclined, from time to time, to revert to its questioning of the government's very legitimacy in order to gain more leverage, in bargaining for fresh financial considerations, for a greater share of power during the transition period, and for an expanded UN presence. It was also necessary, on such delicate questions, to keep referring back to the two presidents: – Tiny Rowland and Mugabe arranging a brief mini-summit between Chissano and Dhlakama in Gaberone on 18–19 September for this purpose, for example. Slowly but surely, however, some advance was made on outstanding fronts, including (albeit in rather rough and often minimally specified terms) the establishment of a new army drawn from both government and Renamo forces, with preliminary arrangements for assembly points around which to regroup this new unified command; new commissions of nationals (drawn from both Frelimo and Renamo) to oversee police and security activities; and the sanctioning of the UN's role in the transition.

Of course, a number of crucial issues were more papered over than resolved for purposes of reaching agreement. For example, "the most difficult problem, one that neither delegation seemed able to address, was how areas with a Renamo presence would be administered after a cease-fire." As Hume continues, "For the time being it seemed reasonable to assume that however this issue was solved in the context of the Rome talks, in fact it would have to be skillfully managed throughout the transition period by the secretary-general's representative, with some flexibility from the parties"! This formulation should be enough, in and of itself, to suggest that the United Nations' task was not going to be an entirely straightforward one in the next round. At the same time, the peace train could by now be considered to be sufficiently on track to meet the deadline set in Rome in August. The two leaders, Chissano and Dhlakama, would now meet again in Rome (after both sides abandoned their original thought that an African site for the final summit might be most appropriate) for last-minute dickering over the precise terms of the agreement. This process found the negotiators (and significant others, notably Herman Cohen and Tiny Rowland[37]) shuffling back and forth between the two leaders in their separate hotels until, finally, the document was ready to be signed by the two leaders, in the presence of President Mugabe and other interested parties, on 4 October.

As noted, the document remained flawed, much remaining to be spelled out in practice – as regards military questions and the cease-fire, demobilization and the creation of a new national military force, reformation of the police and security forces, and the re-establishment of civilian administration in many areas of the country. As Hume concludes, "despite the optimism of the signing ceremony the outlook was guarded.": "The role of the United Nations would now be pivotal," he suggests, while also observing that "because of the defects in the agreements, the process of implementation would have to be constantly preceded or accompanied by a process of renegotiation." As we will see below, this did indeed prove to be the case. And yet the situation – at least in terms of realizing a fresh measure of peace in Mozambique – was also, simultaneously, a rather more optimistic one than Hume's formulation might suggest, albeit in ways that his own approach cannot really illuminate. For both parties to the agreement were by now so mortgaged to Western purposes and paymasters (and had also raised such expectations of peace on the part of their own beleaguered population!) that it would be extremely difficult for them to evade altogether the logic of the peace process, however aggressively they might still seek to advance their own partisan projects within the new context that confronted them.

### RESOLUTION: THE TRANSITION (1992–94)

#### The United Nations ... and Company

Enter, then, the United Nations. As UN Secretary-General Boutros Boutros-Ghali has explained this development, "In the course of the negotiations, the need to secure the services of the United Nations as a partial guarantor of the peace process emerged only gradually. Initially, Renamo was more in favour of the presence of the United Nations than was the Government, which viewed the war as having had an international dimension but also had deeply felt concerns about the implications that a United Nations presence would have in several areas relating to national sovereignty. The government was also concerned by the possibility that Renamo could improve its political status as a result of such United Nations involvement. However, consensus developed on the need for impartial management of the peace process, and the United Nations was clearly the institution that could best provide this."[38]

Thus, only days after the signing in Rome (on 13 October), UN Security Council Resolution 782 (1992) welcomed the General Peace Agreement, while authorizing the secretary-general to appoint a special representative for Mozambique to oversee the UN role (an Italian, Aldo Ajello, was to assume this position) and to dispatch an initial team of military observers. And on 16 December Security Council Resolution 797 (1992) authorized the secretary-general to establish the extensive "United Nations Operation in Mozambique"

(ONUMOZ).³⁹ A vast commitment of resources, in terms of both monetary outlays and the disposition of personnel, was to follow as the UN came to play through ONUMOZ a particularly crucial role, at the humanitarian, the military, and the political levels, in the transition.

But "impartial"? There is certainly room for debate about this, since the fact remains that UN personnel were not to play their "peace-making" role alone. Indeed, a key feature of the peace agreement had been the establishment of a "Supervisory and Monitoring Commission (CSC)," empowered "to supervise the cease-fire and monitor respect for and implementation of the agreements between the Parties within the framework of these negotiations" and "composed of representatives of the Government, RENAMO, the United Nations, OAU, and countries to be agreed upon by the Parties."⁴⁰ In practice the CSC came to include representatives from the Government and Renamo and also from France, Italy, the United Kingdom, the United States, and the OAU (with Germany invited to join later and with the UN Representative in the Chair).⁴¹ In this formal manner, and more informally, the Western powers came to be co-supervisors, with the UN, of the entire peace process. As Boutros-Ghali phrased the point in his report: "As provided in the General Peace Agreement, the Supervisory and Monitoring Commission (CSC) became the key mechanism for sustaining both the momentum and the involvement of the international community. The United Nations chairmanship of the CSC and the other commissions charged with implementing the accords greatly facilitated rapid, objective problem-solving. Whenever difficulties were encountered, the CSC was able to convene negotiations that succeeded in persuading the parties to adhere to their commitments. This form of collective oversight, involving the two parties, the United Nations, the Organization of African Unity and ambassadors of Mozambique's donor countries, allowed for flexible management and for adjustments to the time-table when such recourse became unavoidable."

"Objective"? "Flexible"? Although a Cameron Hume would not, presumably, blink an eyelash at this kind of institutionalizing of the Westernization of the peace process, Joseph Hanlon, one of the most astute and prodigious of writers on Mozambique over the years, sees something quite sinister in it.⁴² And he is not wrong to do so – although we might feel, on closer examination, that he rather misstates the reasons for such suspicions. We have seen the role of the Western powers (and notably that of the United States) to have been expanding throughout the negotiations period, of course, but such a trend was to become intensified during this next, UN-phase of the peace process. Hanlon cites no less an authority than U.S. ambassador to Mozambique Dennis Jett to dramatize the fact (while reaching his own conclusions as to the import of this development): "Ambassadors of the western powers 'dogged the process daily, participating in virtually every decision made affecting the Mozambican transition,' wrote … Jett in his report on the two year Mozambican peace process. In effect, the u.s. Ambassador brags that the UN Operation in Mozambique (ONUMOZ) was carrying out the post-Cold War goals of the u.s. rather than following any balanced directives from the UN." In addition, Hanlon notes the speech by UN Special Representative Aldo Ajello himself (speaking at an "International Workshop on the Successful Conclusion of ONUMOZ" in New York on 27 March 1995), in which he admits that he decided (in Hanlon's paraphrase) "to only act after regular consultation with the ambassadors of the major powers (mainly the u.s., Britain, Italy and Portugal) and [to act] on their authority rather than that of the UN headquarters in New York."

Hanlon also emphasizes the extent to which Ajello and the ambassadors bent over backwards to meet Renamo's demands, citing (again by paraphrasing Ajello's New York speech) "his decision to bolster, financially and politically, one party to the peace accord, namely Renamo." There can be no question that this occurred. In May, 1993, for example, the UN established a Trust Fund for the Implementation of the Peace Agreement, earmarked specifically (in accordance with the peace agreement) to ensuring that "Renamo had the facilities to carry out its political activities in all areas of the country": "The Trust Fund was the response to this requirement and proved critical to the peace process, as it helped to finance the transformation of Renamo from a rebel force into a political party that would be able to campaign effectively in the electoral process."[43] In Hanlon's account establishment of this fund proved possible only after "ONUMOZ sent a secret mission to western capitals to appeal for funds" specifically for such a purpose: "Ajello gave Dhlakama a personal cheque for $300,000 each month," writes Hanlon. Indeed, as Hanlon argues more generally, "from the start, Ajello's view was that the main problem was to keep Renamo playing. This led to a pattern where Renamo or Dhlakama would make a new demand or boycott the various committees set up under the peace accord, and the UN and donors would accede to Renamo demands to get them on board."[44]

Moreover, there can be little doubt that "given the UN's stated commitment to the conclusion of the peace process in accordance with a specific timetable, it was not long before the Mozambicans were using this as a bargaining chip to extract concessions from the UN and international donor community."[45] Nor is there much doubt that this was particularly true of Renamo, who now saw the strength of its military card eroding as peace loomed. But can we really share Hanlon's suspicions, more or less explicit in his writing, that the Americans (and, by extension, the UN) were trying – following a "post–Cold War" agenda – to undermine a progressive Mozambican government in favour of a Renamo victory? To do so one would have to interpret the Frelimo government as representing a great deal more of a threat to Western interests than, in its currently recolonized mode, it was likely that it could or would choose to be. Better, perhaps, to interpret the whole process primarily in terms we have already sketched above (terms which evoke a rather subtler variant of "post-Cold War goals," it might be said). For beyond the desire for peace (and the lifting of the great burdens that war was continuing to impose upon most Mozambicans), the bringing of *a certain kind of peace* had also become for Jett and others part and parcel of the overall project of the stabilization of a new Mozambique and its firm recuperation – including the recuperation of both of its leading combatants-cum-political parties – within the Western orbit, economically and politically.

No doubt this, in and of itself, would have meant special treatment for Renamo since that organization remained the greatest threat to peace and stability[46] – and the one most likely to continue to threaten renewed hostilities in order to gain an edge. Add to that the fact that the movement seemed, so visibly, to be up for sale. For its part, Frelimo moved rather more easily onto the terrain of peace, advantaged in terms of access to resources by its privileged position as the party in power, but also confident (a bit over-confident, as it turned out) that in the sphere of politics-without-the-gun it could easily out-manoeuvre its chief adversary.[47]

Had Frelimo also retained just enough of its original sense of national dignity and high (if authoritarian) purpose to worry some-one like Ambassador Jett? Consider, in this context, the pressure the Americans, in particular, continued to exert on Frelimo throughout the transition process to get it to accept, in advance of the election, some kind of government of national unity-cum-power sharing arrangement with Renamo along the lines of the recent agreements worked out during the South African transition. Although presented as one further means of institutionalizing stability and ensuring peace, this proposed model could also be seen – in line with the central thrust of Hanlon's argument – as a bit of American overkill to further hamstring any new Frelimo government that might emerge with a majority from the elections.[48] In the event, Frelimo, in its confidence and/or arrogance and also in the name of its sovereign rights, rejected this semi-directive, won the election ... and continued with its relatively docile embrace of the apparent logic of post–Cold War global economics.

Not that peace came easily to Mozambique. ONUMOZ itself was slow to establish itself on the ground and the two domestic protagonists were themselves even slower to act on the terms of the cease-fire – although, once again, this was more true of Renamo than it was of Frelimo. Indeed, by June 1993, it was apparent that there was, again, a state of very heightened politico-military tension, Renamo, for its part, digging ever more deeply into certain areas that it continued to control and appearing reluctant to become an active presence in many of the transitional commissions it had agreed to be party to. About this same time, too, it was agreed that the entire transition process would have to be set back one year from the original time-table, the election foreseen for October 1993 now projected to take place in October 1994.[49]

Here the UN sought to profit from its own experience in Angola, writes Boutros-Ghali: "It was apparent to all concerned that Mozambique's planned elections should not take place until the military aspects of the Agreement had been implemented. This conclusion was reinforced by the events following Angola's elections in the preceding weeks; there the failure to complete demobilization had enable the loser of the election to launch an all-out war." But as late as September 1993, "demobilization had not yet started and little progress had been made in drafting an electoral law" and in October, the secretary-general confirms, "the peace process was now badly stalled": "In light of the gravity of the situation, I decided to visit Maputo in order to impress on President Chissano and Mr. Dhlakama the very real possibility of ONUMOZ withdrawal"![50] And this threat, combined with other pressures on both parties from the "international community," did begin to accelerate the pace of the transition, as real progress at last began to be made on a variety of fronts (notably those linked to the cease-fire and to the establishment of electoral arrangements).[51]

One additional word of caution is in order here. It is easy to be cynical about the political projects of Renamo and even of Frelimo as they jockeyed for position during this transition period. It would be quite another thing, however, to overlook the crucial role played in the making of the transition by thousands of ordinary Mozambicans. One thing most observers came to agree upon was the extent to which, below the machinations of their ostensible leaders, such Mozambicans took ownership of the process, not least at the level of the electoral apparatus itself where the UN's role was to remain largely logistical and supervisory and where thousands of Mozambicans, from the supervisor of elections, Brazåo Mazula, on down, actually made the new system function effectively.

More generally, and even more importantly perhaps, there was the dramatic popular embrace of the peace process, creating an atmosphere on the ground across much of the country that, most often, ran well ahead of the practices of the political parties themselves. Thus, Ken Wilson, in documenting the making of a "people's peace," locally and face-to-face, by people on both sides of the politico-military divide, quotes an unnamed UN official as saying (in November 1993): "Well, the peace process goes remarkably well despite the United Nations, Renamo and Frelimo." To which Wilson adds: "This is indeed the case. ... At the grassroots level the desire of ordinary Mozambicans for peace has been the main factor propelling the peace process forwards. While the UN, Frelimo and Renamo have manoeuvred for political advantage, struggled with internal bureaucratic and political divisions, and revealed a limited capacity to deliver what is agreed upon, ordinary Mozambicans – soldiers, churchmen, petty officials, displaced men and women, local chiefs – individually and collectively have grabbed the initiative and created their own 'peace agreements' at the local level."[52] And it was just such a popular mood of disgust with war and passion for peace – a mood at once intangible yet strangely pervasive – that helped frame the election itself when, finally, its moment came.

### Demobilization, Humanitarian Assistance ... and Elections

We have noted the difficulties of establishing an effective cease-fire in Mozambique in the wake of the general peace agreement, difficulties that led to the postponement of the election by a year. However, as also noted above, the secretary-general's intervention in October 1993 saw the agreeing of a new timetable between the Mozambican parties and the CSC and, subsequently (in early November), the Security Council's renewing of the ONUMOZ mandate. The new timetable foresaw acceleration of work on the electoral front but also in the implementation of the cease-fire. In this latter sphere, for example, "the concentration of troops was to commence in November 1993, followed by the start of demobilization in January 1994. Demobilization was due to end in May 1994, by which time the demobilized soldiers would be returned to their home areas. The new Mozambican Defence Force was to be fully operational by September 1994. ... Although a year had passed since the signing of the General Peace Agreement demobilization was finally underway and the electoral process could begin."[53]

Demobilization was not easy ("the most difficult and dangerous phase of the ONUMOZ mandate," writes Boutros-Ghali). The two Mozambican parties were coy about numbers and reluctant to yield up their best fighting units to the process. And Renamo, in particular, put difficulties in the way of firming up assembly areas. Thus, despite the new timetable, demobilization did not really begin until 10 March, and, once under way, produced a vast array of problems, both political and logistical: problems in the provisioning of the sites and in the facilitating of severance pay and reintegration subsidy payments were producing riots and other incidents at the assembly areas well into July and August, for example. Nonetheless, by August assembly points were closed, with November figures eventually to show that demobilization had accounted for 57,540 government and 20,538 Renamo soldiers. Moreover, despite the difficulties, war-weariness and "reintegration subsidy payments" (representing a further eighteen months' pay beyond six months' severance, to be combined with access to retraining programs, and to be sponsored by the UNDP to the tune of $31.9 million) ultimately had taken their toll on the willingness of most Mozambicans to continue to pursue military-related vocations.[54] Indeed, as the process of reconstructing the new Mozambican Defence Force itself moved forward – a force constructed from the blending of both government and Renamo military structures – only one-third of the originally projected troop strength of 30,000 soldiers could be found to volunteer!

There was also the challenge of monitoring the cease-fire and verification of demobilization, and while there were few really serious violations of the cease-fire during the period of the UN mandate ONUMOZ military observers, complemented in their activities by a contingent of international civilian police (CIVPOL) observers, were still discovering arms caches and unregistered soldiers and checking weapons right up to the end of its mandate in December 1994.[55] Moreover, there was one other outstanding problem that, as Boutros-Ghali admits, ONUMOZ never even came close to resolving: the failure to achieve a unified civil administration, in large part because of Renamo's reluctance to cede control of many of the areas it controlled and because of its boycott, after a certain point, of the National Commission on Administration, or CNA. Needless to say, the problem of access to such areas also became one that would haunt the electoral process, qualifying to some degree the claims to openness made on its behalf. Nor was it a problem that would altogether disappear under the newly elected Frelimo government in the post-election, post-ONUMOZ period.

Before turning to those elections, however, it is important to remind ourselves of another very different level of the peace-making process. For one of the most successful aspects of the UN presence, it has been claimed, was the "humanitarian activities" it both mounted and worked to coordinate in Mozambique during the transition. This success, Boutros-Ghali argues, "was critical to the peace process," both helping "to maintain support in the country for the United Nations presence and [demonstrating] the potential advantages of sustained peace."[56] The sums involved were vast, the international community, Boutros-Ghali calculates, contributing "78 per cent of the approximately $650 million required to meet Mozambique's needs for humanitarian assistance during the period of the ONUMOZ mandate."

Moreover, the mechanism for undertaking this work was unique: the establishment, "as the humanitarian component of ONUMOZ" and working closely with such related agencies as the United Nations Department of Humanitarian Affairs, the UNDP, and the UNHCR, of a United Nations Office for Humanitarian Assistance Coordination (UNOHAC), based in Maputo. Key challenges, undertaken either directly by the UN or as the ongoing work of other humanitarian agencies now coordinated, to a greater or lesser degree, by UNOHAC, included: the delivery of emergency relief (and its gradual replacement by a program of reintegration and rehabilitation), the massive resettlement, between October 1992 and December 1992, of some 4.3 million displaced Mozambicans (including some 1.6 million returning from other countries), the reintegration, mentioned earlier, of thousands of demobilized soldiers, the reactivation of health and education programs in the rural areas, and the launching of a program of land-mine clearance throughout the country. Some of these activities also carried UNOHAC into those difficult-to-access Renamo-controlled areas mentioned above, thus providing, in addition to the actual, badly needed goods and services so delivered, some precedent for the possible long-term resolution of the difficult problems thrown up by the existence of such areas.[57]

We have noted that the question of access to such areas (especially by Frelimo campaigners) was to prove a challenge to the electoral process as well, although it must be stressed that it merely qualified the openness of that process rather than compromising it in any fundamental sense. Indeed, once the 1993 political impasse was broken – an impasse that expressed itself vis-à-vis the electoral arena in disputes over the composition of the National Elections Commission (the CNE) and over the terms of the electoral law – the actual organization of the elections ran surprisingly smoothly. This is important, not least, because the day-to-day preparation of the election format and functioning was in the hands of Mozambicans themselves, the CNE now operating under the chairpersonship of Brazão Mazula and comprised of ten members nominated by the government, seven by Renamo, and three by the other, smaller political parties who now came forward to enter the contest. Slowly but surely a dense network of provincial and district commissions was put in place, as were census, civic education, local polling station, and party-based monitoring teams. However, the international role, played, in significant measure, by the UNDP but with substantial financial and other input from the European Union in particular, remained important here as well, in terms of logistical support, technical advice, funding, and observation of the process.[58]

The election (held 27–29 October 1994) was to provide the finishing touch to the peace process, with conflicts once carried out in violent terms now to be domesticated at the polls and rendered pacific.[59] There can be little doubt that many Mozambicans viewed the elections in precisely these terms, as being – with any luck – a "peace election": indeed, large numbers of Mozambicans seemed to be voting, first and foremost, for the very idea of voting itself. Their apparent hope: that the election would prove to be an arena within which political differences might, at last, be resolved peacefully and the violence that has scarred their lives for so long might end. And the immediate result of the election was to do just that. True, there were glitches, the most dramatic being the startling withdrawal of Renamo's Dhlakama from the electoral process for twenty-four hours during the actual balloting. The grounds were trivial, merely serving to rationalize one last bid by Renamo for a further sweetening of the deal, and the response swift: Special Representative Ajello and the Western ambassadors met with Dhlakama, the heads of neighbouring southern states sent warnings, a senior representative of Nelson Mandela's new South African government flew into Maputo for "consultations." And almost at once Dhlakama was back in the electoral fold.

Not only that, Renamo did rather better in the election than anyone had anticipated. To be sure, Dhlakama himself lost to Frelimo's Chissano in the presidential race (gaining 33.73 per cent of the vote to Chissano's 53.30 per cent). But Renamo as a party came closer in the legislative election (Frelimo: 44.33 per cent of the votes and 129 seats, Renamo 37.78 per cent of the votes and 112 seats), carrying a number of provinces in the centre and north of the country. Long-time Frelimo fellow-travellers were rather shocked by the relative closeness of the outcome. But the fact of the matter was that so much had changed in Mozambique. Given this – and with the possibility of peace uppermost in most voters' minds – it is small wonder that, as one South African journalist, Eddie Koch, suggested, the election seemed to be marked by a kind of "moral amnesia": Frelimo's own high purposes at independence now but a distant memory and Renamo's history as first Rhodesia's and then South Africa's brutal cat's paw also obscured by time. In such a context, in fact, the most important result of the election may well have been Dhlakama's confirmation (by phone, on 14 November to Boutros-Ghali) that he was prepared to accept the results. This, and the virtually unanimous view of foreign observers that the election had been both "free and fair"! As Chris Alden concludes: "Despite continuing objections from some politicians, blunted by the international community's acceptance of the results, as well as by Renamo's inability to return to all-out warfare, the end of the long journey to peace seemed at last to have been realized."[60]

It is worth pausing, however, to scan this electoral process a little more closely before drawing any final conclusions about the Mozambican peace process. The election seems to have been productive of peace, at least in the short run, but what other implications did it have for Mozambicans? Here we return to some of the broader questions as to how best to frame any evaluation of the peace process in Mozambique that were raised at the outset of this chapter. Note, in particular, that the process of levelling down the differences between the two parties alluded to by Eddie Koch was reinforced by the fact that, in substantive policy terms, there could really be little enough to divide them. After all, as argued earlier, the scope for national decision-making is (at least for the moment) defined particularly narrowly in a recolonized country like Mozambique. Economic decision-making rests largely in the hands of the World Bank and the IMF, various aid agencies, and a particularly aggressive band of pirate multinationals, while the state, control over which is the ostensible object of electoral competition, is all but eviscerated.

It was also the case that, in ideological terms, much less now separated Frelimo from Renamo than had once seemed possible: both had little choice but to embrace the conventional nostrums of "neo-liberalism" and, apparently, little desire not to do so. Add to this the fact that, at a certain point, the government's own morale seemed to snap, with mounting corruption and the increasingly arbitrary use of power by both military and civilian authorities threatening to drag Frelimo's own project down to Renamo's level. Thus, as noted above, by the time of the 1994 elections, with Renamo finally cajoled (by various international actors, most prominently) into taking up a more conventionally peaceful political role, a great deal of the distance separating the two movements-cum-parties had begun to disappear.

In short, any immediate prospect of political contestation over alternative socio-economic visions had been effectively side-lined. Small wonder, then, that Frelimo, once the proponent of a clear (if controversial) socialist development alternative, should run an electoral campaign centred on "show-micios" (a play on the Portuguese word "comicio") and rallies in which show business (bands, parachutists, and the like), the trivialization of issues, and the glorification of the candidate took precedence over matters of real substance. For its part, Renamo tended to fall back on the quite calculated manipulation of various regional, ethnic, religious, and (advanced in the name of "tradition") gender-oppressive particularisms and animosities in building its own electoral base – thereby setting a number of dangerous precedents for the texture of future political interactions in Mozambique. Can we not argue, more broadly, that the ironic upshot of this final resolution of Mozambique's un/civil war has been the introduction of institutions of pluralist democracy that are, in many ways, *disempowering* for ordinary Mozambicans: rendering them less, not more, able to engage in meaningful debate about the nature of neo-colonial structures in their country and about possible alternatives to them?

### "PEACE, DEMOCRACY AND DEVELOPMENT"?

"ONUMOZ was one of the most effective peace-keeping operations in the history of the United Nations. It brought peace to Mozambique and, equally important, it contributed directly to the profound political transformation that has enabled Mozambique to set a firm course towards greater peace, democracy and development." So concludes Boutros-Ghali's account of the ONUMOZ operation in Mozambique.[61] There can be little doubt that the UN was anxious for a peace-keeping success after a dismal record of recent failures elsewhere in the world and was prepared – with the backing of its principal funders who had a stake of their own in producing a certain kind of peace in Mozambique – to throw a great deal of money at the country in order to produce that success. And (*pace* Hanlon), alongside a number of other factors invoked in this chapter, the UN operation did make a significant contribution to producing that "certain kind of peace."

This is not the place for any full-blown analysis of the politics of post-transition Mozambique. Enough, perhaps, to say that since the 1994 elections the peace in most of its particulars has held. Nonetheless, by way of conclusion, some brief reflection on the precise resonance, under present Mozambican circumstances, of Boutros-

Ghali's final triad – "greater peace, democracy and development" – may be in order. Obviously, to begin, the coming of peace of any sort is not something we should dismiss glibly, not after what ordinary Mozambicans had experienced in previous years. True, the legacy of the war has continued to make itself felt negatively across a wide range of related fronts, the markedly high level of criminality, for example, being as much a reflection of the wholesale availability of arms and of war-induced lack of moral scruple (on the part of many of the recently demobilized former combatants, among others) as it is of the desperate economic situation in which the country finds itself. And land-mines, widely and cavalierly sown across the country during the war, continue to take a deadly toll.[62]

Politically, certain patterns from the past have also carried over. A December 1995 issue of the *Mozambique Peace Process Bulletin* captured some of these contradictions.[63] Certainly, there is a bit too much of a feeling of déjà-vu (sabre-rattling and economic blackmail!) in one of its lead articles, entitled "Renamo Needs Money": " 'The international community is just playing with us,' complained Renamo leader Afonso Dhlakama, and is trying to starve Renamo until it disappears. In an interview in the Sunday newspaper *Domingo* (10 September) he suggested that although he was committed to peace, there were people in the party who might return to war if Renamo did not get more money from the international community." Moreover, the *Bulletin* notes, Renamo continues to control some of its old areas and refuses to yield them up to any process of integrated administration. Not that Renamo, at this late date, has the capacity (or, very likely, the inclination) – it is very different in this respect from its Angolan counterpart, UNITA – to remount a full-scale war. Douglas Patrick Mason seems to capture the post-war mood correctly when he suggests that in the wake of "Mozambique's multi-party elections that capped the negotiated settlement to the civil war, the erstwhile combatants governing Frelimo and opposition Renamo parties have settled into an uneasy relationship in the fledgling democracy. Despite intemperate exchanges, a stand-off over control of the rural areas, and the existence of a not so secret Renamo armed force, both parties have largely accepted the framework of democratic contest."[64]

Peace, then, but what about "democracy"? Some may think it enough to say that establishment of a certain kind of democratic framework did help bring closure to one of the most horrific, chaos-producing wars in Africa: no small accomplishment. Yet we have also presented reasons for scepticism regarding the brand of democracy whose emergence has been witnessed in Mozambique. Closest to the surface in this regard is the fact that – despite the narrowness of its victory – the post-electoral Frelimo government has seemed inclined to operate, rather high-handedly, on a "winner-take-all" basis.[65] And there is also the possibility, as just seen, that Renamo might yet try to play, within limits, a wrecker's role. In short, Mozambique is very far from having consolidated a democratic culture, and there are certainly those, on both sides, who might wish themselves back to the salad days of their more authoritarian pasts.

Still, there are many others who would accept that there are real benefits to be found in consolidating even the most formal of democratic structures: as one erstwhile senior Frelimo politician, himself an architect of some of the most undemocratic features of Frelimo's strategy, admitted to me self-critically, if there had existed the present kind of democratic structures in the old days (including the far greater freedom of the press that now prevails) obvious abuses of authority like the disastrous "Operation Production" of 1983 would not have been possible. And there is also the hope that even the limited, liberal form of democratization now existent in Mozambique will have created terrain, beyond the opportunities/mystifications of the electoral arena, where popular empowerment of a far more meaningful kind might yet be consolidated: empowerment that could spring from the assertions of actors in civil society like trade union and women's movement structures newly liberated from the deadening hand of monoparty control and from the claims advanced by more self-confident peasant activists and agricultural cooperativistas.[66]

And yet, the sense persists that the kind of liberal democracy achieved in the 1994 elections may also, by its own logic, cut precisely against just such a process of empowerment. Thus, for me, there was a particularly sad irony in the recent observation of a Mozambican friend, a journalist and a firm supporter of freedom, not least of the press, in his country. He wished for no return to the bad old days of government dictation of the "party line" to his newspaper. Yet, he confessed, he couldn't escape the feeling that the workers and peasants in Mozambique had actually had more power under the "old" Frelimo regime. Then, he said, the leadership took their interests more seriously (even if it never found ways to institutionalize a genuinely "popular democracy" in any very effective way), and their voices were actually heard more clearly than they are now, under liberal democracy: in the present system their votes are merely canvassed in a competitive manner that has little to do with advancing their life chances or helping them to clarify their socio-economic options.

Recall, too, the international framework of recolonization within which the Mozambican election occurs, a point already alluded to in the previous section. And note, by way of updating and reinforcing this point, the sad description by one new member of parliament of the state of democratic Mozambique in the wake of that election: "The biggest moment of Mozambican politics this year [1995] was when the government went to Paris to meet with the donors. That was where parliament really was held in Mozambique this year, the donor meeting in Paris." Or, as another MP explained: unlike other countries and parliaments "we accept that our budget is really set by donors at the annual Paris conference. We accept that our priority is to develop a donor acceptable budget." The claim he then advanced for elected politicians was correspondingly modest: "But the assembly must be part of that process, that is what democracy means in Mozambique."

And what, finally, of the promise of "development" under such circumstances? Is there any very good reason for assuming that a process of recolonization – however much it may now be consolidated on more peaceful ground and within a rather more stable social order – can actually deliver a level of economic progress that will transform in meaningful ways the lives of the vast majority of Mozambicans? Only his willingness to give a positive answer to this question could possibly ground Boutros-Ghali's confidence that development will flow from the present peace in Mozambique. A far more sceptical response is certainly at least equally plausible. As Colin Leys, cited earlier, has recently written, "For all countries of the world, recapturing control over their own destinies requires the reestablishment of social control over capital and the resubordination of markets to social purposes [and] for the weaker regions of the world, such as sub-Saharan Africa, this is literally a matter of life and death." Recall, in fact, Leys's formulation, cited at the outset of this chapter, to the effect that ideas that might premise such policies "would come to seem rational only in a world that was in the process of rejecting the currently predominant ideology of the market": "While this world must come," concludes Leys, "it is not yet in sight, and meantime the African tragedy will unfold."[67]

Could failure in this sphere mean, in turn, renewed tragedy for Mozambique? Of course, it would be naive at this late date to argue that the era of the old "Frelimo state" – a "left developmental dictatorship" with deeply compromised economic, social, and political policies – did not have its grievous flaws. Nonetheless, reflecting, in 1995, on the first twenty years of Mozambican independence, years most recently marked by destabilization, by "civil war," and by "peacemaking," one might still conclude with the observation that what has been lost, most visibly, from the earliest period of post-independence

Mozambican history is something terribly important. It is, precisely, that strong sense of purpose, social and public, whose loss also Leys decries, a purpose premised on the envisaging of society-wide trans-formations that could actually change the lives of the vast majority of Mozambicans in positive ways. That such commitment to the collec-tive weal has been lost will bring no tears to the eyes of a Chester Crocker, of a World Bank, or even, perhaps, of a Boutros-Ghali. But the fact remains that its loss has been the price both of the kind of war inflicted on Mozambique *and* of the kind of peace achieved there. If development in any meaningful sense is ever to occur in their country Mozambicans will eventually have to rediscover just such a sense of purpose. Without that – and here political economy and political science really do come together in an inextricable manner – the Mozambican society, the Mozambican polity, may merely begin to fragment all over again.

NOTES

1 In my essay, entitled " 'For fear of being condemned as old fashioned': Liberal Democracy vs. Popular Democracy in Sub-Saharan Africa," in a volume on democracy in Africa being edited by Cyrille Daddieh and Kidane Mengisteab (forthcoming).

2 See my "Writing the Thirty Years' War for Southern African Liberation (1960–1990): What Criteria? What Narrative?," paper presented to the 20th Anniversary Conference of the *Journal of Southern African Studies*, University of York, September 1994.

3 Chester Crocker, "Foreword" to Cameron Hume, *Ending Mozambique's War: The Role of Mediation and Good Offices* (Washington, DC: United States Institute of Peace 1994), ix. See also Crocker, *High Noon in South-ern Africa: Making Peace in a Rough Neighborhood* (New York: Norton 1992).

4 I will not dwell at length here on the extraordinary costs – in human terms (death, displacement of population, and the like) and in terms of the destruction of socio-economic infrastructure – of the war to Mozam-bique over the years, but see, inter alia, Africa Watch, *Conspicuous De-struction: War, Famine and the Reform Process in Mozambique* (New York: Human Rights Watch 1992), Hilary Anderson, *Mozambique: A War against the People* (London: MacMillan Press 1992), and Judith Marshall, *War, Debt and Structural Adjustment in Mozambique: The Social Impact* (Ottawa: North-South Institute 1992).

5 Colin Leys, "Confronting the African Tragedy," *New Left Review*, no. 204 (1994), 46; see also Leys, "The World, Society and the Individual," *Southern Africa Report* (*SAR*), 11 no. 3 (1996), pp. 17–21.

6 By far the best overview of Renamo and its role is to be found in William
Minter, *Apartheid's Contras: An Inquiry into the Roots of War in Angola and
Mozambique* (London: Zed Books 1994); see also Alex Vines, *Renamo:
Terrorism in Mozambique* (London: James Currey 1992).

7 From an interview that appeared in the Maputo daily *Noticias* (25 June
1995).

8 It is the subject of some discussion, for example, as to whether the 1983
congress of Frelimo heralded, primarily, the beginnings of a wise tem-
pering and refining of socialist intention or the first strong expression
of the retreat towards the "recolonization" that was to come. On the
ambiguities of Frelimo's project see my *Recolonization and Resistance:
Southern Africa in the 1990s* (Trenton, NJ: Africa World Press 1993),
especially chap. 3, "The Frelimo State: From Revolution to
Recolonization," and also my forthcoming volume, *What Is to Be Learned?
The Rise and Fall of Mozambican Socialism* (in preparation).

9 This interpretation is advanced, most ostentatiously, in Gervase
Clarence-Smith, "The Roots of the Mozambican Counter-Revolution,"
*South African Review of Books* (April–May 1989), and finds echo in Vines,
*Renamo*. See also Christian Geffray, *La cause des armes aux Mozambique:
Anthropologies d'une guerre civile* (Paris: Éditions Karthala 1990); for more
balanced views, see Dan O'Meara, "The Collapse of Mozambican Social-
ism," *Transformation*, no. 14 (1991), pp. 82–103 and, crucially, Bridget
O'Laughlin, "Interpretations Matter: Evaluating the War in Mozam-
bique," *SAR*, 7 no. 3 (Jan. 1992), pp. 23–33.

10 Minter, *Apartheid's Contras*, 283–4. As Minter adds (p. 286), "the fortunes of the internal contenders were decisively influenced by the scale
of external intervention. Whatever may have been the grievances or
goals of Unita [in Angola] and Renamo leaders, their capacity to build
powerful military machines was dependent both on clientship to the
apartheid state and on enrollment in the global Cold War crusade. They
took advantage of existing social cleavages and regime policy failures.
But the fundamental course they and their patrons laid out for the
insurgent armies was to weaken the state by destroying the economic
and human infrastructure of society and maximizing civilian suffering.
The military advantage they gained by fostering insecurity more than
made up for the potential popular support they lost by abusing civilians."

11 Ibid., 284.

12 Joseph Hanlon, *Mozambique: Who Calls the Shots?* (London: James Currey
1991).

13 David Plank, "Aid, Debt and the End of Sovereignty: Mozambique and
Its Donors," *Journal of Modern African Studies* (*JMAS*), 31, no. 3 (1993),
407–30; see also Merle Bowen, "Beyond Reform: Adjustment and Poli-

tical Power in Contemporary Mozambique," *JMAS*, 30 no. 2 (1992), pp. 255–279.

14 Crocker, *High Noon in Southern Africa*, 237. For Crocker (233), Mozambique thus became "one of the first laboratories of Africa's 'new thinking'"!

15 Quoted in my "Mozambique: The Failure of Socialism?," *SAR*, 6, no. 2 (Nov. 1990), pp. 20–24.

16 Crocker, *High Noon in Southern Africa*, 249.

17 See Robert Gersony, *Summary of Mozambican Refugee Accounts of Principally Conflict-Related Experience in Mozambique: Report Submitted to Ambassador Jonathan Moore and Dr. Chester A. Crocker* (Washington, DC: Department of State Bureau for Refugee Programs, 1988). See also William Minter, *The Mozambican National Resistance (Renamo) as Described by Ex-Participants*, Research report submitted to the Ford Foundation and the Swedish International Development Agency, 1989.

18 Vines, in *"No Democracy Without Money": The Road to Peace in Mozambique (1982–1992)* (London: Catholic Institute for International Relations, n.d.), 29, emphasizes the importance of the drought in shaping Renamo's calculations.

19 The two principal accounts of the negotiations phase in Mozambique are Vines, *"No democracy without money,"* and, especially for the period of the Rome talks, Hume, *Ending Mozambique's War*. I have drawn upon these two sources extensively in the present section of this chapter – even though both are almost exclusively concerned with the "political science" of peace-making. (Not surprisingly, given his position as a career American State Department official, Hume's account – especially in its benign and unproblematized presentation of American "peace aims" – is particularly misleading regarding the broader "political economy" that has framed the peace process in Mozambique.) See also Chris Alden and Mark Simpson, "Mozambique: A Delicate Peace," *JMAS*, 31 no. 1 (1993).

20 Vines, *"No democracy without money,"* 6.

21 There was always some question during this period as to just how much centralized control the Renamo leadership actually exercised over its own rather scattered and diverse military apparatus; many observers suspected that this was one reason why the leadership was reluctant to enter into peace negotiations that might actually serve to call its bluff in this regard.

22 From their joint communiqué, quoted in Vines, *"No democracy without money,"* 10.

23 Ibid., 13.

24 Hume, *Ending Mozambique's War*, 49.

25 Vines, *"No democracy without money,"* 16.

26 Ibid., 31–2, where, emphasizing the extent to which "internal dispute within Renamo had often originated over the sharing of booty and resources amongst the leadership," he cites a series of extortionate practices (protection agreements and the like) engaged in by the Renamo leadership throughout its stormy history. He also notes that, as of 1993, "Renamo's public and private requests and demands since the GPA [General Peace Accord] have become its most consistent demand: in part a reflection of the ending of protection payments with peace."

27 Hume, *Ending Mozambique's War*, 92–3.

28 Ibid., 44.

29 I have followed Hume's helpful lead (one that is encapsulated in the format of his successive chapters) in specifying here the several phases of the Rome talks.

30 The Frelimo government nominated the United Kingdom, Congo, the Soviet Union, and France to the commission, while Renamo nominated Kenya, the United States, Zambia, and Portugal.

31 At this point, Renamo actually drew on the advice of experts from several right-wing American foundations to come up, momentarily, with a constitutional proposal of its own.

32 Hume, *Ending Mozambique's War*, 67, 71.

33 See ibid., 65.

34 Ibid., 126

35 There is, of course, considerable truth in this way of formulating the question of the further internationalization of the process (ibid., 93), although, once again, Hume's argument is rendered partial by his unwillingness to look beneath the surface of Western "good intentions" to discuss the underlying premises of such intervention. Note, too, his comment, in this same paragraph, that "so far the international community had not participated in the talks," a most disingenuous and formalistic conceptualization in light of the litany his own account provides of active American involvement in the process throughout.

36 Ibid., 118. Hume emphasizes (129) the extent to which Renamo, in particular, had come to demand an expansive UN role in the transition process, in large part as a way of offsetting the continuing important role in that process of the existing Mozambican government whose "legitimacy" Renamo had had to accept.

37 At this point, writes Hume (ibid., 136), "only Tiny Rowland, who was telling Dhlakama to conclude the deal, seemed able to get through to Renamo's leader."

38 *The United Nations and Mozambique, 1992–1995*, United Nations Blue Books Series, Vol. v (New York: Department of Public Information, United Nations 1995), 17–18.

39 The essential sourcebook for tracking the UN role in Mozambique is ibid., including the important summary introduction by Boutros Boutros-Ghali, the secretary-general, from which I will quote frequently below; resolutions 782 and 797 are documents 16 (p. 130) and 27 (p. 158) in that volume.

40 From Protocol V of the "General Peace Agreement for Mozambique," reproduced as Annexe II in Vines, *"No democracy without money"*, 60.

41 Other commissions established in the agreement that came to be chaired by the United Nations (and that were to have both local and a range of international participation) were the Cease-fire Commission (CCF), the Reintegration Commission (CORE), and the Joint Commission for the Formation of the Mozambican Defence Force (CCFADM).

42 Joseph Hanlon, "No Even-Handed Policy: The United States Used the UN in Mozambique to Pursue Policies Left Over from the Cold War," in *African Agenda*, 1 no. 5 (1995), 15–16.

43 *The United Nations and Mozambique, 1992–1995,* 31–2; ultimately government money, and a special trust fund, were set up to help fund other opposition parties as well, albeit on a much more modest scale than was true for Renamo. For Boutros-Ghali (p. 58), the creation, in May 1993, of the Trust Fund to finance Renamo "was one of most innovative features of the Mozambique operation and was a pivotal factor in maintaining the momentum of the peace process at this stage."

44 Ibid., 16. Hanlon ("No Even-Handed Policy") also cites the revealing momentary glitch in the peace process that resulted from Renamo chief Dhlakama's repeated rejection of "the houses that were offered in Maputo, insisting on something comparable to the house occupied by President Joaquim Chissano": "Eventually Ajello persuaded the EU [European Union] to give Dhlakama the house normally used by its representative, which has a particularly good position overlooking Maputo Bay and is just up the road from Chissano's house."

45 Chris Alden, "The UN and the Resolution of Conflict in Mozambique," *Journal of Modern African Studies*, 33 no. 1 (1995), 115.

46 Writing of the period as late as September 1993, Boutros-Ghali notes (*op. cit.*, p. 35) that "although a return to war was not contemplated, the Renamo leadership was reluctant to give up its military option, while still seeking to gain what it perceived as important political concessions."

47 Indeed, speaking privately, many Frelimo officials were not nearly so exercised about certain of the payments and concessions made to Renamo as is Hanlon, seeing such moves to bring Renamo in from the cold as accomplishing something they had failed to do on the battlefield.

48 Note, however, just how strongly Hanlon ("No Even-Handed Policy," 16) puts his argument on this point: "It was clear that U.S./UN attempts

to build up Renamo would never ensure its election victory. Ajello and u.s. ambassador Jett began pushing for a pre-election deal on 'power sharing' or a government of national unity. Frelimo refused, arguing that it had gone into a u.s.-style winner-take-all election under pressure from the west, and it was not going to change just because it seemed that the western client was about to lose. " *Pace* Hanlon (and his further bold assertion that the UN "backed Renamo at the behest of the u.s."![p. 15]) there is room for considerable debate as to just who represented the most stable and potentially reliable "western client" at this point in Mozambican history. My own hunch is that by now it was Frelimo, and that most Western actors were sophisticated enough to understand this.

49 Compare Hanlon's explanation of this delay ("No Even-Handed Policy," 15): "One year was not enough to turn Renamo into a credible party, so Ajello delayed the election for a year."

50 *The United Nations and Mozambique, 1992–1995*, 34–5; Boutros-Ghali also notes that, at this moment in the peace process, his special representative "publicly warned Renamo that it could no longer try to preserve both a political and a military option."

51 Ibid., Document 46 ("Press Briefing by the Secretary-General in Maputo" of 20 October 1993), 203–4, and Document 48 ("Report of the Secretary-General on ONUMOZ to the Security Council of November 1 and 2, 1993"), 205–12.

52 Ken Wilson, writing in instructive detail of Morrumbula in Zambezia province in his article "The People's Peace in Mozambique," *SAR*, 9 no.4 (March 1994), 22.

53 *The United Nations and Mozambique, 1992–1995*, 37–8.

54 As even Hanlon ("No Even-Handed Policy," 16) – who otherwise acts as a kind of Greek chorus to the UN's official version of its Mozambique operation – acknowledges, "An Ajello-sponsored plan to pay every demobbed soldier for two years played a key role in smoothing the path [towards full demobilization]. This was a genuine UN success."

55 Renamo was particularly guilty of not demobilizing its soldiers and not turning in its arms, practices the UN chose, in Hanlon's opinion, to ignore (ibid., 16).

56 *The United Nations and Mozambique, 1992–1995*, 54; Boutros-Ghali makes the further claim (more difficult to prove) that "politically, the humanitarian effort enabled the Government and Renamo to begin the necessary process of learning how to cooperate with each other."

57 Hanlon ("No Even-Handed Policy," 15) questions this interpretation, however, suggesting that ONUMOZ's willingness to ignore the peace agreement's emphasis on the establishment of a unified civil administration and to work, even for ostensibly humanitarian purposes, through

Renamo structures in Renamo-controlled areas was a betrayal of the peace process.

58 Funding was particularly important, the original election budget of $64.5 million made up of contributions from seventeen countries and international organizations eventually ballooning to something closer to $100 million.

59 I have discussed this election in my chapter, " 'For fear of being condemned as old fashioned,'" cited above, and also in my article, based on first-hand observation of the electoral moment in Mozambique, entitled "Mozambique: The 'Peace Election,'" in *Southern Africa Report*, 10 no. 2 (Dec. 1994, pp. 3–6); I draw from both these texts in the following paragraphs. See also Brazão Mazula, ed., *Moçambique: Eleiçoes, Democracia e Desenvolvimento* (Maputo, 1995).

60 Chris Alden, "The UN and the Resolution of Conflict in Mozambique," *JMAS*, 33 no. 1 (1995), 126.

61 *The United Nations and Mozambique, 1992–1995*, 69. Note, however, both Hanlon's complaint ("No Even-Handed Policy," 16) that "the peace process cost nearly $1 billion, but most of that money left the country in salaries to UN staff and soldiers and other costs," and Alden's litany (in his "The UN and the Resolution of Conflict in Mozambique," 127) of various problems that, in his opinion, blunted the UN's effectiveness: delays in introducing troops ("compounded by the reluctance of member-states to provide soldiers"), "inter-agency conflicts," and "poor procurement procedures," among others.

62 See Human Rights Watch, *Still Killing: Landmines in Southern Africa* (London and Washington, DC: Human Rights Watch 1995), and, for a moving first-hand account by Canadian singer Bruce Cockburn, "The Mines of Mozambique," *SAR*, 11 no. 1 (Nov. 1995), 14–18.

63 *Mozambique Peace Process Bulletin* (published by AWEPA, the European Parliamentarians for Southern Africa), no. 16 (Dec. 1995); meanwhile, it now appears that the process of carrying out local elections – thought to be an important complement to the national elections – are unlikely (the bulletin suggests) to occur for some time to come.

64 Douglas Patrick Mason, "Mozambique's Democracy One Year On: What Next?" (unpublished manuscript), 1. As Mason continues: "Locked in by the new regional geo-political realities and a donor determined policy environment anchored on multi-party democracy and structural adjustment, little substantive ideological or other differences separate the parties other than history and mutual loathing."

65 See the cover story – entitled, quite specifically, "Winner Takes All" – in *Mozambique Peace Process Bulletin*, no. 14 (Feb. 1995), 1–4, and also Joseph Hanlon, "A Democratic One-Party State," *African Agenda*, 1 no. 4

(1995). Fears persist in some quarters that any Mozambican version of the de facto one-party state might prove so provocative as merely to reactivate civil strife – although those who fear this also suggest that Frelimo is relying on the assumption, not altogether inaccurate, that Renamo's military capacity has tended to melt away.

66 See, in this regard, the article by Ken Wilson entitled "More on Mozambique Now" in *SAR*, 11 no. 1 (Oct. 1995), 30–32; this point is discussed further in my chapter, " 'For fear of being condemned as old fashioned,' " where I have also sought to elaborate, more fully, on the distinction between "liberal democracy" and "popular democracy."

67 Leys, "Confronting the African Tragedy," 46.

# PART THREE
## *Protracted Civil Wars*

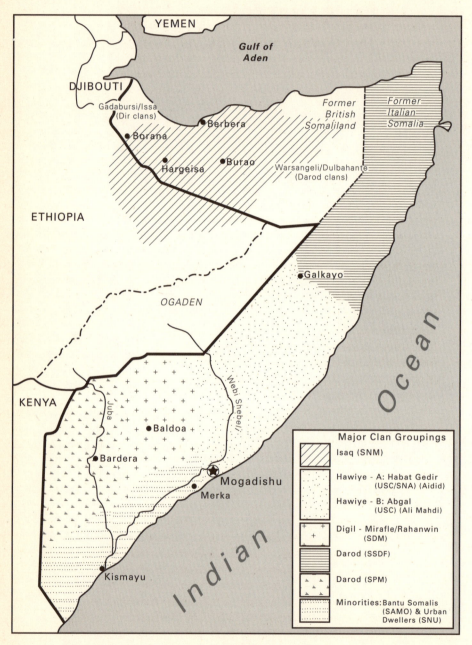

YEMEN

*Gulf of Aden*

DJIBOUTI

Gadabursi/Issa
(Dir clans)

● Berbera

● Borana

● Hargeisa

● Burao

*Former British Somaliland*

*Former Italian Somalia*

Warsangeli/Dulbahante
(Darod clans)

ETHIOPIA

● Galkayo

*OGADEN*

Webi Shebeli

KENYA

Juba

● Baldoa

● Bardera

Merka

★ Mogadishu

*Indian*

Kismayu

*Ocean*

### Major Clan Groupings

Isaq (SNM)

Hawiye – A: Habat Gedir
(USC/SNA) (Aidid)

Hawiye – B: Abgal
(USC) (Ali Mahdi)

Digil – Mirafle/Rahanwin
(SDM)

Darod (SSDF)

Darod (SPM)

Minorities:Bantu Somalis
(SAMO) & Urban
Dwellers (SNU)

Somalia

# 6 Somali Civil Wars

HUSSEIN M. ADAM

In January 1991, Somalia experienced a cataclysmic event, virtually unheard of since the Second World War. For most of Asia, Latin America, and Africa in particular, this period was one of nation- and state-building. By contrast, Somalia witnessed complete state collapse. It saw not simply a military coup, a revolutionary replacement of a decayed and ineffective dictatorship, or a new, radical regime coming to power through a partisan uprising. Somalia's collapsed state represented the literal implosion of state structures and of residual forms of authority and legitimacy.[1] Liberia experienced partial state collapse, and in Rwanda, the rebellious Tutsis represented by the Rwanda Patriotic Front set up some sort of regime in place of the decayed, genocidal Hutu dictatorship. In the former Yugoslavia, a relatively "hard" state – Serbia – preys on neighbouring "soft" states such as Bosnia, Croatia, and Slovenia.

Not many years ago, the Horn of Africa was considered to have a high risk of interstate war, notably between Somalia and Ethiopia.[2] During recent years, an explosion of intra-state wars has led to a radical ethnic restructuring of the Ethiopian state and the total collapse of the Somali state. Somalia has experienced civil strife before – in limited clan wars described in Somali poetry, in the inter-state and intra-state wars of the sixteenth century briefly discussed below, and in the Islamic anti-colonial *jihad* led by Sayyid Muhamed Abdallah Hassan, 1899–1920.[3] Sayyid's Dervish movement began as a pan-clan crusade against British, Italian, and Ethiopian forces, but it soon degenerated into intra-clan warfare as well as intra-elite theological differences. The resulting man-made famine exacerbated environmental problems and weakened Somali societies, especially in the northwest and northeast. Unlike the American Civil War, fought by two relatively conventional armies, the current Somali civil violence has taken the form of a series of civil wars, beginning around 1980 in armed opposition to the clan-based military dictatorship under Major-General Mohamed Siyad Barre. The state collapsed as the decentralized, clan-based opposition groups failed to form governing coalitions. Since conflict among the victors of 1991 unleashed a series of civil wars, "Somali civil wars" is a more appropriate description of the current catastrophe. What has distinguished them from earlier ones has been the abundance of destructive modern armaments. "Weapons were sometimes cheaper than ammunition."[4]

The Somali population of eight to ten million is made up of six major clan-families (Darod, Dir, Hawiye, Isaq, Digil, and Mirifle), each subdivided into six or more clans, and each clan, into subclans and sub-subclans, all the way down to lineages and extended families. Given concentric and interconnected circles, with kaleidoscopic and diffuse attachments, the most stable subunit is the lineage, consisting of close kin who together pay and receive blood compensation in cases involving homicide. In general, the Somali people share a common language (Somali), religion (Islam), physical characteristics, and pastoral and agropastoral customs and traditions.[5] There is, however, a difference between the Somali dialect spoken by the Digil/Mirifle agropastoralists and the other four, predominantly pastoral clan-families.

Clanism is the Somali version of ethnicity or tribalism: it represents primordial cleavages and cultural fragmentation within Somali society. After the Second World War, clanism among Somalis favoured nationalism and a Greater Somalia. At times, however, it has assumed a negative aspect – the abandonment of objectivity when clan and local/parochial interests have prevailed. Clan consciousness is partly a product of elite manipulation – the cooptation and corruption of politicians claiming clan leadership[6] – but at times it is the elite itself, that is manipulated by politicized clanism.

Aspects of clan consciousness, transcending false consciousness, reflect a plea for social justice and against exploitative relations among ethnic groups. Uneven class formation has led certain groups to use clan formations as embryonic trade unions. In such cases, affirmative action–type policies are the best way to overcome discrimination against clans and groups. Clan consciousness tends to rise during periods of extreme scarcities – drought, famine, wars. Clan conflicts are also instigated by memories of past wars for resources or for prestige. However, such disputes take place only between neighbouring clans, and intricate mechanisms have evolved for conflict resolution, because clan territory is often extensive and sometimes even non-contiguous. By far the greatest damage brought about by clan conflicts spread over large geographical areas has resulted from cynical elite manipulation of clan consciousness.

The thesis of this chapter is that deep historical, structural factors – a mismatch between the state and the relatively non-hierarchical Somali civil society – are the underlying cause of the Somali catastrophe. While rooted in historical, socio-economic structures of society, including such factors as ethnic/clan cleavages, the Somali civil wars were the immediate result of the Siyad military regime's style of governance. Its cynical manipulation of these cleavages led bad governance to overwhelm historical, structural factors.

ROOT CAUSES: DOMESTIC FACTORS

For purposes of this study, "civil war" means "large-scale violence among geographically contiguous people concerned about possibly having to live with one another in the same political unit after the fight."[7] It has ended when "the level of violence had dropped below the Small-Singer threshold of 1,000 battle deaths per year for at least five years."[8]

As in most of Africa,[9] the tangible cause of Somalia's civil wars derives from a militarist state and its brutal repression of a vibrant social reality. In a deeper, historical sense, the state's collapse represents a classic mismatch between the post-colonial state and the nature and structure of civil society. In the real world, the conceptual separation between the state and civil society is blurred, though I keep it in this context for purposes of analysis. Imperialism began the commercialization of Somali pastoralism, its subordination to centralized states, and its integration into the global economy.[10] The post-independence parliamentary regime (1960–69) favoured the emerging commercial and bureaucratic petty bourgeoisie as it facilitated political marginalization of the pastoralists and cultivators; it did not go so far as to prevent the clan base from creating contact points between modernism and traditionalism.

The Cold War sustained Siyad's military regime, which kidnapped the emerging state in 1969 and moved on to centralize power, as well as the means of coercion. Siyad used a narrow clan base while condemning and denying political space for other clan bases. In due course, decentralized, clan-based, armed opposition groups rose up to challenge his military dictatorship. The end of the Cold War reduced, even severely limited in some cases, the opportunities for states "suspended" over their civil societies from extracting adequate military, technical, and financial resources from external sources. Somalia became the perfect illustration of this basic contradiction and its collapse, precisely because the Cold War had imposed an exceedingly heavy military regime on a decentralized, relatively democratic civil society, surviving on meagre resources.

Unlike the rest of Africa during the 1960s, Somalia seemed to be a "nation" in search of a "state."[11] Colonial partitions had dismembered the Somali-speaking people into British, Italian, and French (Djibouti) Somalilands; a portion of the Somali population fell under Emperor Menelik's Ethiopia (in the past, the Ogaden, and today, Ethiopia's Region 5) and another, within British-ruled Kenya (the Northern Frontier District or (NFD). British Somaliland obtained independence on 26 June 1960 and voluntarily joined Italian Somaliland to form the Somali Republic on 1 July 1960. The young and fragile republic set out to unite with the three remaining Somali territories.[12]

Even though the potential for irredentism in Africa is relatively high,[13] independent Somalia turned out to be the only consistently irredentist state. In 1963, it encouraged and supported an uprising in Kenya's NFD. In 1964, the Ethiopian army attacked several Somali border posts to dissuade Somalia from supporting a guerrilla uprising within the Ogaden. The relatively pro-Western Somali parliamentary regime turned to the USSR to increase its army from 3,000 to 10,000. On 21 October 1969, Somali military commander Mohamed Siyad Barre overthrew the "artificial democracy" (multi-party parliamentary regime) and instituted a military and personal dictatorship with Soviet support. He increased the army to 37,000 and sought in 1977 to reclaim the Ogaden in a major war with Ethiopia. Ironically, what began as the search to establish a state corresponding with the greater Somali nation ended up with the total collapse and fragmentation of the existing Somali state in January 1991.

Beyond noting the mismatch between the state and civil society, we need to analyse Siyad's military regime, its repressive mechanisms, and its errors of policy and conduct. By re-emphasizing the primacy of political factors over purely historical/structural ones, I am defending the possibility that Somalis can (partly) determine their future beyond the civil wars through careful political choices. Siyad's socialistic measures, including radical nationalizations, were a disincentive for rural producers, especially farmers. Somalia came to produce less and less of its basic food needs and to rely increasingly on imported foods. Constrained domestic economic opportunities intensified the sense of grievance among social groups, especially those suffering clan/regional discrimination.

Like many other African leaders, Siyad installed personal rule.[14] Over time, he was able to manipulate and modify his leadership style, from being a prophetic ruler advocating "scientific socialism" (1970–77), to an autocrat (1978–86), and finally a tyrant (1987–91). During his earlier years, he used mediatory mechanisms that postponed final confrontations, but his prolonged dictatorial rule damaged and distorted state–civil society relations. Later, as an outright tyrant, he applied absolute principles of governance, irrespective of human cost.

Siyad's dictatorial rule did not function in an institutional vacuum. The Somali military structure was considered one of the best in sub-Saharan Africa,[15] and Siyad also understood the importance of controlling other state sectors and civil society through institutions and organizations such as the military, security, paramilitary, an elitist vanguard political party, and so-called mass organizations. As a personal ruler, he had the autonomy to operate above institutions. Ultimately, however, arbitrary personal rule destroys supportive military and related institutions.

*Nomenklatura* involves appointing loyal political agents to guide and control civil and military institutions. The introduction of *nomenklatura* to Somalia by the Soviets involved politicization of institutions that were beginning to function well, relying on education and training, technical competence, specialization, and experience. As early as 1972, the military regime began to appoint political commissars for the armed forces, administrative institutions, social organizations of workers, youth, and women, and cooperatives.

Siyad soon substituted clanism for ideology as criteria for such appointments. Foreign aid provided the glue that held the system together in spite of internal waste and corruption ("selective misallocation"). "Clan-klatura" involved placing trusted clansmen and other loyalists in positions of power, wealth, and control/espionage. It also involved creating "clan-klatura" organizations. One such body, Hangash, conducted military intelligence; the Dabarjebinta, literally, the backbone breakers, were military counterintelligence; then there were the military police, identified by their red berets. The majority of these forces were drawn from the president's clan, the Marehan of the Darod clan-family. In such a situation of divide and rule, state institutions were thrown into gridlock, jealousy, confusion, and anarchy.

From its inception, the regime rested on three clans from the Darod clan-family. Lewis describes how this background was "reflected in the clandestine code name 'M.O.D.' given to the regime."[16] "M (Marehan) stood for the patrilineage of the President, O (Ogaden) for that of his mother, and D (Dulbahante) for that of his principal son-in-law, head of the National Security Service. ... [Though] no one could utter the secret symbol of General Siyad's power openly, the M.O.D. basis of his rule was public knowledge and discussed and criticized in private."[17]

After he dropped "scientific socialism" as his guiding ideology, Siyad did not resort to Islam, as did Numeiri in Sudan. Atavistically, he resorted to clanism. Hardly any members of his clan gained strong bourgeois roots during his long rule – not educational qualifications, economic know-how, or professional competence. Promising clan members were plucked out of educational institutions to fill "clan-klatura" posts. Siyad systematically sought to destroy the bourgeois elements of other clans – sending people to jail or to exile abroad. The damage done to the Somali elite class partly explains both the eventual state collapse and the delay in its renewal.

The "clan-klatura" havoc within state institutions was exported into rural civil societies. After the Ogaden War (1977–78), Siyad practised brutal divide and rule, encouraging clan warfare. At first he used his army to conduct punitive raids, similar to those under early colonial rule. Later his troops armed so-called loyal clans and encouraged them to wage wars against "rebel" clans. The damage caused by negative and destructive elite manipulation of clan consciousness contributed to the inability of civil society to rebound when Siyad fell from power. It will take years to heal these societal wounds.

Young people began to disappear during the early 1980s from regional cities such as Hargeisa in the north, considered rebel territory. This phenomenon, reminiscent of Argentina, continued in other towns, then spread to the capital city, Mogadishu. During 1989 and 1990, Siyad's "clan-klatura" forces massacred hundreds of religious protestors. In July 1989, Siyad's terror squads randomly rounded up and slaughtered on the isolated Jezira Beach (near Mogadishu) a group of forty-seven young northern (Isaq clan-family) youths. Once the armed opposition to the regime grew, Siyad singled out the northern region, inhabited by the Isaq clan-family, for extraordinary, some say neofascist punishment. Perhaps he hoped to unite the south by punishing the north and the Isaq-based Somali National Movement. Previously the conflict between the north and the south generated low-intensity demands for distributional benefits from within a unified political system; however, vindictive warfare led to the current high intensity demand for separate statehood and independence for Somaliland once Siyad's state collapsed. A similar vendetta awaited Hawiye clans, raising a 1989 rebellion across the country. Siyad's vindictive state terror laid the basis for civil wars of revenge that postponed civil society's ability to create a successor state.

Siyad's clan persecutions obliged the opposition to use its own clans as organizational bases for armed resistance. The first clan-based armed opposition group seems to have stumbled into existence. After failing in an anti-Siyad coup attempt in 1978, Colonel Abdullahi Yusuf fled to Ethiopia, where he established the Somali Salvation Democratic Front (SSDF). The front attracted support mostly from his subclan of the Majerteen clan (another part of the Darod clan-family that spawned Siyad). The SSDF, following a burst of cross-border activities, atrophied as a result of heavy reliance on foreign funding from Libya, Abdullahi Yusuf's dictatorial leadership, and Siyad's ability to appease many of the Majerteens as fellow cousins within the Darod clan-family. Eventually, with funds and clan appeals, he was able to entice the bulk of SSDF fighters to return from Ethiopia and participate in his genocidal wars against the Isaq in the north and later against the Hawiye in the south, including Mogadishu. More recently (following Siyad's fall) the SSDF has claimed control of the Bari, Nugal, and parts of Mudug (northeast) regions, under the combined leadership of Mohamed Abshir and Abdullahi Yusuf.

The major opposition clan grouping was the Somali National Movement (SNM), which derived its main support from the Isaq clan-family of the north. The SNM was established in London early in 1981 but soon decided to move its operations to Ethiopia's Somali towns and villages close to the border with former British Somaliland. Because Qadhafi disliked SNM leaders and would not finance their movement, they were obliged to raise funds among the Somali Isaq communities in Saudi Arabia and the Gulf, in other Arab states, in East Africa, and in Western countries. This decentralized method of fund-raising gave the movement relative independence: it also enhanced accountability to its numerous supporters. The SNM evolved democratic procedures. Between 1981 and 1991 it held about six congresses, during which it periodically elected leaders and established policies. In 1988, the SNM conducted several raids and a major military operation in northern Somalia, following a peace accord between Ethiopia and Somalia that removed Ethiopian restraints on SNM operations. The SNM was able to bottle up Siyad's huge army, barricaded in towns and bases, for the next two years. The SNM played an indirect role in the formation of the United Somali Congress (USC), an armed movement based on the Hawiye clan-family that inhabits the central regions of the country, including Mogadishu. It also facilitated formation of the Somali Patriotic

Movement (SPM) by Colonel Omar Jess and other disgruntled Oga-
deni officers from Siyad's army.

The proliferation of proto-political groups or factions (see Table
6.1) is related to the expansion and duration of Somali civil wars. The
term "faction" may be useful when discussing the political groupings,
leaving "clan" for a specific "ethnic" or "kinship" community. Some of
the newer groups – the SDM, SNU and SAMO – represent Rahanwin,
Benadir, and Bantu farmers, respectively, who have suffered dispro-
portionately because of the civil wars. Somalia's shape and size – as
big as Texas – ensured the existence of remote regions, strengthening armed resistance forces and worsening the problems of the
regime in spite of its huge army. The armed opposition did not
emerge for over a decade, as most Somalis hoped that the regime
would allow room for peaceful protest. But once the government
decided to respond through the use of military force, the factions
were easily able to gain access to arms. The availability of arms
enabled repressed groups demanding participation in the state to
resort to war. To combat clan-based armed opposition groups, the
regime created loyal clan militias, thereby heightening the carnage
and disseminating modern armaments and the culture of violence.[18]
The total collapse in 1991 of the over 300,000–strong Ethiopian
army flooded the local markets with huge amounts of modern
armaments and ammunition.

### CONTRIBUTING CAUSES: INTERNATIONAL FACTORS

Military, technical, and financial foreign assistance played a key role
in prolonging Siyad's regime. Somalia's position on the Red Sea and
the Indian Ocean has long attracted foreign interests. Early in Siyad's
rule, the USSR provided substantial military and economic assistance,
including fuel and financing for project local costs that helped
cushion the Somali economy against international economic conditions. After 1977, the United States replaced the Soviets in providing
armaments – unlike the Russians, sending mostly defensive arms –
and, during the 1980s, about $100 million of economic aid per
year.[19] China invested in a series of remarkable projects, including
the north–south tarmac road, a cigarette and match factory, a sports
and theatre complex, and rice and tobacco farms. It also provided
light arms and spare parts.

The military dictatorship also benefited from significant financial
assistance from the United Nations system and the World Bank. Siyad
manoeuvred Somalia into the Arab League in 1974, and the regime

Table 6.1
Groups or factions in Somalia

---

1 Somali National Movement (SNM): Isaq, Republic of Somaliland
2 Somali Salvation Democratic Front (SSDF): Majerteen, Darod
3 United Somali Congress (USC-SNA): Aidid, Habar Gedir, and other Hawiye clans
4 United Somali Congress (USC): Ali Mahdi, Abgal, and other Hawiye clans
5 Somali Patriotic Movement (SPM-SNA): Omar Jess, Ogaden, Darod
6 Somali Patriotic Movement (SPM): General Gabiyo, Ogaden and other Darod
    clans; recently however, the two have reunited as an Ogaden grouping under Jess
7 Somali Democratic Movement (SDM): Digil-Mirifle/Rahanwin
8 Southern Somali National Movement (SSNM-SNA): Dir clans, previously aligned to
    the northern SNM
9 United Somali Front (USF): Issa clan
10 United Somali Party (USP): Dulbahante and Warsangeli, Darod clans
11 Somali Democratic Alliance (SDA): Gadabursi clan
12 Somali National Democratic Union (SNDU): other Darod clans
13 Somali National Front (SNF): former President Siyad's Marehan organization,
    Darod
14 Somali National Union (SNU): based on the ancient Benadir urban dwellers
    outside the clan system
15 Somali African Muki Organization (SAMO): based on the so-called Bantu Somali
    sedentary farmers

---

received generous Arab petrodollar assistance. There was, for example, "an alleged unofficial transfer of substantial sums of money from Saudi Arabia to the Somali government in mid-1990 to ensure that [Siyad] Barre did not side with Iraq."[20] As long as resources did not dry up, Siyad was able to hold on to power. But U.S. congressional criticism of Siyad's human rights record, made dramatic and visible by the war in the north, led to the suspension of American military aid in 1988. In 1989 U.S. economic aid, too, was blocked, and other states and international organizations began to follow suit. The regime collapsed in January 1991.

In the world after the Cold War, internal protests and pressures from external donors can facilitate non-violent transitions in regimes, without engendering state collapse. An abrupt stoppage of all aid to Somalia after the regime collapsed followed a history of too much aid. Modest assistance might have facilitated the formation of a flexible interim administration. In Somalia, international intervention missed the window of opportunity framed by the rising rebellion in the north in the 1980s, the outbreak of urban opposition in 1988–89, and immediate post-Siyad clan warfare in 1991.[21]

International actors helped to worsen state–society relationships in Somalia; their military, technical, and economic aid encouraged the dictatorship to believe that, because of foreign backing, it was capable of imposing its will on society. In spite of losing Soviet military and economic aid in 1977, Somalia continued to receive military aid from the United States, Libya, France, Egypt, Italy, and China.[22] The regime had reason to believe that, with such foreign backing, it could proceed against the opposition with impunity. As in all of Africa's wars, foreign involvement unquestionably raised the level and scope of violence. The armed resistance found shelter in the vast Somali-speaking population of Ethiopia. Ethiopian President Mengistu was only too happy to receive it and provide it with initial armaments and broadcast facilities. He saw this as an opportunity to take revenge against Siyad's irredentist incursion into the Ogaden in 1977. Libya assisted the ssDF with arms and finances but later switched to the side of the dying Siyad regime. Facilitated by the disintegration of Somalia and by Ethiopia's backing, the armed opposition groups managed in time to obtain automatic weapons, ample supplies of ammunition, and anti-tank as well as anti-aircraft weapons from local markets.

COSTS OF SOMALI CIVIL WARS

In 1977, the ruling cliques in Somalia and Ethiopia plunged their impoverished countries into "the most ferocious [conflict] in Africa since World War II."[23] The Siyad regime failed to recognize both American reluctance and Soviet-Cuban readiness to get fully involved in the conflict. This misunderstanding led Siyad to terminate the Treaty of Friendship of 1974 with the Soviet Union and to break diplomatic relations with Cuba. Soon after the Ogaden débâcle, Somalia witnessed the commencement of a series of civil wars. During the Somali–Ethiopian War, Somalia is estimated to have sustained a death toll of 25,000 and, following the war, to have received a crushing burden of 700,000 Ethiopian Somali and Oromo refugees.[24] A coup attempt by officers of a Majerteen (Darod) subclan was foiled on 9 April 1978.

In 1979–80, the ssDF made modest guerrilla forays into Somalia. Siyad retaliated by imprisoning some Majerteen military and civilian leaders and dismissing many others from their jobs. He declared open war on the Majerteen subclan of Abdullahi Yusuf; his army looted its camels, destroyed its *berkeds* (water reservoirs), and confiscated its ordinary arms. In 1981, some members of the Isaq clan-family formed the Somali National Movement (snm) and began similar guerrilla forays into northern Somalia. In 1986 Mengistu and Siyad met in Djibouti and began to work out a deal to rein in armed opposition movements directed against each other's territories. Nevertheless, Mengistu looked the other way as the snm launched a massive attack on government forces in Burao on 27 May 1988 and in Hargeisa on 31 May 1988. Frustrated by efforts to defeat the SNM in direct combat, Siyad's army turned its fire-power, including its air force and artillery, against the civilian population, causing predictably high casualties. Even in those towns spared of SNM attacks, the army engaged in looting on a massive scale; women were raped as hundreds of people were shot and their homes and businesses ransacked. Africa Watch estimates "the number of people killed by government forces in the vicinity of 50,000–60,000. The war has caused over 400,000 refugees to flee, principally to Ethiopia. Another 40,000 refugees are in Djibouti, and tens of thousands have gone to stay with relatives in Mogadishu, the capital, or escaped to the United Kingdom, Holland and Canada. In addition, close to 400,000 people ... are displaced within the Somali countryside, living without any international assistance."[25]

The policy of blanket punishment of innocent "potential" opposition supporters and bystanders continued during the next four years. These measures laid the basis for clan revenge practices as the raw armed youth – the so-called *moryaan* – entered Mogadishu and other towns as the new victors of the anti-Siyad resistance movements. This attack on innocent civilians was but one aspect of the overall policy of poisoning clan relations. In the north, for example, following the 1988 crisis, the regime intensified its policy of recruiting and forcibly conscripting refugees from the Ogaden (Somalis and Oromos). It also financed and armed paramilitary groups among the refugees, using these as a fighting force against the Isaq. Prior to the fall of Mogadishu, Siyad ordered loyal Darod officers to persecute and even massacre Hawiye "sympathizers" of the opposition movement, the USC. In a primordial society, the anticipated reaction followed, as most of the Darod communities had to flee Mogadishu following Siyad's overthrow by the Hawiye-based USC.

As stated above, clan political identities in Somali society are in a state of constant flux. As soon as Mogadishu was "liberated," personal political ambition and personal differences between USC leaders Ali Mahdi (Abgal clan of the Hawiye) and General Mohamed Farah Aidid (Habar Gedir clan) began to surface. It is alleged that the Italian ambassador, Mario Sico (considered highly pro-Siyad), encouraged businessman Ali Mahdi to declare himself "interim president," as Aidid was busy pushing Siyad's remaining forces south of Mogadishu.[26] Aidid's faction of the USC rejected Mahdi's claim, as did the SNM, the SSDF, and other opposition groups. In June, a USC congress elected Aidid chairman in an attempt to get him to accept Mahdi's self-declared position as long as the interim president consulted with the USC's chairman in all major policy decisions and appointments.

This attempt at reconciliation did not receive solid international backing (the UN and diplomatic missions had all left Mogadishu by early 1991), and it failed. Intra-clan fighting resumed in Mogadishu, between Habar Gedir and Abgal forces from 17 November 1991 through March 1992, when the UN managed to broker a cease-fire. Estimates of the number of deaths through March 1992 ranged as high as 30,000, while 500,000 people were estimated as displaced and/or without basic services.[27] Somalia came to resemble Chad, where erstwhile allies were later transformed into violent rivals. This intra-USC conflict reduced Mogadishu to another Beirut, complete with a dangerous "green line."

The SNM supported northern Somalia's decision of May 1991 to establish its region as Somaliland, which added yet another complicated layer to the costs of Somali civil wars. Unfair measures experienced by the north since the 1960 unification, coupled with the savage punishment meted the north by Siyad's formidable military machine, led to the relatively popular decision to dissolve the union of 1960 and declare a Somaliland Republic in May 1991. Ali Mahdi's "grab for power" was seen as the most recent example of "southern arrogance."

Perhaps the most complicated and tragic aspect of Somali civil wars occurred in the southern, more fertile parts of the country. Siyad Barre, unlike Mengistu, did not leave Somalia following his retreat from Mogadishu. He barricaded himself in his clan homeland, on the Somali-Ethiopian frontier, southwest of Mogadishu. From this base, he waged a Renamo-type spoiler war in surrounding areas and launched at least two serious military campaigns to recapture Mogadishu. He failed, the second time in May 1992 disastrously, and had to flee into Kenya with Aidid's forces in hot pursuit. He went into political asylum in Nigeria, where he died on 2 January 1995.

Andrew Natsios sums up the impact of Somalia's civil wars on both farming/livestock activities and access for relief efforts: "Hardest hit by these two deadly circumstances was the area between the Juba River and the Shebeli River further north. This interriverine area contains the country's richest agriculture land and serves as its breadbasket. The area is inhabited by the Bantu and Benadir people who are outside the clan structure and by the Rahanwin clan; ... Rahanwin and Bantu farmers were caught in the clan feud between Darod and Hawiye ... Barre's retreating troops targeted the Rahanwin for massacre. These warring clans took, then lost, and took again this farming area from each other: each time the area changed hands the supplies of food dwindled."[28]

As of June 1995, the UN estimated that some 4.5 million people (in a country of about 8–10 million) were in urgent need of food.[29] By 1992, it was believed that about 400,000 people had died of famine or disease or been killed in the war.[30] Today, that number is steadily climbing towards one million. Relief organizations estimated that by early 1993 one-half of all Somali children under five had died.[31] In the 1991–92 civil war–induced famine, most fatalities resulted from malnutrition-related diseases. "Of the estimated seventy hospitals in Somalia in 1988, only fifteen remain partially operational today, and are totally dependent on external assistance."[32] A study by the U.S. Centers for Disease Control showed that in the city of Baidoa, the centre of Rahanwin communities, at least 40 per cent of the population had died between August and November 1992.[33]

Thus an anatomy of Somali civil wars reveals multiple problems that appear as a single problem in other countries. Since 1984, indiscriminate use of land-mines became a central feature of the army's counterinsurgency policy against the SNM. Somaliland is reported to have inherited at least a million mines, which have maimed and handicapped thousands, especially women and children.[34] It was also estimated that over fifty thousand modern weapons had been abandoned by the army as the civil war reached its peak in January 1991. Militias of stronger, better armed clans and subclans – and opportunistic criminal bands – preyed on weaker groups, causing large-scale transfers of assets as well as protracted insecurity, during which consecutive planting seasons were missed. Food became an instrument of war as thousands perished because of anarchy and the corresponding inability to contain epidemics. War is highly destructive of wildlife, and Siyad made matters worse by financing ivory-smuggling bandits who roamed as far as Kenya to raise funds to fuel his wars. Complete herds were eliminated with machine-guns and even anti-aircraft guns mounted on vehicles. Desperate escapes, especially by the unarmed farming and ancient coastal-city minorities (both outside the Somali clan structure), gave Somalia its own boat people. During 1991–92, frantic refugees in overcrowded, rickety boats sought asylum in Yemen or Kenya, and dozens perished in the sea.

AFTER SIYAD: PROBLEMS AND PROSPECTS

The long-term costs of Somali civil wars and delays in the restoration of the Somali cultures and societies are largely unresearched, but of great significance. In education, for example, Somalia is already losing generations. The visible collapse of the state has lasted half a decade: Somalia has no internationally recognized polity; no national administration exercising real authority; no formal legal system; no banking and insurance services; no telephone and postal system; no public service; no educational and reliable health system; no police and public security services; no electricity or piped water systems; and weak officials serving on a voluntary basis, surrounded by disruptive, violent bands of armed youths. Unlike in Liberia, where the capital at no point fell into rebel hands, chaos and anarchy engulfed Mogadishu. In most of Africa, countries with weak but nominal authorities in the capital city endured civil wars that caused state retraction, but not total collapse. Most states have begun to refuse Somali passports as valid documents. Thus Somalis today, as Eritreans yesterday (who used Somali passports), have to rely on Ethiopian, Kenyan, Yemeni, or Eritrean passports in order to travel abroad!

Writings on the Somali crisis have focused exclusively on the negative aspects of state collapse and militarism. There are, however, certain redeeming features, which, if handled creatively, would facilitate emergence in Somalia of a restored state (or states) that is (are) more indigenous and sustainable than the colonial and Cold War states of the past. There is growing strength in Somali civil society, essentially because the state has collapsed. In the north, and in areas of the country that did not require intervention of foreign troops, the role of "traditional elders" (both secular and religious) has been both visible and positive. Women leaders have also been active, and women and children constituted a majority in demonstrations for disarmament and peace. Throughout the crisis, professionals, especially doctors and nurses who stayed in the country, have served as positive role models. Teachers have begun to revive rudimentary forms of schooling in urban areas.

As an aspect of civil society's strength, the private sector has become revitalized. Gone were the so-called socialistic restrictions imposed by the dictatorship. The thriving, small-scale private sector (in both the north and Mogadishu) has moved far ahead of embryonic regulatory authorities. In most parts of Africa, the state pulls or constrains civil society; in Somalia the embryonic state is challenged to keep up with a dynamic, small private sector. In 1988 there were eighteen Somali voluntary development organizations (VDOs); now the number has grown, and these bodies need help from international VDOs to enhance the non-profit private sector.

There is a palpable spirit of anti-centralism, an atmosphere favouring local autonomy, regionalism, and federalism – and in the north, self-determination and secession. As a corollary, there is a preference for locally controlled police forces rather than a large, standing central army. In Somaliland, and to some extent north-eastern Somalia, there are embryonic manifestations of consociation-al democratic mechanisms, involving consensus, proportionality, and avoidance of winner-take-all confrontations. Somali irredentism has collapsed with Siyad, and in its place one finds broad cooperation and relative harmony between Somalia and Ethiopia. There is also a vibrant, emerging free press – about six papers in Hargeisa and more than sixteen in Mogadishu. Printed in Somali, they are produced by computers and mimeograph machines. Somali minorities, farmers, and Benadir communities have become more self-conscious and willing to stand up for their rights as a result of bitter struggles. They have formed their own political organizations and militia for self-protection, as indicated above.

Perhaps it is still too early to offer a meaningful analysis of the resolution of Somali's civil war. Employing Zartman's analysis, one might conclude that the conditions for "ripeness" and the readiness for conflict resolution have not yet emerged.[35] Based on other cases of civil war, resolutions to the conflicts can emerge under a re-markable variety of conditions.[36] In the following section we examine three attempts at resolution in Somalia since 1991: foreign inter-vention, strongman's hegemony, and consociational, democratic mechanisms.

With the departure of UNOSOM II troops in March 1995, it has become even more obvious that Somali civil conflicts will have to be resolved internally by the parties themselves rather than through external intervention. At present, clan divisions and crude military balances seem to rule out resolution through conquest by a single armed strongman. However, if negotiated settlements continue to fail, the outcome, at least for a while longer, may be protracted, low-intensity conflicts, rather than resolution.

### THE MIRAGE OF FOREIGN INTERVENTION

In 1992 and 1993, many people thought and hoped that massive foreign intervention would resolve Somalia's civil wars and help Somalis restore some semblance of state authority. In 1992, famine-related deaths in Baidoa (Bay region), peaked at 3,000 a week and declined to 1,700 and later to 500 or fewer when outgoing U.S. President George Bush ordered 36,000 troops, including 27,000 U.S. troops, to intervene under UN mandate as Operation Restore Hope (ORH) in December 1992.[37] Deaths reported by mid-1992 by the media and relief organizations galvanized public opinion around the world, causing Bush and the UN Security Council to act. By the summer of 1992, food prices had risen 800–1,200 per cent and relief food could not be adequately delivered on account of looting and banditry.[38] ORH had a narrowly defined mission: to establish a secure environment in the so-called triangle of death (Mogadishu–Baidoa–Kismayu), which covers about 30 per cent of Somalia. The U.S. mission on behalf of the UN cost $2 billion by the time it ended in May 1993; it was followed by direct UN intervention (UNOSOM) from June 1993 till March 1995, at a cost of $4 billion.

What did the United States and UNOSOM achieve at such staggering financial costs? In the short run, perhaps one million people were saved from starvation. Thousands have resumed economic productivity, and Somalia has experienced bumper crops and lower food prices. In 1992, in contrast, "Somalia became the ICRC's largest relief effort since World War II, dwarfing all other NGO efforts combined in Somalia, consuming nearly fifty percent of the ICRC worldwide budget."[39] To deliver food, the International Committee of the Red Cross (ICRC) reportedly hired over 20,000 Somali armed guards before ORH began. "While 465,000 Somali refugees remain in neighboring countries and another 300,000 remain internally displaced, this is down from the nearly two million people who were driven from their homes at the height of the crisis. Morbidity and mortality rates have returned to normal levels."[40] The reality is that the numbers of starving people and of deaths as a result of war have decreased dramatically following the U.S. and UN intervention, and besides relief being received, some progress has been made towards restoring local and regional administration.

However, a more compelling reality remains: despite tremendous cost in funds (and to some extent in lives), ORH and UNOSOM have failed to reduce the level of armaments, to end the civil wars, to promote reconciliation, and facilitate restoration of a reconstructed Somali state (or states). In my view, part of the failure of foreign intervention transcends ORH and UNOSOM; it is failure in preventive diplomacy. The other cause is arrogance resulting from a residual Cold War, conventional-war mentality; lack of impartiality; and the lack of consistent, experienced diplomacy, equipped with local political, social, and cultural knowledge.

Former Algerian ambassador and OAU official Mohamed Sahnoun was appointed by UN Secretary-General Boutros Boutros-Ghali in April 1992 as head of UNOSOM I. Sahnoun argued that foreign intervention could have been more effective in preventing/resolving Somali civil wars in 1988, when the civil war violently erupted in northern Somalia; in 1990, when prominent civilians, risking jail terms, issued a democratic "Manifesto" against the Siyad regime; or in

1991, when the government in Djibouti called a peace conference following the fall of the Siyad regime.[41] ORH lasted from December 1992 till May 1993. Under the acronym UNOSOM II, the UN took charge of Somalia and very soon fell into a destructive war with General Mohamed Farah Aidid and his allies.[42] Aidid's militia was alleged to have killed twenty-four Pakistani UN troops on 5 June 1993, and Admiral Howe, head of UNOSOM, backed by Boutros-Ghali, declared war on Aidid and his supporters, as they sought to arrest him. From June to October 1993, this UN-sponsored and U.S.-backed manhunt put a hold on most of UNOSOM's work at reconciliation and reconstruction. In October, American helicopters were shot down, and, in one street fight alone, eighteen American soldiers were killed, one was captured, and over seventy-five were wounded. This event prompted U.S. President Bill Clinton to shift American policy back to diplomacy and politics, as he ordered an end to the manhunt. These events also caused the United States to ask the UN to reverse policies.[43] Among other things, these destructive engagements postponed the critical task of demobilizing Somalia's clan militias and promoting the political process. This conflict did show, however, that even when formal state sovereignty is lacking, civil society, or its parts, can exercise sovereignty. Following this conflict, the clamour for an "international trusteeship" to run Somalia evaporated.

The issue of disarmament also shows that UNOSOM lacked insight into the general situation. To have succeeded, ORH/UNOSOM disarmament strategy would have needed a demobilization program to provide job-training for the youthful militias; a serious program to train and equip local police forces; a program to equip and restore the legal justice system. On its own initiative, the northern Somaliland Republic has carried out demobilization programs, while UNOSOM failed to promote demobilization during its mandate in southern Somalia. U.S. forces in Somalia, unlike those in Haiti more recently, failed to include a civil affairs program to ensure the success of its military-oriented program. In addition to troops dealing with civil affairs, more than eight hundred police advisers were sent to Haiti.[44]

As early as January 1993, UNOSOM wanted to push Somali elites to set up a juridical Somali state, oblivious of the fact that such pressures contributed to the prolongation of the civil wars. The Addis Ababa Conference of 15–27 March 1993 resisted pressure to form a centralized state and adopted a regional-autonomy approach, based on Somalia's eighteen regions (actually thirteen without the five northern regions). UNOSOM finally backed this plan and speeded up the process, especially after it freed its energies from the hunt for Aidid.

As of 1994, UNOSOM had assisted in the formation of fifty-three district councils out of eighty-one (excluding Somaliland), and eight out of thirteen regional councils (again, excluding Somaliland).[45]

Obviously, circumstances did not allow massive foreign intervention a mediating role. Third-party intervention has been critical in providing relief but conspicuously ineffective in facilitating resolution of the conflicts – some Somalis argue even that outside forces exacerbated matters, thereby delaying, if not reducing the chances of, peaceful settlement. Current experience shows that the UN system is highly inept in resolving civil wars. Unfortunately, the harsh realities of the post–Cold War era have witnessed a mushrooming of such destructive struggles.

### THE PROBLEMATIC OF A STRONGMAN POLITY

Throughout history, states have been established by a conquering strongman, while others have been revived by a winner in civil wars. The fragmented, politicized clan structures and relative military balances in Somalia make it highly unlikely that someone will conquer and pacify the country. Only Siyad, supported by the Cold War antagonists, could temporarily impose a military hegemony over all of Somalia. Even a top–down solution would have to emerge not through decisive armed force but via a negotiated settlement among the warring strongmen – a form of "consociational or power-sharing authoritarianism" or "decentralized Leviathan," if that is not a contradiction in terms. Some of the Somalis who refer to this scenario as "decentralized Siyadism" are willing to consider it not as the best but as the optimal antidote to the Hobbesian "war, where every man is enemy to every man ... and which is worst of all, continual fear, and danger of violent death; and the life of man, is solitary, poor, nasty, brutish and short."[46]

The press has popularized the term "warlords" in reference to Somalia's more notorious strongmen. Unlike the situation in China of 1910–49, where the term received widespread use, Somalia is dominated by clans rather than by a class. The clan-recruited militias are youthful, lack military experience and training, are voluntary, and lack discipline, including the tendency to obey higher authority. Warlords preside over anarchy while attempting to manage chaos. Only in Somalia's clan-based society do we encounter an ex-dictator who has re-emerged as a warlord in his own right. There are those who argue that during the years that witnessed the disintegration of the Somali National Army, Siyad became the first Somali warlord.

Certainly, by mid-1990, barricading himself and his loyal troops in Mogadishu (the press dubbed him "Mayor of Mogadishu"), Siyad had fallen from the pinnacle of national power to the status of regional warlord.

## THE VISION OF A CONSOCIATIONAL POLITY

It is useful to provide at least a rough, working definition of democracy to offer suggestive comparisons with evolving Somali political developments. Larry Diamond et al., in *Democracy in Developing Countries: Africa*, provide a useful definition, containing three main conditions: competition among individuals and organized groups that is both meaningful and extensive; a high level of political participation in the selection of leaders and policies through regular and fair elections; and an adequate level of civil and political liberties.[47] As of 1994, the northern republic of Somaliland began to meet at least some of these conditions within its embryonic consociational or power-sharing political processes and institutions. Southern Somalia is still groping to achieve sufficient reconciliation among competing clans to ensure peaceful political cooperation.

Historically speaking, Somali clans have evolved their own specific forms of politics which "at bottom, means men's cultivation of forms for public power and authority that enable them to meet external challenges and internal needs. Ethnic groups are proving that nations do not have a monopoly on political development."[48] Reconciliation legitimizes and facilitates political cooperation. For the most part, leaders in Somaliland have taken a grass-roots approach to the process. Traditional secular and religious (local) elites, modern elites, representatives of non-governmental organizations, and ordinary citizens have participated in peace and reconciliation conferences held in virtually all the main towns: Berbera, Borama, Burao, Erigavo, Hargeisa, and Sheikh.

Siyad's wars brought conflicts to civil society, and unless these are healed, there will be none of the mutual trust necessary to re-establish state organs.[49] Following the 1992 conflict between two Isaq clans – the Issa Muse and the Habar Yunis – the Sheikh reconciliation *shir* assisted the process of building trust through the use of traditional practices, including group marriages between the two ex-warring clans to demonstrate good faith. This approach has won the support of most non-Isaq clans, and the SNM was therefore able to transform Somaliland from a single-clan to a multi-clan or territorial project. Relying on the territorial basis of the British colonial borders, Somaliland therefore includes a heterogeneous grouping of at least four non-Isaq clans as well as numerous Isaq clans. It is not based only on Isaq claims to clan homogeneity.

Until recently, SNM and Somaliland constitutional practices included leadership rotation and indirect electoral participation within a relatively grassroots approach; in the south, faction leaders hold power without electoral legitimacy. The SNM has proved the most democratic of the insurgency movements. At its 1981 founding in London, it elected Ahmed Jiumale from the Habar Awal clan as its first chair. It raised funds in a decentralized manner from local and expatriate members of Isaq clans and subclans. This saved it from coming under the control of Libya's Colonel Quaddafi, who funded the SSDF. It continued to hold elections regularly, according to its constitution. It enlarged its Central Committee early in 1991 to include, on a proportional basis, representatives of non-Isaq clans, in order that it could serve as the parliament or national assembly of the Somaliland Republic. Membership became pruned and refined enough to constitute a seventy-five-member House of Elders (Guurti) and a seventy-five-member House of Representatives.

It was Arthur Lewis, in his thought-provoking *Politics in West Africa*,[50] who first recommended that Africans drop the winner-take-all electoral principle and form grand coalitions as a more realistic way to operate governments. From ideas such as those of Lewis, Lijphart and other European political scientists have formulated a "consociational" theory of democracy that seeks to avoid the pitfalls of the majoritarian, winner-take-all model.[51] The South African transition from apartheid was achieved through consociational mechanisms. David Laitin has argued that Somalia is in an excellent position to evolve its own unique version.[52]

Somaliland has already taken several steps towards a consociational or power-sharing democracy. The facilitating conditions include the fact that no clan-family or clan can hope to dominate/impose a hegemony (Siyad tried, using the huge national army, which has since evaporated, and there are no plans to establish another one). The clans have recognized leaders who have, at least in the past, cooperated with one another. Traditional Somali society endorses the principle of proportionality, as discussed above. It is also tolerant of the use of a mutual veto for any group that considers a proposed measure vital to its survival and well-being. Segment autonomy, to allow each group sufficient resources, may be achieved through territorial or regional autonomy/federalism, which has already been formally endorsed. Many Somali clans are clustered in given territories, while multi-clan regions might adopt proportional power-sharing. This is one way the new authorities may be able to avoid applying costly, difficult-to-manage preferential policies.[53] The civil service, commissions, committees, and other bureaucratic appointments could be implemented on the basis of merit criteria, combined with the spirit of proportionality. Consociational practices would facilitate clan organizations and clan competition, which might discourage violent clan conflicts. At least that is the hope implied in the vision of a consociational polity.

CONCLUSIONS

The challenge for Somali political development is to transform violent clan conflicts into peaceful competition. Clans cannot simply be wished away, and the current situation represents a basic reality – clans exist, and they need to be harnessed and gradually modified to promote positive political developments. Manipulation of elites by both government and opposition groups provides the major source of clan conflicts. Colonial elites first introduced this practice within a centralized state, leaving a divide-and-rule legacy to be exploited by the post-independence elite. Clanism operates in a defensive manner for those struggling for social justice and equality; the elite and masses are bound together by a consciousness of shared oppression, which is significantly different from forms of "false consciousness" artificially manufactured by a cynical elite.

In the south, the political situation continues to pose dangers of violent clan conflicts, especially in the Kismayu area. More than half of the political factional leaders, including Mohamed Farah Aidid (USC-SNA), Abdullahi Yusuf (SSDF), Umar Jess (SPM-SNA), Abdi Warsame (SSNM), and Umar Masala (SNF), were senior military officers in Siyad's army. Because of the clan factor, today none of them can conquer Somalia militarily. To create a government, they need to compromise and create a coalition of strongmen drawn from different clans along consociational lines.

Somaliland is facing the greatest challenge. Die-hard opposition members decided to circumvent the Borama Conference constitutional process and agreed to abandon the independence proclamation in favour of an unspecified "Somali Federation" with General Aidid's coalition. Somaliland President Egal's term expired in May 1995, but he was able to exploit the crisis to ask the national assembly for an additional mandate of eighteen months. Somaliland's official "hard-liners" have been bolstered by the recent importation of 25,000 tons of newly printed Somaliland currency. The prospects for a power-sharing, democratic resolution of the Somali civil wars in the south are bleak; Somaliland emerged with impressive democratic potential, but recent armed clashes have put a question mark at least on its short-term prospects.

Consociationalism facilitates a form of democracy based on a primordial group – it does not guarantee the substance of democracy. Unbridled petty capitalism since 1991 has unleashed significant productive forces in agriculture, livestock, fishery, and the commercial sector, including a reviving export/import sector (much stronger in the port of Berbera, Somaliland, which now serves larger parts of Ethiopia as well). However, authentic development is more than the sum of individual entrepreneurial action, which, devoid of social regulation, could have large net costs to future Somali society. Somalia's emerging non-profit sector (and, it is hoped, some of the anticipated political parties) will have to evolve social democratic policies to situate development as an activity in which coordination plays a part and that has broad social benefits. The politics of class, gender, profession/occupation, and to a certain extent religion needs to find political space in order to complement and attenuate the divisive politics of clans.

For serious, long-term socio-economic development, Somalia, like its neighbours, will have to rely on an emerging common market in the Horn of Africa, with the Inter-Governmental Authority on Drought and Development (IGADD) manifesting its promise and potential. Since 1994, IGADD, with Eritrea as its newest member, has provided the highest diplomatic forum for attempts to attain negotiated settlements for the Sudanese and Somali civil wars. Most probably the Somali civil wars will have to be resolved internally by the parties concerned, but subregional actors, motivated by a spirit of neighbourliness, could be facilitators.

In the meantime, the layers of problems confronting Somalia continue to get more complicated – for example, fierce wars for land-tenure rights continue to afflict the fertile interriver zone. Perhaps the most crucial lesson one can derive from the tragic and prolonged Somali civil wars is the pivotal role of good governance. After all, commonality of ethnic origins, language, religion, and culture has not ensured for Somalia political unity, peace, and stability, any more than ethnic, linguistic, racial, and cultural heterogeneity has prevented Tanzania from enjoying political unity, peace, and stability.

NOTES

1 Martin van Crevel, *The Transformation Of War* (New York: Free Press 1991).

2 John Drysdale, *The Somali Dispute* (New York: Praeger Publishers 1964).

3 Abdi Sheikh-Abdi, *Divine Madness: Mohamed Abdulle Hassan (1856–1920)* (London: Zed Books 1993).

4 Andrew Natsios, "Humanitarian Relief Interventions in Somalia: The Economics of Chaos," Paper presented to the Princeton University Conference on Somalia, "Learning from Operation Restore Hope," April 1995.

5 I.M. Lewis, *A Pastoral Democracy* (London: Oxford University Press 1969).

6 John Saul, *The State and Revolution in Eastern Africa.* (New York: Monthly Review Press 1979), 391–423.

7 Roy Licklider, ed., *Stopping the Killing: How Civil Wars End* (New York: New York University Press 1993), 9.

8 Ibid., 11.

9 Raymond Copson, *Africa's Wars and Prospects for Peace* (New York: M.E. Sharpe 1994), 74–5.

10 Abdi Samatar, *The State and Rural Transformation in Northern Somalia, 1884–1986* (Madison: University of Wisconsin Press 1989).

11 D. Laitin and S. Samatar, *Somalia: Nation in Search of a State* (Boulder, Col.: Lynne Rienner 1987.)

12 Peter Woodward, "Conflict in the Horn," *Contemporary Review,* no. 231 (Dec. 1977), 281–5.

13 Donald L. Horowitz, *Ethnic Groups in Conflict.* (Berkeley: University of California Press 1985).

14 Robert Jackson and Carl Rosberg, *Personal Rule in Black Africa* (Berkeley: University of California Press 1982).

15 Harold D. Nelson, *Area Handbook for Somalia* (Washington, DC: GPO for Foreign Area Studies, American University, 1982).

16 I.M. Lewis, *A Modern History of Somalia: Nation and State in the Horn of Africa* (Boulder, Col.: Westview Press 1988).

17 Ibid., 222.

18 John Prendergast, *The Gun Talks Louder Than the Voice: Somalia's Continuing Cycles of Violence* (Washington, DC: Center of Concern, July 1994).

19 William J. Foltz and Henry Bienen, *Arms and the African* (New Haven, Conn.: Yale University Press 1985), 100.

20 John Drysdale, *Whatever Happened to Somalia? A Tale of Tragic Blunders.* (London: HAAN Associates 1994), 4.

21 Mohamed Sahnoun, *Somalia: The Missed Opportunities.* (Washington, DC: United States Institute of Peace 1994).

22 Copson, *Africa's Wars and Prospects for Peace,* 106.

23 Woodward, "Conflict in the Horn," 281.

24 Ahmed Samatar, *Socialist Somalia: Rhetorics and Reality* (London: Zed Books 1988), 137 and 139.

25 Africa Watch, *Somalia: A Government at War with Its Own People: Testimonies*

*about the Killings and the Conflict in the North* (New York: Africa Watch Committee 1990), 10.

26 Drysdale, *Whatever Happened to Somalia?*

27 Sahnoun, *Somalia*, 11.

28 Natsios, "Humanitarian Relief," 2–3.

29 Sahnoun, *Somalia*, 18.

30 Dianna Putnam and Mohamood Nour, *The Somalis: Their History and Culture* (Washington, DC: Refugee Service Center, Oct. 1993), 1.

31 Prendergast, *Gun Talks Louder*, 16.

32 Ibid., 16.

33 Ibid., 15.

34 Africa Watch, *Somalia*, 94.

35 William Zartman, *Ripe for Resolution* (New York: Oxford Univrsity Press 1989).

36 Licklider, ed., *Stopping the Killings*, 17.

37 Natsios, "Humanitarian Relief."

38 Ibid., 3.

39 Ibid., 4.

40 Ibid., 14.

41 Sahnoun, *Somalia*, 5–11.

42 Drysdale, *Whatever Happened to Somalia?*.

43 Shoumatoff, Alex, "The 'Warlord' Speaks," *Nation*, 4 April 1994.

44 Admiral Jonathan Howe, "Relations between the United States and the United Nations," Paper presented to the Princeton University Conference on Somalia, "Learning from Operation Restore Hope," (April 1995), 18.

45 HAB, *Horn of Africa Bulletin*, 6 (Jan.–Feb. 1994), 16.

46 Thomas Hobbes, *Leviathan* (New York: Collier Books 1969), 100.

47 Larry Diamond et al., *Democracy in Developing Countries, vol. 2, Africa* (Boulder, Col.: Lynne Rienner 1988), xvi.

48 Cynthia H. Enloe, *Ethnic Conflict and Political Development* (New York: University Press of America 1986), 14.

49 Ken Menkhaus, "The Reconciliation Process in Somalia: A Requiem," Paper presented to the Princeton University Conference on Somalia, "Learning from Operation Hope," April 1995.

50 Sir Arthur Lewis, *Politics in West Africa* (London: Allen and Unwin 1965).

51 Arend Lijphart, *Democracy in Plural Societies: A Comparative Exploration* (New Haven, Conn.: Yale University Press 1977).

52 David Laitin, "A Consociational Democracy for Somalia," *Horn of Africa*, 13 nos. 1 and 2, Jan.–March and April-June 1990, 62–8.

53 Horowitz, *Ethnic Groups*.

# 7 Civil War and Failed Peace Efforts in Sudan

TAISIER M. ALI AND
ROBERT O. MATTHEWS

Africa's longest civil war, in Sudan, has persisted through the country's transition from colonial dependence and through three parliamentary democracies (1956–58, 1964–69, and 1986–89) and three periods of military rule (1958–64, 1969–85, and 1989–present). During the closing days of Anglo-Egyptian rule (1898–1956), societal anxieties and tensions, coupled with administrative overreaction and ineptness, created a highly volatile situation in southern Sudan. Violence erupted in 1955, when the Torit garrison mutinied and was joined by civilians, police, and prison guards. For about two weeks, Equatoria Province became the dying fields for northerners, most of whom were civilians, including women and children. Government punishment was brutal, though many mutineers had fled into the bush or to neighbouring countries.[1]

Memories of the massacre and the subsequent reprisals found a life of their own that continues to haunt the country even now. Before the government talked with the Sudan People's Liberation Movement (SPLM) and Sudan People's Liberation Army (SPLA) in 1990, a state-owned newspaper published an open letter to a peace activist, a half–page-long litany of hate and vengeance based on the Torit events of 1955 and signed by the chief government negotiator.[2] Still, that mutiny and the losses of lives, spiralling antagonisms, massive human displacement, and economic crises are mere symptoms; the civil war is the result of deep–rooted grievances. After independence, hostilities escalated to a full-scale war that has lasted four decades. Fighting has thus spanned the opposite poles of poli-

LIBYA

EGYPT

CHAD

*NORTHERN*

Red
Sea

Port
Sudan

*KASSALA*

*KHARTOUM*

Khartoum ★

ERITREA

*DAHFUR*

*KORDOFAN*

*BLUE
NILE*

Blue Nile

Rosieres

Kurmuk

White Nile

Malakal

*UPPER
NILE*

ETHIOPIA

*BAR EL GHAZAL*

Wau ●

Rumbeck ●

CENTRAL
AFRICAN
REPUBLIC

Bor ●

Pibor ●
Post

*S O U T H E R N   S U D A N*

*EQUATORIA*

Juba ●

Kapoeta ●

Yei ●

Torit ●

ZAIRE

KENYA

UGANDA

| | |
|---|---|
| —— | International boundary |
| —·— | Provincial boundary |
| ★ | Capital |
| ● | Town |

0  50  100  150 miles

0        150 kilometres

Sudan

tical activity from a multi-party system, through the restrictions of one-party rule, to the extreme of military dictatorship. The conflict has survived every form of rule in Sudan.

Though the Addis Ababa agreement of 1972 brought fighting to a halt, it did not lead to peace-building. The second ("May") regime of General Nimeiri failed to take advantage of the momentum of reconciliation to address the roots of the conflict. This unfulfilled promise of a "new deal" inflated frustration with the regime and its high-handed policies. Consequently, when the fighting resumed in 1983, it was much more violent than before. Since then, civil war, and the related famines and diseases, have consumed about a million lives, displaced several million more, and dispossessed the war zone of health, educational, and other social services. Sudan has mastered its own self-destruction.

It is our aim here not to retrace the history of the conflict, or to provide a catalogue of its damage but rather to examine its background in the differing views and situations of the north and of the south; to look at the three failed peace settlements (the Khartoum Round Table Conference of 1965, the Addis Ababa agreement of 1972, and the Kokadam Declaration of 1986); and assess the impasse of the 1990s. This chapter attempts to explain the obstacles to and prospects for peace in the Sudan. This requires the search for answers to the basic questions "why does the war persist?" and "why have all earlier attempts at settlement failed?" Sadly, neither time nor the devastation of the fighting has forged a national consensus on these issues. Yet a considerable measure of consensus exists among southern Sudanese, while in the north, views have remained divided and confused. This latter situation, as we show below, is largely the product of the routine censorship and disinformation spread by successive regimes. Since the military coup of 1989, the deposed traditional rulers have displayed a remarkable shift in their outlook by signing several agreements with the mainstream southern leadership, though legitimate doubts surround this recent conversion of the traditional elite to the cause of peace.

## THE DOMINANT NORTHERN VIEW

Throughout the forty-plus years of independence, the dominant elite and its parties have never questioned their own interpretation of the root causes of the war. Political statements have simply rehashed earlier positions that reduce it to foreign intervention. Whether this is a manifestation of political ineptitude, of social and cultural prejudices, or of total lack of vision is open to debate. Regardless, the ruling elite has never recognized the conflict in terms other than those of a regional mutiny and a local rebellion instigated by foreign powers, or merely a "southern problem." There is no official recognition that what Sudan faces is a civil war and therefore a full-blown national crisis, and as a result there is no sense of urgency. To resolve a crisis, one must first acknowledge that it exists.

The perception of the crisis by northern Sudan's traditional elite has rarely changed. Originally it viewed the 1955 mutiny as another opportunity to whip up popular emotions against colonial rule and pave the way for its ascent to power. The indigenous elite did not attempt to inform the masses about conditions in the south or reflect on the underlying causes of the insurrection or its consequences. As G.N. Sanderson explained, "The most effective weapon in the 'national struggle' was not 'the masses in the streets' ... [P]opular nationalism had no very satisfying part to play. If not quite a mere spectator, it was at most a kind of Greek chorus, reacting to events rather than initiating them."[3] Nor did the elite seriously challenge the reaction of the British governor-general or his government. Instead, after a routine judicial inquiry of Torit's events, it simply accused the British of complicity with the mutineers and pressed on with its manoeuvres to attain "the political kingdom."

Since independence, all regimes, whether civilian or military, have attributed the civil war exclusively to external forces. The ruling elite never even questioned why the fighting continues, despite frequent changes in government and in foreign policy orientation. Accusing fingers have remained readily pointed at colonial policies, imperialist designs, Christian churches, communist plots, Zionist machinations, racist conspiracies, or envious neighbouring states. Rather than abating, the tendency to accuse outsiders has further intensified. Recent statements of the Islamist military government insist that a crusade targeting Sudan's religious orientation has imposed war in the south. In this manner the regime conveniently reduces the conflict to "a plot to undermine the unity of the Islamic state," motivated by "the fears of the enemies of Islam."

Along with evoking a bogus foreign conspiracy, the ruling elite has sought to misinform and confuse citizens about the conduct of the war. None of the post-colonial regimes has ever revealed figures showing lives lost, casualties borne, or prisoners of war taken. Statistics for the massive destruction of agricultural or other civilian property, and of transportation, health, and education facilities, remain cloaked in secrecy. Excluding sparse and vague statements on the desirability of peace, government and ruling-party officials never discuss the real costs of war. State ownership, operation, and control of the principal media organs have reduced news of the war to routine statements by the army's high command. Apart from reports of victories over the "mutineers," or tactical withdrawals in face of rebel advances supported by foreign enemies, no reference appears to the concomitant casualties, waste of national wealth, and lost opportunities for development. All the post-colonial governments have assigned the execution of this policy to a minister of information and national guidance, who supervises radio, television, and the Sudan News Agency. Since 1956, only one southern Sudanese, Bona Malwal, filled this cabinet post, under the exceptional circumstances of the Addis Ababa peace agreement.

Withholding information on the war is not a simple issue of national security. It is an essential component of the state system's arsenal to maintain and reproduce the status quo. As becomes evident below, this status quo allows the northern sectarian-military-bureaucratic establishment to exercise hegemony over the political, socio-economic, and cultural affairs of the whole country. Apparently this dominant power bloc perceives any challenge to the existing order as an immediate threat to its privileges, if not to its very existence. Under such conditions, national interest and national security have come to mean little more than preserving the structures and relations of dominance. It is within this broader context that we understand the determined efforts to conceal the horrendous cost of the civil war.

The governing power bloc remains embroiled in a "Catch 22" situation; for while it is incapable of agreeing to a settlement, it cannot bankroll the war indefinitely. This predicament leads to further complications. The governing elite realizes that its rule cannot survive the popular indignation that would arise if the real human and economic costs of the war were made public. Consequently, data regarding these issues must remain classified, to avoid the risk of a popular backlash and to thwart potential opposition. Confidentiality also placates the army's top brass by allowing it unobstructed access to, and control over, massive funds without scrutiny. War expenditures have always provided the generals of the high command and allied middlemen with private financial gains through local purchases and arms contracts in hard currency, all of which are difficult to audit.

Understandably, official statements by the political and military leadership have remained harmonious. The former group relegates the conflict to the status of an irrelevant and foreign-propelled squabble in the faraway bush, while the latter engages in mopping-up operations against mutineers and bandits. Both groups promote the delusion that a military solution is not only possible but imminent. Whenever the war or other related crises intensify, the ruling elite invariably evokes the ever-present source of all evil – the machinations of foreign intervention. In December 1995, General Basher insisted that Uganda, Eritrea, and the United States had prevented his troops from annihilating the SPLA.[4] The two policy options of playing down the war's impact and ascribing it to external conspiracies dovetail in complete harmony, for they breed apathy about the conflict outside the war-mangled areas and so reduce threats of domestic backlash and upheaval.

During the early years of Sudan's independence, the dominant bloc remained generally insensitive to popular opposition. Governments of the Umma party (UP) and its sectarian twin, the National Unionist party (NUP), later renamed Democratic Unionist party (DUP), have revelled in the religious aristocracy's massive rural following, while military regimes were not as subtle, for they have relied on brute force. The disdain that both types of government showed for public opinion was almost boundless. A case in point was the 1958 change in regimes. In that year, fatigued by inter-party rivalry, the elected prime minister simply asked the commander-in-chief of the army to take over power. Though the military regime survived several coup attempts, an anti-war rally of civilians in 1964 mushroomed into a national strike and a popular uprising that finally forced the officers back to the barracks. Similarly, in 1985 a repeat performance by mass organizations ended sixteen years of Nimeiri's rule. On these two occasions, as again in 1988, the civil war stirred the popular movement to change governments and launch efforts for a peaceful settlement. After each uprising, however, the northern ruling elite managed to abort peace initiatives.

Taking their cue from the sudden collapse of military rule in 1964, the sectarian elite and its bureaucratic-military allies became incessantly sceptical of the popular desire for peace. Concerns of this nature accelerated efforts to control the flow of information on the war. Accordingly, in the following year, a precedent was set by a ministerial decree "to the effect that no reports concerning the security [in the south] should be published before approaching the competent authorities in this respect." From then onward, "Sudanese journalists ... were not permitted to publish their own findings without censor; they had to ... depend on the government reports which were all shamelessly concocted."[5] It is almost unbelievable that these measures were applied by a "democratically" elected government taking office in the wake of a military regime.

"Delinking" the popular movement in the north from the conflict in the south became crucial for sustaining the status quo and for maintaining the continued hegemony of the ruling power bloc. Though the policy was not totally successful, it stunted the growth of a strong peace movement in the north and in so doing retarded settlement. The policies of playing down the effects of the war produced even greater harm in terms of civilian casualties and economic ruin, as they propelled the SPLA to show its muscle and make its presence felt. In the years that followed the reignition of the civil war in 1983, the SPLA launched attacks against high-profile targets such as the Chevron oil-fields, the French consortium dredging the Jonglei Canal, and the regional capitals of Juba and Malakal.

## SOUTHERN PERCEPTIONS

Protracted warfare with the government and the subsequent emergence of "friendly forces" and tribal militias – the creations of Khartoum – have made the south living death for its citizens. Particularly affected are the most vulnerable, the women, children, and elderly who cannot run away. Except during times of military crisis, the dominant northern elite remained oblivious to the south. As Ahmed Sikainga remarks: "The south has always been viewed and treated by the sectarian politicians as an afterthought, an appendage, and a marginalized section of society."[6] Rarely did the vision of this elite extend beyond its power base in the "golden triangle" between the Blue and White Niles. Southern elites recognized that the destruction of life, society, and environment results from the high-handed behaviour of Khartoum's sectarian leaders and their resolve to retain their grip on the region. In reaction to this reality, the southern leaders adopted two quite different courses of action.

Most of the southern elite gravitated towards regional political parties, contested elections, and became entangled in Khartoum's power struggles. Given their narrow base of support and meagre resources, these parties were too weak to influence Khartoum's policies towards the south or other national issues. For the most part, the southern parties failed to challenge the dominant group and remained its hostages. The other faction of the southern elite perceived the roots of war along racial and religious divides and therefore championed the call for secession. As a leading proponent of this view explained to the Khartoum Round Table Conference of 1965, "The Sudan falls sharply into two distinct areas, both in geographical area, ethnic groups, and cultural systems ... [T]here is nothing in common between the various sections of the community; no body of shared belief, and above all, the Sudan has failed to compose a single community." [7]

When it emerged in 1983, the SPLM/SPLA challenged these tactics of the southern elite. This movement linked political marginalization, economic underdevelopment, and cultural domination by the north to national processes. Accordingly, it refused to operate from within these structures of the dominant bloc, expressing a commitment to "end the monopoly of power by a few in Khartoum." The dominant elite may "say there is a southern problem;" but for the SPLM, "the problem in itself is in Khartoum."[8] At the same time, the SPLA rejected secession, on the grounds that the war "is not a fight between northerners and southerners. It is not a fight between Christians and Muslims." In essence, the movement saw its struggle as being against established structures and relations in Sudan. For it, the ferocity of the conflict merely underscores Khartoum's determination to maintain the status quo against what it correctly sees as a threat to its privileged position.

By challenging the existing order and calling for a new Sudan, the SPLM takes the long view. The manipulation and abuse of liberal democracy by the dominant bloc have led the movement to rule out the option of working from within the existing system. Similarly, secession did not seem to provide enough guarantees against future destabilization by the northern elite; the southern elite could not ensure long-term stability, peace, and development. It followed then that the SPLM would have to secure these objectives through its struggle for a more just and democratic new Sudan. Such an endeavour called for "a radical restructuring of the power of the central government in a manner that will end once and for all the monopolisation of power by any self-appointed gang of thieves and criminals, whatever their backgrounds, whether they come in the form of political parties, family dynasties, religious sects, or army officers."[9]

Such sharp declarations by the SPLM served notice that no configuration of the dominant elite will have power in the new Sudan. In reaction to this explicit threat, most of the northern political and bureaucratic elite fiercely opposed contacts with the movement. Of these groups, the sectarian elite found the movement's vision of the future particularly alarming, for the SPLM notion of "Sudanism" maintains that "the Sudan has been looking for its soul, for its true identity. Failing to find it ... some take refuge in Arabism, and failing in this, they find refuge in Islam as a uniting factor. Others ... take refuge in separation. In all of these there is a lot of mystification and distortion to suit the various sectarian interests ... [W]e need to throw away all these sectarianisms and look deep inside our country and the experience of others ... [w]e can form a unique Sudanese civilization that does not have to take refuge anywhere."[10]

Thus this view of Sudan's identity is tantamount to a death sentence to the sectarian elite, for which Islam and the Arabic language are not only ideological weapons but the foundation of its claim to legitimacy. Its importance is made abundantly clear by Sadiq el Mahdi, leader of the Umma party and former prime minister, when he said: "The dominant feature of our nation is an Islamic one and its overpowering expression is Arab, and this nation will not have its entity identified and its prestige and pride perceived except under an Islamic revival."[11] Of course, under the National Islamic Front military regime that came to power in 1989, these issues become even more intractable. Hassan al Turabi, de facto ruler of the country (though he failed to win a seat in the last election), asserts that, without Islam, "Sudan has no identity, no direction."[12]

### BACKGROUND: EMERGENCE OF A DOMINANT NORTHERN ELITE

Sectarian politics, military intervention in the political process, armed struggles in the south, and civil disobedience movements in the north have all figured highly in Sudan since independence. These facets of politics interrelate and feed on each other in a variety of ways. These interconnections antedate national sovereignty. Colonial policy was thought to guarantee stability and was thus adopted after independence as an essential term of reference – an umbilical cord not to be severed.

The conquest of Sudan in 1898 by Great Britain was engineered in response to the threat posed by the Mahdist state (1881–98) and its potential to destabilize conditions in Egypt. This strategic imperative shaped the Anglo-Egyptian administration of Sudan into a militarist and highly centralized mould. Several of these characteristics have survived the transition to independence in 1956 and directly or indirectly influenced developments since then. For example, the overdeveloped colonial state's organs of violence contributed to the advent of military coups and to the mentality that views the conflict in the south merely as a mutiny. Likewise, the colonial economic policies of concentrating investments in the area between the two Niles continued and thereby aggravated the uneven development of the country.

One of Sudan's great misfortunes is that functionaries of this militarist-statist administration commanded the nationalist movement, and they remained locked in its outlook, mentality, and practices. Imbued with the attitudes and dictates of the colonial regime but not its reasoning or mode of thought, the petty bureaucrats-cum-national leaders were not up to the challenges of building a democratic and just society. Independence came in a very similar manner to the conquest, as the result of regional strategic imperatives. The disagreement between Sudan's condominium powers (Great Britain and Egypt) over the country's future resulted in "very heavy pressure upon the [British] Foreign Office from the u.s. State Department to buy Egyptian support for the American cold war strategy by recognising the claims of Egypt."[13] Effectively this meant that independence came before a fully-fledged nationalist movement could develop clear ideas about the future of the country. "The 'national struggle' within the Sudan had itself been conducted throughout as a diplomatic 'game'"[14]

The main local beneficiaries of this diplomatic game were leaders of the two largest religious sects, along with the top operators of their populist political parties. Following as it did immediately on the heels of the theocratic Mahdist rule, the colonial administration had remained particularly sensitive to the role of religious leaders. Colonial policy had nurtured a religious aristocracy that was given massive real estate, agricultural land, and government contracts. At the head of this aristocracy were leaders of the two main sects in the country, whom the British knighted and who later sponsored the country's largest political parties – the Umma and the DUP. At the same time, a budding group of Sudanese bureaucrats, appointed to serve the administration of the colonial regime, realized that it stood to gain from the expansion of private enterprise and accordingly sought closer ties with the religious sects. Out of this close association arose leaders of the dominant political parties: "[T]he bureaucrats never entertained any idea of structural transformation or radical change in Sudanese society. Such notions were out of tune with the training they acquired while serving the colonial agencies of repression, e.g. police, army, local government, etc., and with their education."[15]

The bureaucrats were the architects of these political parties in the immediate postwar period. Reflecting the rigidities of bureaucratic training, the party organizations did not engender genuine democratic practices, popular participation, or the active soliciting of broad-based consensus. Instead of articulating national grievances and aspirations, the political leaders sought to protect the interests of sectarian families, a process that led to further divisions within the

203 Civil War and Failed Peace Efforts in Sudan

north as well as with the south. The religious aristocracy provided not only material backing but, most important, because of its spiritual status, guaranteed the unquestioning, blind, and fanatical following of the larger proportion of the Sudanese people in the north. A close observer, G.N. Sanderson, explains: "In the early 1940s secular nationalism had no resonance, and indeed no meaning, outside a comparatively small circle of white-collar intelligentsia. The nationalist leaders, seeking an ersatz popular following through a link with the Ansar or the Khatmiya, inevitably became bound to the sectarian chariot wheels."[16]

The two main parties had no specific programs of any kind, nor did they collect fixed membership dues. For finances, they relied on the benevolence of the religious aristocracy and its commercial or agricultural investment partners, as well as periodic transfers from foreign sources. From their early formation these parties were more like business enterprises than organs for national liberation. After independence, they remained preoccupied more with political intrigue than with confronting the larger political, social, and economic problems of the country. Never did these parties seem aware of any such urgent needs at all. "The two religious leaders were anything but revolutionaries. Nor ... were even the more militant secular politicians. All concerned aspired to take over the existing system in working order – a goal unlikely to be achieved by the politics of popular insurrection. Indeed, the secular nationalists, most of whom had been career officials, at times tended to identify independence rather narrowly with the Sudanization of the key administrative posts."[17]

Sudanization – the process of replacing colonial administrators by nationals – became a bounty for the bureaucracy and was used by the sectarian parties to reward their clients, to find new ones, and to gain influence within the state apparatus. Planned to end by the early 1960s, Sudanization was executed with record speed, unmatched in the history of the national government, and was completed six years ahead of schedule. The program was an unmitigated disaster for two reasons. First, it amounted to a routine changing of the guard without the least effort being made to reorient the system from its colonial bearings. Second, but more important, it was national in name only, for in essence it was what Peter Nyot called "northernisation of the Sudanese Public Service."[18] Of the eight hundred posts covered by the program, and instead of the forty-odd places that Oliver Albino believes to have been promised to the south, southerners filled only six junior positions. Since then, a pattern evolved by which "the northern bureaucratic elite entrenched and perpetuated itself in the state apparatus."[19]

In view of the orientation of the political parties, their patrons, and their leaders, this débâcle should not come as a surprise. It merely underlines a typical pattern that continues to the present. The Khartoum elite's perception of national issues and of the country remains more often than not reactive, biased, self-interested, fragmented, and therefore limited. Its indifference towards southern protests over Sudanization further fuelled suspicion and contributed to the Torit mutiny. The persistence of the northern elite's misperception, the string of its dishonoured promises, and the series of tragic actions and reactions on both sides have intensified the civil war. A major component of this misperception is its tendency to blame the crises of confidence, if not the entire conflict, on the British colonial "Southern Policy." This plan adopted in the 1930s and 1940s, rendered the south a "Closed District" and barred the travel of northerners into the region without government permits. If the northern elite was so acutely aware of and concerned about the divisive role of colonialism, why did it not introduce confidence-building measures – during Sudanization, for example?

Though this "Southern Policy" was introduced to "protect" the region from exploitation by northern merchants, it did not lead to greater economic activity or self-reliance. Apart from offering traditional tribal leaders some powers and applying certain ridiculous measures to keep out northern influence, it left the south "in a state of 'care and maintenance'. Education remained almost entirely in the hands of foreign missionaries, economic development was virtually non-existent."[20] However, as late as 1946, closed districts were also declared in the north to block merchants' activities. While these areas were quickly reintegrated into the dominant economy by the end of colonial rule, the absence of northern investments in the south reduced interest in the region. The weak economic links between north and south, together with the cultural arrogance of the northern elite, resulted in the north's habitual denial of the real grievances in the south. Accordingly, it has seen the crisis as a mutiny to be out-gunned and defeated. The colonial economic policies of "benign neglect" in the south led to failure to accelerate economic activity and non-development of its productive forces. As a consequence, elite formation in the south was much slower than in the north; its ranks were dominated by traditional chiefs and a small number of missionary-educated southerners. In short, the "separate development" of the south was not only economic but political as well.

BUILDUP OF PRESSURES:
THREE FAILED EFFORTS

In the tumultuous decades following independence, three landmark events offered Sudanese a vision of possible frameworks for peace and reconciliation – Khartoum Round Table Conference of 1965, the Addis Ababa agreement of 1972, and the Kokadam Declaration of 1986. This section describes the context in which they emerged and collapsed.

The growing operations of the colonial government in the north had created the need for not only an indigenous professional cadre but also labourers. Increased exports led to the expansion of irrigation systems, mechanized farming, ginneries, and transport networks to the production areas and the seaport. By the mid-1940s, railway workers, numbering about twenty thousand, initiated the drive for trade union organization, which spread within a decade to most urban areas as well as agricultural projects.[21] The workers were supported by the small but influential Sudanese Communist party (SCP), which also allied itself with unions of farmers, tenants and students. Initially, the sectarian parties offered token financial support to the unions. However, once these parties inherited political power, their relations with the unions deteriorated dramatically. From the early days of the self-rule government in 1953, the unions and SCP formed a broad front to support workers' demands as well as public concerns of civil liberties, democracy, and national economic development.

With political independence in 1956, this loose alliance became more militant in its challenge to the dominant bloc. Encompassing workers, farmers, students, women, professional organizations, and the clandestine SCP, it sought to provide an alternative to the sectarian parties and their unending, petty divisions. However, before these various groups could coalesce and spread outside the urban areas, the ruling elite passed on state power to the military in 1958. After publicly blessing the army take-over, the two sectarian patrons of the Umma and DUP parties allowed members of the deposed cabinet to join in the new council of ministers. The regime detained leading members of the unions and banned their organizations. Through its use of repression, the junta ensured that the opposition of the popular organizations remained uncoordinated and weak.

The army regime continued the policies of Arabicization and Islamization in the south put in place by the previous sectarian government while seeking a military solution to the conflict. But it pursued these policies much more aggressively, particularly the civil war, which was increased to unprecedented levels. Still, the new popular forces of unions and associations continued to intensify their mass-action campaigns against the policies of the regime in the north as well as in the south. Finally, in 1964, following violent demonstrations opposing the war, the unions called for a general strike that paralysed the country and forced the government out of office. It was the unions rather than the parties that brought the military regime down. As historian M.W. Daly noted, "The old political parties had played a much less significant role in these developments than had the trade unions and professional organisations, and the transitional government established in the wake of the generals was dominated by these 'new forces,' whose strength was significantly independent of sectarian support."[22]

Freed from sectarian control, the Unions and Professional Front (UPF) adopted several unprecedented measures – the "first serious attempt at a political settlement of the conflict."[23] The premiership of the new government went to Sirr al-Khatim al-Khalifa, a northern teacher who had served for a decade in the south. Unlike in earlier times, cabinet membership was not dictated by the sectarian patriarchs but was determined by the respective constituencies. Politicians from the south selected their representatives to the council of ministers, which included for the first time workers and farmers. Instead of the traditional marginal positions reserved for southern politicians, they received the major posts of Communications and of Interior, Labour and Transport which went to Ezboni Mondiri and Clement Mboro, respectively.[24] These seemingly simple and uncontroversial steps, as Deng Ruay commented, "attempted a radical departure from the past: a departure from the narrow, chauvinistic and fanatical conception of nationhood to a more flexible and progressive perspective of national unity and national consciousness."[25]

Following these confidence-building measures, the UPF government proceeded with its plans to resolve the national conflict in the south. These efforts culminated in the Khartoum Round Table Conference of 1965, which was attended by exiled leaders from the south as well as leaders from within the country, along with representatives of northern political parties and observers from African countries. The conference represented a bold step, taken in haste and overburdened with great expectations, but lacking adequate political groundwork. The opening sessions were consumed by inflammatory accusations and acrimony, which could have been avoided through earlier, low-level discussions. In the words of Deng Ruay, "The moods and the morale of the Conferees were far from refined and the confidence between them seemed to be wanting."[26] The absence of coherent leadership within the political elite on both sides, north and south, complicated the situation.

Moreover, political parties from both parts of the country shared similar impediments. First, they were riddled with internal divisions and in conflict with each other. Second, politicians from the north and the south seemed worried about accusations of a sell-out by their men in the field – the Sudanese army and the Anya-Nya, respectively. After the gathering dragged on for a week, "it became glaringly evident that no effort could save the Conference from failing in all of its objectives, and it was allowed to collapse."[27] A face-saving resolution was adopted to speed up the resettlement of refugees, the "southernization" of administrative positions, and social and economic development. Dunstan Wai argued that "mutual mistrust, suspicion and lack of statesmanship from both sides" were the prime factors in the round table's failure.[28]

By the end of the conference, the sectarian parties had lost patience with the UPF government and were able to force parliamentary elections. Blessed with the blind support of the religious sects' followers, the sectarian parties returned to power. Again, national politics was dragged back into the pre-1958 quagmire of petty rivalries, endless rifts, frivolous manoeuvres, and total disregard for the real issues of peace and development. The sectarian elite was concerned with issues such as allowing northern merchants to represent the south in the new assembly, the banning of the SCP, and whether the constitution should be Islamic or secular and the government parliamentary or presidential. At the same time, the earlier policies of Arabicization and Islamization were intensified, and the war was allowed to escalate.

Reprisals by government forces against civilians in the south became more vindictive and bloody. With the spread of the war, the sectarian elite's need for financial and military support increased. According to Prime Minister Mahjoub, "the UAR, Algeria, Saudi Arabia and Kuwait, helped us with arms, ammunition and funds."[29] Open support by Arab countries encouraged contacts between the southern armed movement of Anya-Nya and the Israelis, who provided training and equipment. Following Idi Amin's 1971 coup in Uganda, the Israelis became even more deeply involved in the Sudanese conflict. Consequently, by 1970 the Anya-Nya had developed a military organization capable of challenging Khartoum's forces. Success in the field and frustration with the divisions within the southern parties allowed the movement, renamed the Southern Sudan Liberation Movement (SSLM), under Joseph Lagu, to emerge as the major political and military force in the south.[30]

Popular frustration with the sectarian parties and their self-seeking policies had prepared the ground for the 1969 coup d'état by Brigadier Nimeiri and several young army officers. At first, the new junta espoused radical socialist objectives, allied itself with left-wing forces, and battered the traditional sectarian oligarchy. Nimeiri's Revolutionary Command Council (RCC) sought to further restructure the dominant power bloc by purging the army, bureaucracy, and even the private sector. However, when pressure mounted for substantial changes in the country's political economy, Nimeiri balked. Radical elements within the RCC staged a coup in 1971 and detained Nimeiri. Within days, he was reinstated by a counter-coup supported by Libya and Egypt. Before the end of that year Nimeiri had executed the leaders of the Communist party, dissolved the RCC, shifted ideological gears, and advocated wedding Western technology and Arab petro-dollars to Sudanese resources. In a further attempt to break his domestic isolation, Nimeiri formed the Sudanese Socialist Union (SSU) and declared it the sole legitimate party. Instead of mobilizing popular participation, the SSU turned into a government department and a vehicle for corruption. Having alienated both right- and left-wing forces, lacking any strong base of support at home, and cut off from his principal foreign ally, the Soviet Union, Nimeiri found himself isolated and vulnerable.

Ultimately, the search for allies drove Nimeiri to turn towards the south and seek a peaceful settlement of the civil war through the good offices of the World Council of Churches and Ethopian Emperor Haile Selassie. The Anya-Nya too were confronted with an emerging situation, which threatened to undermine their position of strength. Faced with the reality of a military stalemate and the likelihood of a decline in their future capacity to carry on the war, both Nimeiri and the southern Sudanese were prepared to give negotiations a higher priority than they had in the past. By signing the Addis Ababa agreement in 1972, Nimeiri became the peacemaker and won wide support in the south. However, the agreement contained the seeds of its own demise, in that it allowed the south to have an elected regional assembly. In other words, the south emerged as an island of democracy within the autocratic Sudanese state. Granting the south a degree of autonomy and democracy, non-existent elsewhere in the country, disturbed the internal stability of the regime. Also, regional autonomy denied Khartoum immediate control over or easy access to the south's mineral and oil wealth. The regime's need for these resources increased as the national economic crisis deepened. Perhaps fatally, the agreement did not gain broad support in the north, for Nimeiri alone had signed it.

By the mid-1970s Nimeiri seemed invincible, as his security apparatus succeeded in thwarting all coup attempts. However, in 1975 and 1976 his early warning systems failed, and on both occasions he was forced to go into hiding, leaving his lieutenants to save the regime. The latter coup was particularly serious, for the Libyan-trained United Front Force (UFF) of the sectarian parties and the Muslim Brothers (later known as the National Islamic Front) stormed Khartoum and took over government installations. During 1977 Nimeiri reconciled with the UFF, and many of its leaders joined his regime. Eventually, the sectarian patriarchs were alienated by Nimeiri's despotism and began to withdraw their support. The Muslim Brothers party of religious fanatics, however, intensified its collaboration with the regime and was rewarded with several leading posts. More important, this close association allowed them to infiltrate the state apparatus as well as secure extraordinary concessions for their empire of Islamic banks.[31] At the same time as Nimeiri turned towards the Muslim Brothers for local support, he fashioned close ties abroad with Egypt and the United States. Preoccupied with the military threats to Sudan's security posed by Libya and Ethiopia and, behind them, the Soviet Union, Cairo and Washington extended to Khartoum extensive military aid and economic support. Whether they liked it or not, they became identified with Nimeiri and his personal security.

Nimeiri's overconfidence and the regime's intensifying economic difficulties led him to seek direct control over the newly discovered oil resources in the south. Hence, in 1980, he announced plans to redraw the borders between southern and northern provinces. When this proposal was blocked by the regional government in the south, he conveniently created a new province and removed the oil-fields altogether from southern jurisdiction. Nimeiri's greed for power remained unrestrained. In a flagrant breach of the Addis Ababa agreement, he redivided the southern region into three new regions, and the central government began sponsoring, organizing, and arming tribal militias in the south. The justification for this policy was that the state was crippled by economic crisis and was unable to execute its peacekeeping duties. The irony was that these measures were all carried out under the pretext of maintaining unity in the region and consolidating national sovereignty.

The final nail was driven in the coffin of the Addis Ababa agreement in 1983, when Nimeiri imposed his version of Islamic laws – the notorious September Laws. The injection of religion into a long list of government policies abhorred by the majority of the southern population intensified the south's feelings of alienation and estrangement and fanned the flames of the civil war, which was launched again by the SPLM in 1983. Nimeiri's decision surprised only those who believed that the 1972 understanding was motivated by his commitment to peace and national unity. Mansour Khalid, an architect of the document, was not puzzled: "Nimeiri had never been genuinely committed to the principles of the Addis Ababa Agreement."[32] He recalled Nimeiri's own words when asked about procedures for amending the agreement: "The Addis Ababa agreement is myself and Joseph Lagu and we want it that way ... I am 300 per cent the constitution. I do not know of any plebiscite because I am mandated by the people as President."[33]

Basically, Nimeiri's combination of arrogance, despotism, and unpredictability, coupled with the spread of corruption, opened the regime up to opposition in the north from both ends of the political spectrum. The repeated rejections of his plans by the regional assembly in the south may also have increased his frustration and isolation. In face of this rising opposition, Nimeiri coveted the heavenly legitimacy bestowed by Islam on an Imam, and the blind loyalty of all Muslim subjects that came with the title. His were the ambitions of a despot who could observe his powers shrinking. The introduction of the laws was a desperate act. But it was the desperate act of a politician, not a holy man. These laws rendered political opponents ungodly individuals, inspired by the devil. In a further attempt to consolidate his grip on power, Nimeiri declared martial law "... to protect the faith and the fatherland from schemes of schemers and the mischief of Satan."[34]

The manner in which Nimeiri changed directions points out the danger of believing that military rule can enforce the consensus that eludes elected representatives. The decisiveness attributed to men in uniform comes with a high price. Dictators impose their will; they coerce and intimidate. Whatever consensus exists under such regimes is artificial and therefore transient. In 1972, several Western countries, church organizations, and African leaders facilitated the successful conclusion of the Addis Ababa agreement, but they could not prevent its later abrogation. The one lesson that should not be lost from the agreement is best captured by Elias N. Wakson: "Lasting peace, establishing the basis of political stability and good government, cannot be achieved by illegitimate military dictators but only as the outcome of a broad-based dialogue of all the popular political forces in the country."[35]

By early 1985, fighting in the south had escalated to previously unknown levels of death and destruction. Khartoum, like several other urban areas, overflowed with citizens displaced by the conflict in the south and the encroaching famine, all searching for security, shelter, and food. Modern Sudan had not experienced such conditions before, and the state system lacked the material resources to respond effectively since expenditure on the war devoured more than double the allocations for education and health. Meanwhile, the military junta continued to terrorize and humiliate citizens by using the September Laws to detain individuals indefinitely, to carry out public floggings, to amputate hands, and to crucify those charged with heresy. Challenged by these conditions, major trade unions, professional associations, and student bodies formed the Trade Union Alliance (TUA) to coordinate their opposition to the regime.

Within a period of a few months, the unions established an extensive, clandestine network of banned political parties, women's and youth's associations, and cells within the army and police. In April 1985, massive demonstrations preceded a TUA general strike that paralysed the entire country and forced the downfall of Nimeiri. On the eve of the regime's collapse, the TUA and political parties formed a broad front – the National Alliance for National Salvation (NANS) – which agreed on an interim program. Entitled "Charter of April Uprising," the program listed the popular goals of democracy, peace, secular laws, human rights, rule of law, and a national, egalitarian economic policy. Responsibility for implementing these demands rested with the interim cabinet, which was formed by NANS in 1985 and entrusted to hold national elections before the end of its one-year term. However, just as in 1964, the sectarian parties questioned the Transitional Government's (TG) mandate to implement the charter and called for early elections. The UP won a majority of the seats and Sadiq el-Mahdi became prime minister in May 1986.

In an attempt to break the vicious circle of recurrent conflict that had plagued Sudan for almost two decades, the TUA became directly involved in the search for a durable settlement. After about six months of continuous contacts, NANS and the SPLM held meetings in Ethiopia which culminated in the Kokadam Declaration of 1986. The statement affirmed "a democratic consensus by the secular forces of the whole of Sudan on settling the war through a National Constitutional Conference."[36] While all the unions and associations of the TUA showed deep commitment to the peace dialogue, the behaviour of the two main sectarian parties remained at best uncertain. Though the patron of the DUP personally supported the initial contact, a few months before Kokadam he issued a public denunciation of TUA for not informing him of the initiative. Likewise, the UP's representative signed the declaration with the personal approval of his leader, the prime minister, who later claimed in public that he was never consulted.

The Kokadam document was a political landmark in the country's modern history. It proved that there is a national potential and a force for peace in the Sudan. For the first time in the history of the civil war, popular organizations in the north established direct links with the southern armed movement and agreed on a joint peace program. The leader of the SPLM perceived that the declaration had "laid a solid foundation for the peace process. Kokadam is a purely Sudanese experience which will go down in history as a magnificent achievement of great significance, for it proved to the whole world that the Sudanese alone can discuss their problems freely and arrive at concrete proposals regarding their resolution."[37] The agreement took aim at the uneven political, economic, and constitutional relations that reproduced the conflict. In so doing, it challenged the structures that propped up the political elite. By calling for change and linking it to an end in the conflict, peace represented a threat to the established order and to those who benefited from it. Little wonder then that the ruling power bloc could not support the program or its vision of peace and that it intensified its war efforts in the south.

In late 1988, Prime Minister el Mahdi, leader of the Umma party (UP), which had about one-third of the seats in parliament, formed his fourth coalition within two years, in which the extremist National Islamic Front (NIF) became a main partner. This development, explained by el Mahdi in terms of strengthening the internal front (as opposed to the externally supported SPLM), led instead to further divisions. The NIF, the only political organization left out of NANS, had not only broken ranks with the opposition forces in the late 1970s but also staunchly supported Nimeiri's infamous September Laws. El Mahdi, a founding member of NANS, had repeatedly promised to "sweep September Laws to the dustbin of history" and "eradicate all remnants of the May regime."

Indignation against the prime minister intensified mainly because he reneged on earlier pledges and because of his active rehabilitation of the NIF, whose leader secured the same cabinet portfolio of Justice that he had held under Nimeiri. The crisis was further complicated by a jolt from the DUP, which was a partner in the coalition. In a move embarrassing to the prime minister, the DUP signed a peace program with the SPLM. The Sudanese Peace Initiative (SPI) of November 1988 was basically an endorsement of the Kokadam Declaration, to which the DUP had not been a party. Tension within the government mounted following the NIF's angry reaction against the SPI: "[W]e regret the capitulation agreement because it is an unequivocable recognition of the rebellion ... We will not allow anyone with the military establishment to have loyalty to anyone but God and country."[38]

Such setbacks, coupled with the prime minister's indecision about peace and his muddled economic policies, deepened the schism between the sectarian parties and the TUA. Before the end of 1988, an even sharper polarization emerged over increases in the prices of food and the stonewalling of the SPI. These developments reinforced the TUA's links with organizations of women, students, and marginal communities. They launched a campaign involving the writing of memoranda, and the mounting of protest rallies, demonstrations, and strikes to press the prime minister into honouring his commitment to NANS, its charter of April 1985, the Kokadam Declaration, the SPI, and the National Economic Program. Though the massive protests of December 1988 accelerated the peace process, they also drove the NIF into what one of its foreign consultants described as a "now or never" condition.[39]

An extremely unstable and volatile situation induced the army to issue an ultimatum and thus press the prime minister into assembling a broad-based government of national unity. All previous attempts at peace-making by non-Sudanese third parties, whether states, organizations, or individuals, had failed to bring el Mahdi to the bargaining table. In the end, it was the actions of his defence minister and the chief of staff of the armed forces that constituted the turning point. Formed in March 1989, the United National Front Government included NANS and the TUA but was boycotted by the NIF, which subsequently walked out of parliament. Almost immediately the new government remodelled its economic policies and set about implementing the SPI to induce a cease-fire in the south and pave the way for a settlement. A newly formed Peace Ministerial Committee proposed to replace Nimeiri's Islamist Code with a new set of laws drafted by a panel of eminent Sudanese jurists and approved by the attorney general and his assistants. On the day of the emergency meeting called for the cabinet to approve these alternative laws, officers loyal to the NIF, backed by its militias, mobilized units of the army and took over political power.

## TALKING WITHOUT NEGOTIATING: THE 1990S

In one of his first announcements, Brigadier Omar Hassan al-Basher scrapped the SPI as the basis for negotiations, and in the weeks and years to follow his government intensified military operations in the south, with the clear aim of defeating the SPLA. Khartoum was aided in this process by the fall of Mengistu's regime in Addis Ababa and the subsequent expulsion of the SPLA from Ethiopia. Divisions within the ranks of the SPLM further weakened the south to the point that government forces, reinforced by arms from Iran, Iraq, and China, were able to recapture many of the territories previously held by the SPLA.

At the same time as he waged all-out war against the south, Basher stated that his new government's "primary goal is peace," declaring a one-month cease-fire, offering a general amnesty, and arranging for an early meeting in Ethiopia with the SPLA. Indeed, over the next seven years, the regime actively solicited and engaged more third-party mediation than was sought at any other time in the history of the conflict. Yet all these initiatives have come to naught, as the government has remained more interested in talking about peace than in negotiating it.

Of course, the reasons for this tactic are not difficult to understand, given the regime's need to undermine the international community's boycott of Sudan and to divert attention from its escalation of the war. The regime continues to capitalize on the popular yearning and international sentiment for peace talks, as long as they remain just talk. Once discussions move to substantive issues, and negotiations are about to begin, the process comes to a halt. This is the lesson of all past "talks." After all, there are no costs involved in exploiting international goodwill and interest in peace. On the contrary, it provides good press and buys more time. The meetings sponsored by the Organization of African Unity (OAU) in Abuja dragged on from 1992 to 1994, whereas the subsequent Intergovernmental Authority on Drought and Development (IGADD) initiative has entered its fourth year. Both "talks" reached a deadlock. Evidently Bona Malwal was not completely sarcastic when he warned against the "Abujanization of IGADD."[40]

In March 1995, the U.S. under-secretary of state for African affairs informed the U.S. Congress that IGADD was "stalemated" as a result of the regime's intransigence. Not coincidentally, the Sudanese government shifted its attention from IGADD to the good auspices of former U.S. President Jimmy Carter, who arranged a misguided cease-fire. Simultaneously, Khartoum made public overtures for Dutch and Scandinavian mediation. Of course, it would be cynical to suggest that the regime is not interested in peace. Like earlier governments, it wants an end to the conflict, but on its own terms and without the political compromise that peace demands. Members of Basher's junta have publicly acknowledged that their 1989 coup was timed to prevent the government's decision to implement the SPI. Lacking political will to negotiate a genuine settlement, the present regime uses negotiations for public relations purposes. Its uncompromising stance in the peace talks owes more to its doctrinaire commitment than to any power shift on the battlefield.

The NIF regime has transformed the conflict into a religious struggle and a holy war to establish a theocratic state, even to the extent of exporting its own version of Islam to neighbouring states. This is not a new development. Since its inception in 1985 and throughout the parliamentary period that ended in 1989, the NIF has refused to negotiate compromise, opposed every peace initiative, and continued to beat the drums of war. But the influence of the party on the Sudanese state and civil society dates back before even 1985. Nimeiri's national reconciliation policy of 1977 offered the Islamist extremists a major breakthrough, to exercise systematic influence on society. One consequence of such influence, as explained by an American psychologist retained by the NIF for four years in Sudan, was that "[a] culture is created that compels people to adopt to the conflict as an almost permanent feature of life." In that culture "[t]he southerner is reduced to a challenge, an obstacle to be overcome."[41] This perception is explained by a leading NIF politburo member and a former minister of interior in Nimeiri's cabinet: "Most of its [the south's] inhabitants are heathens who worship stones, trees, crocodiles, the sun, etc. ... All this presents a civilised challenge to all of us as Arabs, because there were heathens and Jews at the time of the Prophet, and we know how the Muslims treated Christians and Jews. Southerners are not credited with a sense of historic development or progressive engagement with the world."[42] As the NIF consultant noted, "Not even the language through which the conflict is talked about can be negotiated, let alone the terms of a solution, because the Islamist owes No Allegiance to Anyone But God."[43]

Failure to understand this outlook and its irreconcilability with the alternative vision of the SPLM and the forces of democracy in the north can only perpetuate the pattern of stalemated and deadlocked peace meetings. Those concerned with ending the war in Sudan are advised to seek new approaches to accelerate the process of peace, for as long as the NIF remains in power the process will never amount to anything other than "talks without negotiations."

CONCLUSION

Over the past two decades, the focus of the conflict in Sudan has shifted from "regional protest" against political marginalization, economic neglect, and cultural domination to a clash of visions and competing definitions not just of the south but of the whole country. Failing to understand this phenomenal change, the northern ruling elite has remained incapable of recognizing the necessary elements of any negotiations that are likely to succeed. During 1985–89, in meetings between the SPLM and the ruling Umma party, the latter invariably posed questions about the number of ministerial portfolios that the SPLM would want, instead of examining modalities of restructuring the Sudanese state system. These offers persisted despite the SPLM's rejection of the possibility of its joining the cabinet. While such an approach might have helped to resolve the conflict in 1972, by 1985 it fell short of the minimal requirements.

Consequently, any negotiations in future will have to be qualitatively different from those conducted at any time in the past. Neither the round table of 1965 nor the Addis Ababa framework of 1972 can be repeated, for negotiations in which administrative concessions are handed out are no longer applicable. Any such discussions must begin with the recognition of self-determination for southerners and the acceptance of a secular state. Since all northern opposition forces have recognized these rights, any retreat from these positions will destroy whatever hope is left for retaining a united Sudan.[44]

The ideological divide runs not therefore along north–south lines, but between those who aspire to a new Sudan and those who want minimal changes to the status quo. It is this line that divides the NIF from the SPLM and "new" popular forces. The sectarian and traditional parties indicate at present their solidarity with the new Sudan, but objectively they are a product of the old structures and relations. Their past record certainly does not inspire confidence. After the overthrow of military regimes in 1964 and 1985, they reneged on their prior commitment to peaceful settlement. Not surprisingly, the popular forces are suspicious of the depth of the sectarian parties' commitment to a new Sudan and are fearful that if the NIF were to make the "necessary" amends, an accommodation similar to the one fashioned by the Nimeiri regime could be reached.

Over the past thirty years, since the downfall of Sudan's first military dictatorship, certain institutions of civil society, such as trade unions and women's, students' and professional associations, have played an increasingly dynamic role in national politics. This development, coupled with the rise of the SPLM, has precipitated several realignments within political and popular forces, which in turn have gradually transformed national perceptions of the civil war. In effect, the Kokadam Declaration denoted the changing views of the 'new forces' and their commitment to socio-political and economic restructuring. At the same time, as noted above, the sectarian parties continued to blame external forces and their agents for the war in the south. In this sense, the civil war connotes more than the conflict of identities that Francis Deng examined in his *War of Visions*.[45] Ignoring the existence of these competing views in the north between the popular forces and the sectarian traditional camp cannot be conducive to the search for a lasting peace.

If the conflict is to be resolved, there must be a genuine change in the perception of the roots of the conflict. This requires primarily a shift from the traditional elite's emphasis on external forces to a focus on the internal factors discussed above. The roots of Sudan's civil war are located not in the regional or international environment, but rather within Sudan. External factors have played a role in the civil war, but their influence has tended to be felt once the fighting began. External involvement all too often strengthened the resolve of one or both parties to pursue a military option rather than seek a negotiated settlement. On occasion, notably in 1972, external factors facilitated the reaching of an accord, though the international community might have exerted more pressure on Khartoum than it did to honour the letter and spirit of the Addis Ababa accord and thus build an enduring peace once the war had ended. Since 1985 all third party efforts to resolve conflict have ended in failure.

In the meantime, there is a real and present danger that Sudan may share a fate similar to what has befallen Somalia and Liberia. This danger of collapse does not arise from the civil war alone or its prolongation, though these accelerate the process of disintegration. The cumulative tensions and pressures engendered by the security, economic, and other measures introduced by successive regimes all operate in a rapidly degrading physical and social environment.

For some years prior to the outbreak of the civil war in Doe's Liberia and in Somalia under Siyad Barre the arming of militias became government policy. The same policy was introduced to southern Sudan by Prime Minister Mahjoub in 1965 and was later institutionalized by Nimeiri, who embraced the "Friendly Forces" of Anya-Nya II. However, it was the elected UP government of Sadiq el Mahdi that extended the arming of al-Maraheel tribal militias to western provinces. As this policy coincided with an intensification of the civil war in Chad and an overflow of arms into Sudan, it led to virtual disintegration of legitimate authority in Darfur province. The present NIF military regime rendered the situation even worse by declaring its objective of arming one million Sudanese before the end of 1996. In fact, the militarization of Sudanese society is well under way, with the establishment of militia organizations such as the Popular Defence Forces and Popular Police, alongside well-armed NIF cadres, which participated in the 1989 coup. The recent "peace" agreement between the NIF and Riek Machar's Southern Sudan Independence Movement (SSIM) is a further example of Khartoum's strategy of intensifying armed conflict among southerners.

Clearly these developments bode ill for the country. Sudan's rural economy, which engages about 80 per cent of the population, is facing the disastrous conditions created by government policies, the physical degradation of the soil, encroachment of the desert, and shifting patterns of rainfall. These factors have reduced Sudanese exports by 75 per cent, while "[i]nflation has reached four digits, the national currency has been devalued by 6000%, ... 80% of the factories have closed."[46] Moreover, as a consequence of the state's financial crisis, all basic social, health, and educational services have faded away, and the only non-governmental organizations allowed to operate are those affiliated with the NIF. Evidently the bureaucratic, constitutional, and administrative framework of the Sudanese state cannot meet the needs of its citizens. For many years this fact has been confirmed by the civil war in the south.

The once-vibrant Sudanese trade unions, professional associations, and women's, youths' and regional organizations, as well as all non-NIF associations, were banned. The regime had hoped thereby to subdue the popular forces and undermine their political and social prowess, which was instrumental in the downfall of army rule in 1964 and 1985. Understandably, the NIF purges and reign of terror have reduced the power of these forces and curtailed the autonomy of civil society. It has become increasingly difficult to distinguish between private and public space under the current government. In view of these conditions, the possibilities for reform appear negligible. Yet popular challenges to the government persist, with new forms of activities and new organizational methods emerging. In September 1995 the NIF almost lost control over the capital for several days to rioting students and youth groups. Obviously, the organs of civil society are reconstructing themselves, forging common ground and discovering new civic demands as well as new tactics.

From the NIF's perspective, most menacing of these developments is the creation in 1995 of the Sudan Alliance Forces (SAF). This military and political movement includes many activists from the army, trade unions, professional associations, and police, women's and students' groups involved in the 1985 uprising against Nimeiri and against the war in the south. SAF expresses a view of the country that appears closer to that of the SPLM than to other parties in the north: "Our commitment is to end the civil war in the south and for the resolution of all other conflicts in our country. ... We cannot reach these objectives without addressing the social, economic, racial and cultural injustices and inequalities that are the root causes of these conflicts. SAF is dedicated to a Sudan that is confident of its identity, proud of its diversity and can uphold, promote and protect the human dignity of all Sudanese. Our Sudan is one that is at peace with itself, its neighbours and the rest of the world."[47] In a move that markes a transition in the civil war, SAF has recently opened up a military front along the borders with Eritrea and Ethiopia.

Building an enduring peace is largely dependent on the capacity of these and other forces, in both the south and the north, to converge. The challenge is not only the military defeat of the NIF and the ending of its tyranny, but the articulation of national aspirations for peace, democracy, justice, and development. Attaining these objectives entails also liberation from racial and religious prejudices, mutual fear, and suspicion and the forging of a national identity embracing all ethnic and cultural groups. Ultimately, it is with the popular masses in both the south and the north that resolution of the conflict and the future of Sudan lie.

## NOTES

1 Deng D. Akol Ruay, *The Politics of Two Sudans: The South and the North 1821–1969* (Uppsala: Scandinavian Institute of Africa Studies 1994), 81.

2 *Al-Inqaz Al-Watani* (newspaper) Khartoum, 25 Nov. 1989.

3 G.N. Sanderson, "Sudanese Nationalism and the Independence of the Sudan," in Michael Brett, ed., *Northern Africa: Islam and Modernization* (London: Frank Cass 1973), 106.

4 Al Hayat (newspaper), 4 Dec. 1995,1. Also statement of Sudan embassy in Canada, n.d.

5 Ruay, *The Politics of Two Sudans*, 131.

6 Ahmad A. Sikainga, "Northern Sudanese Political Parties and the Civil War," in M.W. Daly et al., *Civil War in Sudan* (London: British Academic Press 1993), 81

7 Dunstan M. Wai, "Political Trends in the Sudan and the Future of the South," in Dunstan M. Wai, ed., *The Southern Sudan: The Problems of National Integration* (London: F. Cass 1973), 146.

8 Mansour Khalid, ed., *The Call for Democracy in Sudan: John Garang* (London: Kegan Paul International 1989), 130

9 Ibid., 40.

10 Ibid., 127.

11 Ruay, *The Politics of Two Sudans*, 150.

12 Milton Viorst, "Sudan's Islamic Experience," *Foreign Affairs*, 74 no.3 (1995), 46.

13 Sanderson, "Sudanese Nationalism," 105.

14 Ibid., 106.

15 Taisier Mohamed A. Ali, *The Cultivation of Hunger: State and Agriculture in Sudan* (Khartoum: Khartoum University Press 1989), 75.

16 Sanderson, "Sudanese Nationalism," 99.

17 Ibid., 106.
18 Peter Nyot Kok, "The Ties That Will not Bind: Conflict and Racial Cleavage in Sudan," in P. Anyang' Nyong'o, ed., *Arms and Daggers in the Heart of Africa: Studies on Internal Conflicts* (Nairobi: African Academy of Sciences 1993), 43.
19 Ibid.
20 Ibid.
21 Ali, *The Cultivation of Hunger*, 109.
22 Daly, *Civil War*, 14.
23 Ibid., 15.
24 See Mohamed Omer Beshir, *The Southern Sudan: From Conflict to Peace* (London: C. Hurst & Co. 1975).
25 Ruay, *The Politics of Two Sudans*, 111.
26 Ibid., 116.
27 Ibid., 114.
28 Wai, *The Southern Sudan*, 152.
29 Ruay, *The Politics of Two Sudans*, 132.
30 Ibid., 154.
31 Mansour Khalid, *Nimeiri and the Revolution of Dis-May* (London: Routledge & Kegan Paul 1985), 143–53.
32 Ibid., 234.
33 Ibid., 239.
34 Ibid., 258.
35 Elias Nyamlell Wakson, "The Politics of Southern Self-Government 1972–83," in M.W. Daly et al., *Civil War in Sudan* (London: British Academic Press 1993), 48.
36 Khalid, *The Call for Democracy*, 142.
37 Ibid., 169.
38 T. Abdou Maliqaliqalim Simone, *In Whose Image? Political Islam and Urban Practices in Sudan* (Chicago: University of Chicago Press 1994), 146.
39 Ibid., 64.
40 *Sudan Democratic Gazette* (May 1994), 4.
41 Ibid., 74.
42 Ibid., 165.
43 Ibid., 165.
44 Conference of the National Democratic Alliance on Fundamental Issues, *Final Communiqué*, Asmara, Eritrea, 15–23 June 1995.
45 Francis M. Deng, *War of Visions: Conflict of Identities in the Sudan* (Washington, DC: Brookings Institution 1995).
46 Statement by the Secretary General of the National Democratic Alliance (NDA), House of Lords, London, 29 Nov. 1995.
47 Statement by Chairman of the Executive Committee, Sudan Alliance Forces. House of Lords, London, 29 Nov. 1995.

# PART FOUR
## *Civil Wars Forestalled*

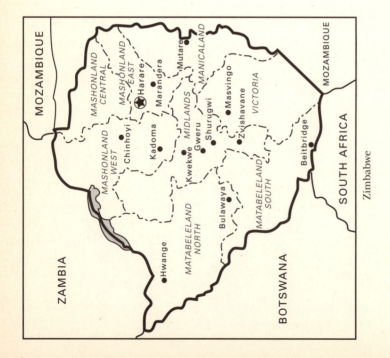

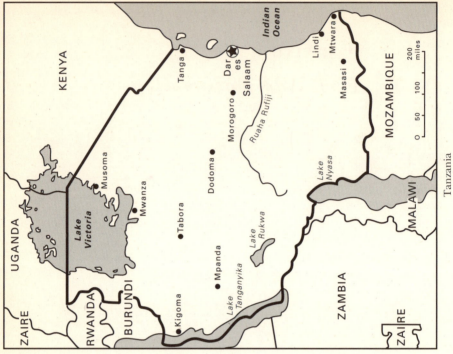

# 8 Leadership, Participation, and Conflict Management: Zimbabwe and Tanzania

HEVINA S. DASHWOOD AND
CRANFORD PRATT

Many former British colonies or protectorates in Africa experienced a depressing, recurrent pattern in the early years of independence. Initially, there was typically a period of enthusiastic political mobilization by means of the nationalist movements that had dominated the struggle for independence, with formal governance being conducted through the parliamentary institutions and the civil services that the British had bequeathed. Then, often swiftly, government became more autocratic and the public service extensively corrupt. Apathy spread throughout the population, particularly in the rural areas. In a growing number of states, ethnic differences were increasingly exploited by political rivals, and regional and tribal divisions severely disrupted the harmony and indeed the peace. Neither imaginative leadership nor conciliatory politics was much in evidence, and disorder, armed unrest, and deep alienation became widespread. Many states abandoned their democratic institutions and became either military dictatorships or authoritarian civilian regimes dependent on the goodwill and support of restless military establishments.

Yet this was not universally the pattern in Africa. Some countries remained under civilian rule, were not primarily dependent on force for the maintenance of order, and continued to enjoy a fair though not a full measure of political freedom. This chapter reflects on

In the writing of this chapter, Dashwood had primary responsibility for the larger section on Zimbabwe, 1980–95; Pratt for the retrospective section on Tanzania, 1961–78; and both authors for the conclusion.

the experience of two such countries, Zimbabwe and Tanzania, in which potential conflict has been contained, in the first case through skilful reconciliatory politics and strong (if increasingly authoritarian) government and in the second through the invention and implementation of a system of rule – the democratic one-party state – that sought to contain the many threats to national unity which challenged the newly independent state, while still providing genuine space for popular participation and a real measure of electoral answerability.

## I ZIMBABWE

By the standard of many African countries, Zimbabwe has been relatively successful in maintaining both political and economic stability. Its independence in 1980 was itself the product of a major civil war (liberation struggle), which culminated in a negotiated settlement, with the signing of the Lancaster House Constitution in December 1979 in London. The settlement ended the war, met the minimal conditions of the major interested parties, and set in place a process for the holding of a national election. The results of the election, in February 1980, were widely viewed as legitimate, even if the results were not welcomed on all sides.[1] However, the termination of the violent racial conflict, which pitted a white settler state against Black nationalists, paved the way for new sources of conflict, which went beyond the confines of the new constitution.

Though racial tensions have continued to simmer, the dominant source of political conflict has been rivalry between the two major political parties that had fought in the liberation struggle – the Zimbabwe African National Union–Patriotic Front (ZANU-PF), led by Robert Mugabe, and the Patriotic Front–Zimbabwe African People's Union (PF-ZAPU), headed by Joshua Nkomo. Mugabe's party is supported predominantly by the Shona speaking people (about 75 per cent of the population), and Nkomo's, largley by the Ndebele-speaking people (about 19 per cent).

Despite early efforts at reconciliation on the part of Mugabe, the struggle over political participation degenerated into disorganized violence in Matabeleland, which was dominated by ZAPU. In 1982, some dissident activity broke out in the predominantly Ndebele-speaking provinces of Matabeleland North and South. Mugabe and his ZANU-PF government used a combination of force and negotiation to end the violent phase of the conflict, culminating with the signing of a Unity Accord between ZANU-PF and ZAPU in 1987. The two parties were formally merged in 1989 at a joint congress of ZANU and ZAPU, at which time ZAPU was subsumed within ZANU.

While the accord secured peace in Matabeleland, it brought to the forefront a second major source of conflict – deciding whether or not Zimbabwe should become a one-party state, controlled by ZANU-PF. Though the agreement specified that the united ZANU-PF should work towards creation of a one-party state, former ZAPU members strongly opposed the idea, as did prominent members of ZANU-PF, opposition parties, intellectuals, students, professionals, and trade unions. They achieved a major victory when ZANU-PF decided in September 1990 not to legislate a one-party state – a goal long held by Mugabe. Nevertheless the 1995 election confirmed the ZANU-PF's monopoly of political power.

The signing of the Unity Accord also brought to the forefront a third source of conflict – class-based divisions over the distribution of wealth and resources, which stemmed from a number of factors. First, there was a crystallization of elite cohesion, symbolized by the joining together of the political elites that signed the Unity Accord. Second, there was inescapable evidence of the acquisitive tendencies of the bureaucratic and political elites; in effect, a Black ruling elite now joined a white economic elite. Third, Zimbabwe adopted an Economic Structural Adjustment Programme (ESAP) in 1991, which has badly harmed the poor majority, while the mostly white entrepreneurial and agrarian elites are clearly perceived to be the main beneficiaries.

Two central features of the Zimbabwean political economy explain the relative success with which these main sources of conflict have been contained. First, notwithstanding an authoritarian tendency, the political leadership has been open to reconciliation with the white minority, ZAPU (at least initially), and societal actors who wish to preserve a formal multi-party democracy. While this democracy may seem to some an "empty shell," the channels of political expression are sufficiently open to maintain political and economic stability; the military takes its cues from the civilian leadership, and overall conditions are conducive to economic development.[2]

Second, an elite accommodation encompasses the ruling elite (senior politicians and bureaucrats), which now constitutes a state-based bourgeoisie; the mostly white elites within the economy – namely, the entrepreneurial elite (the business-owning class) and the agrarian elite (the large-scale commercial farmers); and international capital. These political and economic elites have come to constitute the dominant class, which embraces a capitalist ideology. Hegemonic capitalist rule has in turn reinforced the comparatively open political system, but at the expense of the poor majority.

### Racial Conflict and Reconciliation

In the light of the violent and often brutal nature of Zimbabwe's liberation struggle and the bitter memories that must still prevail less than two decades after it ended, the degree of tolerance between whites and blacks has been quite remarkable. The roots of this tolerance can be traced in part to the terms of the Lancaster House Constitution which paved the way for racial accommodation, by ensuring that the economic security of the whites would not be radically challenged. Such provisions as the preservation of private property rights meant that the new government could not legally expropriate land or other assets.

These constitutional safeguards, however, were insufficient to ensure racial reconciliation unless the new government actively promoted such a goal. Because of the lessons learned from the disastrous departure of whites from Mozambique, which caused economic destruction and increased that country's vulnerability to South African interference, Zimbabwe wanted whites to remain in order to secure economic stability and growth. Thus a combination of strategic, political, and economic factors underpinned Mugabe's policy of racial reconciliation.[3]

The leadership's openness to racial reconciliation was a key factor promoting racial tolerance when peace came. When Mugabe addressed the nation after the 1980 election results were announced, he called for reconciliation and national unity, which went a long way towards calming whites' fears. He further gained the confidence of whites by retaining Peter Walls, formerly commander of the Rhodesian army, as head of the armed forces. Walls was responsible for integrating the three armies that had fought during the liberation struggle – the Rhodesian army, ZANLA (ZANU-PF's military wing), and ZIPRA (ZAPU's military wing). In a further reconciliatory gesture, Ken Flower was maintained as head of the Central Intelligence Office, and Ken Norman, (past president of the Commercial Farmers Union, which represents the white farmers) became minister of agriculture.

Nevertheless, there was much mutual mistrust and suspicion in the early years. As one prominent businessman noted, some whites considered the constitution "just a piece of paper." Even though Mugabe indicated that his government intended to abide by its terms, considerable uncertainty prevailed. Perceptions about Mugabe's intentions were also coloured by ZANU-PF's avowed commitment to

Marxism-Leninism. Certainly, there were contradictions between reconciliation and the expectations of the majority of the population.[4]

ZANU-PF, and in particular Mugabe, displayed considerable consternation over what he perceived as the failure of whites to embrace his gesture of reconciliation. The issue came to a head after the election of 1985. Under the terms of the constitution, the whites had twenty seats in Parliament and a separate voters' roll. The vast majority of whites continued to vote for the Conservative Alliance of Zimbabwe, the renamed Rhodesian Front Party, still led by Ian Smith. Mugabe felt that the system of a separate voters' roll, and the failure of whites to show substantial electoral support for ZANU-PF even after his policy of reconciliation, created a divisiveness in the political system that was unacceptable in majority-rule Zimbabwe. Thus in 1987 he formally abolished the separate voters' roll for whites, which he was legally entitled to do under the constitution.

While abolition of the separate roll might have been considered a major setback for the whites, by 1987 many prominent whites had established growing links with senior decision-makers through informal channels. The entrepreneurial and agrarian elites were among the few societal actors who were consulted by the government prior to the introduction of market-based reforms in 1991. In a seeming paradox, the political influence of whites has increased since the abolition of the separate roll, in large part because of the growing accommodation between the ruling elite and the mostly white economic elites. Thus elite accommodation has helped consolidate racial reconciliation.

Nevertheless the introduction of ESAP in 1991 again brought to the surface racial tensions, with the whites visible beneficiaries of the market-based reforms. Mugabe exploited this fact in the run-up to the 1995 general election, often citing white farmers as the major obstacle to land redistribution. In another example, the president of the students' representative council at the University of Zimbabwe announced an extensive campaign against (white) racism in October 1994, which was to entail the storming by students of nightclubs, schools, restaurants, offices, and clubs alleged to be racist.[5]

The continued high visibility of whites in the economy points to a serious political problem, which could undermine racial accommodation. The permanent fixture of whites dominating the productive sectors of the economy has made many resentful that more blacks have not come to play a greater role in these sectors. This resentment took formal expression in the creation in 1990 of the Indigenous Business Development Centre (IBDC) and, more recently, of the

Affirmative Action Group. Progress has certainly been made in terms of the appointment of blacks to managerial positions. However, many medium-to-small white businesses are family run, effectively preventing black advancement. Furthermore, indigenous entrepreneurs have met with many obstacles in their attempts to set up businesses, and the government has only very recently (and belatedly) come to address their concerns in any serious way.

### POLITICAL CONFLICT: RECONCILIATION OR REPRESSION?

The two major political parties that contested the election in 1980 reflected the two major ethnic groupings among the blacks, with ZANU-PF supported primarily by the Shona, and PF-ZAPU by the Ndebele. However, neither party can be defined merely by its ethnic affinity. Ideological divisions existed both between and within these parties over whether the new government should promote a socialist transformation, or simply remove the racial discrimination that had previously denied the African petty bourgeoisie the opportunity to advance in the economy.[6] These differences reflected also class divisions within the two parties, whose leadership had originated from the ranks of the African petty bourgeoisie.[7]

At the same time, Mugabe and his ZANU-PF were perceived as more radical than Nkomo and PF-ZAPU. This perception can be traced back to the original split in the nationalist movement that occurred in 1963, when a faction of ZAPU broke away and formed ZANU. Though the break contributed to the development of ethnic political cleavages, the original schism occurred over strategy. In particular, there were serious differences over how the struggle against white minority rule should be waged.[8] As the liberation struggle advanced in the 1960s and 1970s, the rivalry between ZANU and ZAPU persisted, even when the two joined forces in 1976 as the "Patriotic Front." The tensions were carried over after 1980.[9]

The difficulties began even before independence, when Mugabe decided to run his party independently of ZAPU in the 1980 election, thereby ending the Patriotic Front alliance. ZANU-PF won a clear majority, taking fifty-seven of the eighty common-roll seats, while ZAPU won twenty.[10] In what appeared to be a gesture of conciliation, Mugabe invited ZAPU leaders to join him in a government of "national unity." Nkomo, who considered himself "Father of the Nation," found electoral defeat especially hard to swallow, and initially refused the offer. Eventually, he accepted the position of minister of home affairs.

The spark that led to the breakdown of the political coalition and the expulsion of Nkomo and other ZAPU members from the government was the discovery in 1982 of a cache of arms on property belonging to Nkomo.[11] Subsequently, more arms were discovered on other properties of Nkomo's or ZAPU's. Relations between ZANU-PF and ZAPU had already been strained by armed clashes in 1980 between former combatants of their armed wings – ZANLA and ZIPRA, respectively. More serious, former ZIPRA cadres tried in March 1981 to stage a rebellion, beginning with a seizure of the armoury at Entumbane Barracks, near Bulawayo.[12]

The dismissal of Nkomo in 1982 was followed by the arrest and detention of Lookout Masuku, commander of ZIPRA, and Dumiso Dabengwa, ZIPRA's intelligence chief. These actions enraged former ZIPRA fighters, hundreds of whom deserted the recently integrated Zimbabwean National Army and took to the bush. They joined others, disillusioned with the new dispensation of power, in Matabeleland, where acts of violence were perpetrated.

### THE REGIONAL CONTEXT

Any discussion of conflict or civil war in southern Africa has to take into account the prominent role of South Africa in the past in fuelling conflict. There is substantial evidence that South Africa did lend assistance to some of the dissidents in Matabeleland.[13] While it now seems that the number of dissidents involved was not that many, the role of South Africa affected the perceptions of Mugabe and his supporters about the seriousness of the conflict. This fact would help to explain, but would not justify, the ruthlessness with which the government handled the dissent.

The security threat posed by South Africa stemmed not only from its support of some of the dissidents. South African acts of military, economic, and political destabilization, most prominently against Mozambique and Angola, had direct negative consequences for Zimbabwe.[14] For example, the disruption to Mozambican transport routes, through which most of Zimbabwe's trade would normally have gone, delayed key imports such as fuel and created stockpiles of export commodities waiting to be transported. In order to protect the Beira Corridor (the rail line and pipeline linking Zimbabwe's eastern border at Mutare to the port of Beira in Mozambique), the Zimbabwean army moved into Mozambique in 1985, incurring additional costs, estimated to be about Z$2.1 billion (roughly Can$300 million) over the period 1980–89.[15]

Even prior to the eruption of violence in Matabeleland in 1982, the government had very real internal and external security concerns. The internal threats stemmed from some whites' refusal to accept Mugabe's victory. While many whites who would not accept Black majority rule simply left the country, mainly for South Africa, a minority chose to attempt to challenge the new government, including several who had been entrusted with certain key positions in the army and security organs of the state after independence.[16]

Of those whites who left Rhodesia for South Africa, a few joined the South African Defence Force (SADF), and others, the Military Intelligence Directorate (MID). There a number of well-placed former Rhodesians inside South Africa were in a position to provide vital intelligence to the South African government. Some of these whites had been loyal to the internal settlement orchestrated by Ian Smith and, according to Johnson and Martin, sought to destabilize Zimbabwe from South Africa.[17] It was they who helped the South Africans in providing assistance to the dissidents in Matabeleland and thus in perpetuating the violence.

His realization in 1983 that elements within South Africa, but not necessarily the government, were helping the dissidents prompted Mugabe to crack down very hard on his opponents. He made no attempt at negotiation and little differentiation between the political and former military wings of ZAPU. It now seems – though much of the information surrounding the events in Matabeleland remain secret – that Mugabe was also fed false intelligence by his own informers about the extent of the dissidents' activity. When amnesty was offered to them in May 1988, just over one hundred people presented themselves.

Mugabe's response was to send in the notorious Fifth Brigade in 1983. This North Korean–trained counterinsurgency unit not only hunted down dissidents but committed terrible atrocities against the local population. (The dissidents were guilty of this as well). These atrocities have not been forgotten. Indeed, in the reopening of a number of mines in Matabeleland in 1992, skeletons were discovered in the mine shafts. This event resulted in demands for apologies from the victims' families and revived memories of what had occurred.[18]

The involvement of South Africa therefore directly affected the perceptions of the ZANU-PF government about the severity of the conflict in Matabeleland. The government's actions in turn produced considerable resentment on the part of the population about the way in which the situation was handled, with lasting implications for the stability of the Unity Accord signed in 1987. Furthermore, many believed that the government, motivated by a desire to crush not only the dissidents but the political organization of ZAPU as well, had overreacted to events in Matabeleland.

## THE UNITY ACCORD OF 1987

The decisive actions of the Fifth Brigade ended the immediate security threat in Matabeleland. Despite real security concerns, however, the manner in which the government crushed not only dissident activity but also ZAPU as a political organization suggests that its motives went beyond removing the security threat,[19] as does its treatment of any source of opposition in Zimbabwe, even where the threat of ethnic violence was absent. Part of the difficulty in assessing the real extent of the dissident threat is that government statements vacillated between assurances that state power was not threatened and attempts to raise public awareness about threats to the nation. It has been argued that this dichotomy can be accounted for by the government's twin aims of justifying extremely repressive measures and assuring the public that the authorities were in control.[20] The government maintained and built on the entire military and security apparatus of the former Rhodesian government, by renewing the state of emergency every six months right up to July 1990 and substantially increasing the power of the Central Intelligence Organization (CIO) and other security organs of the state.[21]

Further doubts about the extent of the danger arise from the fact that, while some dissidents were being assisted by South African elements, unlike the situation with Renamo (known as the MNR in Porguguese) in Mozambique or UNITA in Angola there was no high command organizing the dissidents. Instead, they operated in small bands and were motivated by a variety of aims and grievances.[22] They targeted for intimidation, assault, and murder white farmers, ZANU party officials and members, government officials, foreign tourists, and peasants thought to be "sell-outs." These choices of targets reflected anger about a variety of economic and political factors, including lack of progress in land redistribution, the affluence of white farmers, and the government's treatment of ZAPU officials and attempts to repress the party, its favouring of the Shona over the Ndebele, and its alleged backtracking from its socialist goals. Predictably, the dissidents also tried to exploit ethnic resentment against the Shona, but they generally relied on brute force in order to compel villagers to cooperate.

The extent of Nkomo's role in organizing dissident activity is not altogether clear. Nkomo denied any formal role on the part of ZAPU, and some ZAPU officials openly criticized the dissidents, some of whom referred to themselves as "Super ZAPU." Nevertheless Mugabe clearly had reasonable grounds to question Nkomo's intentions. Certainly, the dissidents themselves were divided over such issues as whether or not to accept help from South Africa and over the treatment of villagers, with some dissidents being considered "good," and others "bad."

The government's efforts to cripple the political organization of ZAPU were therefore not justified by the extent and nature of dissident activity. The only top ZAPU official prosecuted for assisting the dissidents – Sydney Malunga – was acquitted in July 1986. The dissidents never had a large popular base in Matabeleland. Short of banning ZAPU outright (which the constitution forbade), the government went to great lengths to make it impossible for ZAPU to function as a political party. In the run-up to the 1985 election, ZAPU offices were destroyed and supporters assaulted. After the party managed to win all fifteen seats in Matabeleland, disappearances and arrests of ZAPU supporters accelerated.[23]

The harassment of ZAPU prompted a number of defections from ZAPU to ZANU-PF, further weakening the party organisation.[24] ZAPU was effectively bullied into engaging in unity talks with ZANU-PF. Nevertheless, it was also in the interests of ZANU-PF to reach a political accommodation with ZAPU. Despite the government's decisive military action, it was not able to prevent continued acts of banditry by the dissidents, who, as during the liberation struggle, could melt into the bush with either the voluntary or the involuntary help of the peasants. It became clear that only negotiation with ZAPU, even if almost exclusively on ZANU-PF's terms, would bring an end to dissident activity.

Given its military defeat at the hands of the army, ZAPU had an incentive to negotiate with ZANU so that it could participate at the political level. Much as ZAPU members would have liked to negotiate on an equal basis, ZANU was not prepared to allow that. From the start of negotiations in 1985, ZANU determined the agenda and terms of negotiation. Most critically, it was clear that if negotiations were to proceed, it would be to realize Mugabe's dream of uniting the parties and creating a one-party state. In other words, ZANU was not prepared to allow ZAPU to operate as an independent political party.

In deciding to negotiate with ZANU-PF, Nkomo and his followers had accepted union with ZANU. However, negotiations dragged on for two years, from September 1985 until 22 December 1987, when the Unity Accord was signed.[25] Significantly, by that time, there were very few differences on ideology. While ZANU-PF continued to call itself Marxist-Leninist, its development initiatives were far less radical and there was general agreement between the two parties over the government's overall approach to development. ZAPU, recognizing that ZANU's attachment to Marxism-Leninism was purely rhetorical, even agreed to a statement in the accord attesting to the commitment to Marxism-Leninism.

The most serious stumbling block in the negotiations emerged over the name of the new, united party.[26] ZAPU felt strongly that it was important to have a neutral name, such as ZANU-ZAPU, so that its followers would not feel that ZAPU had given in to ZANU. ZANU refused to consider changing its name, however, and in the end ZAPU was compelled to capitulate. In one significant concession, however, the government decided to provide amnesty to the dissidents. Dissidents were given until the end of May 1988 to turn themselves in, and just over one hundred did so. By mid-1988 dissident activity in Matabeleland ceased.

The containment of violence in Matabeleland and the subsequent signing of the Unity Accord present a dilemma for the government and people of Zimbabwe. Clearly, in the absence of peace and political stability, progress in economic development is impossible. However, the manner in which the conflict was resolved, involving as it did a large dose of repression, raises questions in the long term about the stability of the political accommodation. Though Mugabe has attached a high priority to "national unity," the realization of that goal has taken on a repressive and authoritarian character, as evidenced by the lack of tolerance for any serious opposition to ZANU-PF.

## THE SURVIVAL OF MULTI-PARTY DEMOCRACY

The signing of the Unity Accord between ZANU and ZAPU had a contradictory outcome. The political accommodation and the amnesty for dissidents brought about peace in Matabeleland, making it possible once again to promote development in that region. The accord made it possible for attention to be diverted from the destructive ethnic manifestations of political conflict, freeing society to examine critically the government's performance to date.

Among the provisions of the Unity Accord was one that committed the newly united party to work towards creation of a one-party state. That this goal was thwarted is a crucial development in the fledgling democracy that is Zimbabwe. By committing itself to the creation of a one-party state, ZANU-PF had indicated that the price for peace and stability was the stifling of pluralistic political debate. Many Zimbabweans were to show the government that they were not prepared to pay such a price, even though, as the 1995 election revealed, ZANU-PF has a virtual monopoly of political power.

The accord, by resolving the conflict between ZANU-PF and ZAPU, drew attention to the intra-party divisions within ZANU-PF.[27] These differences were ideological, ethnic (there being a number of sub-groups within the Shona), and personal. They came to a head in 1989, when Edgar Tekere, an outspoken critic of government corruption, was expelled from ZANU-PF and established his own party, the Zimbabwe Unity Movement (ZUM). His party ran an election campaign opposing the creation of a one-party state, as well as corruption generally.

The creation of ZUM was significant in a number of respects. Since the party drew support from across the country, it could not be identified with either one of the major ethnic groups. This revealed that political views could be expressed without being cloaked with an ethnic identity. Some of the more serious opposition parties that emerged before the 1995 election also enjoyed support from across the country.[28]

The treatment of ZUM in the run-up to the election of 1990 revealed ZANU-PF's lack of tolerance for any serious opposition, even that which did not threaten to cause ethnic conflict. Prior to the election, ZUM candidates were harassed, and attempts to hold rallies were thwarted by the authorities. More serious was the attempt to murder ZUM candidate Patrick Kombayi, who ran in Gweru Central and threatened to defeat one of the vice-presidents, Simon Muzenda.[29]

Despite the harassment and intimidation of ZUM candidates, the party managed to win two seats. This result encouraged those who were opposed, both in society and within ZANU-PF, to a one-party state. After the election, many segments of society voiced their opposition to a single-party state. Within ZANU-PF, prominent politicians such as Eddison Zvobo and Dumiso Dabengwa (a charismatic former member of ZAPU), publicly opposed the idea.

The degree of opposition was such that it could not be ignored. There can be little doubt that the unity of ZANU-PF itself was at stake. On 22 September 1990 the central committee of ZANU-PF decided not to attempt to legislate a one-party state. This decision, despite the expressed wishes of Mugabe, reveals that though ZANU-PF's authoritarian nature continues to constitute a threat to democracy in Zimbabwe, the popular will is not completely disregarded. This fact, in turn is a function of the continued vigilance of such societal actors as students, unions, civil organizations, professionals, intellectuals, and other courageous individuals.

Unfortunately, developments leading up to the election held in April 1995 confirm that, despite the survival of formal multi-party democracy, ZANU-PF's dominance remains, and the opposition won only two of 120 elected seats. The fate of opposition parties, which are subject to harassment and intimidation, has not been very encouraging. Under a new act introduced in 1992, according to which only parties with fifteen or more seats are entitled to public funding, ZANU-PF is the only party to receive public support. Struggling opposition parties, faced with severe financial constraints, were unable to field candidates in all constituencies. Indeed, prior to the 1995 election, ZANU-PF ran uncontested in fifty-five constituencies. Since Mugabe has the power (under amendments to the constitution made in 1987) to appoint thirty additional MPs, ZANU-PF already effectively had won a majority in the legislature even before the election.[30]

Another factor hindering opposition parties is that they do not differ substantively on policy issues. They have been plagued by what Jonathan Moyo has dubbed the "splinter group" phenomenon. In 1991, for example, a group broke away from Edgar Tekere's Zimbabwe Unity Movement (ZUM) to form the Democratic Party. In September 1994, a group left the Forum Party of Zimbabwe – then considered the most viable opposition party under the leadership of Enock Dumbutshena, the first chief justice – to create the Forum Party for Democracy. In all such cases, the disagreements have been over personalities, not policies, making it difficult for the public to distinguish among parties.

More fundamentally, none of the opposition parties has succeeded in winning a strong basis of support in the rural areas, where the majority lives. Indeed, support for opposition parties tends to come from the urban areas, particularly the middle class, both white and black. (In the 1990 election, ZUM received 30 per cent of the vote in the urban centres of Harare in Mashonaland and Bulawayo in Matabeleland). All the parties supported liberal, market-based reforms, so that ZANU-PF did not have to go on the defensive over the extremely controversial reform program, ESAP.[31]

While ZANU-PF has lost the support it formerly enjoyed from intellectuals and workers, it is still able to command the countryside. While the peasantry has been effectively depoliticized since 1980, that portion of the peasantry that continues to vote still supports ZANU-PF, even though the government has made very little progress on the key issue of land redistribution. Though the government announced in November 1997 that it planned to confiscate 1,000 largely white-owned farms for redistribution, it is not clear who within the peasantry will benefit. Part of the explanation for this continued support lies in the fact that over two million peasants are now permanently dependent on hand-outs of food from the government. During times of drought, which are frequent, the number goes up to over four million.[32]

Though the labour movement would be an obvious candidate to form a party to the left of ZANU-PF, it would face serious challenges in consolidating the necessary support in the rural areas. Morgan Tsvangirai, secretary-general of the Zimbabwe Congress of Trade Unions (ZCTU), has expressed the fear that if a party were formed that was affiliated with the ZCTU, the labour movement would suffer, as it would be targeted for attacks by the government.[33]

For the time being, ZANU-PF's monopoly of power remains unchallenged. However, a number of variables might change this situation, including a battle over the succession to the ageing Mugabe, failure of the economy to generate improvement in the quality of life of the majority, or even a breakdown of the Unity Accord between ZANU-PF and the former ZAPU.

## THE SALIENCE OF CLASS

The weakness of the opposition in Zimbabwe has been a factor in the ability of the government to execute economic policies that are unpopular with the majority of the population. Though market-based reforms were introduced just after the 1990 election, the question of whether to implement economic reforms was not debated during the campaign. Nor was there any serious discussion in Parliament prior to the implementation of reforms, so that broad-based consultation never took place. However, the mostly white economic elites were extensively consulted by the government – a reflection of their class power, stemming from their position in the economy.[34]

The signing of the Unity Accord in December 1987 represented the start of a new period of elite cohesion.[35] The subsiding of the political significance of ethnic divisions in society revealed the growing significance of class divisions, which were no longer neatly demarcated by race. Attention came to focus in particular on the wealth accumulation activities of senior politicians and bureaucrats (the ruling elite). Thus the Unity Accord was perceived by the former rank and file of ZAPU as reflecting the desire of senior ZAPU members to gain access to the advantages that arise from holding state positions.[36]

The process of elite cohesion was not limited to the political elites in ZANU-PF and the former ZAPU. There was also growing cooperation between the black ruling elites and the mostly white economic elites. This effort was facilitated by senior decision-makers' recognition that market-based reforms would benefit the economy – a view long held by the economic elites. Thus by the late 1980s there was a convergence of interests between the ruling and economic elites over market-based reforms.[37]

Equally important to the process of elite cohesion was the transformation of the ruling elite into a state-based bourgeoisie.[38] Masipula Sithole, who emphasizes the salience of ethnic divisions in society, nevertheless points to the ruling elite's "highly developed appetite for accumulation," leading to its "embourgeoisement."[39] In addition to the familiar practice in Africa of corruption, Zimbabwe's relatively well-developed economy has let many politicians and senior bureaucrats acquire private businesses and/or large-scale commercial farms. (Close to one-fifth of the 4,500 large-scale farms in Zimbabwe are now estimated to be owned by blacks).[40]

In 1988, the *Bulawayo Chronicle* began to publish a series of articles detailing the corrupt activities of senior politicians (of both Shona and Ndebele backgrounds) surrounding the sale of cars assembled at the state-owned Willowvale plant.[41] At a time of severe shortage of automobiles, senior politicians were using their political positions to buy cars and then to resell them at grossly inflated prices. Students at the University of Zimbabwe played a prominent role in exposing this corrupt practice.[42] At this time, the labour movement, represented by the ZCTU, began to take an independent stance by joining the students in criticizing the government.

The role of students, intellectuals, and workers in making public the ruling elite's enrichment is very significant, in that they traditionally had strongly supported the governing class. Demonstrations by students and labour have invited violent confrontations with the government; the University of Zimbabwe campus has been surrounded by riot police and closed on numerous occasions since 1988, and the ZCTU's rallies have been disrupted, often violently. The class transformation of the ruling elite has thus contributed to the erosion of the traditional alliance between the ruling elite and workers, students, and intellectuals.

The embourgeoisement of the ruling class has transformed the economic realm as well. Around the time that the Unity Accord was signed, the government began to reconsider its development strategy. The Economic Reform Programme launched in 1991, better known as the Economic Structural Adjustment Programme (ESAP), constituted a dramatic shift from the government's original, social welfare oriented development strategy. The political accommodation facilitated this about-face, as it would have been difficult for the government to implement this major reform had an independent ZAPU been able to take political advantage of this switch in tactics by the government.[43]

The embourgeoisement of the ruling elite, including senior members of both ZANU-PF and the former ZAPU, has led to a loss of the priority that the government had once attached to the welfare of the poor. While ESAP in and of itself may not be detrimental to the long-term interests of the poor majority in Zimbabwe, in the absence of additional policies to meet their basic needs, the poor will not stand to benefit from the reforms initiated after 1990.[44]

A parallel shift also occurred in long-promised land redistribution. The pattern has been for members of the ruling elite to acquire large-scale commercial farms, rather than for these farms to be subdivided into small holdings for distribution to land-hungry peasants. The Land Acquisition Act, as amended in 1992, is actually designed to distribute land to the better off communal farmers, though it is being presented as a major instrument of land redistribution.[45] The poor have also been adversely affected by other recent policy shifts. Since the introduction of market-based reforms, rural peasants have been hurt by the closure of maize collection points, and the urban poor have suffered from the introduction of cost recovery in health and education.

It should not be assumed that these setbacks in Zimbabwe's development strategy are the result of the role of the IMF and the World Bank in financing the reforms. The government itself wanted market-based reforms. Indeed, when it finally included the Social Dimensions of Adjustment component in its reform program, it did so on the urging of the World Bank.[46] In other words, just as the World Bank was beginning to appreciate in the late 1980s the need for giving adjustment a "human face," Zimbabwe's ruling elite, because of its declining commitment to the welfare of the poor, was going in the other direction.[47]

## II TANZANIA, 1961–78

The political stability of Tanzania since 1961 has to be explained in quite different ways from that of Zimbabwe. During the first twenty years after independence, Tanzanian developments tended to receive, save from Marxist commentators, remarkably sympathetic academic analysis. It later became increasingly unfashionable to write positively of almost any public policy in Tanzania. One by one the hallmarks of Tanzanian socialism have been severely discredited – its rural socialism and villagization policies; its pursuit of industrialization; its overreliance on state enterprises; and its continuous attempts, far beyond the capabilities of its public service, to discipline market forces through exchange and price controls and the regulation of imports and exports. All these and much more have been subjected to severe international and domestic criticism.

In this dominant climate of scepticism towards anything Tanzanian, inadequate due has been given the political accomplishments of the Nyerere era. Yet these achievements were major. The Tanzanian leadership reordered its constitution in 1965, abandoning the inherited but rootless Westminster model and replacing it with a domestically designed "democratic one-party state," which at the time seemed very much to fit Tanzanian realities. These arrangements were immediately widely endorsed and continued for several decades to provide a largely unchallenged framework within which Tanzanians ordered their public affairs. Under that system, Tanzania enjoyed continuous, stable civilian rule for some twenty years. Then, peacefully and within that framework of civilian rule, there was not only a change of political leadership but also a near-180 degree change of ideological direction, with Tanzania becoming a more open political society, now in transition to a multi-party system.

Many regard Tanzanian history since the Arusha Declaration of 1967, with its strong commitment to socialism, primarily as evidence, by counter-example, of the appropriateness in tropical Africa of a market-based minimal state, an outward-oriented development strategy, and a competitive party system. However, for anyone interested in the peaceful civilian management of internal conflicts, what is of crucial interest is not so much Tanzania's present ideological resting place as the success with which Julius Nyerere's government, over a long period, maintained political stability. This section on Tanzania is therefore about neither the politics of transition to a competitive party system nor the collapse of a socialist development strategy, both of which have taken place in the last decade and a half or so. It is rather about how Tanzania managed in its early years to create an original, hybrid constitutional order – the democratic, one-party state – which first provided stable and widely popular civilian rule for at least fifteen years and then proved sufficiently resilient and adaptable that, within its framework, fundamental changes towards greater democracy and a more open economy could occur without violence or military intervention. The conclusion to this chapter considers whether the policies and institutions that contributed to this achievement are at all relevant to countries now hoping to move towards a political order that will be stable, democratic, and civilian-led.

One way to approach these questions is to recognize that the leaders of Tanzania, particularly President Julius Nyerere, were aware that their country, like so many others in Africa, faced a profound paradox in its early decades of independence. It had somehow to minimize the adverse consequences of two major political risks that it unavoidably faced. The first was the possibility that its leaders would use their monopoly of power grossly for self-aggrandizing and corrupt ends. The second was the risk that the new force of nationalism would not finally be able to contain the divisive power of ethnic, regional, and religious factionalism and intra-elite rivalries. The paradox for Tanzania was that policies that would help minimize the first risk – such as a genuine safeguarding of freedom of speech and freedom of association – might unleash powerfully divisive social forces that would greatly intensify the second risk. And the converse was also true, for policies that might contain the second risk, such as constraints on these very same freedoms, would increase the chance that those in power would become autocratic and corrupt.

To this awareness by the Tanzanian leadership of this paradox we must add two further influences that shaped the constitutional reforms of the mid-1960s. The Tanganyika African National Union (TANU) had just won for Tanganyika[48] its freedom from colonial rule. Nevertheless Tanganyika was still a very fragile country, facing enormous challenges. TANU and its leader were enormously popular and were indeed the major force that held the country together. Within TANU and generally throughout the country there was an understandable conviction that TANU's great potential to lead the nation forward should not be rapidly dissipated. Many saw this as requiring a single-party system.

Nyerere himself added a final dimension to the diagnosis of Tanzania's political and constitutional needs. He saw Tanzania's social cohesion as being under severe threat from an acquisitive individualism that was rapidly developing, particularly within both the political leadership and the senior government bureaucracy. He saw this characteristic as threatening the fabric of Tanzanian society and destructive of any chance that the nation could pursue economic development in ways that would not generate morally indefensible and socially destructive inequalities. There was thus, in his view, only a short time left in which to develop a national, public ethos that would contain the selfish acquisitiveness of those in power – a modern equivalent to the communitarian values that he felt were typical of traditional Tanzanian societies.

Acting on these deeply felt convictions, Nyerere in the years 1964–5 devised and vigorously implemented an original set of political institutions, making up a democratic, one-party state. These institutions were intended to be sufficiently participatory and democratic as to limit the risk of the regime's becoming severely authoritarian and corrupt, but not so open as to threaten Tanzania's still fragile unity or weaken prematurely the integrating and energizing capabilities of the nationalist movement.[49]

This whole exercise in constitution-building was a brilliant and successful demonstration of democratic leadership. Though Nyerere and the One Party State Commission that he appointed were highly original and innovative in what they proposed,[50] their objectives were close to widely shared popular perceptions that supported a very central role for TANU but wanted its leadership to be answerable to representative party and national institutions.[51]

Nyerere's vision of a democratic society was not that of the pluralist constitutional democracies of Western industrialized states. He sought a modern, national equivalent to the self-governing communities of equals that he felt characterized traditional African societies at least in Tanzania.[52] The single party would be coterminous with the nation. All citizens would be involved in the selection of members of Parliament, and the whole election process would be designed to encourage the choosing of trusted representatives, who would seek to advance the common national good. In addition, the representative institutions within the party were to be structured on the basis of the same principles.

There was thus provision in Nyerere's conception of democracy for governmental answerability, for popular input, and for leadership by example, explanation, and exhortation. As well, it sought to exclude the influence of ideological or personality factions; to rule out the political exploitation of ethnic, religious, racial, or regional identities; and to block the transformation of TANU into a closed, vanguard party, putatively acting on behalf of the workers and peasants but without their immediate, popular involvement.

The main features of the electoral system under the 1965 constitution illustrate well how it was hoped these rather complicated objectives would be achieved. First, membership in TANU was open to anyone willing to accept its aims and objectives – a formal requirement that excluded very few. Second, any member could be nominated for election to the national assembly or to any of the representative organs of the party. Third, in each constituency the annual district conference (ADC), a large and representative meeting, voted its order of preference as among those nominated. Each ballot in each of the constituencies in the national election was to include only two nominees. The National Executive Committee (NEC) of TANU decided which two of the candidates nominated by each ADC would appear on the ballot. From the start it was agreed that the NEC would normally accept the ADC's ranking of candidates. Fourth, the electoral campaigns operated within a set of rules which sought to ensure that the contest was as fair as possible. No candidate was allowed to spend any money campaigning. All election meetings were organized by the party, and each candidate addressed each meeting. No tribal language could be used in electioneering, and no reference could be made to issues of race, tribe, or religion. Finally, no candidate could claim that she or he was supported by any prominent TANU leader, and no one could campaign on behalf of any other candidate or group of candidates.

A second major innovation followed only two years later – the leadership code. Nyerere had been disheartened by the increasing evidence that selfish materialism within the leadership was rapidly overwhelming whatever remnants remained of older, more communal, egalitarian values. By 1966 the values and attitudes of those already in privileged positions in Tanzania had become a national issue. There was increasing evidence that senior party and government officials were beginning to engage in private capitalist activities in addition to their official jobs, though such opportunities were scarce. The most frequent of such activities was the building by party and government leaders of large mansions, which were then rented to foreign embassies or international corporations.

Nyerere saw such developments as the antithesis of the society that TANU was striving to build. He therefore convinced a reluctant NEC to introduce a stringent leadership code.[53] This prohibited any middle- or senior-ranking party or government official from a whole range of self-seeking activities, including holding shares in a private company, being a director in such a company renting one or more houses to others, receiving more than one salary, and employing others to work in income-earning activities. Nyerere was convinced that the code enforced an ethos that was still part of the inherited values of Tanzanian society but needed reinforcement if it was not to be overwhelmed. He told a press conference in 1967: "I think the chances are that all leaders will surrender their personal possessions and remain leaders. The atmosphere in Tanzania is extremely difficult for them to do otherwise. ... This was the right time. Had we delayed you would have discovered two years from now that our leadership had become rather entrenched in the accumulation of personal property."[54]

Tanzania's "democratic, one-party state" and this austere leadership code were the central institutional innovations resulting from

Nyerere's emphasis on nation-building, leadership, participation, answerability, and integrity in government. For over twenty years, these components of the Tanzanian system, widely endorsed throughout society, were accepted features of how the nation governed itself. They are central to the explanation of Tanzania's political stability throughout the Nyerere era. More than that, arguably they helped nurture a political culture that at the least remains less permissive of corruption than most and expects governments recurrently to be answerable through national elections to the people.

### III CONCLUSIONS

Zimbabwe and Tanzania have each been able, since winning independence, to maintain domestic political stability under civilian rule, without primary reliance on repression and with a degree of political participation that distinguishes them from many other African states. They have done so despite having experienced many of the same problems common to other nations on the continent. Each therefore illustrates the importance of political leadership in the early decades of independence. The quality, as well as goals and objectives, of the political leadership clearly had a determining influence on the extent to which political stability was maintained in Zimbabwe and Tanzania. However, the substantial differences in the circumstances of the two countries meant that in each nation the leadership sought to maintain social stability in quite different ways. It is also clear that the existence of a well-entrenched class structure in Zimbabwe helped consolidate the stability of the political and economic system, while its absence in Tanzania has undermined the prospects for sustained economic development.

#### ZIMBABWE

The comparative stability of Zimbabwe since independence could not have been predicted with confidence in 1978. Its powerful white minority was ill at ease with the prospect of living under Black majority rule and was still in a position to undermine the development efforts of the new majority government. Major land reforms and drastic changes in the senior ranks of the bureaucracy and the army were needed to eradicate the legacy of racial domination bequeathed from the colonial decades. A major ethnic division between the Mashona and the Matabele threatened to erupt into civil war. In addition, ZANU had to transform itself from a political movement engaged in an armed struggle into one capable of governing a large state and managing a complex economy.

Nevertheless, despite these severe challenges, Zimbabwe's political leaders have managed to maintain stability and social peace, without primary reliance on repression. Many factors contributed to this success, including a comparatively well-developed economic infrastructure; a more substantial class of educated Blacks than was the case in many other African states; a strong majority party, whose cohesion had been forged through an armed struggle against the earlier white minority regime; a reasonably efficient and professional civil service; and much international development assistance in its early years. Yet by themselves these and other factors might not have been enough to produce the comparatively stable social order that has so far emerged. Two additional factors provide the central explanation: the quality of political leadership and Zimbabwe's developed class system.

As the section above on Zimbabwe illustrated, the Zimbabwean leadership was open to reconciliation. This was especially so in its relationship with its erstwhile rulers, the whites. Mugabe and his colleagues recognized that it was in the interest of the ZANU-PF government to secure the economic cooperation of the whites and thereby prevent a mass exodus, such as had occurred in Mozambique. Strategic considerations included recognition that economic growth and stability would make Zimbabwe less vulnerable to destabilization by South Africa.

The government was also initially open to reconciliation with the rival ZAPU opposition party. This openness soured, however, with the events that led to the outbreak of violence in Matabeleland. Furthermore, ZANU-PF did not have the same strong incentive for reconciliation with ZAPU as it had with the white minority. As the decade continued, it became increasingly clear that ZANU-PF was not prepared to tolerate significant political opposition from ZAPU. This reality was confirmed by the conditions under which the Unity Accord was signed in 1987 and by Mugabe's efforts to legislate a one-party state.

It is highly significant therefore that Mugabe was willing finally to accede to the wishes of those who favoured a multi-party system, by abandoning his long cherished goal. People from all sections of society, including students, professionals, labour, and intellectuals, as well as from within ZANU-PF itself, felt that the multi-party system was worth preserving. Thus, while opposition parties and their leaders are harassed, their presence is grudgingly tolerated, there is a frequently vigorous public debate on government policies, and opposition leaders are not systematically killed, tortured, or detained indefinitely.

This relatively open system is reinforced by the well-defined class system and the multiple-elite coalition described above. This elite accommodation was solidified at the political level by the coming together of elites within ZANU-PF and the former ZAPU in the Unity Accord. The elites within ZAPU were thus able to join members of the ruling elite as they transformed themselves into a state-based bourgeoisie. The embourgeoisement of members of the ruling elite through their acquisition of large-scale farms and ownership of businesses has in turn facilitated elite accommodation at the economic level. As a result, the political and bureaucratic leaders, the commercial farmers, and the domestic capitalist class have come together in an effective coalition that constitutes Zimbabwe's dominant class. An accommodation has also been reached with international capital, as reflected in the introduction of ESAP in 1991, which is financed by the international financial institutions.

This coalition of economic and political elites is strong enough to dominate Zimbabwe's comparatively open political system, and it is therefore happy to see that system continue. Zimbabwe has become a comparatively open political system, which is nevertheless under hegemonic capitalist rule. Commenting on a somewhat similar situation in Namibia, Colin Leys and John Saul quote from Philip Green, who writes that liberal representative democracy as it actually exists "is preferable to most of the immediately available alternative ways of life of the contemporary nation state. But it is not democracy; not really."[55]

Whether the market-based economic policies that will keep that elite coalition intact will at the same time meet pressing mass needs sufficiently to avoid popular unrest is still an unresolved question. Though Zimbabwe has largely avoided sustained internal unrest, its government has recurrently and perhaps increasingly been repressive and is now less responsive than in the early 1980s to the needs and interests of its rural and urban poor.

In conclusion, the emergence of a dominant class that unites ethnic and racial groups has both positive and negative implications for Zimbabwe's political economy. The ruling class has helped to attenuate other sources of conflict, making it possible for economic growth, if not development, to occur. However, the elite accommodation that has emerged has resulted in economic policies that leave little room for meeting the welfare needs of the poor majority. Given the gross inequalities inherited from its colonial past, it seems reasonable to conclude that unless Zimbabwe experiences remarkable rates of economic growth, there is every likelihood that at some point powerful popular opposition forces will challenge the government on its economic and social welfare policies. Such a challenge may undermine the dominant coalition's acceptance of the present, comparatively open and competitive political system, and thereby generate increased repression.

It seems valid also to conclude that the Zimbabwean model, flawed though it may be, is not likely to be relevant to most African states. They do not have a developed and well-articulated class system. They are even less likely to experience high rates of economic growth. They therefore lack the basic prerequisites to that alliance of political, bureaucratic, agrarian, and entrepreneurial elites that constitutes the dominant class that in Zimbabwe, for the moment at least, supports and sustains its form of liberal representative democracy and its ability to contain conflict.

## TANZANIA

Many of the poorest African states today face the same central dilemma as did Tanzania in the mid-1960s. They must balance the contribution to good government that often flows from greater popular participation and fuller respect for civil and political rights against the likelihood that these same democratic features may unleash divisive ethnic, regional, and class divisions, which may shatter the still-fragile unity of the state. It is therefore reasonable to ask whether something like the Tanzanian democratic, one-party system may be preferable for many very poor Third World states than either a competitive party democracy on the Western model or any of the more autocratic alternatives.

How this question might be answered depends in part on one's judgment on whether Tanzania's system helped ease the severe problems that have engulfed the nation since the mid-1970s. In the late 1970s the economy and state began a long and disastrous decline.[56] This situation was in part the result of the impact of the global economic crisis of the mid-1970s and early 1980s. It began with OPEC's several massive hikes in the price of oil, which hit particularly hard low-income countries that lacked their own oil resources, such as Tanzania. It then quickly developed into a global recession, resulting in a simultaneous collapse in world prices for Tanzania's agricultural and resource exports and higher prices for its essential imports.

These circumstances severely hurt the Tanzanian economy, public revenues, and the capabilities and integrity of government. As well, major errors in public policy occurred, which cannot be attributed to the international crisis but were a direct consequence of Nyerere's, and with him the nationalist party's, determined commitment to a socialist transformation of economy and society.

In retrospect, they made three paramount misjudgments. First, in defiance of peasants' profound, almost universal attachment to their family holdings, TANU tried during the mid-1970s, to convince them to emphasize instead the farming of communal land. This effort dissipated much of TANU's support. Second, much of rural Tanzania was alienated when the leadership decided that progress required that Tanzanians move into villages, a plan imposed by force quite widely throughout the countryside. Third, its commitment to a development strategy that would avoid both a widening of the income gap between rich and poor and the extensive foreign ownership of the limited productive capacity brought the government regulatory and managerial responsibilities far beyond its capacity.

It would be hard to argue that these factors, intimately connected to the socialist commitment of Nyerere and TANU, were not substantially responsible for the hardships suffered in those years. Nevertheless, there were commentators at the time, including Pratt, one of the authors of this chapter,[57] who were ready to argue that, but for the major blows to the economy from the global economic crisis, the regime would probably have come to recognize that it had to abandon each of these three policies – compulsory villagization, communal farming, and a heavy measure of state intervention in the economy. On such an assumption, it might therefore be argued that the Tanzanian system offers a balancing of leadership and accountability more appropriate for many Third World countries than any of the known alternatives.

However, in retrospect it seems likely that Tanzania's democratic one-party system had outlived its usefulness by the late 1970s. The system's central failings were two – each a product of destructive oligarchical tendencies that it could not adequately constrain. First the party's institutions gradually lost their democratic and representative character. The most telling example was the failure of its regional and national conferences in the middle and late 1970s to warn the leadership that villagization and rural socialism were profoundly unpopular. Second, the leadership and the controls within the system failed to contain the material self-seeking and oligarchical propensities of the political and bureaucratic elites.

These failings, we suspect, reflect a fundamental weakness in the democratic, one-party state on the Tanzanian model. It now seems almost inevitable that, in the absence of strong popular forces that can insist on greater answerability, democratic, one-party states will finally be unable to check the self-seeking, oligarchical temptations that lurk within them. Ideological commitment, nationalism, exceptional leadership, and even fear of the disastrous consequences of severe intra-elite rivalry seem unable to ensure that the ambitions, abilities, and energies of the new elites serve, rather than undermine, the common good.

The evidence from the Tanzanian experience thus suggests that one-party democracy may well be highly useful for a comparatively short, transitional period in states whose unity is fragile but in which there is a widely popular nationalist party – in consequence perhaps of an independence struggle or the recent overthrow of an oppressive ruler. However, mounting corruption and increasing oligarchical tendencies will probably soon negate its value. Whether at that point it is possible to replace it by a political order that offers greater popular engagement and fuller recognition of civil and political rights, without in turn generating political activities that are highly divisive and socially destructive, can hardly be predicted. The outcome will depend heavily on whether the leadership is committed to a transition to a more fully democratic form of government.

It therefore appears from both the Zimbabwean and the Tanzanian experiences discussed above that one should not expect too much of democratic political institutions, be they modelled after Western competitive party systems or innovative, democratic, one-party systems. Skilful political leadership can certainly use either of these approaches to advance the common good, but each needs much good fortune, wise leadership, and sustained growth if it is not to be overwhelmed by the destructive impact on it of oligarchical love of power, capitalist greed, and ethnic rivalry.

NOTES

1 For a widely respected analysis of the developments leading to peaceful resolution, see Stephen John Stedman, *Peacemaking in Civil War: International Mediation in Zimbabwe, 1974–1980* (Boulder, Col.: Lynne Rienner Publishers 1991). See also Robert Matthews, "From Rhodesia to Zimbabwe: Prerequisites of a Settlement," *International Journal* (spring 1990), 292–233.

2 See Richard Saunders, "A Hollow Shell: Democracy in Zimbabwe," *Southern African Report* (May 1995), 3–4.

3 This argument differs somewhat from that of Jeffrey Herbst, who argues that an implicit racial bargain was struck between the whites and the Black government, whereby whites would be allowed to stay on in order to help run the economy but that their children would be expected to secure their futures elsewhere. See, Jeffrey Herbst, "Racial Reconcilia-

tion in Southern Africa," *International Affairs* (winter 1988–89), 43–54. The continued dominance of whites in the economy, and the benefits they derive from market-based reforms introduced after 1990, raise doubts about the survival of this racial bargain, if it ever existed.

4 As Stedman has aptly observed, reconciliation by its very nature entails a certain degree of continuity with the past and, by extension, the absence of radical change. See Stephen John Stedman, "The End of the Zimbabwean Civil War," in Roy Licklider, ed., *Stopping the Killing: How Civil Wars End* (New York: New York University Press 1993), 159–60.

5 Reported in Economist Intelligence Unit (EIU), *Zimbabwe Report, January 1995*, (London: EIU 1995), 4.

6 These ideological and class divisions are discussed frankly in, ZANU-PF, *Zimbabwe at Five Years of Independence* (Harare: Marden Printers 1986).

7 See Lee Cokorinos, "The Political Economy of State and Party Formation in Zimbabwe," in Michael Schatzberg, ed., *The Political Economy of Zimbabwe* (New York: Praeger 1984).

8 Ibid. See also Stephen Stedman, "The End of the Zimbabwean Civil War," 132–5.

9 For a detailed analysis of the divisions within the liberation movement, see Masipula Sithole, "Zimbabwe: In Search of a Stable Democracy," in Larry Diamond, Juan Linz, and Seymour Lipset, eds., *Democracy in Developing Countries: Africa* (Boulder, Col.: Lynne Rienner Publishers 1988). Sithole places considerable emphasis on the ethnic rivalries between ZANU and ZAPU, and, though these were very real, he tends to play down the ideological divisions both between and within the two parties.

10 For a discussion of the election results of 1980 and 1985, see Masipula Sithole, "The General Elections, 1979–1985," in Ibbo Mandaza, ed., *Zimbabwe: The Political Economy of Transition, 1980–1986* (Dakar: Codesria 1986).

11 This discovery confirmed ZANU-PF's suspicions, dating back to the liberation struggle, that ZAPU might attempt to take military control of Matabeleland, and even the entire country. See Sithole, "Zimbabwe," 238–40. For a concise outline of the immediate causes of the conflict, see Christine Sylvester, *Zimbabwe: The Terrain of Contradictory Development* (Boulder, Col.: Westview Press 1991), 75–7.

12 According to James MacBruce, the rebellion was put down by integrated army units, predominantly former contingents of the Rhodesian army, supported by elements of the air force, manned almost exclusively by former Rhodesians. See James MacBruce, "Domestic and Regional Security," in Simon Baynham, ed., *Zimbabwe in Transition* (Stockholm: Almqvist and Wiksell International 1992), 213. Perhaps ironically, Mugabe continues to maintain former Rhodesian personnel in the army, as a sort of insurance policy.

13 For an exhaustive account of the extent and nature of South African assistance, see Phyllis Johnson and David Martin, "Zimbabwe: Apartheid's Dilemma," in Phyllis Johnson and David Martin, eds., *Frontline Southern Africa: Destructive Engagement* (New York: Four Walls Eight Windows 1988), 69–86.

14 For an excellent account of the impact of South African destabilization on Zimbabwe, see Elipha G. Munkonoweshuro, *Zimbabwe: Ten Years of Destabilization – A Balance Sheet* (Stockholm: Bethany Books 1992). For the impact of destabilization on southern Africa, see Douglas Anglin, "Southern Africa under Siege: Options for the Frontline States," *Journal of Modern African Studies* (Dec. 1988), 549–65. On conflict resolution in post-apartheid southern Africa, see Thomas Ohlson and Stephen John Stedman, *The New Is Not Yet Born: Conflict Resolution in Southern Africa* (Washington, DC: Brookings Institution 1994).

15 Munkonoweshuru, *Zimbabwe*, 16.

16 For example, in 1981, Peter Walls was suddenly dismissed as commander of the Zimbabwe National Army after he apparently revealed that he had plotted a military coup against the new government shortly after it took power. This rendering of the events is given in Masipula Sithole, "Slippery Steps from Racial Domination to Democracy in Zimbabwe," in Peter Anyang' Nyong'o, ed., *Arms and Daggars in the Heart of Africa: Studies on Internal Conflict* (Nairobi: Academy Science Publishers 1993), 166. Not all accounts are consistent, however. According to one, Walls's dismissal was the result of his revelation that a coup had been contemplated against the newly elected government, in order to replace it with more moderate politicians. See Tendai Dumbutshena, "White Exodus, White Return," *Southern African Political and Economic Monthly* (April 1993), 5. Johnson and Martin, in contrast, claim that Walls was dismissed because he revealed that after he learned that ZANU-PF had won the elections in 1980 he asked British Prime Minister Margaret Thatcher to annul the results. See Johnson and Martin, *Frontline Southern Africa*, 61.

17 Johnson and Martin, *Frontline Southern Africa*, 61.

18 Around the same time, demands were also made that ex-ZIPRA fighters be compensated for their share of the contributions that were made to purchase ZAPU properties confiscated by the government after the discovery of arms caches. See "Call to Compensate Ex-Zipra Fighters," *Parade* (Aug. 1992), 13.

19 This argument is convincingly presented in Ronald Weitzer, *Transforming Settler States: Communal Conflict and Internal Security in Northern Ireland and Zimbabwe* (Berkeley: University of California Press 1990), 134–89.

20 Weitzer, *Transforming Settler States*, 163.

21 As Christine Sylvester put it, "One could argue endlessly about the dangers to the new government ... but it was perplexing to see the new government wield the old military apparatuses of the state, much as Smith might have done in a similar situation." See Sylvester, *Zimbabwe*, 77.

22 This paragraph is drawn from, Weitzer, *Transforming Settler States*, 169–71.

23 On the 1985 election, see Sithole, "The General Elections," in Ibbo Mandaza, ed., *Zimbabwe: The Political Economy of Transition, 1980–1986* (Dakar: Godesia 1986), 75–97.

24 These defections have been described by Jonathan Moyo as "opportunistic," and they certainly led to criticisms from the rank and file of ZAPU. See Jonathan Moyo, "The Dialectics of National Unity and Democracy in Zimbabwe," in Ibbo Mandaza and Lloyd Sachikonye, eds., *The One Party State and Democracy: The Zimbabwe Debate* (Harare: SAPES 1991), 91.

25 For a detailed and interesting description of the negotiations leading up to the signing of the Unity Accord, see Willard Chiwewe, "Unity Negotiations," in Canaan S. Banana, ed., *Turmoil and Tenacity: Zimbabwe 1890–1990* (Harare: College Press 1989). Chiwewe was secretary for the Unity Committee, 242–86.

26 Ibid., 264–81.

27 For an excellent recounting of these divisions in the period leading up to the 1990 election, see Jonathan Moyo, *Voting for Democracy: Electoral Politics in Zimbabwe* (Harare: University of Zimbabwe Publications 1992), 31–8.

28 This is the case with the Forum Party of Zimbabwe, formed in 1993 under the leadership of the former chief justice of Zimbabwe, Enock Dumbutshena.

29 See Moyo, *Voting for Democracy*, 49–51.

30 For a pre-election analysis of political developments in Zimbabwe, see "Zimbabwe: Beyond the Elections," *Southern African Political and Economic Monthly* (March 1995), 5–9. The interesting story concerns not so much the 1995 election itself but the primaries leading up to it, which revealed intense factional divisions within ZANU-PF among the subgroupings of the Shona as well as among personalities, as individuals struggled for political power.

31 On opposition politics in Zimbabwe, see T. Deve and F. Goncalves, "Whither the Opposition in Zimbabwe?" *Southern African Political and Economic Monthly* (May 1994), 9–11.

32 The hand-out of food, even in "bumper seasons," is seen to be a form of vote-buying by ZANU-PF. See Lloyd Sachikonye, "Wither the Zimbabwe

Opposition Movement?" *Southern African Political and Economic Monthly* (May 1993), 48.

33 Interview with author, Harare, Aug. 1992.

34 Whites predominate in the productive sectors of the economy, including commercial agriculture, manufacturing, and mining. Though whites lost their twenty separate seats after 1987, they have actually seen their political influence increase, as they are able to consult with the ruling elite behind closed doors in order to advance their economic interests. Their continued political influence is convincingly argued in Sithole, "Slippery Steps from Racial Domination."

35 The term "elite cohesion" was coined by John Makumbe, lecturer, Department of Political and Administrative Studies, University of Zimbabwe, interview with author, Harare, June 1992. The growing convergence of interests between the ruling elite and mostly white elites in the economy has been widely observed. Some commentators even refer to it as a class alliance. See Richard Saunders in an interview with Morgan Tsvangirai, secretary general, Zimbabwe Congress of Trade Unions, *Africa South* (Aug. 1992): 8–9.

36 Moyo, "Dialectics," 91.

37 For a detailed account of the embourgeoisement of the ruling elite and the process of elite accommodation, see Hevina S. Dashwood, "The Political Economy of Transformation: The Evolution of Zimbabwe's Development Strategy, 1980–91," PhD dissertation, University of Toronto, October 1995. This convergence of interests eixsts at the ideological level only, as whites and blacks in Zimbabwe generally do not mingle socially.

38 The acquisitive tendencies of the ruling elite has been facilitated by state participation in the economy, affording new opportunities for directorships, board memberships, and access to information as well as resources. See Lloyd Sachikonye, "From Equity and Participation to Structural Adjustment: State and Social Forces in Zimbabwe," in David Moore and Gerald Schmitz, eds., *Debating Development Discourse: Institutional and Popular Perspectives* (London: Macmillan 1995).

39 Sithole, "Zimbabwe," 244.

40 See Sam Moyo, "Land Tenure Bidding among Black Agrarian Capitalists in Zimbabwe," *Southern African Political and Economic Monthly* (May 1994), 37.

41 For an account of this scandal, see Lloyd Sachikonye, "The Context of the Democracy Debate," in Ibbo Mandaza and Lloyd Sachikonye, eds., *The One Party State and Democracy* (Harare: SAPES 1991), 49–50. A committee of inquiry was set up to look into the matter, and its findings were published in the *Report of the Commission of Inquiry into the Distribution of Motor Vehicles* (Harare, 1989), better known as the Sandura Report.

42 For an account of the students' role, see Welshman Ncube, "The Post-Unity Period: Developments, Benefits and Problems," in Canaan S. Banana, ed., *Turmoil and Tenacity: Zimbabwe 1890–1990* (Harare: College Press 1980), 305–35.

43 This observation was made by one of the participants in the unity negotiations – John Nkomo, formerly of ZAPU and a cabinet minister – in an interview with the author, Harare, Dec. 1992.

44 This is the central hypothesis of Dashwood, "Political Economy."

45 Ibid., 308–12.

46 Ibid., 105.

47 As Colin Stoneman has put it, Zimbabwe met the World Bank "going the other way." See "Home-Grown Trade Liberalisation?" *Africa Recovery* (Oct.-Dec. 1990), 1.

48 Tanganyika became the United Republic of Tanganyika and Zanzibar on 26 April 1964, with the union of these two countries. A year later it became the United Republic of Tanzania.

49 The analysis that follows is based on Pratt, *The Critical Phase in Tanzania, 1945–1968: Nyerere and the Emergence of a Socialist Strategy* (New York: Cambridge University Press 1976), 201–15, where it is more fully elaborated. Tanzania's democratic, one-party state attracted widespread scholarly interest. Other studies that should be consulted by the seriously interested student are Lionel Cliffe, ed., *One Party Democracy* (Nairobi: EAPH 1967); Lionel Cliffe and John Saul, eds., *Socialism in Tanzania* (Dar-es-Salaam: EPAH 1972); Election Studies Committee, University of Dar-es-Salaam, *Socialism and Participation: Tanzania's 1970 Election* (Dar-es-Salaam 1972); and Bismarck Mwansasu and Cranford Pratt, eds., *Towards Socialism in Tanzania* (Toronto: University of Toronto Press 1979).

50 The key public document is *Report of the Presidential Commission on the Democratic One Party State.* (Dar-es-Salaam 1965). As well, the speeches and writings of Nyerere from this period provide major insights into the underlying motivations. Many of these are reproduced in his *Freedom and Unity/Uhuru na Umoja.* (London 1966).

51 Pratt, *The Critical Phase*, 201–5.

52 For an early and hence particularly perceptive analysis of Nyerere's thought, which identifies the communitarian element of his view of democracy, see Harvey Glickman, "Dilemmas of Political Theory in an African Context: The Ideology of Julius Nyerere," in Jeffrey Butler and A.S. Castagno, eds., *Boston University Papers on Africa: Transition in African Politics* (New York: Praeger 1967), 195–223.

53 For a fuller discussion of the leadership code, see Pratt, *The Critical Phase*, 232–7.

54 From the transcript of a press conference given on 4 March 1967. A fuller text appears in Pratt, *The Critical Phase*, 236.

55 As quoted in Colin Leys and John S. Saul, "The Legacy: An Afterword," in their edited volume *Namibia's Liberation Struggle: The Two-Edged Sword* (London: James Currey 1995), 23. The quotation is from Philip Green, *Retrieving Democracy: In Search of Civil Equality* (London: Methuen 1989), 3.
56 The literature on the political and economic crisis in Tanzania in the 1980s is voluminous. Readers are likely to find most helpful Jannik Boesen et al., eds, *Tanzania: Crisis and Struggle for Survival* (Uppsala: Scandinavian Institute of African Studies 1986).
57 See in particular Cranford Pratt, "Tanzania's Transition to Socialism: Reflections of a Democratic Socialist," in Bismarck Mwansasu and Cranford Pratt, eds., *Towards Socialism in Tanzania* (Toronto: University of Toronto Press 1979), 193–236.

# PART FIVE

*Security, Conflict, and Peace*

# 9 Redefining "Security" after the Cold War: The OAU, the UN, and Conflict Management in Africa

JAMES BUSUMTWI-SAM

The end of the Cold War appeared to bring hopes for peace in Africa. The two superpowers that had competed for influence in Africa reduced their competition, and a renewed emphasis on collective security in the United Nations (UN) and in other international forums appeared to herald an era of greater peace. Within Africa, a series of conflicts came to an end: peace accord of 1988 in southwestern Africa led to the independence of Namibia in 1990; agreement of 1991 appeared to bring peace to Angola; another, signed in 1992, ended the war in Mozambique; and the victory of the Eritrean forces in the war in Ethiopia and the resulting peace agreement saw the emergence of Africa's newest independent state of Eritrea at the end of 1992. While the prospects of peace appeared to improve, however, new conflicts were erupting, and older conflicts intensifying. In Liberia, in 1989, a civil war broke out that threatened to spill over into neighbouring countries; in Rwanda, civil war began in 1990; and in 1992, a conflict that had been raging since 1982 in Somalia degenerated into a human disaster of unprecedented magnitude.

This essay examines the role of third parties in the prevention, management, and resolution of armed conflicts in Africa. In it I critically assess the role of the main regional organization – the Organization of African Unity (OAU) – within the overall framework for international peace and security provided by the UN Charter and its collective security mechanisms. My main objective is to identify the conditions that are conducive to effective, multilateral prevention and management of conflict and the most appropriate form of intervention. In examining the role of the OAU in African conflicts and the conditions that make for successful multilateral intervention, I concentrate on two specific tasks. The first is to identify the evolution and changes in the OAU's normative role, as the major regional forum for the articulation of the principles and norms that govern African diplomacy and interstate relations. The second is to assess the OAU's institutional role – the mechanisms and procedures that have recently been devised to manage and resolve conflicts in Africa.

My central argument is that historically, one of the greatest constraints on the OAU's ability to deal effectively with African conflicts, specifically within states, has been the way in which national security in Africa has been defined. Nations have tended to define their security largely in terms of threats emanating from their weakness as states. The primary sources of insecurity have been seen as emanating from the external environment, even where the sources have mainly been domestic, and their emphasis has been on preserving the status quo. As a result, the OAU has been unable to come to grips with the realities of intra-state conflicts. This inability is evident in three principles enshrined in the OAU Charter – a highly restrictive definition of self-determination, the preservation of territorial integrity, and non-interference.

What is required is recognition that a rigid and inflexible adherence to the principles of non-intervention and the inviolability of colonial boundaries is obsolete. The original articulation and institutionalization of these norms are understandable within the historical context of the immediate post-colonial period. While the principles of territorial integrity and non-interference have minimized the incidence of conflict in Africa, they have also helped prolong and intensify of some conflicts by legitimizing preservation of the status quo, delegitimized the grievances of disaffected groups by an overly restrictive definition of self-determination, and thereby hardened the positions of some governments. What if these internal conflicts reflect a legitimate demand by disaffected groups for change? Many African states have no procedures and mechanisms in place for peaceful change in the structures and relations of governance. The problem of civil conflict in Africa is essentially a problem of governance. Thus effective prevention and management of conflict ultimately entails development of norms concerning governance and mechanisms and procedures that can channel demands for change into predictable and manageable directions.

I present and develop my argument in three parts. The first part offers a brief historical survey of the origins, evolution, and effects of the state-centric norms that have governed African diplomacy. To that end I examine the tensions among the principles of self-determination, territorial integrity, and non-intervention, and the kinds of intervention that have occurred in African civil wars, particularly those discussed in this volume. The second part analyses the OAU's new role in African conflicts, outlines the new institutional mechanism that has been devised, and the changes in the norms of African diplomacy. The third part assesses the new mechanism with a view to identifying the conditions required for effective, multilateral prevention, management, and resolution of conflicts.

### THE HISTORICAL RECORD

Throughout the post-independence period, wars have been a major feature of statehood in Africa. Every region has experienced armed conflict at some time since the early 1960s. In the 1960s, civil wars occurred in Congo (Zaire, 1960–5), Nigeria (1967–70), and Sudan (1963–72, 1983– ). In the 1970s war began in Ethiopia (1970), Angola (1975), Mozambique (1979), and Rhodesia (Zimbabwe, early 1970s–1980). Internal conflict in the last three countries was largely sustained and intensified by South Africa's massive involvement. The 1980s was the most destructive decade in Africa, with a total of eleven wars, including the renewal of fighting in Sudan (1983), the beginning of a vicious civil war in Uganda (1980), Somalia (1982), and Liberia (1989). Many conflicts were complicated by foreign military intervention by former colonial powers – for example, by France and Belgium in Congo in 1960 and by the superpowers that acted out their Cold War rivalries in Africa, as in the wars in Angola, Mozambique, Somalia, and Ethiopia.[1] And in many of these situations, the OAU either remained silent, as in Sudan, or sided with the central government, as in the Nigerian civil war.

The reasons for the OAU's actions or lack thereof are to be found in the norms of African diplomacy as enshrined in its charter, developed in response to the perceived realities of independence. In order to explain the origins and the effects of these norms on conflict and its management, and to gauge the extent of any normative shift in these state-centric norms, I first survey briefly the influence of ethnicity and nationalism in Africa and the legacy of colonialism.

*Ethnicity, Nationalism, and the Colonial Legacy*

There is a paradox in the role of ethnicity and nationalism in Africa. On the one hand, ethnic and nationalist identity have been a force for state development, for fostering interpersonal trust, and for enhancing community bonds. On the other hand, they have also led to national disintegration, violence, and war. An increase in ethnic or nationalist tension can produce two outcomes that may lead to war – secessionism and irredentism. Secessionism, or separatism, is the desire by one ethnic or national group for the creation of a new state to represent its interest. Secessionist movements arise from domestic grievances of that group – for example, the Ibo in Nigeria and the Eritreans in Ethiopia. The most common outcome (where these desires are not met) is civil war. "Irredentism" refers to the desire by one ethnic group to annex territory (usually in a neighbouring state) that is populated by people of similar ethnic composition.[2] An example was the Ogaden war of 1977 between Somalia and Ethiopia, sparked by Somalia's bid to annex the Ogaden region of Ethiopia, which is populated mainly by Somalis. The most common result in such situations is interstate war. Of the two destabilizing factors, secessionism has been the greater problem in Africa.

Ethnic and community rivalries existed in Africa before colonialism. Colonialism, however, had the effect of intensifying them. The arbitrary creation of colonial boundaries as a result of the Berlin Act of 1885 divided some ethnic groups and lumped others together in inherently unstable aggregations.[3] The pre-colonial system, which was characterized by migration, fragmentation, incorporation, exchange, and war, gave way through foreign conquest to territorially fixed states, whose shape, balance of forces, population, and so on had little resemblance to what had been evolving prior to colonialism. Thus were the seeds sown for present-day ethnic strife, secessionism, and irredentism. Africa has 103 examples of borders that divide ethnic groups, are the subject of dispute between neighbouring states, or produce secessionist or irredentist conflict.[4]

Yet, as the chapters in this volume show, ethnicity per se cannot on its own offer an adequate explanation of war in Africa. A major factor that has intensified ethnic divisions has been the mode of governance adopted by leaders, especially concerning access to power, allocation and distribution of resources within states, and the handling of ethnic differences by elites and political leaders. The fragility of states, resulting from of colonialism, created a perception of the need for strong states, centralized government, authoritarian control, and repression. State-building by African leaders in some cases intensified ethnic tensions and led to war. The roots of this state-centrism lay in the colonial period, in the colonial system of government, which was authoritarian, repressive, and divisive. This was true of the British system of "indirect rule" in places such as Uganda and Nigeria, which was anything but indirect; the French, of "assimilation"; and the most arbitrary of all, the Belgian, which considered African territories the personal property of the Belgian king.

### Self-determination and Territorial Integrity

The principle of self-determination was conceived as a means of reducing the tensions arising from ethnic/nationalist conflict in Europe by granting ethnic and national groups the right to separate. This principle was enshrined in the League of Nations (1919–39) and found its way into the UN Charter (1945) and the International Human Rights Covenants (1966).[5] Unfortunately, its formulators did not foresee how it could turn out to be a formidable factor in state disintegration and conflict by legitimizing the demands for separation of various groups. Many wars in Africa, such as in Congo, southern Sudan, Nigeria, and Ethiopia, illustrate the dilemmas and contradictions inherent in the concept, in that opposing sides in these civil wars have attempted to justify their positions in the name of self-determination.

There are two main sources of tension. First, how does one define or identify the relevant "self?" Is it coterminous with the entire population of a territory ("nation"), or is it based on more selective criteria, such as language, religion, race, culture, or other bases of ethnicity?[6] What group may legitimately invoke this claim? Even if the relevant "self" can be agreed on, is the claim of self-determination to be exercised only once, or is it subject to continous review? Is there a critical date at which a people entitled to self-determination is fully constituted so as to exclude individuals arriving before or after? Second, what does "determination" mean? How is the right of self-determination to be expressed? Must it be expressed by the people acting as a collectivity, or may a political movement speak on behalf of the collectivity? What about other peoples that are not members of the "self"? Does the "determination" in self-determination entail an unassailable right to separation? Or does it refer to the right of a people to decide on a particular form of government (such as, federal, democratic government) within the existing boundaries of a state? The UN Charter and other international legal documents do not answer these questions. The UN Charter, for example, leaves open the tension between the maintenance of the territorial integrity of a state and the right of a people to separate.

The principle of self-determination was first invoked in the context of African independence at the Pan African Congress in Paris in 1919. However, prior to the end of the Second World War and the advent of the UN, its application was confined to the defeated powers of the First World War – the creation of new nations from the dismantling of the German, Austro-Hungarian, and Ottoman empires. After 1945, beginning with the fifth Pan African Congress in Manchester that year, nationalist movements in Africa embraced the concept as meaning the right to independence from colonial rule.[7] Initially this interpretation and application of self-determination to Africa did not appear to pose any problems. Self-determination meant self-determination vis-à-vis outsiders, or anti-colonialism. The implication was that the principle applied to the entire population of a colonial territory as a single unit, even if the original territorial demarcation had been arbitrary and the population did not share a single ethnic identity.[8]

Thus "self-determination" in Africa was defined conservatively as anti-colonialism. The intention was to ensure the territorial integrity of the newly independent states by precluding the very real possibilty of secessionism and irredentism, given the arbitrary demarcation of colonial boundaries and the multi-ethnic composition of many states. This interpretation was reinforced by a resolution of the UN General Assembly (1514–XV) adopted by consensus on 14 December 1960, as the Declaration on the Granting of Independence to Colonial Countries and Peoples: "All peoples have the right to self-determination; by virtue of that right they freely determine their political status and freely pursue their economic, social and cultural development ... Any attempt aimed at the partial or total disruption of the national unity and the territorial integrity of a country is incompatible with the purposes and principles of the Charter of the United Nations."[9]

This interpretation is also found in the OAU Charter (1963), which affirms the sanctity and inviolability of colonial boundaries within which independence is obtained (uti possidetis).[10] This rendering establishes the primacy of the continuity and territorial integrity of an existing state over the right of specific constituent groups to separation. Self-determination is recognized, but only within the framework of existing states.[11] The right in such circumstances could be exercised only once, by a majority of the population living within the colonial boundaries. As more and more former colonies became independent, the right also correspondingly shrank.

Thus the tension between self-determination and territorial integrity came to be resolved in favour of the latter in the UN General Assembly and regional organizations such as the OAU. Through this process, a normative shift occurred towards restriction of the meaning and applicability of self-determination. This highly restrictive view was supported by the leading Western states (the United Kingdom, the United States, and France) and by the USSR and China, in the interests of international order as well as their own domestic interests. All shared a hostility towards secessionism. Almost without exception from the 1960s up to the end of the 1980s, when the claims of ethnic self-determination conflicted with the principle of territorial integrity, the OAU and the wider international community, as represented in the UN, came down in favour of maintaining territorial integrity. This was the case during Katanga's secessionist bid from Congo in 1960 and Biafra's bid to secession from Nigeria in 1967.

Thus a surprisingly sturdy, regional, customary norm evolved in Africa that reduced the potential for secessionist and irredentist conflict which arose from the tensions between self-determination and territorial integrity. Secessionist wars, specifically in Congo, Ethiopia, Nigeria, and Sudan, and irredentist wars, such as that between Somalia and Ethiopia over the Ogaden, represent exceptions. Yet it is precisely such exceptions that pose the greatest problems and that the OAU's new conflict-resolution mechanism must address. The problem is that there is no universal consensus about the formula to be applied in all circumstances in which self-determination and territorial integrity conflict. In most cases, the issue will have to be decided on the political merits of the case, not on legal grounds.

### External Intervention and the Norms of Non-Intervention

External intervention has been a major feature of Africa's internal wars. Such intervention has assumed many forms, ranging from technical and humanitarian assistance to victims, of civil strife by other governments and non-governmental organizations (NGOs), to covert and overt military assistance by neighbouring states (Tanzania in Uganda), regional powers (Libya in Chad), former colonial powers (France in Chad) and the superpowers (the United States in Somalia and Angola, and the USSR in Ethiopia).[12] It has not, however, been a major cause of these wars, which, it has been argued, result primarily from problems of domestic governance. External intervention, however, has altered the nature, intensity, and duration of civil wars.

Interventions in African wars have intensified conflicts, whether involving covert or overt military support to either side, as in Sudan. Other types of intervention have been designed to reduce or eliminate the conflict, and it is these types that are our focus here. They have ranged from third-party intercession by African and non-African states and regional/international organizations (good offices and mediation) to peacekeeping and the more recent attempts at peace-making. International and regional organizations, including the UN and the OAU, however, have been constrained by prevailing norms in international law that prohibit intervention in states" domestic jurisdiction. The analysis below outlines briefly the reasons for this injunction and its effects on conflict resolution.

At its creation in 1963, the OAU had as one of its overriding priorities the strengthening of African states. The first three of the five purposes listed in article two of the OAU Charter confirm this state-centrism. The order of priorities reflects a conscious desire by the framers to subordinate concerns such as human rights to that of state-building.[13] The principles also emphasize the sovereign equality of member states, non-interference in their internal affairs, and respect for their territorial integrity. The principle of non-interference was restated in resolutions passed in 1965 and 1969.[14] In addition, African states were instrumental in the adoption of three resolutions by the UN General Assembly (UNGA) in 1965, 1970, and 1974, which reinforced non-intervention and strengthened the principle of the non-use of force.[15] For example, according to UNGA Resolution 2131 (1965), the Declaration on the Inadmissability of Intervention in the Domestic Jurisdiction of States: "No state shall organize, assist, foment, finance, initiate or tolerate subversive, terrorist or armed activities directed towards the violent overthrow of the regime of another state or interfere in civil strife in another state."[16]

It is thus hardly surprising that the OAU has shown reluctance to involve itself in civil wars. Its involvement has been restricted to situations where there was clear evidence of external military intervention. A good example was its effort in the conflict in Chad, where there was ample evidence of Libyan intervention. Its hesitation has been evident in all the conflicts examined in this volume.

In the Horn of Africa (Sudan, Ethiopia, and Somalia), for example, for the past thirty years of conflict in this region the OAU has remained for the most part on the sidelines. This was the situation with the internal conflicts in Ethiopia between the central government and the Eritrean Peoples Liberation Front (EPLF). The resolution of that civil war provides a glaring illustration of the OAU's dilemma. The defeat of the forces of the Mengistu government in Ethiopia and its eventual overthrow in 1991 were achieved by an alliance among the EPLF, the Tigrean People's Liberation Army (TPLF), and the Ethiopian Peoples" Revolutionary Democratic Front (EPRDF). The EPRDF was installed as the interim government in Ethiopia and negotiated a settlement, brokered by U.S. mediation, that granted the EPLF the right to create a separate state of Eritrea, which was admitted to the UN in May 1993. Initially, at the Abuja Summit of 1991, the

OAU, in the context of the announcement of the creation of a separate state of Northern Somaliland, reaffirmed its opposition to secession. Even after Eritrea's separation from Ethiopia was recognized by the international communty in 1993, the OAU was still unsure about whether to recognize Eritrea as its newest member.[17]

The conflict in Sudan – Africa's longest civil war – presents perhaps the greatest challenge to the OAU, and its efforts have been poor at best. In 1990 the secretary-general offered his good offices to the government of the National Islamic Front (NIF) and to the Sudan People's Liberation Movement (SPLM) and its military wing, the Sudanese People's Liberation Army (SPLA). Successive OAU chairmen – Yoweri Museveni of Uganda in 1990–91, Babangida of Nigeria in 1991–92, and Diouf of Senegal in 1992–93 – have attempted to mediate.[18] Creation of the new conflict-resolution mechanism in June 1993 suggests, however, that the OAU intends to play a more active role in Sudan.

The OAU's hesitation in the Sudanese conflict stands in contrast to the intiatives taken by other organizations. The Addis Ababa Peace agreement of 1972, which ended the fighting in Sudan (until 1983), was mediated by the World Council of Churches and the All-African Council of Churches. The assistant secretary-general of the OAU and Emperor Haile Sellasie of Ethiopia acted as mediator of last resort.[19] More recently (1994), an initiative was mounted by the Inter-Governmental Authority on Drought and Development (IGADD), a subregional organization comprising countries of east and northeast Africa, with its headquarters in Djibouti. This plan included an attempt to mediate an end to the conflict.[20] This effort follows on IGADD's successful mediation of the conflict between Ethiopia and Somalia in 1988.

Indeed, subregional organizations in Africa have shown greater willingness than the OAU to to deal with civil conflicts. In addition to IGADD, a notable example is the initiative mounted by the Economic Community of West African States (ECOWAS) in the Liberian civil war. In Liberia, a military rebellion in 1989 against the leadership of Samuel Doe ignited a vicious civil war in 1990, which has been complicated by rifts among the insurgents. In August 1990, the sixteen member states of ECOWAS devised a peace plan under the terms of the organization's Protocol on Non-Aggression and sent a peacekeeping force to Liberia (ECOMOG). While this force has not yet ended the conflict, it has reduced the scale of violence. In Liberia, as in Sudan, the OAU has been virtually invisible. It has only provided "encouragement" to ECOWAS and, in concert with the UN, mobilized humanitarian assistance to victims.[21]

The OAU's reluctance to intervene in internal conflicts has affected the types of outside intervention that do occur. States outside Africa have tended to base their responses to conflicts in Africa on the positions taken (or lack thereof) by the OAU.[22] This is not to suggest that foreign military intervention in Africa is the result of the OAU's inaction. However, intervention will occur only if there is a foreign power willing to intervene and where there are circumstances that permit it.[23] Despite the organization's normative injunctions against intervention, especially involving non-African foreign powers, other norms have left the door wide open to such intervention. The OAU is required, for example, to support as the recognized government whatever faction in a civil war claims to be in control of the capital city and to grant that faction the right to invite in outside powers.[24]

### PREVENTION, MANAGEMENT, AND RESOLUTION OF CONFLICT

The development of a new conflict-resolution mechanism by the OAU has proceeded on two fronts[25] – normative and institutional. It is possible to identify stages in the OAU's gradual redefinition of the substantive norms that have governed African diplomacy and inter-state relations, as well as in its creation of new norms regarding domestic governance. As for institutional changes, it began in 1992, led by Secretary-General Salim Ahmed Salim, to create a new frame-work for conflict resolution, which came to fruition at the Cairo Summit in June 1993.

The new framework for preventing, managing, and resolving conflict is contingent on the extent to which OAU member-states clarify the normative context in which the institutions and pro-cedures are to operate, especially with respect to intervention in internal conflicts. The secretary-general and others in the secretariat seem to differ with the OAU's Assembly on the extent of normative change required for effective conflict resolution. This ambiguity, I argue, may undermine the effectiveness of the new mechanism.

### The New Institutional Mechanism

At the Cairo Summit in June 1993, the OAU Assembly issued a decla-ration outlining the principles, objectives, institutions, and pro-cedures that will form the basis of the Mechanism for Conflict Prevention, Management and Resolution (MCPMR). Its objectives (article 14) are to anticipate and prevent conflicts, and, in situations where conflict has occurred, to keep and build the peace. In addition, the OAU may mount and deploy civilian and military missions of observation and monitoring of limited scope and duration.[26] The emphasis is on preventing conflict and/or halting its escalation.

The central organ is the Bureau of the Assembly of Heads of State, consisting of nine member states elected annually, based on regional rotation and headed by the country chairing the OAU for that year. It will act on behalf of the assembly and will be the organ responsible for sanctioning the deployment of military observers and peacekeepers (articles 18–21).[27] At the Tunis Summit in June 1994, the members of this bureau were identified as Benin, Chad, Egypt, Ethiopia, Ivory Coast, Mauritius, Nigeria, South Africa, and Tunisia.[28] Membership in the bureau is confined to African heads of state, supported by ministers and ambassadors. The bureau, as the central organ of the new conflict-resolution mechanism, may be convened at any time by the chairman or by the secretary-general and is to meet at least once a year at the level of heads of state, twice a year at the ministerial level, and once a month at the ambassadorial level. Decisions are made on the long-time OAU basis of consensus (article 20).[29]

A second major component of the MCPMR is the Office of the Secretary-General (article 22). The secretary-general and his or her staff have two main roles. The first is to establish an "early warning" system to gather and analyse information relating to conflicts in order to enhance the mechanism's capacity to detect and thereby intervene to prevent the escalation of tensions into open warfare.[30] The second is to establish contacts and provide initiatives and expertise to facilitate negotiations. The secretary-general may resort to "eminent African personalities" (former heads of state and high-ranking military officers) to conduct fact-finding missions and to provide good offices (article 20).

The two other components of the MCPMR are a revived OAU Defence Commission, which will serve in an advisory capacity, especially for peacekeeping operations, and an Interim Arbitral Tribunal, staffed by "eminent" African jurists. The tribunal will adjudicate territorial disputes pending creation of the African Court of Justice, which was provided for in the treaty establishing the African Economic Community at the OAU Summit at Abuja in June 1991.[31] A special fund, with an allocation of U.S.$1 million, is to pay for the mechanism (article 23).[32]

*The Process and Dimensions of Normative Change*

The proposals outlined above for the MCPMR appear ambitious. Have the norms that have governed interstate relations in Africa for the past thirty years changed in such a way as to allow the new mechanism to achieve its objectives? What conditions will make for effective, multilateral intervention in African conflicts, and what is the most appropriate method of such intervention?

The text of the Cairo Declaration, which created the MCPMR, appears to indicate little if any change in the norms governing diplomacy. Article 14 reaffirms the sovereign equality of member-states, non-interference in their internal affairs, their territorial integrity and the inviolability of borders inherited from colonialism, and the consent of parties to the dispute.[33] Yet the interpretation of these concepts has changed, particularly regarding the thorny issue of intervention in internal conflicts. OAU members seem to have decided that internal wars and the domestic conditions that give rise to them pose the greatest threat to security in Africa, as is evident in the texts of five declarations and agreements and in the debates over these documents.

In June 1990, the OAU Assembly issued the "Declaration on the Political and Socio-economic Situation in Africa," committing leaders to work towards the speedy resolution of all conflicts in Africa. This statement represented explicit recognition that failure to control conflicts would undermine efforts to promote economic development and democracy and to reintegrate an increasingly marginalized continent into a world economic system.[34] It signalled awareness that the OAU should begin to concern itself with intra-state as well as interstate conflicts.

The African Leadership Forum held in May 1991 in Kampala, Uganda, brought together five hundred delegates, including current and former heads of state, to deliberate on a proposal for a Conference on Security, Stability, Development and Cooperation in Africa (CSSDCA,) modelled on the Conference on Security and Cooperation in Europe (CSCE). The resulting Kampala Document offered a framework for governance and development in Africa in the 1990s and beyond. It envisaged far-reaching normative changes in domestic governance, and even though the African Leadership Forum is a non-governmental agency, many of its proposals were endorsed by prominent African figures, such as outgoing OAU chair Yoweri Museveni of Uganda and former Nigerian head of state General Obasanjo.[35] The document's policy proposals included the creation of peacekeeping forces and articulated strong principles regarding domestic governance by identifying democratization, popular participation, and accountability as the key to security and stability. Not surprisingly, a number of leaders, aware that their own governments were not democratic, expressed reservations about some of these proposals.[36]

The meeting of the the OAU Council of Ministers and the June 1991 summit at Abuja in Nigeria debated the proposals contained in the Kampala Document. Leaders decided that the secretary-general should study the proposals with a view to issuing a report to the Council of Ministers and the assembly at the next annual meeting in 1992.[37] Thus the views in the document, while not the official view of the OAU, provided the basis for the secretary-general's proposals on the new conflict-resolution mechanism at the Council of Ministers meeting in May 1992, which were adopted at the Cairo Summit in June 1993.

The debates over the MCPMR reveal the nature of the OAU's attempt to redefine African security. It was at the OAU Council of Ministers meeting in Dakar in June 1992 that the secretary-general first outlined three options – institutionalize the Bureau of Heads of State as an organ of conflict resolution; establish a new organ within the OAU, a sort of African Security Council; or resuscitate the OAU's moribund Commission on Mediation, Conciliation and Arbitration (CMCA). Delegates at the meeting preferred the first option – institutionalizing the bureau.

Three factors influenced this choice. First, there was opposition to the hierarchy among African states embodied in the idea of an African Security Council, modelled on the UN Security Council, which would create permanent seats and the power of veto. This was deemed to be in violation of the OAU's principle of sovereign equality. In contrast, the bureau had a one-year, rotating membership, which would allow all members to be involved at some point. Second, the bureau already had links with the three principal institutions of the OAU (the assembly, the council, and the secretariat), and its use for security would obviate the need for a new body.[38] Third, members explicitly recognized the political rather than legal character of conflict and conflict resolution in Africa.

The dormancy of the CMCA, is the result of the fact that African states engaged in conflict have preferred political to judicial methods of dispute settlement.[39] As Zartman has noted, mediation has been highly personalized – only heads of state/government, not lesser officials, have been acceptable as mediators.[40] Moreover, participants at Dakar recognized that significant ambiguities in international law regarding intervention and domestic jurisdiction precluded an effective judicial approach, especially in intra-state conflicts.

A strictly legal or judicial approach stumbles on the lack of clarity in both the international and the regional norms regarding the conduct of third parties. Judicial processes require agreed-on set of rules. Existing rules in international law, such as those contained in the UN and the OAU charters limit third-party intervention into domestic jurisdiction. Only international or regional consensus to amend these charters could allow specification of when and how such intervention is permissible.

The CMCA became moribund partly because of an article in its protocol that stated that it had jurisdiction only in interstate disputes and that even then its jurisdiction was based on the consent of the states involved. The only way to overcome this injunction would be to amend the protocol, which would be difficult.[41] Rather than attempt to amend the charter of the OAU, the more effective approach was to reinterpret existing norms. This is primarily a political process, and arguably such a process is under way within the UN to make its collective security measures more relevant to the realities of civil conflict in the post-Cold War era.

The UN Charter draws a distinction between the legitimate (defensive) and illegitimate (offensive) uses of force, predicated on a particular conception of threats to international peace and security. Specifically, the assumption was made that the primary danger was aggression (offence) involving the threat or use of force between two or more states – interstate wars. The reality since 1945, however, has been very different – in terms of total deaths/injuries and the frequency, there have been far more internal/civil wars than international wars.[42] This fact has created a problem for the UN in that its Charter provisions – specifically articles 2(4) and 2(7) – appear to restrict its ability to invoke collective measures in the event of violence within a single state. Roughly since the end of the Cold War, the UN has attempted to redefine the norms governing the use of force and intervention and to reinterpret the charter to make its measures more relevant to the realities of conflict and threats to international peace and security in the 1990s.[43]

The UN Charter reflects two clusters of values that overlap and may be in conflict with each other. The first is made up of state-centric norms and principles, which affirm the sovereignty of states and prescribe measures for the preservation and enhancement of the state system – articles 2(4) and 2(7), on non aggression and non-intervention, respectively. The second involves self-determination and human rights values and affirms the rights of individuals and groups of people, not states – articles 1(2) and 1(3). These two sets of values are designed to achieve two objectives. The first is to maintain peaceful relationships between states and preserve the existing state system. The second is to realize autonomy (non-intervention/freedom from external domination). In the past, autonomy was defined in terms of the political independence/territorial integrity of states.

More recently, the emphasis appears to be shifting to the rights of individuals/peoples within state boundaries to organize themselves into political communities and create their own instititions.

The two sets of objectives are complementary to the extent that non-intervention and non-aggression work to promote self-determination and human rights. However, non-intervention and (restrictive) self-determination come into conflict when, for example, a state cites non-intervention as a cover for its violation of the norm of self-determination of peoples/individuals within its own territory.

Since the end of the Cold War, the UN has shown greater willingness to intervene (with varying degrees of force) in such cases of internal conflict. The emerging normative consensus appears to be that when a state is flagrantly violating the self-determination of its own people, non-intervention does not apply – i.e., the consent of the state is not required. The key is the last clause of article 2(7), which exempts enforcement measures undertaken by the Security Council under chapter VII of the charter from the restrictions of non-intervention.

In effect, the Security Council has been more willing to interpret civil conflicts, especially where there is evidence of widespread human rights abuses, as constituting threats to international peace and security, thus allowing for UN intervention, even in the absence of the consent of the states concerned. It set two historical precedents in this regard, imposing sanctions against Rhodesia's unilateral declaration of independence in 1965 and against South Africa in 1977. More recently, the Gulf War and its aftermath – the imposition of protective zones in Iraq – appeared to herald the expansion of the scope of international intervention and the corresponding contraction of domestic jurisdiction. Since then, there has been international intervention, overriding domestic jurisdiction, in a number of cases, including the former Yugoslavia and Somalia.

Legal purists dislike the absence of clarity in the UN's attempt to overcome the limitations of its charter provisions and in the mix of interest, power, and normative principle that motivated its interventions. As one legal scholar notes, "[T]reating like cases alike is fundamental to the evolution of a system based on law rather than on power."[44] While this may be true, it overlooks the fact that the legal mechanisms and procedures in chapter VII have never been implemented. In the two instances where the UN did authorize large-scale use of force – in Korea in 1950 and against Iraq in 1991 – the legal basis was provided not by articles 42–7 of Chapter VII – the core provisions regarding the use of force – but by a loophole in the charter that allows for individual and collective self-defence (article

51).[45] Moreover, its foremost mechanism for conflict management – its peacekeeping role, which is discussed below – has no explicit legal basis in the organization's charter. The very essence of peacekeeping is political, not legal.

Thus the absence of explicit international legal rules regarding intervention in internal conflicts should not by itself preclude the OAU's development of an effective mechanism for conflict resolution, and indeed, it could be advantageous. Supporters of a more interventionist OAU argued that "within the context of general international law as well as humanitarian law, Africa should take the lead in developing the notion that sovereignty can legally be transcended by the intervention of outside forces." And "preemptive deployment should be permitted ... [T]his would transform in real terms, the OAU's expressed commitment to conflict resolution."[46] Primary opposition to creation of the MCPMR came from the leaders of Sudan and Rwanda, whose governments were fighting insurgencies. Sudan's Omar Hassan Al-Bashir argued that such intervention would result in a loss of sovereignty and could lead to conflicts with other states.[47]

Supporters of the MCPMR argued further that the OAU Assembly should redefine the terms of reference for the MCPMR and the secretary-general in order to transform the apparent shift in thinking from theory to practice. As of the Addis-Ababa Summit in June 1995, however, this had not occurred, and none of the resolutions passed there dealt explicitly with intervention.[48] Earlier, at the Tunis Summit in June 1994, the "Tunis Declaration" contained eleven principles, two of which only suggest the possibility of intervention in internal conflicts. Articles 8 and 9 of the declaration commit member-states to take measures to avoid conflict, especially in relation to ethnic and religious differences that may lead to conflict within states.[49]

CONDITIONS FOR EFFECTIVE MULTILATERAL
INTERVENTION

The objectives of the OAU's new MCPMR are to prevent, manage, and resolve conflicts. Prevention is elimination or control of the factors that lead to conflict. Management involves reduction of the means of conflict, with a view to preventing escalation. Resolution is the settlement of the basic issues of conflict.[50] The relationship among these tasks, however, is not as clear-cut as the above definitions indicate, as is reflected in the various strategies and methods envisaged in the MCPMR. The debates of 1992-93 over its creation emphasized preventive strategies. By 1995, however, the OAU had come to realize that it should be prepared for more immediate and interventionist responses, including mediation and peacekeeping/preventive deployment.[51] The discussion below outlines the conditions for success in these methods and assesses the ability of the OAU's new mechanism to meet these conditions.

### Conflict Prevention and Peace-Building

There is a close parallel between conflict prevention and peace-building. Peace-building in this regard involves a longer-term, preventive strategy that focuses on the potential causes of insecurity as well as post-conflict reconstruction designed to prevent the recurrence of conflicts.[52] If one of the principal sources of conflict in Africa is the allocation and distribution of socioeconomic resources, then a key aspect of conflict prevention and hence peace-building lies in the promotion of equitable economic growth and the mitigation of the negative impact of global economic forces on disadvantaged groups. The proposition here is that equitable economic development will eradicate many of the socioeconomic conditions that lead to conflict, and mitigation of the socio-economic conditions that lead to conflict will be conducive to economic development. From this perspective, economic and social policies and programs, as well as policies with respect to human rights and distributive justice, have as significant an effect on national security in Africa as do policies on national defence and the use of force.

It is certainly no accident that African countries experiencing high degrees of civil strife and conflict are also those whose economic, social, and political institutions are crumbling. The OAU Assembly, at its annual summit in Addis Ababa in June 1995, reaffirmed the "Cairo Agenda for Action," which was issued by the Council of Ministers in March 1995 and recognized the link among socio-economic development, governance, and peace and security.[53] The socioeconomic aspect of conflict prevention, however, cannot be managed by the OAU acting alone. It must be spearheaded by the international financial institutions (IFIs) through their policies and programs of lending and investment. Though they are not concerned primarily with security, there is no doubt that the structural adjustment programs that are being implemented throughout the continent affect economic, social, and political variables that influence national security. In this regard, effective conflict prevention and hence peace-building in Africa will require improved coordination among the OAU, the UN, the IFIs, and regional development banks. What is needed from the IFIs working with African governments, is the construction of "safety nets" to ease the effect of global economic forces on vulnerable groups and of bridging social capital to cushion the impact of the transition to a market economy.

There is another more immediate aspect of conflict prevention in which the OAU is uniquely placed to play a major role. This lies in the detection of conditions within African countries that contain the potential to deteriorate into open conflict, particularly with respect to tensions among groups arising from resource scarcity and the manipulation of ethnic differences and exploitation, which are often signs of impending conflict. The organization envisages the creation of a continent-wide early warning network, with member-states as the focal points, and including subregional organizations, the UN and its specialized agencies, academic and research institutions, and NGOs.[54]

The two major issues in operationalizing the network are how to obtain information about potential or actual conflicts and what to do with that information after it is obtained. For early warning to be effective, the MCPMR must obtain up-to-date and timely data. A recent report from the MCPMR identifies lack of speedy exchange of details on conflict as a major shortcoming that has further complicated some difficult situations and impeded decision making.[55]

What to do with the information obtained? The OAU has outlined options that include deployment of forces for peacekeeping, and a more active role in mediation, both are discussed below.

### Conflict Management and Resolution: Peacekeeping and Preventive Deployment

The OAU's MCPMR can deploy forces either to manage an existing conflict or to prevent rising tensions from breaking into open warfare. I have based my analysis of the conditions for the success of these strategies on an evaluation of the models of peacekeeping provided by UN operations in Somalia and Rwanda, OAU operations in Chad and Rwanda, and the peacekeeping efforts of ECOWAS forces in Liberia.

When should the OAU deploy peacekeeping forces? What about the nature and the ability of the forces deployed? The difficulty in practice is that of determining which conflicts warrant intervention, what the objective is (selectivity); and what form of intervention will achieve the desired objective (capacity). This is a lesson that emerges from Somalia, where the UN Observer Mission (UNOSOM II) was forced to withdraw (February–March 1995), and ECOMOG in the Liberian conflict. The major problem in both cases is a blurring of the distinction between enforcement and traditional peacekeeping.

Enforcement is primarily legal, not political action, authorized under chapter VII of the UN Charter and using force to suppress aggression. It involves collectively identifying an "aggressor" and then marshalling resources in a rising "ladder" of force until the aggression is stopped.[56] Thus collective security as envisaged in the UN Charter is effectively "internationally sanctioned war."[57] There are no precise legal foundations for peacekeeping in the UN Charter; the practice lies somewhere between chapters VI and VII. As long as the basis remained the consent of the parties in a dispute, it did not matter what its legal basis was. But the requirement of consent has been eroded in more recent UN peacekeeping operations.

Traditional peacekeepers attempted to overcome problems of co-ordination between belligerents. Their primary role was to deter new fighting by ensuring that parties to a dispute understood agreed-on rules and that compliance or deviation would be made transparent by a force interposed between the belligerents to monitor cease-fires and observe frontier lines. Governing principles included consent of the parties, the impartiality of the peacekeepers, and the non-use of force except in self-defence.[58] In contrast, the newer UN operations – the establishment of the "No Fly Zones" in Iraq in 1991, the establishment of the UN Protection Force in Bosnia (UNPROFOR) in 1992, the UN Observer Mission in Somalia (UNOSOM II), and the Security Council resolution establishing the Unified Task Force (UNITAF) that authorized deployment of U.S. forces in Somalia – lack consent and appear partial.[59] This is also the case with ECOWAS forces in Liberia. In addition, the role of the forces sent to these conflicts appears to be not deterrence/transparency but compulsion/enforcement.

In the case of Somalia, on 27 July and 28 August 1992, the UN Security Council adopted Resolutions 767 and 775, respectively, authorizing deployment of a UN force of 3,500 troops (UNOSOM I). The force's mandate was to create a secure environment for the delivery of humanitarian aid and monitor the cease-fire established in February 1992. Up to this point, the UN had deployed forces in Somalia with the consent of the warring factions.[60] On 3 December 1992, Operation Restore Hope was launched by Security Council Resolution 794, in response to the worsening human disaster and the stepped-up hijacking of aid shipments by the warring parties.

Resolution 794 authorized the secretary-general to "use all necessary means to establish as soon as possible a secure environment for humanitarian relief operations in Somalia." Most significantly, it made explicit reference to chapter VII and declared that the "magnitude of the tragedy caused by the conflict in Somalia ... constitutes a threat to international peace and security."[61] It resulted in the creation of UNITAF, a U.S.-led force of 37,000 troops to secure the delivery of aid, which was deployed in Somalia from December 1992 to March 1993. On 26 March 1993, Resolution 814 created UNOSOM

II to take over the responsibilities of UNITAF. The transition was completed in May 1993. However, U.S. forces remained in Somalia as part of UNOSOM II until March 1994.[62]

The later deployment of forces in Somalia departed from traditional peacekeeping in three ways. First, in contrast UNOSOM I, UNITAF and UNOSOM II received no consent. Second, the resolutions creating these forces authorized the use of force – "all necessary means" – by reference to chapter VII. Third, there was no principle of impartiality. On 6 June 1993, following the killings of UN troops in Mogadishu, the Security Council adopted Resolution 837, which authorized UN forces to take actions against the parties responsible, including their arrest and detention for prosecution, trial, and punishment. It identified the faction led by General Farar Aidid as the party responsible for the killings. The UN's failed attempt to capture him severely injured the credibility of the UN forces and invited the hostility of those whom the forces had been sent to protect. In addition, there was confusion surrounding the mandate of UNOSOM II. There were disagreements among its national contingents – most publicly, between the U.S. and the Italian forces. Though nominally under UN supervision, the countries deploying troops were determined to keep a degree of control over their contingents, reflecting differences in military strategies and national interests.[63]

In Liberia, the forces deployed by ECOWAS – the Ceasefire Monitoring Group (ECOMOG) also departed from previous practices. Though ECOMOG was labelled a peacekeeping operation, with a mandate to monitor a cease-fire, the forces were initially deployed in August 1990 with no cease-fire to monitor.[64] There was considerable confusion regarding the mandate of ECOMOG and strong opposition to its deployment by several ECOWAS member-states, including Burkina Faso, the Ivory Coast, and Mali.[65]

ECOMOG was also unusual in terms of the principles of consent, impartiality, and use of force. One of the three warring factions, the National Patriotic Front of Liberia (NPFL) led by Charles Taylor, refused to give its consent to the force's deployment. The assassination of the Liberian president, Samuel Doe, at the headquarters of ECOMOG by NPFL rebels in September 1990 was an embarrassment that forced a change in mandate. ECOMOG launched a full-scale offensive against the NPFL, thereby abandoning the semblance of impartiality, and found itself siding with the Armed Forces of Liberia (AFL), and the Independent National Patriotic Front of Liberia (INPFL) against the NPFL. Its full-scale offensive in the fall of 1990 shifted its mandate closer to enforcement, though ECOWAS members described the actions as "self-defence."[66]

Thus, in civil conflicts such as those in Somalia and Liberia, with multiple and overlapping warring factions and widespread cease-fire violations, traditonal peacekeeping becomes next to impossible, necessitating greater use of force in the effort to restore order. This situation blurs the distinction between peacekeeping and peace enforcement. The resulting peacekeeping-cum-enforcement in effect constitutes compulsion, but the forces have the capacity only to perform deterrence. Enforcement requires clear identification of an "aggressor" and a greater commitment of resources and force. Thus the OAU must be careful to maintain the distinction between peace-keeping (preventing resumption of fighting after a cease-fire has been established), or preventive deployment (preventing tensions from expanding into open warfare) and deploying forces where fighting is in progress and no cease-fire has been reached. The last-named task is far more ambitious and will move the OAU's new mechanism into the realm of enforcement, for which the OAU does not have the resources or capability. When a conflict does require measures closer to enforcement, the OAU should seek the assistance of the UN, under of chapter VIII of the UN Charter.

There are at least six requirements for successful peacekeeping. (1) There must be a ceasefire and clear front lines dividing the parties; (2) the forces should be impartial; and there must be (3) a clear political goal that can be reflected in the mandate of the forces, (4) there must be a precise mandate that specifies the rules of engagement, (5) reasonable assurances about the safety of the peace-keepers, and (6) adequate financial and logistical support.[67] In the light of these conditions, it is not difficult to see why the OAU's peacekeeping operation in Chad in 1981–82 failed. In November 1981, the OAU, in response to an intensification of the war in Chad and increasing Libyan intervention, decided to send a pan-African force to separate the warring factions. This effort – the first of its kind in Africa – was short-lived because of financial problems, lack of commitment among the warring factions, and disagreement among OAU members about appropriate action and goals.[68]

For successful preventive deployment, John Ruggie has outlined what he terms the "D3" strategy – deter, dissuade, and deny.[69] The sponsor must deploy forces that pose a credible threat (deter) and convince all parties that violence will not succeed (dissuade), by bringing enough force to bear not to defeat, but to neutralize the local forces (deny). The political objective is to prevent parties in a potentially explosive civil conflict from resorting to force as the means to settle their dispute and to convince them that the only viable alternative is through negotiation.[70] Thus preventive deployment is part of a wider strategy of preventive diplomacy, involving mediation and confidence-building measures, with the emphasis on achieving a negotiated settlement.[71]

In Rwanda, it has been argued that timely deployment of about five thousand troops would have prevented the bloodshed that occurred between April and June 1994.[72] The evidence, however, is inconclusive. What is not in doubt is that the UN and the OAU could have done more in support of the Arusha peace process. The Arusha Accords of August 1993 appeared to herald an end to the fighting, which began in 1990 with the incursion into Rwanda by rebels of the Rwanda Patriotic Front (RPF) in an attempt to topple the government of President Juvenal Habyarimana. The signing of the accords represented the culmination of mediation efforts involving the Great Lakes Region Heads of State, the OAU, the UN, the United States, and France. The OAU's involvement was led by Senegal's Abdou Diouf and the secretary-general Salim.

Negotiations began with the cease-fire that was part of the N'sele agreement signed in March 1991, following mediation by the Great Lakes Region Heads of State, including Mobuto Sese Seko of Zaire, Mwinyi of Tanzania, and Museveni of Uganda. The establishment of a Neutral Military Observer Group (NMOG) under the auspicies of the OAU was one of the key components of the N'sele cease-fire. Concerns about whether the OAU had the capacity for such an operation led the secretary-general in April 1993 to seek UN assistance. Thus the United Nations Assistance Mission in Rwanda (UNAMIR) was created, replacing the OAU forces. Its 2,500 troops had a mandate to monitor the cease-fire and assist in the implementation of the accords. Between April 1993 and April 1994 the reforms agreed to at Arusha appeared to have a good chance of being implemented with the assistance of UNAMIR. However, the assassination of the Rwandan president and the president of Burundi, Cyprian Ntarymira, on 6 April 1994 derailed the process and plunged Rwanda into genocidal violence.[73]

The UN's response to this outbreak of violence is further evidence of the dilemmas posed by the requirements of selectivity and capacity. The outbreak of violence in reaction to the deaths of the two presidents produced a change in UNAMIR's mandate. However, in contrast to Somalia, this change in mandate did not invoke chapter VII but instead involved a reduction in the size of the contingent, even though the UN commander in the field, General Roméo Dallaire, had requested a larger force, with an expanded mandate, to act as a deterrent in order to prevent civilian deaths.[74] The reduced UNAMIR forces could thus do little but watch as the genocide unfolded. It was not until mid-May 1994 that the Security Council adopted Resolution 918, which authorized deployment of 5,500 troops and expanded the mandate of UNAMIR along the lines requested by Dallaire.

Why did the Security Council fail to respond in a timely and effective manner to the request by UNAMIR's commander? The answer may lie in the experiences of the UN in Somalia. Disillusionment over that UN operation may have confirmed for the UN the wrong lesson about the relationship between selectivity and capacity in the deployment of forces. Selectivity does not imply inaction or narrow self-interest. The wrong response here is to preclude the deployment of forces into civil conflicts or to link participation in any future peacekeeping operation to the realization of strategic interests. The latter is implied by the U.S. Presidential Decision Directive 25 of 5 May 1994, issued by Bill Clinton in the context of the operation in Somalia, which outlines the conditions for any future U.S. involvement in peacekeeping.[75] For Rwanda, a timely expansion in the mandate of UNAMIR might indeed have prevented the carnage of April–June 1994.

Inevitably, the OAU's deployment of forces for peacekeeping or preventive deployment must be selective. The OAU cannot hope to cover all actual or potential conflicts in Africa. In addition, it does not have the capacity to perform the deterrence, dissuasion, and denial essential to the effective deployment of military forces without the UN's assistance. Indeed, it is unrealistic to expect the OAU to shoulder these kinds of commitments by itself. Though under certain conditions military forces from other African countries deployed by the OAU may be more effective in dealing with a conflict in Africa than troops from elsewhere, the OAU should not hesitate to draw on the experience and resources of the UN should the need arise. Selectivity, however, should not pose a problem in so far as it is non-discriminatory – that is, the organization should not show a preference for certain countries or regions in Africa over others. This fact must be recognized if the OAU's capacity in peacekeeping and preventive deployment is to be created and enhanced.

*Mediation*

Mediation involves the intervention of third parties as intermediaries, usually by invitation and the concurrence of the parties to a dispute, arrived at achieving a negotiated settlement.[76] Zartman has argued that in the African context mediation by third parties, usually other African states, has been quite effective in bringing disputing parties to negotiation.[77] African mediators have operated mainly in the first two of the mediator's three main roles – communication, formulation, and manipulation – involving the reduction of the risk and uncertainty that impede reconciliation and agreement. To what extent can the OAU's new conflict resolution mechanism mediate in African conflicts? Zartman argues that the existence of a hurting stalemate in a dispute is a necessary condition for effective mediation, and mediation, a necessary response to stalemate.[78] The only leverage available to African mediators has been their ability to help disputants out of their stalemate.

The main role of the OAU in the conduct of mediation is to establish the norms or parameters within which mediators may place their proposed solutions.[79] With the creation of the new mechanism and the recognition of the political nature of conflict, the OAU may overcome the limitations of the judicial approach envisaged in the moribund CMCA. Operation by the bureau, assisted by the secretary-general's office, may reduce a major limitation on mediation attempts in the past – namely, competition among mediators acting in their private capacity.[80] A multilateral approach would insulate the mediation process from the dynamics of regional politics in Africa by functionally separating the role of mediator from that of legitimizer of any outcome.[81] In addition, the resources available through the centralized bureau and the secretary-general's office could assist the mediator in his/her role as the agent of trust and the assessor of risk.

In this regard, the recent attempt by IGADD to mediate the Sudanese conflict is instructive. In May 1994 the Mediation Committee of IGADD (Ethiopia, Eritrea, Kenya, and Uganda) presented a Declaration of Principles (DOP) as the pillar of the peace process to the principal factions – the NIF government and the SPLM/SPLA. The DOP represents an attempt to clarify the normative context of negotiations by recognizing both the right to self-determination of the southern Sudanese and the upholding of national unity in Sudan as a priority. A formula was devised to reconcile the tension between the two principles. This envisaged an interim period, during which attempts at maintaining national unity would be made, including secularization of the state and creation of a multi-party democracy. After this period, a referendum would be held in which the people of the south would be asked whether to continue the interim arrangements or adopt new ones, including the right to create a separate state.[82]

These proposals, especially recognition of the right to self-determination and secularization, were rejected by the NIF, which is intent on creating and maintaining a unified Islamic state. In addition, three of IGADD's mediators – Eritrea, Ethiopia, and Uganda – have come into conflict with the Sudanese government over its allegations of their subversive activities. Since September 1994, the mediation process has been stalled, and the Mediation Committee, in an effort to keep the negotiations alive, has sought the support and collaboration of the OAU and the wider international community represented in the UN.

Strongly articulated norms within the OAU would assist IGADD's initiative in Sudan and in other negotiations by narrowing the area of uncertainty and influencing the behaviour of the parties to a conflict. Well-articulated norms may help to clarify the bargaining situation by clarifying what the stakes in dispute are by supporting either the legitimacy of the side upholding the status quo or the side demanding change. Thus the key role for the OAU lies in what may be termed "soft" mediation, or a process of legitimization, as distinct from "hard" mediation, or the attempt to find specific solutions to specific disputes.[83] This appears to be the intention behind the hard-line position taken by the OAU against the government of Sudan in September 1995.[84]

Legitimization, while it may involve legal or moral aspects, is ultimately political.[85] Conferring or withholding legitimacy will not guarantee that all behaviour will conform to principle, but it will introduce a systemic bias into the negotiating process by shifting the burden of proof onto the side whose actions deviate from the accepted norm or standard. Thus the effectiveness of the multilateral approach to conflict management and resolution envisaged in the OAU's MCPMR, whether in the form of mediation or some other method of peacemaking, is contingent on the clarity of the norms governing intervention.[86]

### CONCLUSION

The efficacy or otherwise of the OAU's new mechanism for conflict prevention, management and resolution depends ultimately on the extent to which African countries can redefine or have redefined security and stability. In other words, they must see the sources of internal conflicts as residing in demands for change rather than as aggression. Redefining reinterpreting the norms of African diplomacy and governance can facilitate multilateral intervention in states" domestic jurisdiction.

Sovereignty, as the defining norm of the Westphalian international system, is not sacrosanct. Increasingly, states are being permeated by global economic, technological, environmental, and political forces that narrow their jurisdiction. While the norms that constitute and regulate the exercise of state sovereignty should be upheld, less attention should be paid to the formal legal limits on intervention into states' domestic jurisdiction. There are forms and degrees of intervention that need not entail wholesale rejection of existing norms. The world requires recognition of the political, not legal nature of armed conflict and development of a formula that reassesses the balance between the rights of states and the rights of persecuted groups and individuals in a civil war in such a way as to permit collective intervention and override domestic jurisdiction.

The key is to interpret the norms in a way that recognizes that in certain circumstances, when norms of non-interference and territorial integrity conflict with the rights of persecuted and oppressed groups within states to self-determination, the balance should tilt in favour of the latter. In some extreme cases, colonially demarcated borders will have to be redrawn, as has occurred of Ethiopia and Eritrea. In this regard, serious consideration should be given to the discussion and analysis of the conditions under which separation may legitimately and peacefully occur.

This form of normative reinterpretation is already under way within the UN, as evidenced in the dramatic increase in the number and types of its interventions since 1988 and the changes in the role of UN peacekeeping. Though a new interpretation of the norms of African governance and diplomacy alone will not guarantee more security and stability or necessarily make the OAU more effective, a normative redefinition along the lines described above is a necessary pre-condition for any attempt at creating effective mechanisms for multilateral prevention, management, and resolution of conflicts.

NOTES

1 Raymond W. Copson, *Africa's Wars and Prospects for Peace* (New York: Sharpe 1991), chaps. 1 and 2.
2 Donald L. Horowitz, "Ethnic and Nationalist Conflict," in M.T. Klare and D.C. Thomas, eds., *World Security: Challenges for a New Century* (New York: St Martins 1994), 175–87.
3 Keith Sommerville, *Foreign Military Intervention in Africa* (New York: St Martins 1990).
4 Ibid, 2–3; Copson, *Africa's Wars*, 26–73; and Jeffrey Herbst, "The Creation and Maintenance of National Boundaries in Africa," *International Organization*, 43 no. 4 (fall 1989), 673–92.
5 See Patrick Thronberry, "Self-Determination, Minorities, Human Rights: A Review of International Instruments," *International and Comparative Law Quarterly*, 38 (1989), 867–89. See also Benyamin Neuberger, *Na-*

*tional Self-Determination in Post-Colonial Africa* (Boulder, Col.: Lynne Rienner 1986), 3–10.

6 See Ali A. Marzui, *Towards a Pax Africana* (London: Wiedenfeld 1967), 3–20; Crawford Young, in Francis Deng and I. William Zartman, eds., *Conflict Re Southern Africa* (Washington, DC: Brookings Institution 1991), 321–2. 321–2.

7 Neuberger, *National Self-Determination*, 5–7.

8 Ibid, 8–9.

9 *Yearbook of the United Nations, 1960*, 49. This resolution passed by eighty-nine votes to nil, with nine abstentions.

10 This means the territorial continuity of a political unit, irrespective of the international legal merits of its original demarcation and the transfer of sovereignty. See Michael-Cyr Djiena Wiembou, "The OAU and International Law," in Yassin El-Ayouty, ed., *The OAU after Thirty Years* (Westport, Conn.: Praeger 1993), 16.

11 Michael Akehurst, *A Modern Introduction to International Law*, 6th ed. (London: Routeledge 1992), 294–5.

12 Copson, *Africa's Wars*, 103–55.

13 These purposes are to promote the solidarity of African states; to co-ordinate and intensify their cooperation and efforts to achieve a better life for the peoples of Africa; to defend their sovereignty, their territorial integrity, and independence; to eradicate all forms of colonialism in Africa; and to promote international cooperation, having due regard to the Charter of the United Nations and the Universal Declaration of Human Rights.

14 Wiembou, "The OAU," 16.

15 These UNGA resolutions are no. 2131 (1965), Declaration on the Inadmissability of Intervention in the Domestic Jurisdiction of States; no. 2625 (1970), "The Declaration of Principles of International Law Concerning Friendly Relations and Cooperation among States"; and no. 3314 (1974), The Definition of Aggression.

16 *Yearbook of the United Nations, 1965*, 94. This resolution passed by a vote of 109 to nil and was reaffirmed by the International Court of Justice *Nicaragua v. the USA*.

17 James C. Jonah, "The OAU: Peace Keeping and Conflict Resolution," in Yassin El-Ayouty, ed., *The OAU after Thirty Years* (Westport, Conn.: Praeger 1993), 10–11.

18 Berhanykun Andemicael, "OAU-UN Relations," in ibid, 124–5.

19 I.W. Zartman, "Inter-African Negotiations," in J. Harbeson and D. Rothchild, eds., *Africa In World Politics* (Boulder, Col.: Westview 1991), 273.

20 Francis M. Deng, "Mediating the Sudanese Conflict: A Challenge for the IGADD," unpublished paper.

21 "Resolution on Liberia," CM/Res. 1499. UN Document A/48/322, 19 Aug. 1993, 23. Also Andemicael, "OAU-UN Relations," 124–5.

22 Andemicael, "OAU–UN Relations," 11–12.

23 For a discussion of the reasons for foreign intervention in African conflicts, see Sommerville, *Foreign Military Intervention*, 185–6; Alain Rouvez, *Disconsolate Empires: French, British and Belgian Military Involvement in Post-Colonial Sub-Saharan Africa* (Lanham, Md.: University Press of America 1994), 1–29; and Peter J. Schraeder, *United States Foreign Policy toward Africa* (Cambridge: Cambridge University Press 1994), 1–50.

24 William J. Foltz, "The OAU and the Resolution of Africa's Conflict," in Francis Deng and I.W. Zartman, eds., *Conflict Resolution in Africa* (Washington, DC: Brookings Institution 1991), 356–61; Sam Amoo, "The Role of the OAU: Past, Present and Future," in David R. Smock, ed., *Making War and Waging Peace*, (Washington, DC: U.S. Institute of Peace Press 1993), 254.

25 OAU, *Resolving Conflicts in Africa* (1992), 17.

26 Article 15 of the "The Declaration of the Assembly of Heads of State and Government on the Establishment within the OAU of a Mechanism for Conflict Prevention, Management and Resolution." UN Document A/48/322, 19 Aug. 1993, 109.

27 UN Document A/48/322, 110.

28 FBIS-AFR-94-116, 16 June 1994, 3–4.

29 UN Document A/48/322, 111.

30 UN Document, A/48/322, 111–12; OAU, *Resolving Conflicts in Africa*, 21.

31 OAU, *Resolving Conflicts in Africa*, 22–3.

32 "Combining against Conflict," *Africa Report*, 37, no. 5 (Sept.–Oct. 1992), 22–3.

33 UN Document A/48/322, 109.

34 See Statement by Secretary-General Salim Ahmed Salim, in OAU, *Resolving Conflicts in Africa*, 4.

35 FBIS-AFR-91-098, 21 May 1991, 1–3.

36 Africa Leadership Forum, jointly with the secretariats of the OAU and the ECA, *The Kampala Document: Towards a Conference on Security, Stability, Development and Cooperation in Africa. Kampala, Uganda: 19–22 May 1991*, 2–3 and 9–10; and FBIS-AFR-91-098, 21 May 1991, 1.

37 Kampala Document, 4.

38 FBIS-AFR-92-123, 25 June 1992, 2–3.

39 Ibid.

40 Zartman, "Inter-African Negotiations," 271.

41 FBIS-AFR-123, 25 June 1992, 2–3.

42 Eighty-five per cent of wars since 1945 have been within rather than between states. See E. Marks and W. Lewis, *Triage for Failling States* (Washington, DC: Institute for Strategic Studies 1994), 12.

43 The argument developed in this section is based on information from the following sources: Report of the Commission on Global Governance, *Our Global Neighbourhood* (Oxford: Oxford University Press 1995), 85–93; B. Boutros Ghali, *An Agenda for Peace* (New York: United Nations 1992); Lori Fisler Damrosch, ed., *Enforcing Restraint: Collective Intervention in Internal Conflicts* (New York: Council on Foreign Relations Press 1993); Adam Roberts, "The Crisis in UN Peacekeeping," *Survival*, 36 no. 3 (fall 1993), 93–120; Ruth Gordon, "UN Intervention in Internal Conflicts," *Michigan Journal of International Law*, 15 no. 2 (winter 1994); and Stanley Hoffman, "Out of the Cold: Humanitarian Intervention in the 1990s," in Charles W. Kegley and E. Wittkopf, eds., *The Global Agenda* (New York: McGraw-Hill 1995), 200–4.

44 Damrosch, ed., *Enforcing Restraint*, 361.

45 Johan Kaufmann et.al., *Testing the UN's Capacity* (New York: ACUNS 1991), 20–6.

46 OAU, *Resolving Conflicts in Africa*, 17; *Africa Report*, 37 no. 5 (Sept.–Oct. 1992), 23.

47 FBIS-AFR-92-125, 29 June 1992, 2–3; FBIS-AFR-128, 6 July 1992, 2; *Africa Research Bulletin*, 1–30 July 1992, 10636.

48 OAU, Draft Resolutions, AHG/Draft/Res.1–11 (XXXI), 26–8 June 1995.

49 *Africa Research Bulletin*, 1–30 June 1994, 11464.

50 Adapted from Zartmann, "Inter-African Negotiations," 274.

51 OAU, Council of Ministers, CM/1851 (LXI), Part 1,. "Introductory Note to the Report of the Secretary General," Addis-Ababa, 23–7 Jan. 1995, 7; OAU, "Statement by the Secretary General," 26 June 1995, 4–6.

52 Gareth Evans, "Cooperative Security and Intra-State Conflict," *Foreign Policy* no. 96 (fall 1994),:11.

53 OAU, "Relaunching Africa's Economic and Social Development: The Cairo Agenda for Action," Draft Resolutions AHG/Draft/Res 1–11 (XXXI), 26–8 June 1995.

54 OAU, Central Organ/MEC/MIN/3 (IV), "OAU's Position towards the Various Initiatives on Conflict Management: Enhancing the OAU's Capacity in Preventive Diplomacy, Conflict Resolution and Peacekeeping,." Addis Ababa, OAU, April 1995, 4–7.

55 OAU, Central Organ/MEC/MIN/3 (IV) Annex I, April 1995, 1–2.

56 John Ruggie, "Wandering the Void," in Charles W. Kegley and E. Wittkopf, eds., *The Global Agenda* (New York: McGraw-Hill 1995), 207.

57 S. Hoffman, "Out of the Cold: Humanitarian Intervention in the 1990s," in Charles W. Kegley and E. Wittkopf, eds., *The Global Agenda* (New York: McGraw-Hill 1995), 204.

58 Ruggie, "Wandering the Void," 208; Roberts, "The Crisis in UN Peacekeeping," 95–7.

59 This erosion of the requirement of consent is evident in the UN secre-

tary-general's definition of peacekeeping contained in his *Agenda for Peace.*

60 Mark R. Hutchinson, "Restoring Hope: UN Security Council Resolutions for Somalia and an Expanded Doctrine of Humanitarian Intervention." *Havard International Law Journal,* 34 no. 2 (spring 1993), 624–40; Jeffrey Clark, "Debacle in Somalia," in Lori Fisler Damrosch, ed., *Enforcing Restraint: Collective Internveion in Internal Conflicts* (New York: Council on Froeign Relations Press 1993), 222.
61 UN Document S/RES/794, 3 Dec. 1992.
62 Roberts, "The Crisis in UN Peacekeeping," 100–5.
63 Ibid, 105–6.
64 David Wippman, "Enforcing the Peace," in Lori Fisler Damrosch, ed., *Enforcing Restraint: Collective Internveion in Internal Conflicts* (New York: Council on Froeign Relations Press 1993), 157–203.
65 FBIS-AFR-167, 28 Aug. 1990, 1.
66 Wippman, "Enforcing the Peace," 168–75.
67 This list is derived from the Statement by the President of the UN Security Council, discussing the Secretary General's Report, "Improving the Capacity of the UN for Peacekeeping," UN document S/PRST/1994/22, 3 May 1994; and Boutros Ghali, *An Agenda for Peace,* 29–31.
68 Amadu Sesay, "The Limits of Peacekeeping by a Regional Organization: The OAU Peacekeeping Force in Chad," *Conflict Quarterly,* 11 no. 1 (winter 1991), 7–26. Also, D.R. Smock and H. Gregorian, "Introduction," in David R. Smock, ed., *Making War and Waging Peace* (Washington, DC: U.S. Institute of peace Press 1993), 208.
69 Ruggie, "Wandering the Void," 208.
70 Ibid, 208.
71 Boutros Ghali, *An Agenda for Peace,* 13–19.
72 This argument was advanced by the UN commander in Rwanda, Major-General Roméo Dallaire, at a talk given at the University of Toronto in March 1995.
73 "Report on Rwanda," *Africa Report* (May–June 1994), 14–19.
74 UN Document S/1994/470, 20 April 1994, 17; *Globe and Mail,* 29 April 1994, A13.
75 U.S. Department of State, No. 10161, May 1994. See also Roberts, "The Crisis in UN Peacekeeping," 108–9.
76 Mark Hoffman, "Third Party Mediation," in John Baylis and N.J. Rengger, eds., *Dilemmas of World Politics* (Oxford: Oxford University Press 1992), 261–86; Smock and Gregorian, "Introduction."
77 Zartman, "Inter-African Negotiations," 269.
78 I. William Zartman, *Ripe for Resolution: Conflict and Intervention in Africa* (New York: Oxford University Press 1989); Zartman, "Conflict Reduction: Prevention, Management and Resolution," in Francis Deng and

I.W. Zartman, eds., *Conflict Resolution in Africa* (Washington DC: Brookings Institution 1991), 299–321; Zartman, "Inter-African Negotiations," 271–2.

79 Zartman, "Inter-African Negotiations," 269.

80 Ibid., 275.

81 Sam G. Amoo, "Role of the OAU," in David R. Smock, ed., *Making War* (Washington, DC: U.S. Institute of Peace Press 1993), 245.

82 M. Deng, "Mediating the Sudanese Conflict," 15.

83 Jerome Walker, "International Mediation of Ethnic Conflicts," *Survival*, 31 no. 1 (spring 1993), 102–17.

84 *Africa Research Bulletin*, 1–30 Sept. 1995, 11973.

85 See Innis Claude Jr, "Collective Legitimization as a Political Process of the United Nations." *International Organization*, 20 no. 3 (1966), 367–79.

86 Amoo, "Role of the OAU," 245.

# 10 Conclusion: Conflict, Resolution, and Building Peace

TAISIER M. ALI AND
ROBERT O. MATTHEWS

In a recent volume on African conflicts, Peter Nyot Kok suggests that most conflicts go through three distinct phases: incubation, conflictual intercourse, and conflict resolution.[1] We have chosen to talk about those phases as the roots of conflict, the eruption of conflict, and conflict resolution. We believe that there is a further step – peace implementation. After the conflict has been resolved and a settlement reached, there remains the problem of building peace. As we have seen in at least two of our case studies above, if peacemakers ignore this final stage in managing conflict, there exists a very real likelihood that the settlement will collapse and violence erupt once again. With peace-building we come full circle, to the stage that preceded the outbreak of hostilities, for there is little difference between peace-building and the preventive measures that might avert violent conflict in the first place.

## ROOTS OF CONFLICT

For most Africans, political independence did not bring the prosperity that so many had expected. Over the past few decades, the quality of life for most people on the continent has deteriorated dramatically. Brutal military or civilian rulers, economic mismanagement, famine, and environmental, political, and societal degeneration visited most countries. In the 1980s, civil wars symbolized the latest in a series of crises causing untold human suffering and destruction of social and economic infrastructure as well as the threat of state collapse.

Past discussions of civil wars in Africa have tended to emphasize the role of outside forces over domestic conditions. More often than not, observers presented internal conflicts as "the machinations of the various global protagonists of the Cold War or, sometimes, those of a neighbouring 'rogue state' on the continent itself."[2] Explanations of this type also mirrored the reaction of ruling elites to domestic challenges to their authority. These elites tended to blame their own failings on imperialist conspiracies or plots by subversive elements, fifth columnists and traitors. While these explanations clearly exaggerate the influence of external factors, outside intrusion in domestic affairs has been frequent and often destructive. Evidence suggests a complex mix of internal and external factors operating at various stages of conflict and conflict resolution.

Surely colonial policies had a tremendous influence on the structures and relations of African societies. All the case studies in this volume, but particularly those on Liberia, Rwanda, Sudan, and Uganda, point out that colonial rule polarized African society along ethnic, religious, or regional lines. Nevertheless the civil wars studied above, except for Mozambique, have deep domestic roots. Even where colonial powers did set the stage for the conflict, the influence of colonialism was not solely, or even in large part, the cause. Colonialism cannot permanently be held responsible for every failure. Conflict in Africa may well be inevitable, as one astute observer noted,[3] but civil wars are not. Political leaders do have a choice, either to weave together often diverse peoples into a cohesive society, and thus strive for a stable social order, or to exploit ethnic and cultural differences in an attempt to hold onto power. It is to the policies and practices of the ruling elites that we must look for the roots of civil war.[4]

In his examination of Somalia, for example, Hussein Adam explained how the Darod clan-family–based regime of Siyad Barre had "armed so-called loyal clans and encouraged them to wage wars against 'rebel' clans. The damage caused by negative and destructive elite manipulation of clan consciousness contributed to the inability of civil society to rebound when Siyad fell from power."[5] In Liberia, similar policies implemented by Samuel Doe led to the "overt tribalization of politics and the militarization of society."[6] At the end, Dunn concludes "that it was Doe's insistence on favouring his Krahn group that turned most other groups, including American Liberians, against him."[7] Again, in Rwanda, Habyarimana's favouritism towards and dependence on his Bushiru Hutu clan led to the destructive consequences with which we are all too familiar. Members of this subclan dominated the only legal political party in the country and occupied

80 per cent of senior posts in the army. In the words of Bruce Jones, "It was extremist members of this akazu (Little House), as it became known, who planned and controlled the genocide of 1994."[8]

Members of the political elite intensified and manipulated narrow regional, ethnic, and sectarian cleavages in other countries as well. Mengistu Haile Mariam mobilized Ethiopia's population against Eritrea largely by appealing to ethnic chauvinism, while the successive regimes of the northern ruling elite in Sudan have flagrantly exploited religious and ethnic sentiments to justify and to bolster their war efforts. In Uganda, the long history of political turmoil preceding Museveni's regime was the result of failure by the political elite to build a consensus-based political community. Instead of pursuing "a type of politics that emphasized negotiations, compromise, and inclusion," the country's leaders tended to aggravate "existing anxieties" or create "new ones." As John Kiyaga-Nsubuga remarks, "[P]olitical control was sought either through tactical coalitions ..., or through the use of the state's coercive machinery to reduce political space for contending elites."[9] Even in Mozambique, according to John Saul, "the Frelimo leadership ... proved itself far too insensitive to the cultural complexities of the situation" in which it found itself. Instead of forging political alliances across social cleavages, Frelimo "tended to ride roughshod over the various regional, ethnic, racial, and quasi-traditional faultlines that cut across Mozambican society."[10]

Fortunately there have been a few cases where leaders dared to take up the challenge of consolidating national unity. Cranford Pratt identifies the policy paradox that Julius Nyerere recognized in Tanzania at independence – namely, that policies which ensured wide political participation increased the risk of strengthening divisive ethnic, regional, or religious forces and intra-elite rivalry. Pratt then describes the imaginative constitutional arrangements that Nyerere devised in order to maintain democracy in a formal sense while ensuring the unity, mobilization, and momentum that the nationalist movement had provided. In a related case, Hevina Dashwood examines the manner in which Robert Mugabe contained the racial and ethnic threats to Zimbabwe's national unity posed by the liberation struggle and later the rebellion in Matabeleland.[11] Other African countries too have successfully managed communal competition through the judicious use of political alliances and patronage relations.[12]

If unchecked, the tensions generated by various forms of factionalism and elite rivalry will continue to bedevil a nation and threaten its stability even after a civil war has apparently ended. The peace established in Sudan by the Addis Ababa agreement of 1972 was undermined by Nimeiri's manipulation of the ambitions of elites in both the north and the south. The possibility of rekindled hostilities emphasizes the need for proactive initiatives in that country. Regimes that come to power at the conclusion of a civil war must adopt preventive measures so as to avert the re-emergence of civil strife. Uganda is particularly instructive in this regard. John Kiyaga-Nsubuga explores how, following the divisive inter-elite struggles that led to civil war, the NRM regime under Yoweri Museveni facilitated intra-elite cooperation and moved towards more inclusive participation, thereby lessening the tension between political control and political liberalization. By contrast, in Ethiopia, the ruling EPRDF sponsored ethnic-based organizations for each major nationality, thus pitting pro-EPRDF groups against older, established ethnic opposition movements. As a result the major opposition parties withdrew from the governing coalition and boycotted the 1995 national election.

Internal conflicts are neither self-igniting nor irrational. Most post-colonial regimes in Africa lacked a sense of purpose other than to stay in power. Their track record of economic decline, famine, violation of human rights, and political decay points out that they made little or no effort to create a stable social order. Often ruling elites were made up of self-seeking cynics with no vision for the future of their countries. They perpetuated their power by maintaining the inherited structures and policies of the colonial state, by manipulating ethnic loyalties, and by trampling on the economic, cultural, and political rights of marginalized communities. In so doing they nurtured the seeds of conflict and perpetuated the conditions that invited outside intervention.

Moreover, the character of the regime in power seems to influence the state's reaction towards domestic conflicts and conflicts in neighbouring countries. In Ethiopia, Liberia, Somalia, and Sudan, for example, internal conflicts have rapidly intensified under military regimes, whereas Tanzania and Zimbabwe, which have avoided civil war, had civilian-led governments. This difference is more than just a coincidence. Army officers are more inclined to view internal dissent as a military challenge that should be out-gunned and defeated. Also, their regimes are more inclined than civilian counterparts elsewhere to intervene in the internal disputes of their neighbours. Consider, for example, the involvement of General Nimeiri in Eritrea, or that of Qadhafi in Chad and Liberia. Yet we should avoid generalizations, for not all civilian regimes are capable of reaching a peaceful settlement as is evident in Ethiopia under Haile Selassie, in Obote's Uganda, or in Sudan under Sadiq el-Mahdi.

The conflicts examined in this volume thus strongly suggest that most civil wars in Africa derive from internal rather than external sources. Even in Mozambique, where external intervention was most marked, John Saul concludes that, while the civil war was initiated primarily by outside interference from Rhodesia and South Africa, in time it became much more internally rooted, with two protagonists fighting over the spoils of war.[13] Nevertheless external involvement in African civil conflicts has often increased once all-out war has erupted. While foreign interests may not set off the conflicts, they often act as catalysts, exacerbating existing differences and prolonging hostilities. As Francis Deng and William Zartman point out in *Conflict Resolution in Africa*, the causes of African conflicts "are nearly always domestic or regional but ... the effects or the operational aspects involving the means, whether in weapons or the financial ability to procure them, are usually external."[14]

Our cases also challenge the widely held view that the causes of civil strife lie in the deeply rooted socio-economic structures of post-colonial society. Ethnic and regional cleavages, economic disparities, and weak state institutions are often underlying causes, but not sufficient explanations. It is the manner in which governing elites treat ethnic conflicts and identities that determines whether or not conflicts erupt into violence and become civil war. It is their vision of the future (or lack thereof) that decides whether the underlying structural problems will be managed, even settled, or simply allowed to fester and ultimately explode. Leaders dedicated to inclusive policies, to the broadest participation in the political process, and to removal of abject poverty and widespread economic disparities will probably avoid the horrors of civil war. By contrast, those whose vision is limited to personal aggrandizement and the narrow interests of the few and to the concerns of a single region or one ethnic or racial group will in time face a violent uprising.

This conclusion corresponds closely to the argument advanced by Michael Brown in his recent study of internal conflicts. He suggests that "most major, internal conflicts were triggered by internal, elite-level forces." Driven by ideological or power struggles these "bad leaders," as he calls them, engage in actions and make decisions that propel their societies towards war.[15] In a similar fashion, Raymond Copson sees Africa's wars as rooted in the failure of the state "to respond to Africa's 'heterogeneous social reality.'"[16] Faced with a widening gap between state and society, some governments "refused to permit broad participation in the state" and lacked the ability "to impose their policy decisions on reluctant ethnic, regional and other groups."[17] It is in these errors of policy and conduct that Copson too finds the proximate causes of Africa's civil conflicts.

In short, civil wars in Africa stem largely from failure in governance – from a government's mismanagement of ethnic, racial, religious, and regional cleavages.[18] While structural factors do count, it is what leaders in fact decide to do or not to do "that ultimately matters."[19]

## THE ERUPTION OF CONFLICT

What are essentially domestic conflicts easily and quickly become internationalized. As the fighting escalates, the various sides to a civil war seek support from abroad. Foreign powers are often only too happy to help, hoping thereby to enlist allies in their own struggles, whether that be the Arab–Israeli conflict, the Cold War, or civil strife in neighbouring countries in a region. Thus foreigners become actively engaged in civil wars, and their presence, as one observer noted, "unquestionably raise[s] the level of violence."[20] Even though external actors and forces may not be the cause of Africa's civil wars, "without ... external sources, armed confrontation would be constrained, and conflicts, even if they exploded into violence, would be less destructive."[21]

We can see this process of internationalization and increasing conflict in the case studies above. While Mengistu received substantial support from the Soviet Union and Cuba, the Eritreans were openly backed by Arab countries, including Ethiopia's neighbour Sudan. In Mozambique, the Soviet bloc constituted a major source of material support to Frelimo in the decolonization struggle and continued to play an important role in the period after independence, whereas its chief protagonist, Renamo, was a creature of first Rhodesia's security forces and later, the South African military. External forces have at different moments fuelled the flames of war in Sudan, with Arab countries and Israel major actors before the Addis Ababa agreement of 1972; the United States, Egypt, Libya, and Ethiopia after the civil war resumed in 1983; and Iraq, Iran and China since the NIF came to power in 1989. In Liberia the competing factions found sanctuary, training, and support in neighbouring states and in Libya, while in Rwanda the government received assistance from France, Belgium, and Zaire to repel the Uganda-backed RPF. Finally, the widespread availability of weapons from earlier Soviet and American military aid programs accelerated Somalia's slide into anarchy. Only in Uganda, which was considered largely irrelevant by the Cold War rivals, did foreigners play a minor part in the civil war. As one observer recently noted, the NRA achieved military victory there "without continuing access to external resources."[22]

In examining the role of external actors, it is useful to distinguish between neighbouring states and "external," non-African powers. It is obvious that few, if any civil wars are "hermetically sealed"; the vast majority of those examined above have affected or involved neighbours states "in one way or another."[23] Even when neighbours wish to remain detached, they can rarely escape influxes of refugees, economic disruption, military insecurity, and political instability. But, as Brown notes, neighbouring countries are rarely "passive victims."[24] For ideological reasons in some instances, self-defence in others, neighbours and nearby nations have often provided assistance (arms, training, sanctuary, or a route for military aid from afar) to dissident forces. As a result, pairs or groups of countries such as Sudan and Ethiopia (before 1991), Sudan and its neighbours Eritrea and Uganda (in recent years), Rwanda and Uganda, Liberia and Sierra Leone, and Somalia and Ethiopia have become locked in "reciprocal patterns of interference."[25] Civil wars do tend, almost inevitably, to become regionalized, thus inviting regional solutions.

Actors from outside Africa have also contributed to civil wars on the continent, often intensifying and prolonging the fighting. The Soviet Union provided massive military assistance to the governments of Ethiopia and Mozambique, while the United States backed regimes in Liberia, Somalia, and Sudan. Given the substantial level of this support, coupled with official statements of endorsement by either Washington or Moscow, it is not surprising that, as Copson remarked, "[t]he regimes in all these countries ... had reason to believe that they had a superpower on their side and could proceed against the internal opposition with impunity."[26] The end of superpowers' rivalry and their proxy confrontation encouraged Ethiopia and Mozambique to find a peaceful end to their conflicts, but its effect on other conflicts was negligible. Either through stockpiles of weapons from earlier wars or with alternative sources of supply (private or governmental), factions in the Liberian, Rwandan, Somali, and Sudanese civil wars were still able to secure continuing supplies of arms.

In choosing to support one side or the other in these civil wars, regional and global powers have frequently intensified and prolonged the conflicts. As long as both sides can count on access to the means to continue the struggle, and even to win, they are more likely to seek a solution by force than through peaceful negotiations.[27] Only when external links are severed or substantially reduced are the parties likely to consider a negotiated settlement. It was not until

1971, when faced with a military stalemate and the likelihood of a decline in their future capacity to carry on the war, that both President Nimeiri and the southern Sudanese insurgents, the Anyanya, entered into negotiations, which resulted in the Addis Ababa agreement of 1972. Similarly, the collapse of both apartheid and the Cold War meant that neither South Africa nor the Soviet Union was willing any longer to bankroll Renamo and Frelimo, respectively; without external support both sides were willing to consider negotiations seriously. The ending of foreign engagement will not by itself ensure a political settlement, but in many instances it will help deflate the conflict and increase the chances of an early resolution.

## CONFLICT RESOLUTION

Not all conflicts are managed or resolved. Several analysed in our volume have dragged on in a seemingly endless manner. Though Somalia's no longer figures in the world press, it remains unresolved. Various efforts have been made to bring the many parties together and to form a new national government, but with the exception of the republic of Somaliland – the northern section of Somalia, which has declared its independence and established a modicum of stability – the inter-clan fighting continues, especially in and around Mogadishu, and the structures of a central state remain in a state of collapse. Similarly, the conflict in Sudan has now entered its fifteenth year since its renewal in 1983. The principal parties have proclaimed their desire for peace and have been brought together on several occasions by other African states or statesmen, but each time the talks broke down. Indeed, it is difficult not to question the commitment of the government of Sudan to peace, except on its own terms.

The drawn-out negotiations over Sudan sponsored by General Babaginda at Abuja in 1992 and 1993 and by the IGADD states since 1993 provide a classic example of talks without negotiations. In such instances, one or both parties to a conflict enter into pre-negotiations to create the impression of interest in peace while actually pursuing hostilities on the battle-field. Such talks are thus a form of propaganda, directed at an anxious domestic public and a concerned international community, not a preliminary stage in negotiations.[28] As long as the NIF-backed government remains in power in Khartoum, valuing more highly the development of an Islamic state than the costs of pursuing the war, there seems little prospect of resolving Africa's longest civil war.[29] In the case of Somalia, the issue is less "the shape of the settlement" sought by the factions than the large number of parties engaged in the civil war, each of which seems unwilling "to consider power sharing arrangements with its opponents." Under such circumstances, civil wars "are characterised, at least for a time, by considerable levels of violence and are remarkably resistant to negotiated settlements."[30]

The other conflicts discussed in this volume have all ended; hostilities have been terminated, even if a lasting settlement has not been reached and fully implemented. In three instances, military victory by one of the parties finished the violent phase of the conflicts. Despite a last-minute attempt by Kenya's president, Daniel arap Moi, to bring the warring parties together, the civil war in Uganda was ended with Museveni's defeat of the opposing forces in the early months of 1986. Fighting still continues in the north, along the Sudanese border, but for the most part peace has been restored. Surrender by the Derg forces in Asmara in May 1991 brought an end to the civil war in Eritrea and the eventual collapse of Derg rule throughout Ethiopia. The collapse of the Soviet Union and the expiry of its massive military assistance, together with u.s. intervention, hastened Mengistu's departure and facilitated a relatively smooth transition from Derg rule.[31] Ultimately, however, it was the military success of the two major liberation movements – the Tigrayan People's Liberation Front and the Eritrean People's Liberation Front – that terminated Ethiopia's civil war.

On 18 July 1994 the Rwandan Patriotic Front (RPF) declared victory and a unilateral cease-fire, thus ending the genocide that engulfed Rwanda after 6 April 1994. African and Western states had brokered the Arusha Accords of August 1993, which had called for a cease-fire; return of the Tutsi refugees; demobilization of the RPF and the Hutu-dominated militia in Rwanda and their reorganization into a national army; and establishment of a broad-based, transitional government of national unity. However, as Bruce Jones so persuasively argues, that agreement – specifically its exclusion of Hutu extremists from the new government and the absence of an international force to control extremist Hutu militias – contributed to the genocide that followed. This case underlines the fact that a negotiated accord does not in itself ensure permanent peace, unless the parties are resolved or compelled to respect its terms.

While three of the civil wars described in this volume ended with decisive military victory, two were settled through negotiations, with active mediation by both regional and global third parties. When Joaquim Chissano became president of Mozambique in late 1986, following the death of Samora Machel, it was apparent that the government could not win the war and that, if the military stalemate were to be ended, it would have to negotiate with Renamo. But, as John Saul eloquently points out, it was not sufficient that the two principal protagonists saw themselves as entrapped in a "hurting stalemate." Other, more powerful actors would have to become involved before peace could be restored. For quite different reasons, South Africa and the Soviet Union retired to the sidelines. It was to presidents arap Moi of Kenya and Mugabe of Zimbabwe that the two sides first looked. These two leaders initiated preliminary talks in Nairobi, but by 1990 their role as mediators had become problematic. Other, non-African actors became engaged at this stage, the most visible being the Community of Sant'Egidio and the Italian government. As Mozambique abandoned its progressive policies and became more and more subject to Western influence, a process described as "recolonization," Washington too came to see the Frelimo regime as "a new 'partner' in the global enterprise of peace, capitalism, and democracy." Though not one of the four mediators that facilitated the peace accord, the United States was actively engaged in cajoling both sides into making compromises and, along with a United Nations force (ONUMOZ), in overseeing implementation of the final agreement.[32]

In Liberia, hostilities appeared finally to have been ended through negotiations when an accord was signed in Abuja, Nigeria, in August 1995. The sporadic outbreaks of violence that followed in Monrovia signalled not its collapse but merely the last in a series of setbacks to a final settlement, reached in 1996. To the surprise of most Liberians, the United States remained aloof from the conflict, except to send a ship to remove American citizens from Monrovia and to provide some funding for the west African peacekeeping operation. It was states from the region that sent a peacekeeping force (ECOMOG) and brokered a settlement. But as Elwood Dunn describes in painful detail, ECOMOG became involved in the internal rivalry of Liberian politics and thus helped delay a political settlement. And yet, as he concludes, paradoxically, "without ECOMOG Liberia risked descending in the short run into greater chaos." Neither the OAU nor the UN helped end the hostilities. Only in 1993, over three years after the civil war had erupted, did they agree to supporting roles. The UN secretary-general appointed an "eminent person" to provide liaison with the ECOWAS secretariat, while three states from eastern Africa agreed to supply troops to ECOMOG, in an attempt to address the charge of impartiality levied against the west African force. The precarious nature of the Abuja agreement is in part a reflection of the general lack of interest from the international community and its unwillingness to support significantly the west African peacekeeping force. It also illustrates quite vividly how difficult it is to enforce a negotiated settlement.

There seems to be a consensus, among practitioners and academics alike, that civil wars are much more likely to end by decisive military victory than by negotiated settlement.[33] As they are often perceived as "zero-sum" in nature – in effect, total wars – reaching a compromise is difficult, if not impossible. Neither side is willing to share power with its opponents, nor prepared to disarm, as this action may put it at the mercy of its erstwhile enemy.[34] Civil wars are indeed very "resistant to negotiated settlement."

None the less civil conflicts are sometimes ended through negotiations. Of the cases analysed in this volume, two were settled peacefully – Mozambique, after several years of talks, and Liberia, though the continuous outbursts of violence in Monrovia placed the negotiated settlement in temporary jeopardy. Negotiated settlements did bring an end to fighting elsewhere – in Sudan for eleven years and in Rwanda for eight months. But in both cases the governing party openly violated the terms of the settlement, thus ushering in a return to armed struggle.

If ending civil wars through negotiations is indeed a rarity, what accounts for the positive outcomes in these four instances of peaceful settlement? There appear to have been at least two factors that in each case encouraged peaceful resolution – a painful stalemate and third-party mediation. First, the parties found themselves in what William Zartman has termed a "hurting stalemate."[35] Both sides feared that they stood to lose a great deal if they were to continue fighting. As Roy Licklider summarized the evidence of seven instances of negotiated settlement in his edited volume on ending war, "... both [sides] must *perceive* the current situation as untenable and unlikely to improve in the future."[36] As the military option becomes less attractive, the parties became at least willing to consider negotiated settlement.

In Mozambique, the collapse of the Cold War, the end of apartheid, and a devastating drought in 1992 combined to raise the costs of war for both parties, prompting them to reach a peace agreement.[37] By the spring of 1995 the major factions in the Liberian civil war were deadlocked and weary of the ongoing war.[38] In Rwanda, a timely show of force by the RPF demonstrated to the Rwandan delegation at the peace talks in Arusha that if the war continued, the Hutu-led government was more than likely to lose further ground. Given the RPF's superior field position and Rwanda's continued economic decline, the government concluded that an agreement, however distasteful, was preferable.[39] And in Sudan, between July 1971 and March 1972, shifting alliances in the region and the world at large created conditions conducive to a peaceful resolution of the civil war. Nimeiri had broken ties with the Soviet bloc and had not yet established links with the West, while the Anyanya realized that their arms supply from Israel was seriously threatened as both Ethiopia and Uganda were preparing to patch up their differences with Khartoum.[40] In all our cases then, while both sides did prefer military victory, both faced a military stalemate and the likelihood of a decline in their future capacity to carry on the war. But a "hurting stalemate" was not enough.

Second, peaceful solution required as well active and prolonged third-party mediation. Bringing to the table a mixture of threats, promises, and good ideas, disinterested third parties helped fashion agreements that met the needs of both parties. For Mozambique this mediating role was played by the Community of Sant'Egidio, the Italian government, and several other major donor countries; for Liberia, by President Rawlings of Ghana's timely initiative and the west African peace force supported by the UN; for Rwanda, by a group of African and non-African states; and for Sudan, by the World Council of Churches, the All-African Council of Churches, and the Ethiopian emperor.

Negotiated settlements are notoriously unstable. Concerned about the possible effects of an agreement on their security and even their very survival, one or both parties may abandon the peace option and take up arms again. On other occasions, failure to achieve objectives at the bargaining table may send the parties back to war. In still other instances, the commitment of the parties to negotiations may not be genuine but a temporary tactic, designed to win time to recuperate and rearm before relaunching a military offensive. Agreements, however solemnly agreed on, are therefore precarious and easily overturned. It is this feature that explains the on-again, off-again talks in Monrovia; the collapse of the Arusha Accords of 1993 for Rwanda, where Habaryimana accepted the arrangements for transition with great reluctance, and the more extreme members of his party, not at all; and the eventual breakdown of the Addis Ababa agreement for Sudan in 1983, once Nimeiri had established an alliance with the Islamic absolutists in the north and insisted on imposing the Sharia law throughout the entire country.

Many observers had hoped that the end of the Cold War would dampen conflict in Africa: the Soviet Union and the United States would no longer have any interest in pursuing their rivalry through active engagement in regional and civil conflicts. This decline in interest and the corresponding drop in their support for opposing sides to a conflict would, it was expected, create an environment more conducive to peaceful settlement. As one author has put it, "[W]ithout the United States and the Soviet Union battling each other for influence in the region, it is easier to devise solutions in which all parties can win."[41]

In fact, the reduction in tensions has been a mixed blessing. Though the Soviet Union never served as mediator in any of the conflicts analysed in this volume, by the late 1980s Moscow had begun to cut back its military assistance to Ethiopia and Mozambique, thereby pressing Mengistu and Frelimo, respectively, to pursue a non-military approach to their conflicts. The United States was more active in that role, yet it has been selective, focusing attention and resources on countries previously aligned with the Soviet Union and committed to socialist development. For instance, Washington took an active hand in the negotiations that led to the flight of Mengistu and to the 1992 settlement in Mozambique, but it remained curiously silent over Liberia, with which it had been closely aligned; withdrew its troops from Somalia once it had sustained casualties; and refused to support a more active role for the UN in Rwanda in the spring of 1994 other than to send "humanitarian relief to the refugees in Zaire once the killings had ended."[42] No longer driven by the strategic rivalry of the Cold War, the United States seems less likely to assign a high priority to intervening in civil wars in Africa unless such action appears to further an overriding strategic interest. One author explains American unwillingness to be a leader in ending such wars as the result of the U.S. public's inward focus on domestic issues, the opposition of the U.S. military to anything other than decisive actions, with clear objectives, to which overwhelming force can be applied, and to "an assertive Congress."[43] Clearly the American débâcle in Somalia made an enduring impression on policy-makers in Washington, who for the most part are reluctant to intervene abroad in internal conflicts unless vital U.S. interests are engaged.

The end of the Cold War created an expectation that the UN and the OAU would become more active in preventing, managing, and resolving conflicts in Africa. In the past, provisions in their charters upholding the sovereignty and territorial integrity of member-states and prohibiting intervention in domestic jurisdiction kept international and regional organizations from intervening in internal conflicts. However, the renewed post--Cold War emphasis on collective security in the UN and the development of a new mechanism in the OAU for resolving conflicts seemed, in the words of James Busumtwi-Sam, "to herald an era of greater peace."

The earlier reluctance of these two organizations to intervene in internal conflicts is borne out in this volume. Both the OAU and the UN remained on the sidelines during the civil wars in Sudan, in Uganda, in Ethiopia, and, until 1992, in Mozambique. But, as predicted, since the end of the Soviet–American rivalry, UN peacekeeping forces have been inserted into Mozambique (1992) to guarantee the peace process, in Somalia (1992) to create a secure environment for the delivery of humanitarian aid and to monitor a cease-fire, and in Rwanda (1993) to monitor the cease-fire and to assist in the implementation of the Arusha Accords. In Somalia, the UN was even prepared to authorize the use of force by both UNITAF (December 1992) and UNISOM II (March 1993). However, it was not always so willing to tackle internal conflicts: even in Somalia, the UN force did not resolve the underlying political issues, and once it withdrew chaos was quick to return. In 1994 the international response to genocide in Rwanda was, as Bruce Jones notes, "non-existent"; fearful that Rwanda might turn into a peacekeeping disaster like Somalia, the UN never seriously considered "the option of reinforcing UNAMIR." Lacking the "will to address the root causes of the conflict and to use force decisively," as another observer remarked, the leading members of the Security Council "simply treated the humanitarian symptoms of strife, and did so in a half-hearted manner."[44] In Liberia the UN remained largely on the side, limiting itself to a supporting role vis-à-vis the ECOWAS force, while in Sudan it has restricted itself to providing food aid and to criticizing the government's human rights record.

This mixed record of UN engagement is perhaps not so surprising. In a sense, it simply reflects the reluctance of the leading members of the Security Council, particularly the United States, to become involved in civil wars in countries and a region in which their interests are not heavily engaged. In effect, we need only be reminded that "the United Nations itself is simply an instrument in the hands of its member states, particularly the P-5 (permanent members of the Security Council)."[45] If the UN fails to act, or acts in a half-hearted manner, or withdraws before achieving its original objectives, then we need look only at the policies of the UN's leading members to find an explanation.

The OAU's record is even less praiseworthy. At the Cairo Summit in June 1993, the OAU Assembly did create a new Mechanism for Conflict Prevention, Management and Resolution, but to date it remains on paper only. In Liberia, Mozambique, Rwanda, Somalia, and Sudan, the OAU has played at best a secondary role; more often than not it has remained invisible. A number of subregional organizations took the initiative in dealing with civil wars – for example,

IGADD, in the case of Sudan; ECOWAS, in Liberia; and the Great Lakes Heads of State, in Rwanda. If the new mechanism is to become effective, African states must, as James Busumtwi-Sam asserts, redefine or reinterpret "the norms of African diplomacy and governance, [so that they] can facilitate multilateral intervention in states' domestic jurisdiction."[46]

But, as Sam Amoo has convincingly argued, improving "the OAU's conflict management practices ... will hardly constitute an adequate response to the current dynamic of African conflict."[47] Many of the civil wars studied in this volume require resources and skills in which the OAU is particularly deficient. What may therefore be required, in addition to the normative changes of which Busumtwi-Sam has written, is "a multilateral approach coordinated and spearheaded by the UN with the OAU playing a complementary role as an important but junior partner."[48] While the leading members of the United Nations may be reluctant to send troops to Africa, they may be prepared to support African forces.

BUILDING PEACE

Signing a peace accord is not the end of the peace process but merely a way station along the road. Though such accords are an important, even essential part of that process, there remain a number of critical steps that war-torn societies must take in order to ensure that peace has firmly been established. For some, the emphasis is on designing a program for the demobilization of soldiers and insurgents and their reintegration into civilian life.[49] For others, the task of promoting peace and rebuilding society is much broader in scope, involving a complex set of measures that include consolidation of peace, provision of emergency relief, and establishment of the political, social, economic, juridical, and psychological foundations of sustainable development.[50] Whether dictated by an internationally sanctioned settlement or undertaken by the victorious party, peace-building is likely to include many tasks – development of a political system that offers all groups effective participation in governance, holding of open and free elections, reform of the civil service, institutionalization of respect for human rights, demobilization of military forces and their reintegration into civil society, elimination of surplus weapons, and social and economic rehabilitation and reconstruction.

Peace-makers ignore at their own peril the significance of this phase, which has been termed "peace-building."[51] A flaw in the settlement, lack of resources, or failure to monitor implementation may bring the collapse of peace and the resumption of civil war. In at least two instances examined in this volume a negotiated settlement broke down because of insufficient attention being given to the consolidation of the peace. The Addis Ababa agreement of 1972 brought an end to the Sudanese civil war for eleven years. It did not resolve the underlying sources of the conflict, but it did provide a framework of regional autonomy for the south within which north-south differences could be addressed. During the entire period the accord was in effect no effort was made to confront the social, economic, and political problems of the south, and once it ceased to serve Nimeiri's immediate political needs, he did not hesitate to abrogate it. Not surprisingly the civil war erupted again in 1983.

In the other example, that of Rwanda, while the Arusha Accords of August 1993 brought a brief end to the fighting, its very terms set the stage for its ultimate demise and the genocide that followed. Bruce Jones summarized the flaw in the agreement in this way: "[H]aving effectively removed ... the akazu (Hutu exremists) from power on paper, the international peace-makers should have conceived of means of pushing them out of power in fact – by disarming them or removing them from Kigali, under the supervision of a peace-enforcement force."[52] UNAMIR, in other words, should not have been sent in as a (UN Charter) chapter VI neutral operation, but under chapter VII, with a mandate to neutralize and disarm the opponents of the peace process. As the genocide began, the Security Council reduced the size of UNAMIR. Only when the RPF was on the verge of winning a military victory did the UN approve a new mandate. The new, Tutsi-led government now faces the enormous task of meting out suitable punishment to those involved in the genocidal attack on the minority Tutsis while it reaches out, with compassion and forgiveness, to the majority Hutus, most of whom have returned from refugee camps in Zaire. Only with such reconciliation can anything approximating peace be eventually restored.

The failure to build peace in Sudan and Rwanda contrasts sharply with the manner in which peace was consolidated in Mozambique, Uganda, and, to a lesser extent, Ethiopia. Though John Saul is critical of the peace produced in Mozambique, he leaves no doubt that the UN and the Supervisory and Monitoring Commission (CSC), which included representatives of the OAU, the UN, and major donor countries, carefully monitored the process and even threatened the two parties, Frelimo and Renamo, when they resisted demobilization of their best troops. Though the Rome agreement was defective, the UN and major Western states kept pressure on the two parties during implementation to renegotiate new terms. The international community thus constituted what Boutros Boutros-Ghali has called a "form of collective oversight." Through the UN, as well, massive humanitarian assistance was launched, with the world community providing over one-half billion dollars for emergency relief, resettlement of over four million displaced Mozambicans, reintegration of demobilized troops, reactivation of health and education programs, and clearance of land-mines. Finally, a general election in late October 1994 provided what Saul describes as "the finishing touch to the peace process." Saul notes that the peace has held. Whether or not it endures, he argues, depends on the consolidation of a democratic culture among Mozambicans and on the ability of the new government to develop a strong sense of purpose that promises to improve the lives of most of its citizens.

Though the civil war in Uganda was ended by military force rather than negotiated settlement, Yoweri Museveni could not avoid the difficult task of peace-building.[53] Had he not undertaken to broaden the political process, thereby including previously marginalized groups, and to promote economic development, he would have faced the resumption of civil war. As part of his politics of inclusion, Museveni coopted representatives of various political tendencies within a broad-based cabinet; incorporated fighters from other armed groups within a greatly expanded National Resistance Army; promoted grassroots discussions through the development and expansion of people's resistance committees (PRCs) across the country; and solicited widespread participation in the drafting of a new constitution. At the same time, the National Resistance Movement regime turned the economy around, reorganizing the public sector, reducing inflation to single-digit figures, rehabilitating infrastructure, and expanding both agricultural and industrial production.

What distinguished Uganda's experience from Mozambique's was not the concrete steps undertaken to build peace, but the nature of the political process. Unlike in Mozambique, where a political settlement was hammered out in negotiations mediated by powerful third parties before the consolidation of peace began, Museveni had to launch reconstruction in the absence of what John Kiyaga-Nsubuga describes as "intra-elite consensus" on the rules of political competition. While allowing for substantial participation in the political process, the government was not prepared to give up overall control of that process. In Kiyaga-Nsubuga's view, where there exists no prior agreement among the major actors over the distribution of power and the rules of the game, a measure of centralized control is essential to the peaceful development of the country. However, that control must be tempered by a strong measure of liberalization, without which citizens will not feel themselves part of a shared enterprise, and those who see themselves as being on the outside will resort again to armed struggle.

The experience of Ethiopia following the victory of the TPLF/EPRDF highlights the same tension between political control and political liberalization. Born in the context of a struggle for survival, the TPLF, the principal liberation front in Ethiopia, adopted a siege mentality and a vision of rural-based development and mobilization. Once it had acquired the reins of power following the defeat of the Mengistu regime, it displayed intransigence towards those who opposed its vision. To counter opposition groups in various regions, the TPLF nurtured satellite liberation fronts organized along ethnic lines. As John Prendergast and Mark Duffield point out, these largely ethnic parties "were placed in command of the local administrations and treated favourably over the older established ethnic opposition movements during the transition phase." By the end of the transition period the major opposition groups had withdrawn from the political process and, fearing defeat at the polls, refused to participate in the 1995 national election.

To ensure the long-term stability of Ethiopia, the newly elected government will have to allow for more political liberalization than it has at present. (Because of their close links with the government, forged during the liberation struggle, NGOs and donor countries have a special role to play in pressing the government in this direction.) In the absence of political reconciliation, the central government will probably have to resort to increasing repression to ensure its control over Ethiopia.

In two other civil wars studied in this volume, peace-building is only in embryonic form. In Liberia, an agreement reached in 1995 envisages the sharing of power among the major players during an interim period. This accord thus sets the stage for what Elwood Dunn calls the "crucial element of faithful implementation." The outburst of fighting in the streets of Monrovia clearly put peace-building temporarily on the back burner; this breakdown of order highlights the importance of demobilization as a pre-condition for elections and the danger involved in not providing international "collective oversight."[54] In the case of Somalia, all efforts, local or foreign, to re-create the structures of the collapsed state have failed and are likely to fail, pending a negotiated settlement among competing clan leaders. While noting this failure, Hussein Adam does point hopefully to the growing strength of civil society and to the earliest signs of "consociational democratic mechanisms." Both Liberia and Somalia now face the daunting task of building an enduring peace. In preparing for that undertaking, they might usefully draw on the experience of not only Mozambique, Uganda, and Ethiopia, but also Zimbabwe and Tanzania.

Hevina Dashwood and Cranford Pratt reflect on the initiatives undertaken by these two countries to maintain domestic political stability. That those nations were able to avoid large-scale political violence while experiencing most of the problems facing other African states does underscore the significance of political leadership and the usefulness of a policy of inclusion. Both Mugabe and Nyerere envision a political society in which all people are able to participate. That each followed a different set of policies in maintaining social stability – one relying on "skilful reconciliatory politics and strong (if increasingly authoritarian) government," and the other, on invention and implementation of democratic, one-party rule – also suggests that preventive diplomacy must be fashioned to fit the special circumstances of each country. These studies in successful conflict management underline also the fact that prevention and resolution of domestic conflict must be linked to the underlying causes of those conflicts. Failure to address the root causes of any conflict, whether it be potential or real, can result only in the eruption or continuation of civil strife. Finally, the policies that a country pursues to prevent conflict from erupting into violence, such as Mugabe and Nyerere introduced, are not too different from those designed to build an enduring peace after a conflict has ended. Conflict prevention and peace-building are not at opposite ends of a straight-line continuum but are adjoining points in a circle of policy options.

Students engaged in the analysis of peace-building might usefully examine more closely the institutions (new and reformed) that countries such as Ghana, Tanzania, Zambia, and Zimbabwe have fashioned and the policies they have pursued in their attempts to deal with the problems associated with political development. By examining carefully the normal, day-to-day activities of such governments, we should be able to see how they have dealt with the demands and grievances of ethnic, religious, and regional groups, distributed resources with some measure of equity, and maintained the legitimacy of governmental institutions. In effect, we should heed Bill Zartman when he calls for "a better understanding ... of the processes of successful prevention, so they can be replicated."[55] By examining above the successes of countries such as Tanzania and Zimbabwe and the failures of countries such as Rwanda and Sudan we hope to have provided a beginning.

NOTES

1 Peter Nyot Kok, "The Ties That Will Not Bind: Conflict and Racial Cleavages in Sudan," in Peter Anyang' Nyongo, ed., *Arms and Daggers in the Heart of Africa* (Nairobi: African Academy of Sciences 1993).

2 John Saul, chapter 5 above, 123. In a study of "Causes and Regional Effects of Internal Conflicts," which includes civil wars, Michael Brown notes that much of "the scholarly literature on causes of internal conflict emphasizes the importance of ... two sets of factors: internal, mass-level factors such as economic development and modernization; and external, mass-level factors, which are usually characterized as 'contagion' or 'diffusion' effects." See Michael Brown, ed., *The International Dimension of Internal Conflict* (Cambridge, Mass.: MIT Press, 1996), 575.

3 James O'Connell, "The Inevitability of Instability," *Journal of Modern African Studies*, 5 no. 2 (1967), 181–91.

4 While Stephen Stedman recognizes that the "roots of Africa's violence" can in part be attributed to the economic and political conditions found at independence, he stresses as well "the policies pursed by elites to gain and consolidate power." Stephen John Stedman, "Conflict and Conciliation in Sub-Saharan Africa," in Michael Brown, *ed., The International Dimension of Internal Conflict* (Cambridge, Mass.: MIT Press 1996), 236, 238.

5 Hussein Adam, chapter 6 above, 174.

6 Elwood Dunn, chapter 4 above, 95.

7 Ibid., 101.

8 Bruce Jones, chapter 3 above, 60.

9 John Kiyaga-Nsubuga, chapter 1 above, 16.

10 Saul, chapter 5 above, 128.

11 Hevina Dashwood and Cranford Pratt, chapter 8 above, 223–54.

12 See, for example, James R. Scarritt, "Communal Conflict and Contention for Power in Africa South of the Sahara," in Ted Gurr, ed., *Minorities at Risk: A Global View of Ethnopolitical Conflicts* (Washington, DC: U.S. Institute of Peace 1993), 252–89.

13 Raymond Copson argues that from the very beginning Frelimo had alienated many elements of Mozambican society, and it was from these segments that the Rhodesian security forces were able to draw recruits for Renamo and foster armed resistance. See Raymond Copson, *Africa's Wars and Prospects for Peace* (New York: Sharpe 1994), 76–7.

14 Francis Deng and I. William Zartman, eds., *Conflict Resolution in Africa* (Washington, DC: Brookings Institution 1991), 10. Similarly, Copson, *Africa's Wars*, 103, argues that "the causes of every war were, at their root, internal, and that the international factor played [only] a contributory role."

15 Brown, "Causes and Regional Effects," 580.

16 Copson, *Africa's Wars*, 74.

17 Ibid., 76.

18 Stephen Stedman, "Conflict and Conciliation," in Francis Deng and I. William Zartman, eds., *Conflict Resolution in Africa* (Washington, DC: Brookings Institution 1991), notes (373) that all the contributors emphasize that "conflict in Africa stems primarily from crises of national governance," whether from the elites' restriction of political participation, their unequal distribution of economic resources, or their overall unresponsiveness to societal needs and demands.

19 René LeMarchand, "Managing Transitional Anarchies: Rwanda, Burundi, and South Africa in Comparative Perspective," *Journal of Modern African Studies*, 32 no. 4 (1994), 604.

20 Copson, *Africa's Wars*, 104.

21 Deng and Zartman, eds., *Conflict Resolution*, 10–11.

22 Christopher Clapham, *Africa and the International System: The Politics of State Survival* (Cambridge: Cambridge University Press 1996), 213.

23 Brown, *International Dimension*, 572.

24 Ibid., 25.

25 Ibid., 27.

26 Copson, *Africa's Wars*, 104.

27 In her conclusion to a study of external involvement in Sudan, Ann Mosely Lesch notes that the intervention of outside powers "has helped harden the government's stand by bolstering the government's military and diplomatic position." Military and economic support, she argues, acted "as a brake on negotiations," conveying to Khartoum's successive governments "that if only they could obtain more arms they could prevail militarily and avoid negotiations." See her "External Involvement in the Sudanese Civil War," in David R. Smock, ed., *Making War and Waging Peace* (Washington, DC: U.S. Institute of Peace 1993), 98. LeMarchand, "Managing Transitional Anarchies," 603, draws a similar conclusion with respect to French military support for the Hutu government in Rwanda in the early 1990s. By strengthening its military capabilities, France created "major disincentives for the Habyarimana clique to make concessions to the opposition." And, finally, Roy Licklider in the conclusion to his edited book *Stopping the Killing: How Civil Wars End* (Boston: South End Press 1994), 312, concludes that "strong external military support to governments seems to militate against a negotiated settlement."

28 See Robert O. Matthews, "Talking without Negotiating: The Case of Rhodesia," *International Journal* (winter 1979–80), 91–117, as well as Fred Ikle, *How Nations Negotiate* (New York: Praeger 1967), chap. 4.

29 Jane E. Holl, "When War Doesn't Work: Understanding the Relationship between the Battlefield and the Negotiating Table," in Roy Lick-

lider, ed., *Stopping the Killing: How Civil Wars End* (Boston: South End Press 1994), 277, points out that civil wars are likely to be protracted when at least one side values "the shape of the settlement" over the costs of pursuing the war.

30 Ibid., 275.

31 For an analysis of the factors surrounding the collapse of Derg rule, see Paul Henze, "Ethiopia and Eritrea: The Defeat of the Derg and the Establishment of New Governments," in David R. Smock, ed., *Making War and Waging Peace* (Washington, DC: U.S. Institute of Peace 1993), 53–77.

32 See also Witney W. Schneidman, "Conflict Resolution in Mozambique," in David R. Smock, ed., *Making War and Waging Peace* (Washington, DC: U.S. Institute of Peace 1993), 219–38.

33 According to Stephen Stedman, "Between 1900 and 1980 fifteen per cent of civil wars ended through negotiations." See his "Negotiations and Mediation in Internal Conflict," in Michael Brown, ed., *The International Dimension of Internal Conflict* (Cambridge, Mass.: MIT Press 1996), 343. See also Stedman, *Peacekeeping in Civil Wars: International Mediation in Zimbabwe, 1974–1980* (Boulder, Col.: Lynne Rienner 1991) and Paul Pillar, *Negotiating Peace: War Termination as a Bargaining Process* (Princeton, NJ: Princeton University Press 1983), especially 16–26. Since 1989 a significant number of civil wars in the world have ended through negotiations. It still remains to be seen whether or not there has been a noticeable shift in the way in which the fighting is stopped since the end of the Cold War.

34 See Stedman, *Peacekeeping in Civil Wars*, 343, and Holl, "When War Doesn't Work," 275.

35 See I. William Zartman, *Ripe for Resolution* (Oxford: Oxford University Press 1985).

36 Roy Licklider, "What Have We Learned and Where Do We Go from Here?" Roy in Licklider, ed., *Stopping the Killing* (Boston: South End Press 1994), 309.

37 See Thomas Ohlson and Stephen Stedman, *The New Is Not Yet Born: Conflict Resolution in Southern Africa* (Washington, DC: Brookings Institution 1994), 121.

38 Elwood Dunn, chapter 4 above, 113.

39 See Bruce Jones, chapter 3 above, 70.

40 See Nelson Kasfir, "Southern Sudanese Politics since the Addis Ababa Agreement," *African Affairs*, 76 no. 393 (April 1977), 143–66; Ann Mosely Lesch, "External Involvement in the Sudanese Civil War," in David R. Smock, ed., *Making War and Waging Peace* (Washington, DC: U.S. Institute of Peace 1992), 79–105; and Donald Rothchild and Caroline Hartzell, "The Peace Process in the Sudan, 1971–1972," in Roy Lick-

lider, ed., *Stopping the Killing: How Civil Wars End* (Boston: South End Press 1994), 72–4.

41 Schneidman, "Conflict Resolution," 235.

42 Ivo H. Daadder, "United States and Military Intervention in Internal Conflicts," in Michael Brown, ed., *The International Dimension of Internal Conflict* (Cambridge, Mass.: MIT Press 1996), 235.

43 Ibid., 465–80.

44 Chantal de Jonge Oudraat, "The United Nations and Internal Conflict," in Michael Brown, ed., *The International Dimension of Internal Conflict* (Cambridge, Mass.: MIT Press 1996), 501.

45 Ibid., 526.

46 James Busumtwi-Sam, chapter 9 above, 281.

47 Sam Amoo, "The Role of the OAU: Past, Present and Future," in David R. Smock, ed., *Making War and Waging Peace* (Washington, DC: U.S. Institute of Peace 1993), 255.

48 Ibid.

49 For an analysis of these programs and their particular application in Ethiopia, Namibia and Uganda, see Nat Collette, Markus Kostner, and Ingo Wiederhofer, *The Transition from War to Peace in Sub-Saharan Africa* (Washington, DC: International Bank for Reconstruction and Development 1966).

50 For such an overview, see *States in Disarray: The Social Effects of Globalization* (New York: United Nations Research Institute for Social Development 1995), especially chap. 7.

51 The concept of "peace-building" was first defined by the UN secretary-general as "Action to identify and support structures which will tend to strengthen and solidify peace in order to avoid a relapse into conflict." Boutros Boutros-Ghali, *An Agenda for Peace* (New York: United Nations 1992). For an update see Boutros Boutros-Ghali, "Supplement to *An Agenda for Peace*," Position Paper of the Secretary General on the Occasion of the Fiftieth Anniversary of the United Nations), Document A/50/60-S/1995/1, 3 Jan. 1995.

52 Bruce Jones, chapter 3 above, 79.

53 It is sometimes argued that building peace is much more difficult if war has ended through negotiations than if it has been brought to an end by military victory. The political outcome, in the former cases, is what Robert Harrison Wagner calls a "balance of power," in which "all the adversaries retain some semblance of their organizational identities after the war, even if they are disarmed." See R.H. Wagner, "The Causes of Peace," in Roy Licklider, ed., *Stopping the Killing: How Civil Wars End* (Boston: South End Press 1994), 261. While Wagner may be correct in identifying the particular problem for those who have negotiated an end to war, he seems to have ignored the knotty predicament that John

Kiyaga-Nsubuga has noted in chapter 1 above, in Uganda, where the civil war was ended by force – how to liberalize the political process amidst continuing instability without losing control altogether. The most likely outcome for a non-negotiated ending to a civil war may well be what Wagner terms (261) "the supremacy of state," in which all but one faction in the civil war is disarmed and "the organizational identity of the losers" is destroyed. Like the balance of power, however, this outcome is very unstable.

54 The experience of peace-building in Mozambique and elsewhere reveals the essential role of the international community in monitoring and verifying compliance by all parties with terms of the negotiated accord. See Ohlson and Stedman, *The New Is Not Yet Born*, 123.

55 I. William Zartman, "Bilateral Management and Resolution," in Francis Deng and I. William Zartman, eds., *Conflict Resolution in Africa* (Washington, DC: Brookings Institution 1991), 319.

# Contributors

HUSSEIN M. ADAM is an associate professor of political science at the College of the Holy Cross in Worcester, Mass. He served as chair of Social Sciences at the Somali National University and in 1981 founded and directed the Somali Unit for Research on Emergencies and Rural Development (SURERD). He has published numerous articles, book chapters, and a monograph and edited volumes on Somalia and Somali studies.

TAISIER M. ALI is currently a visiting scholar at the University of Toronto, where he is writing with R.O. Matthews a study of the civil war in Sudan. Formerly an associate professor at the University of Khartoum, he has published several articles and a book on Sudanese politics.

JAMES BUSUMTWI-SAM is an assistant professor at the Department of Political Science, Simon Fraser University, where he teaches international politics and international law and organization. He is currently engaged in research on the role of international and regional organizations in preventing conflict in Africa.

HEVINA S. DASHWOOD is an assistant professor at the Department of Political Science, University of Windsor. Her research interests include international development and the Third World in international affairs. The *Journal of Southern African Studies* in March 1996 published a condensed version of her recent doctoral thesis on the political economy of transformation in Zimbabwe.

MARK DUFFIELD has a background in anthropology and political economy. Between 1985 and 1989 he was Oxfam's country representative in Sudan. He is currently a senior lecturer in the School of Public Policy at the University of Birmingham, England. His major area of specialization is so-called complex political emergencies. His many publications include a volume written with John Prendergast, *Without Troops and Tanks: Humanitarian Intervention in Ethiopia and Eritrea* (1994).

D. ELWOOD DUNN is professor of political science, University of the South, in Sewanee, Tennessee. He has taught at Seton Hall and Fordham universities and served 1974–80 in the government of his native Liberia, becoming a cabinet minister. He was editor 1985–95 of the *Liberian Studies Journal.* Among his numerous publications he is co-author with Byron Tarr of *Liberia: A National Polity in Transition* (1988).

BRUCE D. JONES is a PhD candidate at the London School of Economics. He has published several articles and book chapters on conflict in Rwanda and was contributing author of the conflict management report of a recent multi-donor evaluation of emergency response in Rwanda. He has worked as a consultant with training, development, and conflict-resolution agencies in Canada and the United Kingdom.

JOHN KIYAGA-NSUBUGA has degrees from universities at Makerere, Cambridge, and Toronto. He is assistant professor of political science at Makerere University. His research interests include the dynamics of political instability in sub-Saharan Africa and problems of reconstructing shattered societies.

ROBERT O. MATTHEWS is professor of political science at the University of Toronto, author of several articles on inter- and intra-state conflict in Africa, and currently working on a study of the civil war in Sudan with Taisier M. Ali.

CRANFORD PRATT is professor emeritus in political science at the University of Toronto, author of *The Critical Phase in Tanzania, 1945–68; Nyerere and the Emergence of a Socialist Strategy* (1976), and, with Bismark Mwausasu, editor of and contributor to *Towards Socialism in Tanzania* (1979).

JOHN PRENDERGAST is USIP Fellow at the National Security Council, Washington, DC, and is a visiting fellow at the University of Maryland's Center for International Development and Conflict Management. His publications include *Frontline Diplomacy: Humanitarian Aid and Conflict in Africa* (1996) and *Crisis Response: Humanitarian Band-Aids in Sudan and Somalia* (1997).

JOHN S. SAUL, who teaches at York University and is a member of the editorial working group of *Southern African Report*, has written or edited some twelve volumes on eastern and southern Africa since 1972. His new book, *What Is to Be Learned? The Rise and Fall of Mozambican Socialism*, will appear soon.

# Index

Addis Ababa agreement of 1972, 8,
    195, 205, 208, 210, 216, 217, 265,
    295, 299, 303. *See also* Sudan
Aidid, General Mohamed Farah, 179,
    185, 189, 276. *See also* Somalia
Alden, Chris, 154
All-African Council of Churches, 265,
    299
Amin, Idi, 16, 207
Angola, 229, 231, 259
Anya-Nya, 207, 208, 295, 299
Arusha Accords/process, 54, 66–71,
    72–6, 78–9, 278, 296, 299, 303. *See
    also* Rwanda

Barre, Major-General Mohamed Siyad:
    external support to, 176–8; leader-
    ship style of, 170, 171, 172, 173,
    174, 175; opposition to, 179, 180,
    184, 185, 186, 187, 189
Basher, Brigader Omar Hassan, al-,
    213, 214
Boutros-Ghali, Boutros, 143, 145, 146,
    149, 151, 154, 155, 158, 159, 184,
    185, 303

Brown, Michael, 292, 294

Carter, Jimmy, 214
Chissano, Joaquim, 131, 149, 296; and
    churches, 134–5; and elections,
    153; and Western powers, 136
Clapham, Christopher, 89, 98
Cohen, Herman, 64, 136, 138, 144
Cold War: end of, 8, 78, 123, 299–300,
    and Ethiopia, 37, and Liberia, 92,
    and Rwanda, 56, 64, 78, and So-
    malia, 171–2, 177; impact of, 5,
    259, on Mozambique, 130, on
    Somalia, 171; U.S. ambivalence
    following, 106, 114
colonialism, impact of, 4, 14–16, 44,
    281; on Liberia, 91–3; on Mozam-
    bique, 123–6; on Rwanda, 57,
    84n26; on Somalia, 172; on Sudan,
    201; on Uganda, 14, 15–16, 289
Community of Sant'Egidio (Rome),
    137, 297, 299
conflict resolution, 4–8, 258–62,
    295–300; attempts at, in Ethiopia,
    42–3, 45, in Rwanda, 60–2, 64–5,

70, 79–81, in Somalia, 184–7, 190, in Sudan, 189–95, 197–205; in Uganda, 17–19, 21–2; by negotiations, in Liberia, 112–15, 116–17, in Mozambique, 130, 133–50. *See also* ECOWAS; OAU; UN
Copson, Raymond, 292, 294
Crocker, Chester, 64, 78, 115, 125, 131–2, 133, 159

Dallaire, Brigadier-General Roméo, 73, 77, 278. *See also* Rwanda
Daly, M.W., 206
Deng, Francis, 216, 292
Dhlakama, Afonso, 136, 138, 140, 141, 142, 144, 147, 149, 153, 154, 156
Diouf, Abdou, 265, 278
Doe, Samuel, 91, 93, 95, 96, 110, 265; assassination of, 276; and Krahn hegemony, 100, 101, 289; and Nigeria, 104; and Quaddafi, 106; and religion, 101

Economic Community Military Observer Group (ECOMOG), 297; bias of, 104; formation of, 103, 275, 276; model of, 116; and Nigeria, 106
Economic Community of the Countries of the Great Lakes (CEPGL), 61–2, 278, 302
Economic Community of West African States (ECOWAS), 7, 297, 302; inadequacies of, 104–5; instrument of peace-making, 103–5, 110, 112–14, 116; and Rawlings, 113
Eritrean People's Liberation Front (EPLF), 35, 37, 40; economic and social policies of, 38, 39; military success of, 264, 296; multi-party politics, 43; relations with NGOs, 50
Eritrean Relief Association (ERA), 37, 40–2

Ethiopia, 6, 257, 259, 260, 263, 282, 291, 294, 299; Ad hoc Committee for Peace and Development in, 43; causes of conflict in, 290; federalism, 47–50; negotiations in, 42, 43; participation in IGADD, 280; and opposition parties, 44, 45, 49
Ethiopian People's Revolutionary Democratic Front (EPRDF), 43, 291; affiliated parties, 46, 50; development strategy, 47; electoral democracy, 48; ethnic federalism, 48–9; and national army, 46; opposition to, 44–5

Frente da Libertaco de Mocambique (Frelimo), 124, 132, 134, 135, 139; and elections, 154; government of, 158; leadership of, 290; party project of, 128; and peace talks, 140–2, 148; in postwar period, 157; and Rhodesia, 124; and shortcomings, 127–8

governance, 4, 116, 225, 226, 248, 250, 258, 260, 292–3; and management of elite rivalry, 14–16, 289–91

Habyarimana, Juvenal, 55, 59, 278; assassination of, 75–6; and ethnic politics, 60, 61, 62, 80, 289; and negotiations, 67–8, 70, 76, 299. *See also* Rwanda
Hanlon, Joseph, 146, 147, 148, 155
Hume, Cameron, 138–9, 142, 144, 146
hurting stalemate, 70, 127, 134, 297, 298, 299

Inter-Governmental Authority on Drought and Development (IGADD), 302; in Somalia, 190; and Sudan, 214, 280–1
international financial institutions

(IMF/World Bank), 273; in Mozambique, 130–1, 154, 159; in Rwanda,
60; in Somalia, 176; in Uganda, 26;
in Zimbabwe, 238
International Monetary Fund (IMF). *See*
international financial institutions
intervention, 7–9, 267–8, 293, 294; in
Ethiopia, 37, 43; in Liberia, 101–5,
106–7, 114–15; in Mozambique,
123–5, 127, 130; in Rwanda, 59,
61–2, 66, 70–1, 77; in Somalia, 171,
176–8, 183–6; in Sudan, 204,
207–9, 214; in Uganda, 16. *See also*
Liberia; Mozambique; Rwanda;
Somalia

Kagame, Major-General Paul, 58, 77,
83n17
Kasfir, Nelson, 16, 22
Kegley, C.W., Jr, 90
Khadiagala, Gilbert, 13
Khalid, Mansour, 210
Koch, Eddie, 154
Kok, Peter Nyot, 288

Laitin, David, 188
Lewis, Arthur, 188
Lewis, I.M., 173
Leys, Colin, 158
Liberia, 6, 7, 257, 259, 298; Abuja
Peace Agreement of 1995 (Abuja I)
and of 1996 (Abuja II), 89, 111–12,
117, 305; Akosombo Accords, 113;
All-Liberia Conference, 111; Banjul
peace talks, 105, 109; economic
crisis in, 93; Interfaith Mediation
Committee (IFMC), 104, 108–9;
political parties in, 93–7, 109–11,
276; rice riots, 89; role of foreign
states in, 102, 106, 113–14; triggers
of conflict in, 96, 291
Licklider, Roy, 298

Lijphart, Arend, 188

Machel, Samora, 130, 134, 296
Mahdi, Sadiq, al-, 211, 212, 213, 217,
291
Malwal, Bona, 197, 214
Mamdani, Mahmood, 18
Mechanism for Conflict Prevention,
Management and Resolution
(MCPMR). *See* OAU
Mengistu Haile Mariam, 35, 37, 264;
and ethnicity, 290; and Somalia,
178, 180; and Soviet support, 293;
and Sudan, 213
Mobutu Sese Seko, 59, 62, 63, 278
Moi, Daniel arap: and Mozambique,
135, 136, 297; and Uganda, 17, 296
Mozambique, 6, 7, 257, 259; changing
nature of conflict in, 129, 298; and
Contact Group, 139; demobilization
in, 150; democracy in, 156–8; elections in, 152–5; external sources of
domestic conflict in, 123, 229, 231,
289; internal sources of conflict in,
128, 290, 292; negotiations in
Rome (1990–92), 136–45; Nkomati
Accord, 133–4; post-conflict period
in, 155–6; pre-negotiations in
(1984–88), 133–5; recolonization
of, 125–6, 130, 131–2, 157; role of
Western countries and institutions
in, 125, 130, 132, 136, 138, 142,
143; and South Africa, 136; and
Soviet Union, 125; Supervisory and
Monitoring Commission (CSC), 146;
Tiny Rowland in, 135, 144; UN
operation in (ONUMOZ), 146–50,
152, 155, 297
Mugabe, Robert, 225; and Matabeleland, 230, 232, 233, 234; and
Mozambique, 135, 136, 144, 297;
and one-party state, 224, 234; and

policies of reconciliation, 226, 227,
290
Museveni, Yoweri, 13, 56, 268; and
1995 elections, 24; and politics of
inclusion, 290, 291, 304; and
Rwanda, 57, 59, 61, 62, 72, 278;
and Sudan, 265

National Resistance Movement (NRM,
Uganda), 13; alliances of, 19; and
competitors, 23–4, 26; drafting of
constitution by, 21; and peace-
building, 18; and political participation, 18, 22, 23, 291; and
resistance committees, 20–1, 22;
and Rwanda, 58
Natsios, Andrew, 180
Nigeria, civil war in, 259, 260, 263
Nimeiri, Gaafar Mohamed, 174, 207,
215, 299; and the Addis Ababa
agreement of 1972, 195, 208–10,
291, 295; and Islam, 212, 213; and
militias, 217
Nkomo, Joshua, 224, 231, 232
Nyerere, Julius, 8, 240–1, 242, 246–8,
290

Obote, Milton, 13, 16, 291; and constitution, 21; downfall of, 17; and
Rwandans, 56, 58; second regime
("Obote 2"), 20n27, 22, 23, 25
Oloka-Onyango, J., 22
Operation Restore Hope, 183, 184,
185, 275
Organization of African Unity (OAU), 8,
214, 269, 270; basic norms of,
261–5; institutional and normative
roles of, 258; in Liberia, 103,
106–7, 297; Mechanism for Conflict
Prevention, Management and Resolution (MCPMR), 62, 272, 274, 281,
301, 302; in Mozambique, 146;

record in conflict resolution,
301–2; in Rwanda, 56; in Sudan,
214; summits of, 266, 267, 269,
272, 273

Patriotic Front–Zimbabwe African
People's Union (PF-ZAPU), 224,
225, 228, 229, 231, 232, 233, 238
peace-building, 5, 13, 14, 17; assessment of, in Ethiopia, 47, 305; in
Liberia, 305–36, in Mozambique,
155–9, 303–4, in Somalia, 305–6,
in Uganda, 19–25, 25–6, 304–5,
310–11n53; failure of, 30; meaning
of, 302; relationship with conflict
prevention, 273–4, 288, 306

Quiwonkpa, Thomas, 91, 93, 94, 101,
108

Rawlings, Jerry, 113, 299
Relief Society of Tigray (REST), 37,
40–2
Resistencia Nacional Mocambicana
(Renamo), 7, 124, 132, 134, 135,
137, 139; and elections, 154;
ideology of, 128; links to Rhodesia
and South Africa, 127, 231, 293;
and peace talks, 140–2, 143, 148,
149; in postwar period, 156, 157;
and Western powers, 138
Ruay, Deng, 206

Rwanda, 6, 7, 257, 289, 298–9; Akazu,
60, 72, 74, 80, 290; Arusha process,
54, 66–71, 72–7, 78–9, 278, 296,
299, 303; Broad Based Transitional
Government of, 71, 72, 74, 76;
Dallaire, Roméo, 73, 77; ethnic tension in, 57; genocide in, 76–8;
Neutral Military Observer Group
(NMOG), 62, 63; N'Sele agreement,

62; refugee movement in, 57–8; role of Belgium, 61, of France, 65–6, of Tanzania, 66–7, 70, 71, of United States, 63–4; root causes of war in, 54–5, 59, 61; UN Assistance Mission (UNAMIR), 73, 74, 75; UN failure in, 77–8; and UNHCR, 62

Rwanda Patriotic Front (RPF), 55; and Burundi, 73; formation of, 58, 169; military superiority of, 70, 296; in talks, 6, 63; and UN, 76

Salim, Salim Ahmed, 62, 75, 266, 278
Sanderson, G.N., 196, 203
Sawyer, Amos, 96, 104, 105, 110
Sikainga, Ahmed, 199
Somalia, 6, 7, 178–9, 180, 181, 187, 188, 259, 291; Addis Ababa Conference, 185; Borama Conference, 189; civil society in, 182–3; clanism in, 170, 171, 183, 189, 289; clanklatura, 173, 174, 175; emergence of political factions, 176, 177; Ethiopia, war with, 169, 172, 178, 260, 263; foreign intervention of: Soviet Union, 178, UN, 183–6, United States, 183–5; prospects for consociationalism in, 187–9, 190; state collapse in, 169, 181–2
Somaliland, 180, 181, 182, 187, 188, 189, 190
Ssemogerere, Paul, 24, 30n28
Sudan, 6, 8, 259; Abuja talks, 214; Addis Ababa agreement of 1972, 8, 195, 205, 208, 210, 216, 217, 265, 291, 295, 299, 303; Anya-Nya, 207, 208, 295, 299; colonial legacy in, 204, 289; dominant elite, 201–4, 205, 207; Ethiopian cross-border relief, 37, 41; external intervention in, 207, 209, 213–14, 217, 263, 293, 29; hurting stalemate in, 208, 299;

Kokadam Declaration, 195, 205, 211–12, 213, 216; National Islamic Front, 201, 209, 212, 213, 214, 215, 216, 217, 218; northern view of conflict, 195–9, 290; popular forces, 198, 205, 206, 207, 216, 218; Round Table Conference, 195, 199, 205, 206; sectarian parties, 198, 200, 201, 202–4, 205, 207, 208, 211, 216; September laws, 209, 211, 212; Southern Sudan Independence Movement, 217; southern view of conflict, 199–200; Sudan Alliance Forces, 218–19; Sudanese Peace Initiative, 212, 213, 214; Torit mutiny, 194, 196; Trade Union Alliance, 211–13; tribal militias in, 199, 217
Sudan People's Liberation Army/Movement (SPLA/SPLM), 194, 198, 199, 216; and external support, 37, 213, 214; peace talks, 265, 280; political vision, 200, 218

Tanzania, 8, 291; Arusha Declaration, 239; conflict contained in, 224, 290; democratic one-party state in, 239–42, 247–8; electoral system in, 241–2; leadership code, 242; Nyerere, leader of: on communal values, 240, on democratic one-party state, 240–1, on leadership code, 242, major policy failures, 246–8; oligarchic tendencies, 240; salience of class in, 240, 242; Tanganyikan African National Union, 240; villagization in, 247
Taylor, Charles, 91, 102, 105, 108, 276; and elections, 117; and foreign business, 107; in Nigeria, 107; relations with Sierra Leone and Gambia, 104

Tigrayan People's Liberation Front
(TPLF), 35, 264, 296; economic and
social policies of, 38, 39–40;
political philosophy of, 43, 44, 47;
and relations with NGOs, 50
Tolbert, William, 192; and social
cleavages, 99–100
Tubman, William, 93; and cleavages,
98–9; unification and Open Door
policies, 99

Uganda, 6, 259; armed opposition to
NRM in, 23, 26; Buganda, prominence of, 15, 21; Constitutional
Assembly elections, 21; federal/
unitary structures, legacy of
colonialism in, 14, 15–16, 289;
intra-elite conflict, 24, 27, 290;
Okello regime, 17. *See also* National
Resistance Movement (NRM)
United Nations (UN), 257, 261, 262,
301; in Liberia, 107, observers at
talks, 142, role in transition, 143–4,
145–50; in Mozambique: operations (ONUMOZ), 145–6, 147, 149,
151, 152, 155, 297, 304; Observer
Mission for Uganda–Rwanda
(UNOMOR), 72; in Rwanda: UN
Assistance Mission in Rwanda
(UNAMIR), 73, 74, 75, 81, 278, 279,
303, response to genocide in, 77–8;
in Somalia, 8, 180, 183–6, 274, 275,
276, 277
United States, policy towards: Ethiopia,
43, 264; Liberia, 106, 113, 114,
294, 297, 300; Mozambique, 132,
136, 142, 297, 300; Rwanda, 63–4,

66, 278, 300; Somalia, 183–5, 294,
300; Sudan, 209, 293, 294

Vines, Alex, 133, 134, 136, 138, 139

Wai, Dunsten, 207
Wakson, Elias N., 210
Waltz, Kenneth, 90
World Bank. *See* international financial
institutions
World Council of Churches, 208, 265,
299

Zartman, I. William, 18, 269, 279, 280,
292, 298
Zimbabwe, 8, 291; class, salience of, in,
236–8, 244–6; conflict contained
in, 224, 290; constitutional safeguards, 226, 227; corruption in,
237; dominant class in, 225, 236–8,
245; elections in (1995), 235–6;
elite accommodation in, 225–6,
227, 234–8; Lancaster House Constitution of, 224, 226; Land
Acquisition Act in, 238; multi-party
democracy in, 233–6; political conflict, 228–31; potential source of
conflict in, 224–5; racial reconciliation in, 226–8; role of South
Africa in, 229–30; structural adjustment program, 225, 235, 237; Unity
Accord, 224–5, 230, 231–3, 236,
237
Zimbabwe African National Union–
Patriotic Front (ZANU-PF), 224, 225,
226, 227, 228, 229, 230, 232, 233,
234, 238